Contested Conventions

CONTESTED CONVENTIONS

The Struggle to Establish the Constitution
and Save the Union, 1787–1789

MELVIN YAZAWA
University of New Mexico

Johns Hopkins University Press
Baltimore

Johns Hopkins University Press
2715 North Charles Street
Baltimore, Maryland 21218-4363
www.press.jhu.edu

Library of Congress Cataloging-in-Publication Data

Names: Yazawa, Melvin, author.
Title: Contested conventions : the struggle to establish the constitution
and save the union, 1787–1789 / Melvin Yazawa.
Description: Baltimore : Johns Hopkins University Press, 2016. |
Includes bibliographical references and index.
Identifiers: LCCN 2015037770| ISBN 9781421420264 (pbk. : alk. paper) |
ISBN 9781421420271 (electronic) | ISBN 1421420260 (pbk. : alk. paper) |
ISBN 1421420279 (electronic)
Subjects: LCSH: United States. Constitutional Convention (1787) |
United States—Politics and government—1783–1789. | United States.
Constitution. | Constitutional history—United States.
Classification: LCC E303 .Y39 2016 | DDC 342.7302/9—dc23 LC
record available at http://lccn.loc.gov/2015037770

A catalog record for this book is available from the British Library.

*Special discounts are available for bulk purchases of this book. For more
information, please contact Special Sales at 410-516-6936 or specialsales
@press.jhu.edu.*

Johns Hopkins University Press uses environmentally friendly book
materials, including recycled text paper that is composed of at least
30 percent post-consumer waste, whenever possible.

To Jack P. Greene

CONTENTS

Constitution Day

Senator Robert C. Byrd of West Virginia, who famously claimed that he always carried a copy of the Constitution with him, amended a federal spending bill in 2004 to include a provision for a national observance of Constitution Day. Among other things, Byrd's amendment required all schools receiving federal funds annually to "hold an educational program on the United States Constitution on September 17." In its tribute to Byrd and his fifty-one years of service in the Senate, the *New York Times* reported that the West Virginian, who won acceptance as the unofficial constitutional scholar of Congress, was "particularly proud" of this 2004 amendment. The Constitution "defines us as Americans," Byrd reasoned, and to "preserve" it, we must "make it an active part of our lives."[1]

The mandate and the celebrations that followed were well intentioned, to be sure, but they were fraught with difficulties that rendered them potentially misleading if not downright confusing. At the most basic level, the date itself conceals as much as it commemorates. September 17 was the day on which thirty-nine delegates signed the document they had created at the Federal Convention. It was the capstone event of the business at Philadelphia and therefore perhaps the obvious episode to celebrate. Since World War I, September 17 has been the preferred day for localized public festivities. In 1919, eighty-five years before Byrd introduced his amendment, the National Security League, self-appointed guardians of "100 percent Americanism," tried to get September 17 declared a national holiday. However, there was nothing magical about the date. The signing of the Constitution on the last day of the convention did not settle its fate. That came nine months later. The delegates themselves said as much. During the debates over the relative merits of the Virginia and New Jersey plans, when proponents of the latter questioned whether the convention was authorized to do more than to revise the Articles of Confederation, James Wilson made what became the standard justification for ignoring Congress's directive. The convention was merely drafting a proposal,

1. Adam Clymer, "Robert C. Byrd, a Pillar of the Senate, Dies at 92," *New York Times*, June 29, 2010; Robert Byrd, "A Constitution Day Message from Senator Byrd," September 17, 2006, Robert C. Byrd Center.

he explained, and was therefore "at liberty to *propose any thing*" because it could in fact "*conclude nothing*." James Madison agreed. What they had written at the Pennsylvania State House, he declared, was "nothing but a dead letter, until life and validity were breathed into it by the voice of the people, speaking through the several state conventions." In light of sentiments such as these, perhaps June 21, 1788, when New Hampshire became the ninth state to ratify, thereby formalizing the establishment of the new Union under the Constitution, would be more appropriate than September 17, 1787, as the date to memorialize.[2]

A second difficulty with Constitution Day is a consequence of the first. The focus on September 17 privileges the thirty-nine signers of the Constitution, ignoring the contributions of George Mason, Edmund Randolph, and Elbridge Gerry, the three delegates who refused to affix their names to the document on the last day of the convention. It also dismisses the thirteen others who left Philadelphia before September 17. Most of the lesson plans developed by various organizations, public and private, to assist teachers and school administrators in meeting the requirements of the new federal regulation reflect this bias. The best plans, those sponsored by the National Constitution Center at Independence Mall in Philadelphia and the National Archives in Washington, DC, avoid the error by identifying all fifty-five delegates to the Federal Convention as our "founding fathers." But even this more inclusive list is insufficient. If we are to believe Madison and Wilson, the men who ratified the Constitution deserve at least as much attention as those who drafted the document. In other words, to the roster of thirty-nine or fifty-five "founders," we should add the names of the more than sixteen hundred delegates to the thirteen state conventions. Surely, John Hancock, Samuel Adams, and Patrick Henry, all of whom chose not to attend the Federal Convention but who were enormously influential at their respective state conventions, ought to rank higher among the "founders" than Richard Bassett, John Blair, Thomas Fitzsimons, Alexander Martin, Thomas Mifflin, and others who were in attendance at Philadelphia but said little or nothing while there and served on no committees. For the same reasons, Melancton Smith of New York and Willie Jones of North Carolina, whose actions shaped the decisions of their states, should join the first ranks of the "founders." Ultimately, however, even the designation "founders" may be of questionable utility. The sixteen hundred state convention delegates, after all, were supposed to represent the "voice of the people," as Madison said. If so, then the influence exerted by the masses of ordinary farmers and tradesmen, the "unruly Americans" who were politicized by the Revolution

2. Michael Kammen, *A Machine That Would Go of Itself* (New York, 1986), 220; Farrand, 1:253; *Annals of Congress*, 42 vols. (Washington, DC, 1834–56), 5:776.

and remained active in 1787, should not be discounted in favor of the so-called founders.[3]

Finally, Constitution Day festivities, and by extension the popular understanding of the Philadelphia Convention, take too much for granted. Absent is an appreciation of contingency in these formulaic demonstrations of affection for the "greatest event in our national history." Progress toward "a more perfect union" under the newly created Constitution seems a foregone conclusion. The Union, already secure, needed only to be perfected. But this was not how the participants themselves viewed their situation. On the contrary, their dominant mood was one of apprehension about the state of the Union. Alexander Hamilton expressed this mood best in an anxious letter he wrote to George Washington in 1783. Anticipating Washington's resignation as the Continental Army prepared to disband in the wake of the signing of the preliminary articles of peace between Great Britain and the United States, Hamilton beseeched the general to remain active in the public arena. The successful conclusion of the Revolutionary War was not enough to secure the blessings of independence, he said, because the "seeds of disunion" in America were "much more numerous than those of union." Ahead lay the "arduous work" of establishing the foundations necessary "to perpetuate our union," and Washington's continued presence would be indispensable. Only he, already cast in the public's imagination as the iconic savior of the nation, could pull the people together. Washington's exertions would be "as essential to accomplish this end as they have been to establish independence," for, lamentably, "the centrifugal is much stronger than the centripetal force in these states."[4]

Hamilton's appeal reflected his core belief that the prevailing situation was unacceptable and that unless it was attended to immediately, it would end tragically for Americans. Centrifugal forces had to be weakened and centripetal strengthened. Otherwise, a fragmentation of the Union must take place, and disunion would be followed by "dissensions between the states themselves." Past grievances, disputed territorial claims, commercial rivalries, the public debt, and other sources of conflict, rooted in human nature and therefore too numerous to name, would be reinvigorated by the separation into competing entities. Competition, in turn, would breed suspicion, which would lead to discord, then to infractions, next to reprisals, and finally to appeals to the "sword." And following the first armed engagement, no state could possibly resist popular demands for the establishment of a standing army to repel or deter invasions

3. Clinton Rossiter, *1787: The Grand Convention* (New York, 1966), 251; Woody Holton, *Unruly Americans and the Origins of the Constitution* (New York, 2007).

4. Kammen, *A Machine That Would Go of Itself*, 221; Alexander Hamilton to George Washington, March 24, 1783, *PAH*, 3:304; Garry Wills, *Cincinnatus: George Washington and the Enlightenment* (New York, 1984), 4–16; Barry Schwartz, *George Washington: The Making of an American Symbol* (New York, 1987), 13–39.

by rapacious neighbors. "To be more safe," the people "become willing to run the risk of being less free." Unfortunately, the necessity of standing armies "enhances the importance of the soldier, and proportionately degrades the condition of the citizen," encouraging the people to consider the "soldiery not only as their protectors" but eventually as their "masters." This descent from disunion to militarism to despotism was inevitable, Hamilton said, because it traced a "natural and necessary progress of human affairs."[5]

This book is an extended examination of these themes, and it argues that the overriding concern of the framers and ratifiers of the Constitution were the centrifugal forces driving Americans apart. The problem with the Confederation government was not simply that it lacked the power to tax or to enforce its decisions. If that had been the case, a revision of the Articles of Confederation, granting these powers to Congress, would have sufficed. No, the problem with the Confederation was that it was too weak to contain the centrifugal forces threatening to render the Union "no more than a rope of sand." Unless a stronger central government was "obtained," one frustrated member of Congress reported as that body staggered from crisis to crisis without closure, "a dissolution of the Union must take place." The impetus for the Annapolis Convention, which preceded and issued the call for the Federal Convention, was the inability of Congress effectively to control the separate and often competing commercial laws of the several states. To James Monroe, the regulation of trade by the central government was absolutely "necessary to preserve the Union. Without it, it [the Union] will infallibly tumble to pieces." What mattered was not whether such laws hurt domestic traders while benefiting foreign interests. Rather, as Madison explained, it was the "multiplicity" of laws in general, commercial or otherwise, that was an "evil" because it reinforced as well as reflected existing divisions within the nation.[6]

What follows, then, is not a comprehensive account of the creation and ratification of the Constitution but rather an exploration of the sense of crisis that made its establishment possible. Part 1 examines the creation of the Constitution by concentrating on the two most divisive questions before the Philadelphia Convention: whether states would be represented equally or proportionally in the proposed federal legislature and whether slaves would be counted in the

---

5. *Federalist* nos. 6, 108–11, 7, 114–18, and 8, 119–24; Melvin Yazawa, "Republican Expectations: Revolutionary Ideology and the Compromise of 1790," *Republic for the Ages: The United States Capitol and the Political Culture of the Early Republic*, ed. Donald R. Kennon (Charlottesville, VA, 1999), 5–35; Melvin Yazawa, "Dionysian Rhetoric and Apollonian Solutions: The Politics of Union and Disunion in the Age of Federalism," *Empire and Nation: The American Revolution in the Atlantic World*, ed. Eliga H. Gould and Peter S. Onuf (Baltimore, MD, 2005), 179–80.

6. Timothy Bloodworth to the governor of North Carolina [Richard Caswell], September 4, 1786, *LMCC*, 8:462; James Monroe to James Madison, September 3, 1786, *PJM*, 9:114; James Madison, "Vices of the Political System of the United States," April–June 1787, *PJM*, 9:354.

allocation of seats in the House of Representatives. The confrontations over these two issues, and these alone, led delegations to threaten to leave the Convention and to put an end to the effort to construct a new frame of government. The debates relative to the other branches of government, especially the executive, were contentious, but disagreement over these issues never put the continuance of the convention at risk. No delegation said it would leave Philadelphia because it disagreed with decisions pertaining to the method of electing, eligibility for reelecting, or term of office of the president. Similarly, no delegation said it would abandon the convention because it feared that the federal judiciary would undermine the jurisdiction of the state courts. We return, therefore, to the great divisions over size and slavery. Why did the delegations remain in Philadelphia after issuing their ultimatums? Compromises, of course, but why would delegates sacrifice their self-described principles for the sake of appeasing their opponents? The answer is to be found in their conviction that the Philadelphia meeting afforded the best chance, perhaps the last chance, of securing the Union. Allowing a small state to have the same number of senators as a large state struck Madison as unfair, and counting three-fifths of the slave population in the rule of representation struck Elbridge Gerry as indefensible, but the alternative, disunion and the downward spiral toward civil war, was unacceptable to both men and their cohorts.

Part 2 follows the lead of those at Philadelphia who argued that the more consequential part of the story of the Constitution would take place at the various state conventions. The logical separation here is between the first nine states to ratify and the other four, because Article 7 stipulates that ratification by nine states "shall be sufficient for the establishment of this Constitution." Chapter 3 surveys the first nine conventions, focusing in particular on the Massachusetts convention. The Boston meeting attracted the most attention among contemporaries, and for good reason. Massachusetts was the second largest state in the Confederation, the dominant polity in New England, and the scene of the first closely contested convention. Also, the adoption of recommendatory amendments by the Boston convention, a maneuver that helped the friends of the Constitution finally to prevail, set a precedent for similar actions taken in four other states.

Once New Hampshire became the ninth state to ratify, the question before the remaining states changed fundamentally. Objections to specific provisions or clauses of the Constitution mattered only if they were serious enough to justify nonratification, a predicament that confronted every previous convention, but now a refusal to ratify was tantamount to refusing to join the newly established Union under the Constitution. The question before a nonratifying state was whether it was better to become a part of the United States or to remain an outlier. Were the perceived dangers posed by the Constitution greater than those associated with a solitary existence? Chapter 4 deals with the Virginia convention, where the outcome was too close to call and where Patrick Henry and George Mason stood powerfully in the opposition. But even among delegates supremely confident in the majesty of their beloved state, the prospect of being left out proved too much to bear.

Whereas the supporters and opponents of the Constitution were nearly evenly divided in Massachusetts and Virginia, Antifederalists held a commanding two to one majority in New York. Chapter 5 analyzes the factors that enabled Federalists to secure ratification despite this huge initial disadvantage. Timing was a crucial consideration. Virginia's decision to ratify removed any lingering doubts that the new Union was a reality. Two weeks after the Richmond convention adjourned, the Confederation Congress set a date for its own expiration and the inauguration of the new federal government under the Constitution. New Yorkers had to act quickly to avoid being overtaken by swiftly moving events.

All of the factors that figured into the Virginia and New York decisions were at play in North Carolina, which is the subject of Chapter 6. The first North Carolina convention, meeting in Hillsborough, had a two to one Antifederalist majority and voted against ratification on August 2, 1788. Thus when the First Federal Congress met in March 1789, North Carolina was not represented. The fear of being relegated to the status of a "foreign" state coupled with Congress's drafting of the Bill of Rights, a move orchestrated by Madison to split the ranks of the Antifederalists, persuaded the delegates to the second North Carolina convention, meeting in Fayetteville, to ratify the Constitution in November 1789. The Union was now whole, except for Rhode Island, and more than a few exasperated Americans thought it was "of very little moment whether she comes in or not."[7]

On a lazy morning at the Kennedy compound back in 1961, the president queried his guest as he lit a cigar. How did a "sort of backwoods country like this, with only three million people," John Kennedy asked, repeating a question recently posed to him, produce some of the "great geniuses of the eighteenth century"? Gore Vidal, on the receiving end of this query, had no answer for the president that day, at least not a satisfactory one, and it troubled him. More than four decades later, having "pondered" the question intermittently throughout the intervening years, Vidal offered a more considered response. But his meandering discussion of Washington, John Adams, and Thomas Jefferson is a disappointment. Vidal himself seems to apologize for his effort, saying at the end, "this volume is my hardly definitive answer." He, and we, would have been better served had Vidal taken his cue from "dear Jack." After

---

7. Richard Platt to Winthrop Sargent, August 8, 1788, *DHRC*, 21:1351.

posing his question, Kennedy went on to comment, "You know in this, uh, job . . . I get to meet everybody——all these great movers and shakers and the thing I'm most struck by the lot of them is how second-rate they are. Then you read all those debates over the Constitution . . . nothing like that now. Nothing." What impressed the president about these debates? Were the debates of 1787–89 deserving of such high praise? Who reads these debates anymore?[8]

8. Gore Vidal, *Inventing a Nation: Washington, Adams, and Jefferson* (New Haven, CT, 2003), 187–88.

ABBREVIATIONS USED IN THE NOTES

Bailyn, *Debate*	Bernard Bailyn ed., *The Debate on the Constitution: Federalist and Antifederalist Speeches, Articles, and Letters during the Struggle over Ratification.* 2 vols., New York, 1993.
DHRC	Merrill Jensen, John P. Kaminski, et al., eds., *The Documentary History of the Ratification of the Constitution.* 24 vols. to date. Madison, WI, 1976–present.
Elliot	Jonathan Elliot, ed., *The Debates in the Several State Conventions on the Adoption of the Federal Constitution.* 2nd ed., 4 vols., Washington, DC, 1836.
Farrand	Max Farrand, ed., *The Records of the Federal Convention of 1787.* Rev. ed., 4 vols., New Haven, CT, 1966.
Federalist	Benjamin Fletcher Wright, ed., *The Federalist.* Cambridge, MA, 1961. Cited by essay and page number.
Letters of Madison	William C. Rives and Philip R. Fendall, eds., *Letters and Other Writings of James Madison,* 4 vols., Philadelphia, 1865.
LMCC	Edmund C. Burnett, ed., *Letters of Members of the Continental Congress.* 8 vols., Washington, DC, 1921–36.
PAH	Harold C. Syrett and Jacob E. Cooke, eds., *The Papers of Alexander Hamilton.* 26 vols., New York, 1961–79.
PGM	Robert A. Rutland, ed., *The Papers of George Mason, 1725–1792.* 3 vols., Chapel Hill, NC, 1970.
PJM	William T. Hutchinson, Robert A. Rutland, et al., eds., *The Papers of James Madison.* Chicago and Charlottesville, VA, 1962–present.

Republic of Letters   James Morton Smith, ed., *The Republic of Letters: The Correspondence between Thomas Jefferson and James Madison, 1776–1826.* 3 vols., New York, 1995.

Veit   Helen E. Veit, Kenneth Bowling, and Charlene Bangs Bickford, eds., *Creating the Bill of Rights: The Documentary Record from the First Federal Congress.* Baltimore, MD, 1991.

Writings of Madison   Gaillard Hunt, ed., *The Writings of James Madison,* 9 vols., New York, 1900–1910.

PART ONE

CREATION
The Critical Period of American History

In 1888, on the centennial of ratification of the Constitution, the philosopher-historian John Fiske published a history of the United States under the Articles of Confederation. Entitled *The Critical Period of American History, 1783–1789*, Fiske's study described the five years following the end of the Revolutionary War as "the most trying time of all." As soon as the need for concerted action against a common enemy had passed, the several states began to pursue their own separate agendas. In the absence of a long-standing attachment to union, "unspeakably stupid and contemptible local antipathies" once again reigned supreme, leaving the newly independent states "ripe for endless squabbling." Competing commercial interests, mutually discriminatory trade legislation, economic distress, territorial disputes, and wild speculation prompted by personal extravagance and the demand for paper currency threatened to break the Union into thirteen separate pieces. Congress, disregarded and underfunded, could not check the "drift toward anarchy." Finally, and fortunately when judged by its outcome, the added pressure of an armed rebellion in western Massachusetts brought this "great chain of events" to an end by getting "people of all shades of opinion . . . to agree upon one thing—that something must be done, and done quickly."[1]

The Critical Period set the tone for much of the writing on the Confederation for the next half century. It was not until 1950 that a full-blown refutation of Fiske's interpretation appeared. In *The New Nation*, the historian Merrill Jensen painstakingly and systematically questioned every one of Fiske's major arguments. Economic recovery was already under way before the Federal Convention met; reciprocity and cooperation among the states was the rule rather than the exception in matters of trade and navigation; the Articles of Confederation prescribed a method for settling interstate disputes, which several states used successfully to resolve their differences; paper money was not automatically prone to depreciation, and the contest over its issuance did not simply pit debtors against creditors; states refused to respond to federal requisitions after

1. John Fiske, *The Critical Period of American History, 1783–1789* (Boston, 1888), 55, 57, 62, 98, 94, and 134–86 passim.

Congress failed to arrive at an accurate system of accounting that balanced such requisitions against each state's contributions during the war; and although Massachusetts had to endure Shays's Rebellion before enacting debtor and tax relief laws, other states were variously addressing similar problems well before 1786. Fiske's portrayal of the period as "one of stagnation, ineptitude, bankruptcy, corruption and disintegration," Jensen concluded, was "grossly distorted."[2]

That Jensen was a far better historian than Fiske and that the *New Nation* is far superior to the *Critical Period* are beyond dispute. Jensen makes a compelling case for dispensing with the idea that the Confederation was beset by a great chain of unresolved and latently lethal difficulties. And yet, as Gordon S. Wood notes, a "desperate sense of crisis" was endemic in the new nation. Regardless of whether they were rooted in reality, the fears "were real, intensely real." Indeed, there was nothing original even in Fiske's use of the phrase "critical period" to describe the years after the Treaty of Paris. The belief that the 1780s marked the "really critical period of the entire Revolution was prevalent everywhere," and talk of impending doom was so common as to be redundant. Fiske is best understood, then, as an anachronism. His unabashed identification with the Revolutionary generation placed him squarely within the ranks of the patriot historians of a century earlier rather than alongside the first of the professional historians of the 1880s. The *Critical Period* was a throwback to much of the literature produced by the Revolutionaries themselves, and this is what makes it useful and instructive.[3]

In *The History of the American Revolution*, one of the best and most widely read narratives on the era, published after eleven states had ratified the Constitution and the First Congress had commenced its proceedings in 1789, South Carolina physician David Ramsay summarized the prevailing mood of the period in a manner that a century later still resonated with Fiske. After spending the first 650 pages of his two-volume work describing the "actors" and the "great scenes" associated with the Revolution, Ramsay sounded a note of despair. In his last chapter, Ramsay told the victorious Americans that all was not well, that they were to blame and needed to mend their ways, and that there was still much work to be done to secure the blessings of independence. The "distresses of the states after the peace" resulted from the "selfish passions" set loose once the dangers posed by the war were removed. The economy languished because the Confederation Congress could not regulate commerce

2. Merrill Jensen, *The New Nation: A History of the United States during the Confederation, 1781–1789* (New York, 1950), xii–xiii, 246, 342, 423, 337, 343, 321, 376–79, 245–345 passim.
3. Gordon S. Wood, *The Creation of the American Republic, 1776–1789* (Chapel Hill, NC, 1969), 394, 395; Peter Novick, *That Noble Dream: The "Objectivity Question" and the American Historical Profession* (Cambridge, 1988), 47–60; Lester H. Cohen, *The Revolutionary Histories: Contemporary Narratives of the American Revolution* (Ithaca, NY, 1980), 185–211.

and the states would not tolerate any restrictions, even temporary restraints intended for the good of the whole. The public debt, money owed to foreign and domestic creditors, could not be retired because Congress had no taxing powers and most states ignored their revenue obligations. Interstate relations deteriorated because commercial interests clashed and territorial disputes continued unresolved. "Confidence between man and man received a deadly wound" because private contracts were violated by consumers who insisted on living extravagantly, "exceeding what either prudence or policy could justify." Clearly, this "deranged state of public affairs" had to be set straight, if the new republic was to last. For Ramsay, the problems of the Confederation were "evils" needing to be addressed.[4]

A Luxuriancy of Legislation

Ramsay may well have been inspired by James Madison. In 1787, before the meeting of the Constitutional Convention and in preparation for it, Madison wrote a long explanatory memorandum entitled the "Vices of the Political System of the United States." Beginning with their refusal to go along with congressional requisitions, Madison listed the failures of the states "both during the war and since the peace." Encroachments on federal authority, violations of treaties, trespasses against one another, want of concert in matters of common interest, a multitude of commercial laws, paper money emissions, and factions unrestrained were undermining the Union. But these were more than examples of political or economic delinquency; they were "vices." Madison used "fallacious," "selfish," "perverseness," "pestilent," and "vicious" in reference to actions taken by the various states or their representatives. Like Ramsay, however, the descriptive Madison preferred above all others was "evil," a word he used a half dozen times to describe the "alarming symptoms" of the "present system."[5]

The sense of crisis associated with the Confederation period, in other words, cannot be accounted for simply by examining, as Jensen so masterfully does, the "remarkable variety of opinions" expressed on the complicated political and economic issues of the day. Madison's preference for the word "evil" indicates as much. It must be traced instead to the conviction that the Articles of Confederation could not preserve the Union. The separate actions of the states too clearly proved that whenever it was to their advantage or "where any favorite object" was involved, states served themselves even at the expense of the good of the whole. Virginia and Maryland entered into "unlicensed compacts"

---

4. David Ramsay, *The History of the American Revolution*, ed. Lester H. Cohen, 2 vols. (Indianapolis, 1990), 1:xliv; 2:648–56.
5. James Madison, "Vices of the Political System of the United States," April–June 1787, *PJM*, 9:348–57.

that attempted to regulate commercial traffic on the Potomac and in the Chesapeake. Pennsylvania and New Jersey tried to do the same on the Delaware River. New Hampshire, New York, Connecticut, Pennsylvania, and Virginia enacted protective tariffs that affected goods arriving from foreign countries as well as from other states. To be sure, as Jensen argues, state officials often did not enforce such laws, and Massachusetts and Rhode Island did restrict their duties to foreign imports. The larger and more important point, however, was not whether states discriminated against one another or how successfully they resolved their differences. What concerned Madison was that these states acted on their own without the supervision of Congress.[6]

A "luxuriancy of legislation," which resulted "naturally from the number and independent authority of the states," was the main cause of Madison's alarm. The experience of "every similar Confederacy" throughout history demonstrated that the "multiplicity and mutability of laws" characteristic of a "league of sovereign powers" was always "destructive of the general harmony" because one state's self-serving laws may "be deemed aggressions on the rights of other states" and provoke "retaliating regulations." It mattered little whether some of these laws were better than others or that bad laws went unenforced. The problem was the sheer number itself. Among the Confederation states, the "short period of independency" had "filled as many pages" in the statute books "as the century which preceded it," and "every year, almost every session, adds a new volume." These variable codes were a "nuisance," but they were more than just legislative humbug, for they were "a nuisance of the most pestilent kind." The abundance of existing state laws, of which only about "one tenth" were "necessary and useful," promoted disunion. A luxuriancy of legislation exacerbated the "centrifugal" forces that Alexander Hamilton had earlier warned would undo the Union if left unchecked. "How indeed could it be otherwise?" Providing for the good of the whole occasionally obliged the general government to enact laws that "necessarily bear unequally hard on some particular member or members of it." If states selectively ignored certain acts at will in favor of those passed by their own legislatures and partial to their own interests, the result must be "adverse to the spirit of the Union."[7]

Irregularities and the Treaty of Paris

The divisiveness of multiple and mutable laws and the barriers they erected against the advancement of a uniform national policy was nowhere more apparent than in the realm of postwar diplomacy, when the self-interested behav-

6. Jensen, *New Nation*, 245; James Madison, "Vices of the Political System," April–June, *PJM*, 9:348, 349.
7. James Madison, "Vices of the Political System," April–June, *PJM*, 9:354, 348, 353, 350; Alexander Hamilton to George Washington, March 24, 1783, *PAH*, 3:304.

ior of the states jeopardized existing treaties. "From the number of legislatures, the sphere of life from which most of their members are taken, and the circumstances under which their legislative business is carried on, irregularities of this kind must frequently happen," Madison observed. This was soon evident in the ways that states responded to their obligations under the Treaty of Paris. Although the treaty stipulated that Congress "earnestly recommend" to the states that they make allowances for the restitution of all confiscated estates and that Loyalists and loyalist sympathizers "meet with no lawful impediment" in the collection of prewar debts or the "prosecution of their just rights," the states in varying degrees were reluctant to comply with these instructions. In New England, the expressions of bitterness directed at them notwithstanding, Loyalists fared relatively well. In New York and Pennsylvania, where large populations of Loyalists remained after the war, acts of suppression were more forceful. And throughout most of the South, reaction to the treaty's leniency was strong, especially among indebted merchants and planters, and punitive measures remained in effect until 1787.[8]

Such "irregularities" had repercussions, most of them bad. American violations of the treaty were countered by the British violations. George III, for example, refused to withdraw his forces "with all convenient speed" from garrisons in the Great Lakes region. John Adams, who as the American minister to the Court of St. James presented a memorial calling for a speedy withdrawal, could not get even a speedy response. He waited three months before hearing from Lord Carmarthen, the thirty-five-year-old British minister of foreign affairs. And then he received a lecture from the young man, whose demeanor, even Thomas Jefferson inferred, communicated an "aversion to have anything to do with us." Carmarthen began by enumerating "all the acts of the several states which militate against the treaty, with great precision," and concluded by telling Adams that "whenever America shall manifest a real determination to fulfill her part of the treaty, Great Britain will not hesitate to prove her sincerity." This scolding by a supercilious minister sixteen years his junior must have rankled Adams, but he had himself condemned as disgraceful all impediments to the collection of legitimate debts and was appalled to learn that Massachusetts was among the offending states. For Adams, Carmarthen's argument that "it would be folly for one party to carry its engagements into effect while the other neglected theirs" was not without merit.[9]

---

8. Articles 4 and 5, Treaty of Peace, Richard B. Morris, *The Peacemakers: The Great Powers and American Independence* (New York, 1965), 461–65, quotations at 463, 464; James Madison, "Vices of the Political System," April–June, *PJM*, 9:349; Jensen, *New Nation*, 265–81.

9. Article 7, Treaty of Peace, Morris, *Peacemakers*, 464; James Monroe to Richard Henry Lee, May 24, 1786, *LMCC*, 8:365; William Grayson to George Washington, May 27, 1786, *LMCC*, 8372; David McCulloch, *John Adams* (New York, 2001), 354, 365–66.

There appeared to be no way for the Confederation to end the standoff. It lacked the strength to remove British troops from American soil, and Congress lacked the power to force the states to abide by the terms of the treaty. Compounding this problem was another matter related to the treaty that, as Madison observed, had a "more dangerous root." The Paris agreement declared that the Mississippi River "shall forever remain free and open to the subjects of Great Britain and the citizens of the United States." Spain, however, was not a party to that agreement and contested the right of either nation to navigate freely on the Mississippi. The British claim was based on a provision in the 1763 Treaty of Paris, which ended the Seven Years' War. But as far as the Spanish were concerned, their declaration of war on Great Britain in 1779 invalidated that earlier privilege. "They totally deny our right to navigate that River or the right of Great Britain to grant it to us," North Carolina representative Richard Dobbs Spaight protested.[10]

The Mississippi Question

Americans might rail against the unfairness of the situation, insist that they were "entitled" to free navigation on the Mississippi, and denounce Spain's refusal to honor that entitlement as a "national outrage," but Spain conceded nothing. Madison's "dangerous root" reached back to the Revolutionary War, when Congress sent John Jay to Madrid in hopes of securing an alliance with Charles III. Jay quickly discovered that while the king was committed to expelling the English from the east bank of the Mississippi, he was equally determined to keep the Americans away. Thus Jay never secured an understanding, and the principal reason for his failure, he was informed through the office of the king's chief minister, the Conde de Floridablanca, was that the United States "did not seem inclined to gratify Spain in the only point in which she was deeply interested," that is, abjuring any claim to navigation on the Mississippi. William Carmichael, who as Jay's secretary was intimately involved in the protracted negotiations, confirmed that the Mississippi question was the "sole" obstacle to an alliance.[11]

The peace treaty Spain signed with Britain in 1783 made no mention of free navigation of the Mississippi. On the contrary, that agreement ceded West Florida to Spain, which gave the Spanish government effective control of both banks of the river over the course of its last two hundred miles to New Orleans and the Gulf of Mexico. Concerned about the heightened threat posed by

10. James Madison to James Monroe, January 8, 1785, *PJM*, 8:220; Article 8, Treaty of Peace, Morris, *Peacemakers*, 464; Richard Dobbs Spaight to the governor of North Carolina [Alexander Martin], December 6, 1784, *LMCC*, 7:622.
11. Samuel Hardy to the governor of Virginia [Patrick Henry], December 5, 1784, *LMCC*, 7:620; Morris, *Peacemakers*, 233.

American expansionism, Spain was not willing to grant in 1783 what it had refused during the war. And in fact, Spain closed the Mississippi to American traffic in June 1784, the howls of protest from states with extensive western lands awaiting development notwithstanding. "Nature has given the use of the Mississippi to those who may settle on its waters, as she gave to the United States their independence," Madison declared. The "impolicy of Spain may retard the former as that of G. Britain did the latter. But as G. B. could not defeat the latter, neither will Spain the former." To ask the United States to accept the "occlusion of the Mississippi" would therefore be the equivalent of asking them to commit "treason against the very laws" of nature "under which they obtained & hold their national existence." Thus the action taken by Spain was "dishonorable to her character" and destined to be futile.[12]

What Madison only hinted at was more brazenly stated by others. Spain's ideas regarding navigation on the Mississippi differed "so widely from ours," North Carolina's Spaight declared, "that one of the nations must recede from their opinions or a war will be the consequence." Hugh Williamson, Spaight's North Carolina colleague, had mixed feelings about the impact of the Mississippi traffic on "mercantile connections" with the inhabitants of "our Western territory," but agreed that the "strange proceedings" of the Spanish government were "dangerous." Virginia representative Richard Henry Lee, complaining to Madison about the tardiness of Congress in getting things done, thought that the "momentous concerns" raised by Spain's action had to be speedily addressed "or else a war may be the consequence." Fellow Virginian Samuel Hardy shared Lee's frustration and felt humiliated that legislative lethargy prevented the Confederation from standing up to the Spanish "insult," but, he warned, "with nations as with individuals there is a point of forbearance beyond which neither can yield. . . . Heaven forbid that Spain should drive us to this point." Nevertheless, the Comte de Montmorin, France's ambassador to the court of Madrid, was confident that Spain would not let up. "Spain looks upon the United States as prospective enemies before very long," he wrote, and therefore "she will omit nothing to keep them away, and specifically from the banks of the Mississippi."[13]

Jay-Gardoqui Talks

Shortly after Jay accepted appointment as the Confederation's secretary for foreign affairs in 1785, Congress charged him with negotiating a settlement

---

12. James Madison to the Marquis de Lafayette, March 20, 1785, *PJM*, 8:251–52.

13. Richard Dobbs Spaight to the governor of North Carolina [Alexander Martin], December 6, 1784, *LMCC*, 7:622; Hugh Williamson to Thomas Jefferson, December 11, 1784, *LMCC*, 7:624; Samuel Hardy to the governor of Virginia [Patrick Henry], December 5, 1784, *LMCC*, 7:620; Morris, *Peacemakers*, 220.

with Spain on matters pertaining to trade and territorial boundaries. Jay met with Don Diego de Gardoqui, whom Floridablanca had sent to New York as a special minister plenipotentiary to address these same issues. Gardoqui was new to America but no stranger to Jay. From 1780 to 1782, as Jay tried in vain to secure a formal alliance with Charles III, Gardoqui had been one of his most important diplomatic contacts in the Spanish ministry. The main issue in contention was also familiar to both men. Jay was instructed by Congress to claim for the United States free navigation on the Mississippi "from the source to the ocean, as established in their treaties with Great Britain." Gardoqui's instructions, however, explicitly removed from the bargaining table Spain's exclusive control over the last two hundred miles of the river.[14]

Based on his earlier experience, Jay knew that no progress could be made unless Congress softened its claims to navigation rights. He also knew that Congress might be willing to make certain concessions. In 1781, at the tail end of his negotiations for a treaty of alliance at the court of Madrid, Congress had authorized him to cede the right of navigation in hopes of averting a separate peace between Spain and Britain. Jay conveyed the offer to Floridablanca, but at his own discretion he imposed a time limit on the cession, a revision that quickly gained the approval of Congress. The Spanish minister still refused to conclude a formal alliance, thus spurning the American offer temporarily to forgo any claim to navigation rights. Now, in 1786, eager to break the deadlock between the two nations, Jay was willing to renew the offer. In exchange for what amounted to a most-favored nation trade relationship, the United States would agree "to forbear the use of the Mississippi for 25 or 30 years, the term for which the treaty shall last."[15]

Jay submitted his proposal to Congress on May 29, 1786, which set off a heated debate that highlighted sectional divisions to the detriment of the Union. Southern representatives in general accepted James Monroe's assessment of the exchange as a "very disadvantageous one" and shared his sense of outrage. "This is one of the most extraordinary transactions I have ever known," Monroe exclaimed, "a minister negotiating expressly for the purpose of defeating the object of his instructions." Monroe's anger was personal as well, fueled by the fact that he was the principal draftsman of the instructions that denied Jay any authority to compromise on this issue, specifically requiring him to secure free navigation rights on the Mississippi. South Carolinian Charles Pinckney joined the opposition and issued a warning. The "sacrifice" of navigation rights properly belonging to the United States in order to "obtain

---

14. Richard B. Morris, *The Forging of the Union, 1781–1789* (New York, 1987), 236.
15. Morris, *Peacemakers*, 242–43; James Monroe to the governor of Virginia [Patrick Henry], August 12, 1786, *LMCC*, 8:423.

a trivial commercial advantage" for northern merchants would "weaken if not destroy the union by disaffecting the southern states."[16]

Northern congressmen saw it differently. There was nothing trivial about the commercial advantages Jay had negotiated, Rufus King of Massachusetts claimed in rebuttal. With an "ungrateful soil and no staple but what they drew from the sea," the New England states "depended on a market" for their catch, and "the best market was Spain." Pinckney's assertion that "nothing was offered by the treaty but what might be enjoyed without it" was therefore completely uninformed, for "our fish, and every article we sell in Spain, is sold upon the footing of the most favored nation in that country." This special status "could not be secured but by treaty." On the other hand, the supposed sacrifice made by the country in ceding navigation rights "was of no great consequence." Pinckney might argue that the United States was giving up "far more than an equivalent" in the exchange of trading privileges for navigation rights, but Jay and King begged to differ. Given the sparseness of the population in the western districts and the current pace of economic development in the region, there was no need to insist on free navigation now. It was, Jay said, "not *at present* important." The United States, King said, agreed to give up "that which we could not at present enjoy." In twenty-five or thirty years, the story would be different, but by then the nation would be more capable of imposing a solution and Spain less able to resist. Henry "Light-Horse Harry" Lee understood the logic of the proposal. By "agreeing to the occlusion of the navigation of the Mississippi, we give in fact nothing, for the moment our western country becomes populous and capable, they will seize by force what may have been yielded by treaty." Therefore, the "extensive good consequences" of a most-favored commercial relationship with Spain outweighed any claim to navigation rights, since "we only give what we cannot use."[17]

Seven versus Five

Lee was one of a few. Southerners by and large did not share his sentiments, and Lee knew why. A treaty between the Confederation and Spain promised "advantages very great" but not so much "to the whole as to a part," he told a receptive Washington. Lee's Virginia colleague William Grayson was among the "popular declaimers" who "depreciated" the merits of the proposed treaty on precisely these terms. "Whatever the advantages might be," Grayson argued, "they were confined to the Eastern states." New England would "find a

16. James Monroe to the governor of Virginia [Patrick Henry], August 12, 1786, *LMCC*, 8:423, 424; minutes of proceedings, August 16, 1786, *LMCC*, 8:428.
17. Rufus King to Elbridge Gerry, August 13, 1786, *LMCC*, 8:425; minutes of proceedings, August 16, 1786, *LMCC*, 8:428, 429; Morris, *Forging the Union*, 241; Henry Lee to George Washington, August 7, 1786, *LMCC*, 7:417.

market for the fish," but it would be gained "wholly at the expense of the Southern states." Pennsylvania's Arthur St. Clair responded that although the "immediate benefits will be reaped by one part of the Union," those benefits "will redound to the advantage of the whole Union" due to their ripple effect throughout the entire domestic economy. Lee interrupted the debate before it could progress much further. The arguments on both sides were familiar enough, having been repeatedly made during the week, and he saw no point in continuing the exchange over "whether the advantages were great or small, equal or unequal." Indeed, there was every reason to discontinue the debate before it destroyed the Union itself. The disagreement over the treaty had thrust "other considerations" of "more weight" to the forefront.[18]

What concerned Lee became apparent in a string of votes over the disposition of the proposed treaty. Because Congress had instructed Jay to secure navigation rights, the vote in Congress was not on the treaty per se but on Jay's instructions. Massachusetts moved that the clause enjoining Jay to secure free use of the Mississippi be expunged from his instructions. In effect, the alteration granted the secretary for foreign affairs ex post facto authorization to forgo navigation rights. On a strictly sectional vote of seven states in favor of the change and five opposed, the motion carried, as far as the northern majority was concerned. However, the southern minority objected. Monroe said that the vote on August 29 settled nothing because the five dissenting states—Virginia, Maryland, North Carolina, South Carolina, and Georgia— challenged the "right of 7 either to instruct or ratify." Under the Articles of Confederation, treaties required the assent of a supermajority of nine states, and southern representatives argued that instructions to treaty negotiators had to meet this same requirement. It followed that "alterations made in instructions upon this subject" could not be effected by a mere seven states. As the "removal of a positive restraint confers a positive authority" in the manner of the original commission, it required a "similar concurrence of nine states."[19]

Monroe informed Patrick Henry that the southern delegations were prepared to "throw every possible obstacle in the way" of the proposed change in Jay's charge, and they did. On August 30, Charles Pinckney moved that Jay be told not to "negotiate upon different principles than those under which he was formerly instructed" in as much as the partial repeal voted upon the previous afternoon gained the assent of only seven states "when nine were alone competent to such alteration." By a seven to five vote, Pinckney's motion was defeated. Next Monroe, in a convoluted maneuver, moved to amend an amendment to

18. Henry Lee to George Washington, August 7, 1786, *LMCC*, 8:417; minutes of proceedings, August 18, 1786, *LMCC*, 8:438–40.

19. *JCC*, 31:595–96, 598–99; James Monroe to the governor of Virginia [Patrick Henry], August 12, 1786, *LMCC*, 8:424.

the original resolution so as to disallow any occlusion of the Mississippi. That motion was also defeated, seven to five. Finally, Monroe moved that if, during the course of his negotiations, Jay decided it was necessary for the United States to forbear use of the Mississippi for a set period, that concession must be accompanied by a statement of principle asserting American rights "to use and navigate the said river" and disavowing Spain's "exclusive" claims to the same. Again, by a vote of seven to five, the motion failed. The same bloc of seven, comprising the four New England states plus New York, Pennsylvania, and New Jersey, voted against these motions. Meanwhile, the same five Southern states voted for them. The division in each instance was as predictable as the entire controversy was unnecessary. In the end, whether seven or nine states were needed to alter Jay's instructions was irrelevant. Treaties required the approval of nine states, there was no disputing that, so whatever Jay negotiated under the authority of his new instructions would require the support of a supermajority in Congress. With the unwavering opposition of five states, there was no chance that Jay's proposal or any other settlement that impeded the use of the Mississippi could succeed.[20]

A Rope of Sand

Confrontations, even gratuitous and inconclusive ones, have consequences. Although the Jay-Gardoqui talks went nowhere and no accord on navigation rights was ever reached between the Confederation and Spain, the mutual allegations and suspicions incited by the Mississippi question deepened the crisis of union. Before the vote on August 29, North Carolina's Timothy Bloodworth said Jay's proposal had generated such "great divisions in the Eastern and Southern delegates" that he feared "no small disquietude will attend the decision should it terminate against us." After the votes of August 29 and 30, Bloodworth remarked that the "unhappy division" was rapidly becoming "firm and immovable." Henry Lee, who supported Jay's proposed exchange, regretted that the "decided difference" reflected in the several votes was felt "in every part of the Union." The whole "affair" had instilled "an intemperance" on each side that was "always injurious to the interest of the public."[21]

For Bloodworth and Lee, the "unhappy dispute" over Jay's proposed treaty was the latest evidence of the necessity of granting "additional powers to the confederation." Unless a "more efficient government" was instituted, one capable of managing divisive state and sectional interests, Bloodworth argued, "a dissolution of the Union must take place." He thus lent his support for an

---

20. James Monroe to the governor of Virginia [Patrick Henry], August 12, 1786, *LMCC*, 8:423–24; *JCC*, 31:596–607.

21. Timothy Bloodworth to the governor of North Carolina [Richard Caswell], August 16 and September 4, 1786, *LMCC*, 8:433, 462.

upcoming convention, which, at the urging of Lee's Virginia, was scheduled to meet in Annapolis on September 11, hopefully to recommend commercial regulations for the sake of promoting "permanent harmony" among the states of the Confederation. The alienation resulting from the profusion of state laws coupled with the protracted division over navigation rights on the Mississippi signified that the status quo was no longer sustainable. Something had to be done and done soon to offset the emerging impression that the "Confederated compact is no more than a rope of sand."[22]

The convention was a bust. Although nine states responded positively to Virginia's call, only five—Virginia, New York, Pennsylvania, New Jersey, and Delaware—made an appearance at Annapolis. A disappointed Madison, who arrived several days in advance, reported on September 8 that "the prospect of a sufficient number to make the meeting respectable is not flattering." To Monroe, Madison was even more pessimistic, telling him not to expect any help from the convention with regard to the quarrel over the Mississippi. Notwithstanding the legitimacy of Monroe's complaints about seven states attempting to repeal Jay's instructions, there was no "prospect here" of correcting the "injury" or "insult" perpetrated by the northern majority. The problem was inattendance; the absence of a "more respectable number" of state delegations at the Annapolis meeting prevented it from addressing any problems that threatened the harmony of the Confederation.[23]

Gentlemen Talk So Lightly of a Separation

The Annapolis Convention adjourned on September 14, after four days of futility. The committee appointed on September 11 to propose "measures proper to be adopted" concluded it would be "inexpedient for this Convention, in which so few states are represented, to proceed in the business committed to them." Accordingly, the twelve assembled delegates recommended only that another "Convention of Deputies from the different states" be convened in Philadelphia "on the second Monday of May next" for the "sole purpose" of devising a "plan for supplying such defects as may be discovered to exist" in the current Confederation. Few observers were surprised by this disappointing outcome. In fact, many had been skeptical from the outset. Rufus King was initially optimistic about the gathering and hopeful that "wisdom will govern their deliberations, and that their result will produce an union of opinions on the subject of commercial regulations through all the states." But two months be-

22. Timothy Bloodworth to the governor of North Carolina [Richard Caswell], September 4, 1786, *LMCC*, 8:462; Resolution Authorizing a Commission to Examine Trade Regulations, *PJM*, 8:471.

23. James Madison to Ambrose Madison, September 8, 1786, and James Madison to James Monroe, September 11, 1786, *PJM*, 9:120, 121.

fore the convention was scheduled to meet he was already singing a different tune, informing John Adams that he doubted whether the delegates would be capable of effecting "those measures essentially necessary for the prosperity and safety of the states." King's congressional foil, William Grayson of Virginia, was equally unenthusiastic, but for different reasons. A "partial reformation" of the Confederation, which was the most that could be accomplished in Annapolis, "will be fatal" to the Union, Grayson said, and therefore it might be better for the convention to leave things "as they are" rather than to "produce anything decisive." Madison himself, often credited with being the moving force behind the convention, was lukewarm about the idea of an interstate assembly to address the "subject of general [trade] regulations." In late January, after the Virginia legislature voted overwhelmingly in favor of just such a meeting, Madison called it an "expedient" and predicted that it would "probably miscarry." He went along with the proposal, however, thinking it was "better than nothing."[24]

Theodore Sedgwick of Massachusetts disagreed with Madison. He thought it better to do nothing than to answer Virginia's call. Suspected of being one of the leaders of the unprincipled "Eastern men" who were conspiring to give up navigation rights on the Mississippi in order to retard western development and thus to keep the "weight of government" centered in New England, Sedgwick returned the favor. "No reasonable expectations of advantage can be formed from the commercial convention," Sedgwick declared, because the "first proposers designed none." Rather than seeking to promote harmony by instituting a federal system of commercial regulation, their sole intention was to defeat the "enlargement of the powers of Congress. Of this I have the most decisive evidence." For Sedgwick, then, the preferred course of action for the "eastern and middle states, who are in interest one," was to avoid the Annapolis meeting and instead "seriously to consider what advantages result to them from their connection with the Southern states." Those states "can give us nothing," he said, except "participation in their commerce," which "they deny to us." It was time, therefore, "to contemplate a substitute" for the Confederation. His recommendation to his friend Caleb Strong, the Hampshire County lawyer who was one of the principal drafters of the Massachusetts Constitution of 1780, was a withdrawal from the present Union followed by the creation of a smaller confederation of northern states supervised by a "real and an efficient government."[25]

24. Egbert Benson, minutes, September 11, 1786; address of the Annapolis Convention, September 14, 1786, *PAH*, 3:686n1, 688–89; Edmund Cody Burnett, *The Continental Congress* (New York, 1941), 666, 667; James Madison to James Monroe, January 22, 1786, *PJM*, 8:483.

25. James Monroe to the governor of Virginia [Patrick Henry], August 12, 1786, *LMCC*, 8:24–25; Theodore Sedgwick to Caleb Strong, August 6, 1786, *LMCC*, 8: 415–16.

James Monroe had heard these and other separatist sentiments being expressed by "the Eastern people." During "conversations at which I have been present," he confided to Patrick Henry, New Englanders "talk of a dismemberment." He hoped that "wise and temperate men" everywhere would work to prevent a division of any sort, and yet, he cautioned, "I do consider it as necessary on our part to contemplate it as an event which may possibly happen and for which we should be guarded." How? In their conversations, New Englanders invariably included Pennsylvania as part of their confederation and "sometimes all the states south to the Potomac." Prudence dictated that Virginia not allow a separation along these lines, for such "a dismemberment . . . would throw too much strength into the Eastern Division." A breakup of the Confederation "should be so managed, (if it takes place) either that it should be formed into three divisions, or if into two, that Pennsylvania if not Jersey should be included in ours." Lest the governor doubt the accuracy of the information he was receiving, Monroe reported that his observations were "founded on authentic documents" and that New Englanders themselves admitted their "intrigues" were not "confined to a few only."[26]

Henry Lee was aware of the huddled exchanges occurring outside chamber doors, but unlike his fellow Virginian he was genuinely "sorry to find gentlemen talk so lightly of a separation and dissolution of the Confederation." The Annapolis Convention had done little to discourage such loose talk. If anything, it seemed to have fostered more distrust among an already divided people. And yet "Light-Horse Harry" Lee, whose Revolutionary War experiences and service in the Continental Congress had convinced him that the Articles of Confederation had to be amended or replaced, refused to give up on the idea of a stronger central government. Lee considered the "existence" of the United States "as a nation to depend on our Union," and he "was sensible that to preserve that Union, the powers of Congress should be enlarged." The Confederation government was too weak to keep a disunited people from fragmenting further, too ineffectual to keep acrimonious rivalries from escalating into acts of violence, and too impotent to ensure that such violence did not lead to self-destructive civil wars.[27]

Shays's Rebellion

In early September 1786, while Madison anxiously awaited the arrival of more delegates at Annapolis, Lee was worried. "The period seems to be fast approaching when the people of these U. States must determine to establish a

26. James Monroe to the governor of Virginia [Patrick Henry], August 12, 1786, *LMCC*, 8:425.

27. Minutes of proceedings, August 18, 1786, *LMCC*, 8:439; Charles Royster, *Light-Horse Harry Lee and the Legacy of the American Revolution* (New York, 1981), 88–96.

permanent capable government or submit to the horrors of anarchy and licentiousness," he wrote Washington. Lee had just learned of the "commotions" in western Massachusetts, where armed protesters had begun to challenge the authority of local courts to dish out penalties and were demanding legislative relief from creditors and burdensome taxes. Abigail Adams reacted harshly to the "tumults," which she attributed to the actions of demagogues. "Ignorant, restless desperadoes, without conscience or principles, have led a deluded multitude to follow their standard," she wrote Jefferson, "under the pretense of grievances which have no existence but in their imaginations." Lee was a bit more understanding. "The decay of their commerce leaves the lower order unemployed," he explained, and in their "idleness," they become more susceptible to the "intriguing exertions of another class whose desperate fortunes are remediable only by the ruin of society."[28]

Massachusetts governor James Bowdoin, who found the disturbances "alarming" and also blamed "evil and designing men" for alienating the "affections of the people," appealed to Henry Knox, the Confederation's secretary at war, for assistance in quelling the insurgency. Knox managed to persuade Congress in late October, as the militants became better organized and more numerous, to request $530,000 from the states in order raise a force of over thirteen hundred soldiers. None of this came to pass because with the exception of Virginia, every state, Massachusetts included, refused to ante up its share of the congressional requisition. Consequently, Bowdoin was forced to appeal to the wealthy merchant-speculators of Boston, whose reluctance to part with their money was trumped by their fear of the undeserving poor endangering all forms of property. Within two months, a privately funded army of three thousand men was ready to march against the insurgents, and, as it turned out, Bowdoin's volunteer force was more than a match for the rebels. By the end of the first week of February, the government's troops, commanded by former Revolutionary War general Benjamin Lincoln, had defeated and dispersed the Shaysites.[29]

In the meantime, however, Lee complained frequently and openly as Congress slowly did nothing. He thought Americans everywhere ought to be concerned about the commotions in western Massachusetts. Although the turmoil was currently concentrated in one locale, the problem could not be "confined to one state or to one part of a state, but pervades the whole." Indeed,

---

28. Henry Lee to George Washington, September 8 and October 17, 1786, *LMCC*, 8:463, 486; Abigail Adams to Thomas Jefferson, January 29, 1787, *The Adams-Jefferson Letters: The Complete Correspondence between Thomas Jefferson and Abigail and John Adams*, ed. Lester J. Cappon, 2 vols. (Chapel Hill, 1959), 1:168.

29. James Bowdoin, *An Address from the General Court to the People of Massachusetts* (Boston, 1786), 3, 4; David P. Szatmary, *Shays' Rebellion: The Making of an Agrarian Insurrection* (Amherst, MA, 1980), 82, 84–86, 98–106.

"every day brings new information" about the "designs and preparations of the malcontents," including their attempts at "forming connections with their neighboring states." To Madison, Lee declared it "unquestionably true that present appearances portend extensive national calamity—the contagion will spread and may reach Virginia." A swift and forceful response, for "the discontents will never be settled but by the sword," was long past due. Unfortunately, Congress failed to summon the needed resources, and congressional inaction, the "impotency of government," encouraged the "malcontents" while providing no restraints on the "licentious." All of this too clearly demonstrated that "a continuance of our present feeble political form is pregnant with daily evils."[30]

The Business of May Next

News of the rebellion in western Massachusetts, along with conjectures about "how far the Eastern disorders will spread," coincided with the circulation of the Annapolis delegates' recommendation that another convention, "with more enlarged powers," meet in Philadelphia for the sole purpose of rendering the "constitution of the Federal Government adequate to the exigencies of the Union." Washington, who was a frequent recipient of Lee's missives, linked the two concerns and eagerly endorsed the idea of an interstate meeting in May. Intelligence he had received from Henry Knox, who was sent by Congress to assess the situation in Massachusetts, was full of "melancholy information," Washington said, enough to convince him that "we are fast verging to anarchy & confusion!" "Without some alteration in our political creed," he wrote to Madison, "the superstructure we have been seven years raising at the expense of much blood and treasure, must fall." Congress must not be allowed to stagger feebly from crisis to crisis. "Prejudices, unreasonable jealousies, and local interest" must "yield to reason." The Articles of Confederation must be subjected to "that calm & deliberate attention which the magnitude of it so loudly calls for at this critical moment."[31]

Washington knew, of course, that Madison needed no persuading. They were kindred spirits on this particular issue. Madison was the principal author of the Virginia bill authorizing the state legislature to appoint seven delegates to attend the Philadelphia Convention, where they were enjoined to cooperate with deputies from the other states "in devising and discussing all such alterations and further provisions as may be necessary to render the federal Constitution adequate to the exigencies of the Union." Like Washington, Madison believed that the time had come for Americans to decide whether they would

30. Henry Lee to James Madison, October 25, 1786, *LMCC*, 8:492–93.
31. Edward Carrington to the governor of Virginia [Patrick Henry], December 8, 1786, *LMCC*, 8:516; address of the Annapolis Convention, September 14, 1786, *PAH*, 3:689; George Washington to James Madison, *PJM*, 9:161.

"by wise and magnanimous efforts reap the just fruits of that Independence which they have so gloriously acquired, and of that Union which they have cemented with so much of their common blood." The "auspicious blessings" anticipated as a result of the Revolution would not be realized unless local "jealousies and prejudices" gave way to wider "fraternal & affectionate sentiments." The United States would never be "as happy in peace as they have been glorious in war" until "partial and transitory interests" were cast aside, to be replaced by "noble and extended" motives.[32]

On December 4 the Virginia General Assembly elected the state's seven delegates to the upcoming Federal Convention. Madison, presently a member of Congress but also one of the seven chosen by the legislature, undertook almost immediately the challenge of doing what he could to improve the chances of a successful meeting in Philadelphia. An essential first step was to persuade Washington to participate. A month before the assembly made its appointments, he forewarned a seemingly reluctant Washington that "your name" will be placed at the head of the Virginia delegation in order "to give this subject a very solemn dress, and all the weight which could be derived from a single state." Three days after his and Washington's election, Madison resumed his cajoling, reminding the general "of the mission and its acknowledged preeminence over every other public object." Furthermore, it was the unanimous "opinion of every judicious friend whom I consulted," Madison continued, "that your name could not be spared from the deputation to the Meeting in May in Philadelphia." This was not simply a matter of local importance. Other states were watching with great interest and would take "having your name in the front of the appointment as a mark of the earnestness of Virginia, and an invitation to the most select characters from every part of the Confederacy."[33]

When Washington demurred, citing his recent refusal to attend a May meeting of the Society of Cincinnati, a fraternal organization established in 1783 by former officers of the Continental Army, and the awkwardness of his being in Philadelphia "on another public occasion during the sitting of this Society," Madison sympathized but remained undeterred. The "posture of our affairs," the dire circumstances in which the nation found itself, should be more than enough to silence "every criticism on the situation which the contemporary meetings would place you in." However, he understood completely the "difficulties" to which Washington alluded, and therefore asked only that "a door . . . be kept open for your acceptance hereafter, in case the gathering

32. Bill Providing for Delegates to the Convention of 1787, November 6, 1786, *PJM*, 9:163–64.
33. Resolution to Select Commissioners for a Federal Convention, November 30, 1786, *PJM*, 9:187; Edmund Randolph to James Madison, December 6, 1786, *PJM*, 9:198; James Madison to George Washington, November 8 and December 7, 1786, *PJM*, 9:166, 199.

clouds should become so dark and menacing as to supersede every consideration." Meanwhile, he kept Washington apprised of the darkening clouds: the "thinness of Congress," that is, the absence of so many members, was an insurmountable "obstacle to all the important business before them," including securing "full compliance" with the Treaty of Paris and ensuring that "money comes into the Federal Treasury"; General Lincoln's forces had restored "calm" in western Massachusetts, but there was "a great distrust of its continuance"; and the "business of the Mississippi begins to ferment," as inhabitants throughout the West remained in "great agitation by the reported intention of Congress" to curtail traffic on the river.[34]

It was a familiar litany of the "evils" that plagued the nation. Fortunately, as he reported to Jefferson, plans for the Philadelphia meeting were progressing splendidly, and "appointments for the Convention go on auspiciously." By late March, all of the states, except Connecticut and Rhode Island, had chosen their delegates or enacted measures for doing so, and "it is not doubted" that those two "will follow the example of their neighbors." Patrick Henry's refusal to take his place in the Virginia delegation was "ominous," to be sure, a clear indication that this influential troublemaker was "keeping himself free to combat or espouse the result of it according to the result of the Mississippi business." But George Wythe, the dean of the Virginia legal establishment, and John Blair, a distinguished member of the state supreme court, were committed to attend, and Edmund Randolph, recently elected to succeed Henry as governor, had already turned his "thoughts towards the business of May next." Additionally, the famously private George Mason, revered above all other Virginians save one, seemed reconciled to accept his most public appointment. And most importantly, although Washington declined to commit himself openly, he was poised to step "into that field if the crisis should demand it." The health of the country was "becoming every day more & more critical," but at least the upcoming convention would be well attended, comprising, as Madison later recalled, some of the "most enlightened & influential patriots" from the several states, and fully prepared to address the "malignity of the disease."[35]

34. George Washington to James Madison, December 16 and 24 and November 1, 1786, *PJM*, 9:215–16, 224, 155; James Madison to George Washington, March 18 and February 25, 1787, *PJM*, 9:315–316, 285; James Madison to Edmund Randolph, February 25, 1787, *PJM*, 9:299.
35. James Madison to Edmund Randolph, March 25, April 8, and February 25, 1787, *PJM*, 9:331, 369, 299; James Madison to Thomas Jefferson, March 19, 1787, 9:318–19; James Madison to George Washington, April 16, 1787, 9:383; James Madison, preface to debates, Farrand, 3:545.

CHAPTER ONE

A Union of Large and Small States

The delegates slowly began to arrive in Philadelphia, much too slowly for James Madison. The Constitutional Convention, scheduled to begin on May 14, had been forced to adjourn without conducting any business because only the members of the Virginia delegation were present in sufficient numbers. Over the next week, delegates from other states trickled into the Pennsylvania State House. Charles Pinckney and John Rutledge from South Carolina attended on May 17, Alexander Hamilton and Robert Yates from New York on May 18, and William Few of Georgia and George Read of Delaware the following morning. Still, at the start of the second week, only three states—Virginia, New York, and Delaware—were ready to proceed. Even the Pennsylvania delegation was officially absent. "There is less punctuality in the outset than was to be wished," Madison complained to Thomas Jefferson. His complaint was cast in a manner characteristic of his "most agreeable style of conversation," but even Madison's "remarkable sweet temper" must have been sorely tested as adjournments continued day after day for most of that second week until a quorum was finally achieved on May 25.[1]

The twenty-nine delegates from seven states dealt expeditiously with routine matters of housekeeping on the first day. Robert Morris on behalf of the Pennsylvania delegation nominated George Washington as president of the convention. South Carolina's John Rutledge seconded the motion, confident "that the choice would be unanimous" but withholding further commentary because, he said, Washington's presence forbade such praises that "might otherwise be proper." Rutledge's explanation was as gratuitous as his gesture of genteel reserve. Laudatory observations on Washington's behalf were unnecessary, and everyone at the Pennsylvania State House knew it. They had entered Philadelphia largely unnoticed; Washington could not avoid the fanfare. Befitting the arrival of the celebrated "deliverer of his Country," church bells rang, cannons fired, and crowds cheered as soon as the "Commander in chief of the late American Army" had approached the city the previous Sunday evening.

1. James Madison to Thomas Jefferson, May 15, 1787, *Republic of Letters*, 1:477; Farrand, 3:95, 587–90.

Following his election, Washington was escorted by Morris and Rutledge to his seat at the front of the Assembly Room. He thanked the other delegates "in a very emphatic manner" for the honor they had bestowed on him, asked to be excused for any errors he might commit "as they would be unintentional," and reminded them of the "novelty" of the business they were about to undertake.[2]

Convention Rules

The next day the delegates proceeded to adopt the standing rules of the convention with so little debate that their significance might easily be overlooked. A few of these were simple matters of etiquette—do not talk or read when someone is speaking, speak only once on an issue in order to give others a chance to be heard, do not cross in front of someone addressing the president, refrain from "reprehensible" behavior, and stand in place upon adjournment until the president has passed—but there were four rules of far greater significance that had lasting consequences. First, the convention agreed that the presence of seven states would constitute a quorum. According to George Read, who rented a room in the same boardinghouse with Madison and Edmund Randolph, the Virginians had become increasingly uneasy by the end of the week after May 14 due to the "backwardness of individuals in giving attendance." That uneasiness was partly rooted in the memory of the irregular attendance that plagued the Confederation Congress, making it difficult to achieve a quorum let alone gain the assent of nine states, which the Articles of Confederation required for deciding such matters as waging war, raising an army or navy, appointing a commander in chief, commissioning privateers, coining or borrowing money, and entering into treaties. Even the treaty ending the War of Independence was left in limbo because, as Jefferson pointed out in December, 1783, three months after the Paris signing, "we have no certain prospect of nine states in Congress and cannot ratify the treaty with fewer."[3]

Second, the convention allotted to each state one vote irrespective of its size or the size of its delegation. The Philadelphia Convention, in other words, would operate in the same manner that Congress did under the Articles of Confederation. That this rule generated little or no discussion is somewhat surprising. Many if not most of the representatives of the self-described "principal States" bridled at this aspect of the Confederation Congress. George Mason, second only to Washington in the esteem he commanded among Vir-

2. Farrand, 1:1, 3–4, 3:94; James Madison to Thomas Jefferson, May 15, 1787, *Republic of Letters*, 1:477; Richard Beeman, *Plain, Honest Men: The Making of the American Constitution* (New York, 2009), 30.
3. Farrand, 1:11–12, 3:25; Jack N. Rakove, *The Beginnings of National Politics: An Interpretive History of the Continental Congress* (New York, 1979), 198–200, 354–59.

ginians, identified the practice of equal representation as the most objectionable feature of the "present federal system." Madison believed that the "inequality of importance and influence in the States" ought to be reflected in the "principle of Representation in the federal system." That a vote from Delaware not "be of equal value with one from Massachusetts or Virginia" was simply "just." But when some Pennsylvania delegates, led by Gouverneur Morris, pressed the Virginia delegation to join them "in firmly refusing to the small States an equal vote" in the convention, they were "stifled." Why? Because the Virginians had made a calculation of the risks involved. To insist on a change in the manner of voting to which the "little States" had grown accustomed "might beget fatal altercations" and cause them to withdraw from Philadelphia before the convention had really begun. It was better, that is, more "practicable," Madison reasoned, to trust the convention to do the right thing, especially because "a majority of the States" would be "gainers" as a result of the change in government and would therefore realize that their own selfish interests dictated an abandonment of the practice of equal representation.[4]

Third, unlike the Confederation Congress, which required a supermajority of nine states to authorize actions on major issues, the Philadelphia Convention agreed that "all questions shall be decided by the greater number of these [states] which shall be fully represented." But what did the "greater number" mean? Did the winning side need more than 50 percent of the votes cast, abstentions included? Initially, there was some confusion over the application of this rule. This became apparent on June 1, when the convention took up the question of the national executive's term of office. The debate pitted Pennsylvania's James Wilson, who argued for a three-year tenure with the possibility of reelection, against South Carolina's Charles Pinckney, who favored a single term of seven years. On Pinckney's motion, the vote was five states for, four opposed, and one delegation divided. "A question was asked whether a majority had voted in the affirmative?" The delegates turned to Washington for clarification, and "the president decided that it was an affirmative vote." Less than a week later, on a motion by South Carolina's John Rutledge to deny the federal government the power of establishing lower courts, the vote was five for, four opposed, and two delegations divided. However, there was no confusion this time. The precedent having been established, no one questioned whether Rutledge's motion had carried.[5]

Finally and most famously, the convention adopted a rule of secrecy. Delegates were cautioned to ensure that "nothing spoken in the [Pennsylvania State] House be printed, or otherwise published or communicated." Washington,

4. George Mason to George Mason Jr., May 20, 1787, *PGM*, 3:880; James Madison to Thomas Jefferson, March 19, 1787, *Republic of Letters*, 1:470–71; Farrand, 1:10–11n4.
5. Farrand, 1:11, 64, 69, 118, 125.

above all, expected strict compliance on the part of the membership. On one occasion in mid-June, after Pennsylvania's Thomas Mifflin presented him with a copy of some notes that an unidentified delegate had mislaid in the assembly room, a visibly upset Washington laid the document on the table in front of him and announced that "one Member of this Body has been so neglectful of the secrets of the Convention as to drop in the State House a copy of their proceedings." The president's demeanor was "so severe," Georgia's William Pierce said, "that every Person seemed alarmed." Pierce himself "was extremely so" until he saw that the notes in question were in the "hand writing of another person." Mason understood Washington's distress, believing as he did that the free exchange of ideas required a certain degree of confidentiality and anonymity. The act of creation was bound to be messy. Ideas initially may be "crude and undigested," but delegates should feel free to express them openly without the threat of popular "misrepresentations." The exclusion of the public also removed the temptation some delegates might otherwise feel to play to an audience, concerning themselves more with popularity than with posterity. Madison, who confessed to being mortified because he could not disclose anything about the proceedings of the convention to Jefferson, nevertheless honored the rule, promising his friend to "make amends" for his "silence" as soon as he was at liberty to do so. Years later, like Mason, Madison continued to insist that "no Constitution would ever have been adopted by the convention if the debates had been public."[6]

One consequence of the secrecy rule has been that subsequent generations of Americans have been left with only one full account of the daily proceedings of the Philadelphia Convention. Fortunately, that account was written by Madison. Situating himself next to the president's table at the front of the chamber, and thus in a "favorable position for hearing all that . . . was read from the Chair or spoken by the members," Madison took "lengthy notes of every thing that . . . passed." In order to ensure that he caught every "single speech," he did not miss "a single day, nor more than a casual fraction of an hour in any day." And true to his reputation for "industry and application," which, as Georgia's William Pierce observed, "he possesses in a most eminent degree," Madison painstakingly reconstructed each day's events from his "abbreviations & marks," with hardly a moment's relief in the after hours "between the adjournment & reassembling of the Convention." Never robust to begin with, this strenuous regimen began to take its toll on Madison's health, but, as he informed Jefferson in mid-July, two months into the convention, he meant "to go on with the drudgery" unless some "indisposition obliges me to

---

6. Farrand, 1:15, 17, 3:28, 33, 86–87; James Madison to Thomas Jefferson, July 18, 1787, *Republic of Letters*, 1:483–84; Clinton Rossiter, *1787: The Grand Convention* (New York, 1966), 167.

discontinue it." More than three decades later, as he recalled his four-month ordeal in Philadelphia, Madison reportedly said that "the labor of writing out the debates, added to the confinement to which his attendance in Convention subjected him, almost killed him."[7]

The Virginia Plan

The "main business" of the convention started the morning of May 29, when Edmund Randolph addressed the delegates in a "long and elaborate speech," presenting what came to be known as the Virginia Plan. Beginning with a review of the "defects" that contributed to "the prospect of anarchy from the laxity of government every where" and portended the "fulfilment of prophecies of the American downfall," Randolph proceeded to outline a remedy in fifteen resolutions. Of these, the most carefully conceived and most controversial were the five that dealt with the new legislative branch. Unlike the Confederation Congress, the National Legislature would be bicameral, and representation in both houses would be proportioned according to each state's "contribution" toward federal revenues or to the "number of free inhabitants" residing within its borders. This suggested alteration, as Mason explained, had long been contemplated by the large-state deputies and reflected their "most prevalent idea."[8]

The end of the one vote per state rule in favor of proportional representation signaled a radical redefinition of the federal presence in the new Union. The Articles of Confederation empowered the legislatures of each state to direct the appointment of its congressmen, but the Virginia Plan stipulated that the people were to elect their representatives to the "first branch," which in turn would choose the deputies of the "second branch" from a "proper number of persons nominated by the individual [state] legislatures." The membership of the National Legislature, as Madison saw it, would thus embrace the "alternative of a government which instead of operating on the states, should operate without their intervention on the individuals composing them." Furthermore, the powers of this differently constituted bicameral legislature would be greatly enhanced under the Virginia Plan. Whereas the Confederation Congress "could not defend itself against the encroachments from the states"—a necessary consequence of the Articles being not "paramount to the state constitutions"—the National Legislature would act as a superintending body, checking state laws that might disturb the "harmony of the United States." Included in the description of this superintending capacity was an early rendering of what became the federal supremacy clause, authorizing the

7. Farrand, 3:94, 550; James Madison to Thomas Jefferson, July 18, 1787, *Republic of Letters*, 1:484.

8. Farrand, 1:20, 23; George Mason to George Mason, Jr., May 20, 1787, *PGM*, 3:880.

exercise of a veto over state laws that "in the opinion of the National Legislature" were inconsistent with the new "articles of Union."[9]

Taken together, these provisions of the Virginia Plan amounted to a repudiation rather than a revision of the Articles of Confederation. Robert Yates, who shared a table with Alexander Hamilton as a member of the New York delegation but distanced himself from his colleague's nationalist aspirations, grew increasingly agitated as he listened to Randolph. In a journal that he kept sporadically until "discontent & disgust" caused him to abandon the convention in early July, Yates did not even bother to summarize the resolutions before going on to claim that the Virginia governor "candidly confessed" in closing that his resolutions "were not intended for a federal government." According to Yates, Randolph and presumably the rest of the Virginia delegation admitted that their real intention was to establish "a strong *consolidated* union, in which the idea of states should be nearly annihilated." That Randolph made such a confession is highly dubious, to say the least. Neither the official journal of the convention nor any other set of notes taken by any other delegate makes any mention of what would surely have passed for intentionally inflammatory remarks. Madison dismissed Yates's journal as the unreliable product of a "zealous partisan," whose fragmented notes crossed the line between recording and editorializing so routinely that "parts of sentences explaining or qualifying other parts might often escape the ear." Such qualms aside, Yates's comment accurately reflected the reactions of those delegates who were committed to the Articles of Confederation and to the principle of equality of representation.[10]

There Cannot Be Two Supremes

Advocates of the Virginia Plan knew that it amounted to much more than a revision of the existing articles of union. As soon as the May 30 morning session began, Randolph moved that three alternative propositions be considered in lieu of the first resolution of the Virginia Plan, which called for the "Articles of Confederation . . . to be so corrected & enlarged, as to accomplish the objects proposed by their institution." That resolution was potentially confusing and almost certainly "unnecessary," Yates claimed Gouverneur Morris responded, because "the subsequent resolutions would not agree with it." Of the three new propositions, the first two preempted any effort to revise the Articles. A "union of the States merely federal" would not be able to guarantee the ends for which governments were established, the first proposition declared, "namely common defense, security of liberty, & genl. welfare." Second, no al-

9. Farrand, 1:19, 20, 21; James Madison to Thomas Jefferson, October 24 and November 1, 1787, *Republic of Letters*, 1:496.

10. Farrand, 1:24; James Madison to N. P. Trist, December [?], 1831, and James Madison to W. C. Rives, October 21, 1833, in Farrand, 3:516–17, 521.

liance of sovereign states, whatever the configuration, "would be sufficient" to these ends. In other words, the Union created under the Articles was so fundamentally flawed that it was beyond salvation. The third proposition pointed to a remedy for the ills of the Confederation: "a *national* government ought to be established consisting of a *supreme* Legislative, Executive & Judiciary."[11]

Madison noted that "some verbal criticisms were raised against the first proposition, and it was agreed . . . to pass on to the third." But his disjointed summary fails to do justice to the "criticisms." Yates's journal and the notes taken by Maryland's James McHenry give us a more complete picture of the morning's action. After Randolph made his motion, the delegates sat momentarily in silence, perhaps stunned by the boldness of the proposal to do away with the Articles of Confederation. George Wythe, "the famous Professor of Law at the University of William and Mary" whose "too favorable opinion of men," according to William Pierce, made him "no great politician," inferred "from the silence of the house" that the delegates were ready to "pass on the resolution." Pierce Butler of South Carolina rose immediately to protest that "he had not made up his mind on the subject" and would welcome any "light which discussion might throw on it."[12]

The ensuing discussion quickly brought matters to a head. The convention had been authorized by Congress to meet in Philadelphia "for the sole and express purpose of revising the Articles of Confederation." All of the state commissions likewise spoke of "alterations," and several, including those of New York, Massachusetts, and Connecticut, repeated the qualifying phrase of the congressional charge. Mindful of these very particular circumstances, South Carolina's Charles Cotesworth Pinckney, "generally considered an indifferent orator" but one who proved effective when "warm in debate," challenged the delegates to explain under what authority they might proceed with "a discussion of a system founded on different principles" from the Articles. To proceed under Randolph's first proposition would take the delegates beyond the scope of their appointment, which was "to revise the present confederation, and to alter or amend it as the case might require." For the first time, the Assembly Room resonated with the words that the nationalists dreaded most to hear. If the convention voted for Randolph's initial proposition, Pinckney announced, "their business was at an end."[13]

Pinckney's "remark had its weight, and in consequence of it, the 1st and 2d resolve was dropt." The convention moved on to the third, but it too had its "difficulties." Charles Pinckney, second cousin to Charles Cotesworth Pinckney, wanted to know what the terms "national" and "supreme" signified. Was

11. Farrand, 1:38, 33, 39, 40, 41.   12. Farrand, 1:33, 34, 3:94.
13. Farrand, 3:14, 96, 1:34, 39.

Randolph seeking "to abolish the state governments altogether"? Randolph said he had no such wish and that the third proposition was intended only "to give the national government a power to defend and protect itself." It would take from the states "no more sovereignty than is competent to this end," thereby restoring the proper balance between the central government and the states. Gouverneur Morris elaborated further with an explanation that harked back to the imperial crisis of the 1760s and 1770s, when radicals began openly to articulate a response to the assertion that Parliament was sovereign within the empire. The "distinction between a *federal* and *national, supreme* Govt.," Morris said in support of the first and third propositions offered by Randolph, was that the former relied "on the good faith of the parties," whereas the latter had "*compulsive*" power. And the power of compulsion was the sine qua non of a sovereign government. Congress under the Articles of Confederation was neither national nor supreme because it lacked this power "to compel every part to do its duty." It was as if there were two sovereign entities in the Confederation, the federal government and the states, and such an arrangement violated a maxim of politics: There cannot be "two *supremes*" in a single polity. "In all communities there must be one supreme power, and one only."[14]

Morris's summary statement amounted to a defense of Sir William Blackstone's definition of sovereignty, first issued in 1765, the year of the Stamp Act crisis, which held that there must be one indivisible and absolute authority in every government. The logic of the colonists' resistance to parliamentary measures in the 1760s and 1770s, complemented by the autonomy to which the colonies had grown accustomed during most of the half century preceding the Seven Years' War, seemed to contradict Blackstone's classic formulation. However, the proven ineffectiveness of the Confederation Congress in the 1780s necessitated a reconsideration of the prevailing emphasis on state sovereignty. George Mason, Randolph's senior colleague, understood and endorsed the distinction made by Morris. Not only was the present confederation "deficient in not providing for coercion & punishment against delinquent states," Mason argued, but the federal government under the Articles "in the nature of things" could not punish the "states collectively." What was needed and what Randolph's third proposition recommended was a national government that "could directly operate on individuals."[15]

Other delegates were not willing to go as far as Morris and Mason. To push the distinction between federal and national systems to their extreme would

14. Farrand, 1:39, 42, 33–34.
15. Jack P. Greene, *Peripheries and Center: Constitutional Development in the Extended Polities of the British Empire and the United States, 1607–1788* (Athens, GA, 1986), 153–211; Farrand, 1:34.

lead them back to the same objections over congressional authorization and state commissions that Pinckney had raised in conjunction with the first of Randolph's propositions. Elbridge Gerry cautioned the delegates to avoid settling on Morris's distinction. If he understood them correctly, the proponents of Randolph's resolution were advocating a "government totally different" from the one prescribed by the Articles of Confederation. If so, it would justifiably lead to questions about the very "foundation of the convention," for in the given context "if we have a right to pass this resolution, we have a right to annihilate the confederation."[16]

Too Great Inroads on the Existing System

Waiting uneasily for a chance to speak was Roger Sherman, who had taken his seat with the Connecticut delegation just before Randolph presented his three propositions. As a member of the Continental Congress in 1776, Sherman had served on the committee that had drafted the Articles of Confederation and thus had a personal investment in the government it established. More importantly though, the act of the Connecticut legislature under which he held his appointment specified that he and his two colleagues, William Samuel Johnson and Oliver Ellsworth, were to attend the Philadelphia Convention "for the sole and express purpose of revising the Articles of Confederation." Sherman was not about to abuse that trust. He readily admitted that the Articles "had not given sufficient power to Congress and that additional powers were necessary," but Randolph's propositions, even with, indeed perhaps especially with, the clarifications offered by Morris and Mason, went too far, and he was not "disposed to make too great inroads on the existing system."[17]

Sherman's comments were bound to have an impact. By 1787 the self-educated lawyer and one-time shoemaker had achieved a reputation for "thoughts that are wise and useful." He was ungainly and often socially awkward, "the reverse of grace," according to John Adams, and his lack of formal schooling was betrayed by his inability to "embellish" his speeches with classical allusions, but he won over admirers with his intelligence and common sense. Even William Pierce, whose Georgian sensibilities recoiled at Sherman's unpolished "New England cant," which he deemed "grotesque and laughable," came to conclude that "there is something regular, deep and comprehensive" in the Connecticut delegate's "train of thinking." Pierce was also impressed by Sherman's ability to adjust to changing circumstances and by his influence over others, which he attributed to his having overcome the "lowness of his condition" in early life. As he "progressed upwards," Sherman had learned to

16. Farrand, 1:42–43.   17. Farrand, 3:585, 1:34–35.

be "extremely artful in accomplishing any particular object," Pierce noted, and "it is remarked that he seldom fails."[18]

Using Sherman's reservations to his advantage, Delaware's George Read moved that consideration of Randolph's third proposition be postponed, recommending instead a resolution stating simply that "a more effective government consisting of a Legislative, Executive and Judiciary ought to be established." Gone were references to a "national" government and to its "supreme" branches. Read's motion would have removed two roadblocks to the convention's progress: it would have preempted further disagreement over the implications of the disputed terms in Randolph's resolutions and it would have forestalled questions concerning the authority of the delegates to act in contravention of their state commissions. It could accomplish this, however, only by backing away from the Virginia Plan and pursuing, as Read's Delaware commission put it, "such alterations and further provisions as may be necessary" to render the Articles of Confederation "adequate to the exigencies of the union." But Read, whose voice was so "feeble and . . . articulation so bad that few can have patience to attend to him," could not persuade a majority of the state delegations to abandon the Virginia Plan. When the vote on his motion was taken, the convention was evenly split, four in favor and four opposed, and so the "motion to postpone for this purpose was lost." The convention finally called the question on Randolph's third proposition, which carried by a vote of six states in favor, including Read's Delaware; one opposed, Sherman's Connecticut; and one divided.[19]

Delaware's Threat to Withdraw

It was well past noon before the delegates moved on to the second resolution of the Virginia Plan, and they had been sitting at their assigned tables since ten o'clock that morning. But there was no respite for the weary. The apportionment of seats in the new National Legislature based on a state's revenue contributions or the number of its free inhabitants was a more direct assault on the Articles of Confederation, and the small-state delegates wanted none of it. Anticipating a vigorous opposition on several fronts, the supporters of the Virginia Plan agreed to postpone further consideration of the second resolution because its reference to "free inhabitants" tended, as Madison explained, to divert attention away from the question of "whether the principle of representation should be changed." Randolph then proposed, and Madison seconded, a more straightforward resolution: "that the rights of suffrage in the national legislature ought to be proportioned." Even this seemingly unambiguous statement

18. Farrand, 3:88–89; Bernard Bailyn, *To Begin the World Anew: The Genius and Ambiguities of the American Founders* (New York, 2003), 28–30.
19. Farrand, 3:574, 93, 1:35, 30–31.

of principle, however, generated some controversy, especially among those who were opposed to the equal distribution of votes prescribed by the Articles. In an effort to appease them, a friendly amendment attached the phrase "and not according to the present system" to the end of Randolph's motion. Now it was the small-state delegates turn to be heard. They moved to delete the words "to be proportioned," so that the resolution would read: "that the rights of suffrage in the national legislature ought not to be according to the present system." That rendering could conceivably leave them enough wiggle room to justify equal representation of the states, as long as it was not exactly the same as the one-vote-per-state arrangement that prevailed under the Articles.[20]

Unable to arrive at a consensus, the delegates postponed further consideration of the Randolph-Madison motion. But Madison, who remained convinced that "if a majority of the larger states concur, the fewer and smaller states must finally bend to them," refused to be deterred. In what he described as an attempt to get the delegates beyond their present "difficulties," Madison offered a resolution that could not be misinterpreted: "that the equality of suffrage established by the Articles of Confederation ought not to prevail in the National Legislature, and that an equitable ratio of representation ought to be substituted." Seconded by Gouverneur Morris of Pennsylvania, the motion was "generally relished, [and] would have been agreed to" according to Madison, had George Read not abruptly interjected with a protest. Disappointed that he had failed to waylay Randolph's third proposition earlier in the morning, Read objected to Madison's new motion and asked that the whole issue relating to representation be postponed. Delaware's delegates, he reminded the convention, "were restrained by their commission from assenting to any change of the rule of suffrage." The deputies from New York and Connecticut may have felt constrained by commissions authorizing them to be in Philadelphia for the sole purpose of revising the Articles of Confederation, but the representatives of Delaware operated under even greater restraints. The state legislature expressly prohibited them from agreeing to alterations of the fifth article of the Articles of Confederation, which declared that "in Congress assembled, each State shall have one vote."[21]

Read did not view this prohibition as a burden; to the contrary, he endorsed it as a "prudent measure" devised to preserve "our existence as a state." Writing to John Dickinson in anticipation of their appointment to the Philadelphia Convention, Read noted that public discussions and private conversations had already indicated that the "voice of the states," that is, their mode of voting in the federal legislature, "will be one of the subjects of revision" at Philadelphia,

20. Farrand, 1:36.
21. James Madison to Thomas Jefferson, March 19, 1787, *Republic of Letters*, 1:471; Farrand, 1:36–37.

and it behooved the smaller states not to count on the "generosity or ideas of public justice" of the larger states. "Trust nothing" of consequence to them, Read advised his more accomplished colleague. In this situation, it was advantageous for Delaware's representatives to have their hands tied by the dictates of the state assembly. Without any authority whatsoever to modify Article 5, they were saved from ever having to enter into "disagreeable argumentation" on the matter. Read's reminder to the other delegates, therefore, came with a warning. If the majority decided to change the "rule of suffrage," then the Delaware delegation might be obligated "to retire from the Convention."[22]

Gouverneur Morris reacted strongly to the threatened "secession of a state." Mustering the combination of talent and charm for which he was known and which reportedly made "the labor of reasoning easy and pleasing," Morris staked out an unyielding position. The possible withdrawal of Delaware was regrettable, a cause for "real concern," he declared, but the change in the one vote per state rule was "so fundamental . . . that it could not be dispensed with." Madison, less commanding than Morris as an orator but more effective in debate because his preparation made him, in William Pierce's estimation, "the best informed man of any point," tried to be more understanding. Confident that Delaware stood alone in this confrontation and seeking to save its delegates the "embarrassment" of being forced to act on their threat, Madison suggested that the vote on his motion be taken informally in the committee of the whole rather than formally in the convention. The lopsided result in the informal poll might so overwhelm Read and his companions that they would back away from the reckless position they had staked out. But nothing worked "to satisfy Mr. Read." Rather than agreeing to a straw poll or making any other concessions, he moved for a postponement of the whole issue relating to the principle of representation.[23]

That Delaware should seek a postponement is hardly a surprise, but why would the other delegations go along with Read's motion? What would explain their willingness to bend to the will of tiny Delaware? The threat to withdraw from the convention was cause for some concern, to be sure, but Rhode Island withheld its participation, and few seemed to have fretted over its absence. Moreover, when this confrontation took place on the afternoon of May 30, Maryland and Georgia could not vote because they had not achieved a quorum in their respective delegations, and New Hampshire's deputies did not bother showing up for another month and a half. What made Delaware special? The short answer is that it was not. Morris was being diplomatic when he said that the departure of Delaware's delegates would be lamentable because

22. George Read to John Dickinson, January 17, 1787, in Farrand, 3:575–76n6; 1:37.
23. Farrand, 3:92, 1:37–38.

the convention would miss "the valuable assistance of those members." Morris and most of the large-state nationalists were more concerned with what Read, Dickinson, and their associates might be compelled to do after their withdrawal than with the loss of their contributions to the convention itself. The Delaware legislature would surely demand a reason for their leaving Philadelphia, and in justifying their action the appointees would gladly violate the rule of secrecy to which they had been bound. Once the general public learned about the Virginia Plan and the repudiation of the Articles of Confederation, the business of the convention was in danger of being brought to an untimely end. Read might have been bluffing, but why take the chance? It made more sense for the nationalists to agree to a postponement than to provoke a crisis. Hopefully, their retreat would buy them enough time to convince the Delawareans that "no just construction" of their commission "could require or justify a secession."[24]

A Federal Veto

On June 9, after more than a week had elapsed, the convention resumed consideration of the rule of representation in the proposed National Legislature. Since the May 30 postponement, the convention had addressed all of the remaining resolutions of the Virginia Plan and reached a consensus on a number of them. The majority had agreed tentatively that there would be a single national executive, chosen by the National Legislature for a term of seven years with no possibility of reelection, empowered with a veto that could be overridden by a two-thirds vote in each house of the legislature and subject to impeachment by a process still to be determined. They had also agreed that the National Judiciary would consist of one or more supreme tribunals and such lower courts as the National Legislature at its discretion might create, that federal judges were to hold their offices during good behavior, and that the method of their appointment be left "blank" in order to allow for "maturer reflection." The rules of order adopted at the outset of the convention allowed motions to reconsider, meaning that questions previously debated and voted on could be revisited and earlier decisions reversed, revised, or left unchanged after additional discussion. Hence the configuration of the executive and judicial branches would be modified in the months ahead, but substantial progress had been made on these issues by the time the delegates returned to the thorny question of representation in the National Legislature.[25]

William Paterson introduced the subject with a simple motion on June 9 that the convention "resume the clause relating to the rule of suffrage." Paterson's

24. Farrand, 1:37–38.
25. Farrand, 1:120, 13, 16, 17, and 45–173 passim.

action caught only the most inattentive by surprise, coming as it did on the heels of three days of heated exchanges on the National Legislature, especially with regard to its power to veto state laws. On the morning before Paterson's motion, Charles Pinckney moved to reconsider a previously agreed-to clause in the Virginia Plan that allowed federal legislators to veto state laws they deemed to be in violation of the "articles of union." Pinckney wanted the scope of this veto power enlarged to include the authority "to negative all [state] laws which they should judge to be improper." Madison, who seconded the motion, argued that a federal veto was "absolutely necessary" to curb the "constant tendency" of the states to act irresponsibly, ignoring their obligations under national treaties and encroaching upon the "rights & interests of each other." Left unchecked as they were under the Articles of Confederation, the state governments had demonstrated a tendency "continually [to] fly out of their proper orbits" to the detriment of good order and harmony. Thus the federal government must have the power to "control the centrifugal tendency of the states," and to be effective, this power had to be "indefinite." Attempts to enumerate specific instances in which the veto power should apply proved impracticable even in theory; in practice they would "be a fresh source of contention between the two authorities."[26]

An impressive lineup of speakers then addressed the merits of the motion. Elbridge Gerry of Massachusetts did not object to the federal veto per se but questioned the "extent of such a power" and whether Madison's conceptualization of it might not "enslave the states." Sherman understood the logic of the argument against an enumeration of applicable cases but thought it was at least worth a trial "for that purpose." Pennsylvania's James Wilson supported the motion, contending that one of the "vices" of the Articles of Confederation was "the want of an effectual control in the whole over its parts." But it was when John Dickinson of Delaware spoke in favor of the Pinckney-Madison motion that the whole context of the debate shifted. Arguing that it was "impossible to draw a line between the cases proper & improper for the exercise of the negative," Dickinson told the delegates that they had to choose between two alternatives: "either subject the states to the danger of being injured by the power of the Natl. Govt. or subject the latter to the danger of being injured by that of the states." For his part, Dickinson "thought the danger greater from the states."[27]

The Consequences of Disunion

Gunning Bedford, also from Delaware, was incensed by his colleague's apparent defection. Dickinson, whose *Letters from a Farmer in Pennsylvania* written

26. Farrand, 1:176, 31, 54, 164–65.   27. Farrand, 1:165, 166, 167.

to protest the 1767 Townshend duties had won him intercolonial fame and whose committee in the Continental Congress had drafted the Articles of Confederation, was not a political lightweight. Nevertheless, when Dickinson chose to favor the federal government over the states, Bedford issued a sharp retort. Suspecting, perhaps, that Dickinson's affiliations ran deeper in Pennsylvania than in Delaware—Dickinson had ties to both and had served as chief executive of Delaware (1781–82) as well as Pennsylvania (1782–85)—Bedford reminded him of the "smallness of his own state which may be injured at pleasure without redress." The motion was part and parcel of Pinckney and Madison's earlier effort "to strip the small states of their equal right of suffrage" and was thus hostile to the very existence of the small states. For Delaware, the repercussions of a switch from equal to proportional representation would be disastrous. "Delaware would have about 1/90 for its share in the General Councils, whilst Pa. & Va. would possess 1/3 of the whole." Given their competing interests, especially the "rivalship of commerce . . . [and] manufactures," such a gross imbalance of power would allow "these large states [to] crush the small ones whenever they happened to stand in the way of their ambitions." Small wonder that the Pennsylvania and Virginia delegates were promoting a system in which they would have a dominating influence, but, surely, Dickinson must appreciate the dangers this "monstrous" arrangement posed for "his own state."[28]

Madison, even more than Dickinson, was stung by Bedford's attack. Although they had been classmates at Princeton, Madison and Bedford were never friends and could not have been more unlike one another in both physical appearance and political preferences. Described as "very corpulent," "very commanding," "warm and impetuous in his temper, and precipitate in his judgment," Bedford stood in stark contrast to the slight Virginian, who successfully blended "the profound politician with the scholar." Madison was an even-tempered man whose carefully prepared arguments made him a "convincing speaker," William Pierce observed, but never a commanding orator. More dissimilar still were their politics. Madison made his reputation on the national stage with his dedicated service in the Confederation Congress from 1780 to 1783. Bedford preferred to remain in Delaware. First elected to Congress in 1783, he attended its sessions only sporadically until 1785 and not at all in 1786. Whereas Madison considered the federal government's power to veto state laws in "all cases" as indispensable to a "perfect system," Bedford's first priority was the protection of his state's interests against all challenges of whatever origin.[29]

28. Farrand, 1:167.
29. Farrand, 3:92, 94–95, 1:164, 165; Rakove, *Beginning of National Politics*, 220, 225,229; *LMCC*, 7:lxiv, 3:lxxxiv.

But Bedford's criticism went beyond the pale when he questioned the motives of the Pennsylvania and Virginia representatives. He had insinuated that they were not acting with candor, and Madison demanded before any votes were taken that he be allowed the courtesy of a response to the "difficulties which had been started." Staring directly at the Delawarean seated a few feet to his left, Madison "asked Mr. B. what would be the consequence to the small states of a dissolution of the Union." Bedford claimed that any plan proposing to change the one vote per state rule was an "impossibility," but Madison said it was inconceivable that the current "defective system" of representation could hold the states together much longer. A substitute had to be found, and to be "effectual" it had to be based on the principle of "proportional suffrage." Did Bedford really think that his beloved Delaware would be better off alone? "If the large states possessed the avarice & ambition" that Bedford claimed were their motivating passions, what would guarantee the security of the "small ones in their neighborhood" after the Union was dissolved and the protections it once offered were removed?[30]

The delegates sensed that the exchange between the former Princeton classmates was pointed but peripheral to the original motion to empower of the National Legislature to veto all "improper" state laws. The question called, the motion "for extending the negative power to all cases" was defeated on a vote of three states for the extension, seven against, and one divided. It is worth noting that the split delegation was Delaware's. Read, who was now "against patching up the old federal system," and Dickinson were for the motion, while Bedford, who spoke early and often, and Richard Basset, who had "modesty enough to hold his tongue" and never made a speech in the convention, were opposed. Fresh off this defeat, Pinckney moved to amend the fourth resolution of the Virginia Plan, which dealt with the lower house of the national legislature whose members were to be popularly elected. For the purpose of apportioning seats in this house, Pinckney proposed dividing the states into "three classes, the 1st. class to have 3 members, the 2d. two & the 3d. one." Bluntly stated, the number of representatives a state would be "entitled to" would be a reflection of its "comparative importance" in the Union. The convention treated Pinckney's motion as an afterthought and adjourned without further discussion. But the proposal, because it seemed to confirm Bedford's suspicions about the link between the movement to increase the power of the national government and proportional representation schemes, served as an introduction to Paterson's motion the next morning.[31]

30. Farrand, 1:168.
31. Farrand, 1:136, 169, 3:93; Rossiter, *Grand Convention*, 251.

Paterson and Wilson

William Paterson had been present for all of the sessions since May 25 but sat so quietly, "with looks that bespeak talents of no great extent," that he went almost unnoticed for nearly two weeks. First impressions, of course, can be deceiving. Paterson had been busily taking notes in preparation for his address on June 9, true to his habit of never speaking until "he understands his subject well." Sometime after the close of business on June 7, he wrote two drafts of his impending speech, complete with references to the preceding days' arguments of others, whom he identified. His notes for these drafts included specific clauses of the Articles of Confederation, a citation taken from the charge under which the Massachusetts delegation operated, a table projecting tax quotas and numbers of delegates to be accorded to each state in a proportional representation scheme, and bullet points critical of the idea of representation based on individuals rather than states. Indeed, Paterson's notes included prompts that present-day politicos might understand as "talking points": "Ambition goads him on," "impulse is progressive," "enlarge his Prospects, and you enlarge his Desires," and "nature of Govts."[32]

After his New Jersey colleague David Brearley seconded his motion to resume deliberations on the mode of representation, saying "he was sorry" that an issue that had been "rightly settled" when the Confederation was formed was again being "agitated," Paterson rose to deliver his lengthy inaugural speech. As an experienced former attorney general keen on the rule of law, he began by challenging the convention to explain the authority under which it was allowed to pursue its present course of action. The February 21 congressional resolution authorizing the convention specifically stipulated that the delegates of the several states were to meet in Philadelphia "for the sole and express purpose of revising the Articles of Confederation." Several state commissions "recited" these very words in their own charges. To drive this point home, Paterson asked William Jackson, the secretary of the convention, to read aloud the relevant portion of the credentials submitted by Massachusetts. The Articles of Confederation ought therefore to be the "basis of all the proceedings of the Convention," and because the "idea of a national government as contradistinguished from a federal one" dispensed with it, any proposal to that effect took the convention beyond its proper limits and was tantamount to a "usurpation" of power.[33]

Having questioned the legitimacy of the proceedings related to the Virginia Plan, Paterson moved on to question the wisdom of its many provisions,

---

32. Farrand, 3:90, 1:185–91. 33. Farrand, 1:177, 178, 182.

especially as it pertained to proportional representation. "There was no more reason that a great individual state contributing much should have more votes than a small one contributing little, than that a rich individual citizen should have more votes than an indigent one," Paterson argued. It was a matter of equity. Would anyone contend that because "the rateable property of A was to that of B as 40 to 1" that "A for that reason [ought] to have 40 times as many votes as B"? As others had done, Paterson identified three large states— Virginia, Massachusetts, and Pennsylvania—and categorized the remaining ten as small states. "Give the large states an influence in proportion to their magnitude, and what will be the consequence?" Paterson's draft notes and talking prompts supplied an answer: "The mind of man is fond of power— Enlarge his prospects, you increase his desires." His speech to the convention reflected these notes: "Their ambition will be proportionally increased." Moreover, if his estimation of the votes to be accorded to each state in a proportional representation scheme based on revenue contributions was fairly accurate, the three large states together would control in excess of 45 percent of the total. The "impulse" to dominate being "progressive," once unleashed it would strike "at the existence of the lesser states." Working up to a dramatic climax, Paterson declared that New Jersey, in danger of being "swallowed up" by the larger states, "will never confederate on the plan before the Committee." And he personally would "rather submit to a monarch, to a despot, than to such a fate."[34]

Paterson was a modest man, "one of those kind of men whose powers break in upon you and create wonder and astonishment," an admirer wrote. Wonder and astonishment, of course, are not unambiguously positive responses, and James Wilson, whom Paterson had singled out for criticism, may have been astonished by the New Jersey delegate's arguments but not favorably impressed. Outside of Pennsylvania, Wilson was best known for his carefully argued pamphlet entitled *Considerations on the Nature and Extent of the Legislative Authority of the British Parliament* (1774), which posited that what linked the American colonies to the empire was their allegiance to the king and not to an unrepresentative Parliament. Inside the Assembly Room, he garnered attention and gained considerable influence "not by the charm of his eloquence," according to William Pierce, "but by the force of his reasoning." This was on full display when Wilson responded to Paterson with an argument befitting the Philadelphia lawyer that he was. If Paterson truly believed, as he had argued, that "we must follow the people," then he must accept the political maxim that "equal numbers of people ought to have an equal number of representatives." The Confederation "improperly violated" this principle "owing to the urgent circumstances of the time," but circumstances had changed and

34. Farrand, 1:187, 190, 177–79.

so it was time to correct that error. "Are not the citizens of Pennsylvania equal to those of N. Jersey? does it require 150 of the former to balance 50 of the latter?"[35]

Robert Yates, the New York delegate whose editorial remarks were often more revealing than his observations, depicted a much angrier Wilson. After illustrating the size differential between the two states, Wilson asked, according to Yates, "Shall New Jersey have the same right or influence . . . with Pennsylvania?" and answered, "I say no. It is unjust—I never will confederate on this plan." He was a proponent of a simple solution to the question of representation: "The state who has five times the number of inhabitants ought, nay must have the same proportion of weight in the representation." Paterson had been "candid" in declaring his hatred for the scheme proposed in the Virginia Plan, claiming it portended a fate worse than despotism for the smaller states. "I commend him" for his candor, he said, adding that he would be equally frank. Repeating his earlier declaration but with a personal twist this time, Yates's Wilson concluded, "I never will confederate on his principles." If the convention chose to side with the New Jersey delegate and "depart from the principle of representation in proportion to numbers," then the whole purpose of the Philadelphia meeting was lost, in which case, "a majority, nay even a minority, of the states have a right to confederate with each other, and the rest may do as they please." Whether Yates accurately recorded Wilson's speech is open to question; however, his rendering of the debate, especially the allusion to separate confederations of large and small states, reflected the emotions at play that afternoon.[36]

The long day was winding down as the delegates prepared to cast their votes on the resolution for proportional representation in the Virginia Plan. Paterson, sensing that a small majority stood against him, asked for a postponement—he said "till tomorrow," perhaps forgetting that it was Saturday afternoon and the convention did not meet on Sundays. The stakes were so high, "so much depended" on the outcome of the voting, that putting off the decision for at least another day seemed advisable. Tempers had begun to flare. After Wilson suggested that the larger states might have to confederate among themselves, Paterson himself had supposedly shouted, "Let them unite if they please, but let them remember that they have no authority to compel the others to unite." Informal meetings over dinner after adjournment, a good night's sleep, and a more leisurely Sunday, might allow cooler heads to prevail. The convention agreed unanimously to adjourn.[37]

35. Farrand, 3:90, 92, 1:178, 179–80; Samuel Eliot Morison, ed., *Sources and Documents Illustrating the American Revolution, 1764–1788* (1923; repr., New York, 1965), 105–15.

36. Farrand, 1:183.

37. Farrand, 1:179–80.

First Decisions

Roger Sherman opened the Monday morning session with a solution to the dilemma over the rule of representation. If he had seldom known failure in the past, he experienced more than his fair share of them during the week leading up to June 11. He was on the losing side of a string of important decisions: he opposed the popular election of the members of the lower house, favored having the chief executive appointed by the National Legislature and "absolutely dependent on that body," opposed the idea of an executive veto, favored the creation of an executive council akin to the privy council, and opposed the proposal to allow the new Constitution to be ratified by state conventions. Where he stood on the contentious issue of equal versus proportional representation was unclear. Sherman had said nothing on June 8 and 9, when Madison and Bedford and then Paterson and Wilson had exchanged barbs that included hints of disunion, but his silence was not for the want of sympathy or thought. "No man has a better heart or a clearer head," Pierce said of Sherman, and these attributes made him an "able politician" and a "useful" one as well.[38]

Sherman's skills as a practical politician were evident on June 11 as he positioned himself to be the first speaker that morning and tried to head off another round potentially ruinous charges and countercharges between the large-state and small-state delegates. His solution was a compromise: whereas representation in the lower house would be proportional "according to the respective numbers of free inhabitants," representation in the Senate would be equal, with "each state . . . [having] one vote and no more." Sherman's proposal fell on deaf ears. Rufus King, the Massachusetts lawyer who was a friend of Madison's, decoupled the twin components of Sherman's compromise "in order to bring the question to a point." King's motion, seconded by Pennsylvania's Wilson, dealt only with the lower house and resembled the proposal Randolph and Madison had made before the postponement two weeks earlier. Representation in the "the first branch of the national legislature ought not to be according to the rule established in the Articles of Confederation, but according to some equitable ratio of representation."[39]

Benjamin Franklin then rose to be recognized, and for a second time in eight days the eighty-one-year-old Pennsylvanian had his prepared speech read for him by his younger colleague James Wilson. Anticipating some verbal fireworks, Franklin pleaded for a return to the "great coolness" that, he claimed, had characterized discussions until the matter of "proportion of representation came before us." They were gathered in Philadelphia "to *consult* not to *contend*

38. Farrand, 1:48, 65, 68, 99, 105, 122, 3:89.   39. Farrand, 1:196.

with each other," Franklin reminded the delegates, and a fixed determination "never to change" one's mind was productive of "warmth on one side" which "naturally beget their like on the other." So far, so good, but the legendary scientist turned statesman then came out in favor of the doctrine that "the number of representatives should bear some proportion to the number of the represented; and that the decisions should be by the majority of members, not by the majority of states."[40]

Franklin, whose understanding of "all the operations of nature" was so great that, according to one commentator, "the very heavens obey him," could not command the attention, let alone the compliance, of the convention when it came to his complicated formula linking equal representation to revenue raising, a plan best described as a mishmash of mandatory contributions to be determined by the amount the "weakest state" could afford to give coupled with additional voluntary sums supplied by the "richer and more powerful states." As had happened earlier when Franklin's speech was read by Wilson, the delegates listened politely to his proposition—on that occasion Franklin argued that the national executive be paid no salary whatsoever—and then proceeded to ignore it. No debate followed the venerable Pennsylvanian's conclusion because the delegates viewed his proposal "with great respect, but rather for the author of it, than from any apparent conviction of its expediency or practicability." Wilson, after delivering Franklin's address, moved immediately to amend King's motion by clarifying what an equitable ratio of representation in the lower house meant: representation "in proportion to the whole number of white & other free citizens & inhabitants[,] . . . including those bound to servitude for a term of years and three fifths of all other persons." The amended motion, seconded by South Carolina's Charles Pinckney, passed by a vote of nine in favor and only New Jersey and Delaware opposed.[41]

What followed was a quick succession of votes to settle the rule of representation in the National Legislature. Sherman, trying to salvage his proposed compromise, moved that a vote be taken on "whether each state shall have one vote in the 2d branch," that is, in the Senate. "Every thing he said depended on this. The smaller states would never agree . . . on any other principle than an equality of suffrage in this branch." The vote was six to five against, with Virginia, Massachusetts, and Pennsylvania leading the opposition. Next, Wilson moved that representation in the Senate "be according to the same rule" as in the lower house. That motion carried with a final tally that was the mirror image of the preceding vote: six states, led by the big three, supported Wilson's proposal. In short order and with no debate the convention had seemingly

40. Farrand, 1:197–98.   41. Farrand, 3:91, 1:199–200, 81, 85, 201.

reached a consensus on an issue that had vexed the delegates from the very beginning.[42]

New Jersey Plan

On June 13 the convention received the revised Virginia Plan, now expanded to nineteen resolutions from the original fifteen and updated with all of the modifications that had been adopted by the committee of the whole since May 30. The delegates made copies of the document before adjourning for the day in order "to give an opportunity for other plans to be proposed." The next morning, William Paterson announced that he intended to take advantage of the opportunity on behalf of "several deputations, particularly that of N. Jersey," to present the convention with an alternative that was "purely federal, and contradistinguished from the reported [Virginia] plan." But he needed more time to complete his work and requested another adjournment, promising to be ready by the following morning.[43]

On June 15 Paterson opened the session by laying before the convention a plan that he and several other delegates "wished to be substituted in place of that proposed by Mr. Randolph." The convention referred Paterson's alternative, better known as the New Jersey Plan, to the committee of the whole, and for the sake of a "due comparison" agreed that the Virginia Plan "should be recommitted." At the urging of New York's John Lansing and "some other gentlemen," the convention also agreed to adjourn until the next day in the interest of giving the proponents of the new plan time to prepare their defense and all others a chance to study its provisions.[44]

In truth, the delay was unnecessary and may have provoked the North Carolina delegation to ask the state for an additional two months' stipend because the business of the convention seemed "to promise a summer's campaign." A moment's study should have been enough to reveal the essential difference between the two plans. The New Jersey proposal was an elaboration of the legitimacy argument Paterson had broached in his inaugural speech a week earlier. Thus its first resolution proclaimed that the "Articles of Confederation ought to be so revised, corrected & enlarged, as to render the federal Constitution adequate to the exigencies of government & the preservation of the Union." And the eight remaining resolutions attempted to do just that. They addressed three of the principal weaknesses of the Confederation by authorizing Congress, first, to raise a revenue by levying duties on foreign imports and imposing a stamp tax on "paper, vellum or parchment"; second, to regulate all trade, foreign and domestic; and third, to direct the collection of requisitions among

42. Farrand, 1:201–2.   43. Farrand, 1:239–40.
44. Farrand, 1:242.

noncomplying states. Indeed, addressing the problems posed by recent treaty violations, especially with regard to the dispensation of confiscated Loyalist property as provided for in the Treaty of Paris, the New Jersey Plan included a supremacy clause. Its sixth resolution declared that all acts of Congress and all treaties made under the authority of the United States "shall be the supreme law of the respective states[,] . . . laws of the individual states to the contrary notwithstanding." If a state blocked the execution of such acts or treaties, the resolution empowered the newly created federal executive "to compel an obedience."[45]

John Lansing of New York, who probably had a hand in drafting the New Jersey proposal, began the June 16 session by asking the secretary of the convention to read the plan's first resolution. After the reading, Lansing repeated that the arguments Paterson had made on June 9. The New Jersey Plan fell within the limits set by the act of Congress for the Philadelphia meeting in that it sought to revise the Articles, whereas "that of Mr. Randolph destroys it." Several states predicated their participation in the convention on the expectation that it would strictly adhere to the congressional charge; the proof of this lay in their appropriation of the very words used by Congress. "N. York would never have concurred in sending deputies to the convention," Lansing declared, "if she had supposed the deliberations" would go further than "an augmentation of the powers of Congress." Lansing and his colleague Robert Yates later justified their fleeing Philadelphia for good on July 10 in exactly the same terms. Their charge bound them to the task of "preservation" rather than "subversion," that is, they were supposed to amend the Articles of Confederation, not replace it with an entirely new frame of government. Paterson, mindful of his earlier remarks and determined to avoid repetition "as much as possible," added that if the delegates were convinced that the existing frame of government was "radically wrong," so "radically defective" as to be beyond repair, then they must return to their respective states "and obtain larger powers, not assume them."[46]

At Liberty to Propose Anything

Wilson's answer to the challenge posed by the first resolution of the New Jersey Plan became the standard response of the nationalists. "With regard to the *power of the Convention*," he explained, the delegates were "authorized to *conclude nothing*, but . . . at liberty to *propose any thing*." Pinckney reiterated this point, contending that "the Convention [was] authorized to go [to] any length in recommending" remedies for the "evils" of the Confederation because, as

45. North Carolina delegates to Governor Caswell, June 14, 1787, in Farrand, 3:46, 1:242–45.
46. Farrand, 1:249–50, 258.

the Virginia Plan provided, its recommendations would take effect only upon ratification by "assemblies of representatives . . . expressly chosen by the people." Edmund Randolph likewise argued that the business of the convention "consists in recommending a system of government, not to make it." But Randolph was more forceful than Wilson in making this point. He "painted in strong colors," as Madison put it, the "imbecility of the existing confederacy" and declared that "when the salvation of the Republic was at stake, it would be treason . . . not to propose what we found necessary."[47]

In *Federalist* no. 40, Madison elaborated on this response to the legitimacy question. The February congressional act declared that delegates were to meet in Philadelphia "for the sole and express purpose of *revising the Articles of Confederation*" in order to "render the federal Constitution *adequate to the exigencies of government and the preservation of the Union*." Paterson and the other proponents of the New Jersey Plan saw no complications in this charge, even when coupled with the acknowledgment by Congress, in the same act, that the convention would "be the most probable mean of establishing in these states *a firm national government*." But what if the defining authority of the convention proved to be ambiguous? What if "a *national* and *adequate government* could not possibly, in the judgment of the convention, be effected by *alterations* and *provisions* in the *Articles of Confederation*"? What if the congressional charge contained expressions that were "irreconcilably at variance with each other"? Under this scenario, was it more important to preserve the Union and disregard the Articles or to preserve the Articles and disregard the Union? "Let the most scrupulous expositors of delegated powers[,] . . . the most inveterate objectors against those exercised by the convention, answer these questions." Ultimately, however, the people would decide. The powers of the convention "were merely advisory and recommendatory," Madison concluded, and therefore its final product would "be of no more consequence than the paper" it was written on, "unless it be stamped with the approbation of those to whom it is addressed."[48]

But why would the New Jersey Plan's fix for the Articles of Confederation not be sufficient? Why would the Union still be in jeopardy after the powers of the general government were increased to include the power to tax, regulate trade, and compel obedience to federal laws and treaties? Because legitimacy was never the central issue; it was a distraction. "The true question," Randolph said, "is whether we shall adhere to the federal plan, or introduce the national plan." In the former, as Yates has Paterson explaining, "independent societies confederate for mutual defense . . . and . . . each state for those purposes must

---

47. Farrand, 1:253, 22, 262, 255.   48. *Federalist*, no. 40, 286–88.

be considered as *one* of the contracting parties." The size of each party is im-material because the Union is in the nature of an alliance among equally sov-ereign polities. "Destroy this balance of equality" and the compact itself is destroyed. "On this ground, representation must be drawn from the states to maintain their independency, and not from the people composing those states." By contrast, in a national union, Wilson reportedly argued, all power being derived from the people, they "ought to participate equally in the bene-fits and rights of government" according to the "proportion of their numbers." The contracting parties were not the states but, indeed, the people of those states. Equality was a measure affixed to individual citizens rather than to col-lective bodies of them residing in separate states. Choosing not to repeat the remarks he had made earlier on the rule of representation, Wilson summarily noted "that an inequality in it, has ever been a poison contaminating every branch of government."[49]

Inadmissibility of the Jersey Plan

For the nationalists, the modifications proposed by the New Jersey Plan not only failed to remedy the evils of the Confederation but made them worse. Wilson announced that under the current arrangement he would receive any enhancement of the powers of Congress with "extreme reluctance." An "inad-equate" assembly "in point of representation," its unicameral structure com-pounded the likelihood of abuse. "Despotism comes on mankind in different shapes," explained Wilson, "sometimes in an executive, sometimes in a military." The accelerator was always the absence of effective checks on the wielders of power. An undivided legislature, such as the Confederation Congress, was the equivalent of an unrestrained ruler. "Is there no danger of a legislative despo-tism?" Some seemed willing to place their trust in the "virtue & good sense" of its members, but these had proven to be notoriously unreliable restraints throughout history. Ironically, the reason Congress had not become despotic was due to its feeble powers, the very "imbecility" that the New Jersey Plan sought to correct. But increase the power of this structurally unchecked legislature, in particular enable it to compel obedience, and the danger of oppression would become all too real.[50]

On June 19, James Madison delivered what turned out to be his longest speech to the convention. Picking up where Wilson had left off two days ear-lier, Madison said that he "was not anxious to strengthen the foundations on which it [the Confederation] now stands." The articles that Paterson's plan sought to bolster were too deeply flawed to preserve the Union and provide for

49. Farrand, 1:255, 258–59, 253, 261.   50. Farrand, 1:253–54, 256, 261.

the exigencies of government. Recapitulating many of the observations that he made in his "Vices of the Political System of the United States," a memorandum he completed shortly before traveling to Philadelphia in May, Madison concentrated on the "evils" of the states rather than on the failings of Congress. The New Jersey Plan was unacceptable because it did nothing to curtail the misdeeds of the states. "Mr. Paterson's plan" proposed to increase the powers of Congress, granting it the authority to pass laws that taxed imports and regulated trade, but Madison knew that such legislation, under the existing Articles of Confederation, required the votes of nine states. Given the recent history of Congress, how likely was it that such legislation would be passed? These were paper powers only and would leave "the will of the states as uncontrouled as ever." The same held true for "trespasses of the states on each other." Paper money emissions, debtor relief laws, preferential treatment of their own citizens at the expense of others, retaliatory acts, and "other kindred measures" continued to threaten the "harmony . . . [and] the tranquillity of the Union," but the New Jersey Plan, by not allowing a federal veto, "a negative on the Acts of the states, left them as much at liberty as ever to execute their unrighteous projects against each other." Indeed, not only did Paterson's plan leave the states open to interstate transgressions, but it did nothing to prevent the states from encroaching on federal authority. The provision that acts of Congress and federal treaties "shall be the supreme law" was meaningless because ratification remained the responsibility of the individual state legislatures rather than "the people at large." In other words, the states remained sovereign. Consequently, "acts of Congress" could not be "even legally *paramount* to the Acts of the States." Finally, whatever its perceived merits or demerits, the New Jersey Plan, as with any proposal to amend under the Articles, required the acceptance of "the legislatures of every state." In view of the actions taken by the convention and the objections voiced during the three days of debate since Paterson had spoken, the chances of achieving such unanimous consent were slim.[51]

After Madison had resumed his seat, the convention voted to postpone further deliberations on the first resolution of the New Jersey Plan, which called for the Articles of Confederation to be revised and enlarged. Only New York, with Yates and Lansing outvoting Hamilton, and New Jersey opposed the postponement. Rufus King then immediately moved that "Mr. Randolph's propositions be re-reported without alteration." His motion carried on a vote of seven in favor, three opposed—Delaware, New Jersey, and New York—and Maryland divided. Everyone understood, Madison noted, that King's motion "was in fact a question whether Mr. R's [resolutions] should be adhered to as

51. *PJM* 9:348–57; Article 13 of Articles of Confederation; Farrand 1:314–19.

preferable to those of Mr. Paterson." Yates agreed: the outcome amounted to a decision by the convention regarding the "inadmissibility of the Jersey plan."[52]

The Affair of Representation

During the week after June 19 vote, the convention methodically took up each of the nineteen resolutions of the modified Virginia Plan as submitted by the committee of the whole on June 13. It made quick work of the first five, which dealt with the composition and election of the members of the National Legislature. But on June 27, when the convention came to the sixth resolution and the enlarged powers to be exercised by this newly formed legislature, John Rutledge of South Carolina moved for a postponement, so that the convention might move on to "the 7 & 8 which involved the most fundamental points." The seventh resolution called for representation in the first house of the National Legislature to be based on population, and the eighth stated that representation in the second house would follow "the rule established for the first." For proponents and opponents alike, the decisions on these two resolutions would determine the extent of the powers they were willing to grant to the National Legislature. Rutledge's motion passed without dissent.[53]

The ensuing confrontation over what Madison referred to as "the affair of Representation" revealed that the delegates had been anticipating, eagerly or otherwise, the resumption of debate on this contentious issue, and that, if anything, their positions had hardened in the interval. Confined to the Assembly Room from about ten in the morning until three in the afternoon, six days a week for over a month, many of them were understandably tired, and in their fatigue less willing to be generous toward their antagonists. When Luther Martin of Maryland monopolized the June 27 session, rambling on for more than three hours on matters that had been raised before by others and then begged leave to resume his speech the next morning because "he was too much exhausted he said to finish his remarks," Madison was less than sympathetic. He briefly summarized the substance of Martin's first day's effort and was dismissive of the "residue," recording that it "was delivered with much diffuseness & considerable vehemence." Madison might be forgiven for this unkind cut, for Martin lubricated his imposing intellect with immoderate doses of brandy almost daily, becoming "so extremely prolix," William Pierce observed, "that he never speaks without tiring the patience of all who hear him."[54]

In his own address to the convention on June 28, Madison responded to the argument, highlighted first by Paterson on June 9 and repeated most

---

52. Farrand, 1:322, 328.
54. Farrand, 1:321, 438, 445, 3:93.

53. Farrand, 1:334–435, 236, 436.

recently by Martin, that the large states, specifically Virginia, Massachusetts, and Pennsylvania, would be dangerously advantaged under the rule of proportional representation. Martin went so far as to claim that the "smaller states would be equally enslaved" by the three larger states, and therefore rather than accommodating the seventh and eight resolutions of the Virginia Plan, he would prefer the "dissolution of the Union." Speaking on June 19, Madison had "begged" the small-state delegates to consider the logical implications of their arguments. If the larger states were driven solely by "ambition & power," as they contended, would the smaller states be more secure outside of the Union as independent but weaker neighbors? Now, more than a week later, he reiterated this warning, explaining that in the aftermath of a "perfect separation," the states "would be independent nations subject to no law, but the law of nations."[55]

But Madison did more in his June 28 speech to question the primary assumption made by Paterson, Martin, and their cohorts. Were there sound reasons for their belief that Virginia, Massachusetts, and Pennsylvania were bound together as allies "from the mere circumstance of similarity of size"? Experience had shown that size alone was never the deciding factor in the formation of coalitions. "It had never been seen," for example, "that different counties in the same state, conformable in extent, but disagreeing in other circumstances, betrayed a propensity to such combinations." Similarly, in the Confederation Congress, Virginia, Massachusetts, and Pennsylvania had never formed a "peculiar association" among themselves. And this was unsurprising because "in point of situation they could not have been more effectually separated from each other by the most jealous citizen of the most jealous state." Virginia, Massachusetts, and Pennsylvania represented three fundamentally different religious, cultural, and economic establishments. Indeed, "they were as dissimilar as any three states in the Union."[56]

The Union Will Go to Pieces

Shortly before adjournment on June 28, Benjamin Franklin bemoaned the "small progress we have made after 4 or five weeks close attendance & continual reasonings with each other." In fact, however, except on the issue of representation, quite a lot of progress had been made since May 25. And William Samuel Johnson, the scholarly and aristocratic lawyer from Connecticut, offered a solution to that conundrum as soon as the convention opened for business on June 29. In his trademark tone of voice that was "not pleasing to the ear" but consistently clear, Johnson proposed the same compromise that his rough-hewn colleague, Roger Sherman, had suggested nearly three

55. Farrand, 1:445, 320, 449.   56. Farrand, 1:447, 448.

weeks earlier. "The controversy must be endless" as long as the nationalists insisted that the states were "districts of people composing one society," and their opponents maintained just as vehemently that the states were separate and equal "political societies." Both were correct but not entirely. The states as well as the people at large were constituent parts of the government to be formed. Therefore, "the two ideas embraced on different sides, instead of being opposed to each other, ought to be combined." In one house of the National Legislature, "the *people* ought to be represented; in the *other*, the States."[57]

Once again the rest of the delegates ignored Connecticut's appeal for a compromise and forged ahead with their separate agendas. Madison took notice of and agreed with Johnson's contention that the "mixed nature of the government ought to be kept in view," but he quickly returned to a subject he had introduced earlier, only this time with as much passion his "great modesty" allowed. The "confessedly unjust" position taken by the representatives of the small states "could never be admitted," he declared, because it "must infuse mortality into a Constitution." The unavoidable result of such an infusion was that the Union would "go to pieces." Madison then went on at length, as he had never done before, describing the fateful consequences of disunion. With each state relying solely on its own resources for security, the dangers posed by foreign powers and jealous neighbors would increase exponentially. Living under the "constant apprehension of war," the newly independent states would be forced to accept "high toned governments" with "a standing military force." This transformation might begin with the smaller states, those less powerful and therefore more vulnerable to invasion, but their example would perforce be followed by others, setting off an eighteenth-century-style arms race, until the change was "universal." Unfortunately, the tragedy would not end there, for these increasingly militarized regimes would actually instigate armed conflicts. Madison, whose understanding of human nature and political behavior was influenced most by the Scottish philosophers, and especially David Hume, explained why this unwanted outcome was inevitable: "The same causes which have rendered the old world the theatre of incessant wars & have banished liberty from the face of it, would soon produce the same effects here."[58]

Other delegates picked up on the same theme, and it came to underlie all of the exchanges generated by the contest over representation until mid-July. Hamilton warned of the consequences of failure. Upon the dissolution of the

---

57. Farrand, 1:450–51, 461–62, 3:88.
58. Farrand, 3:95, 1:464–65; Douglass Adair, "That Politics May Be Reduced to a Science: David Hume, James Madison, and the Tenth Federalist," in *Fame and the Founding Fathers: Essays by Douglass Adair*, ed. Trevor Colbourn (New York, 1974), 93–106.

Union the separated states would form alliances with the "different rival &
hostile nations of Europe . . . that would foment disturbances among ourselves
and make us parties to all their own quarrels." Knowing what was at stake, the
delegates must act and act with due dispatch. The "habits of union" were still
intact, Hamilton warned, but they were growing "feebler" and the difficulties
of maintaining them becoming "greater" with each passing day. The present
moment was therefore "critical" and should not be squandered away because
such an opportunity was not likely to arise again. That they were gathered in
Philadelphia and engaging in "tranquil & free deliberations" was a "miracle."
To count on another convention would be "madness." Besides, Elbridge Gerry
added, to do nothing but adjourn in hopes of scheduling another meeting at
a later date was not a viable option because the present Confederation was
already "dissolving," and should the convention "not agree on something, few
delegates will probably be appointed to Congress." In short, the "fate of the
Union will be decided by the convention."[59]

Political Negotiators

As the convention prepared to vote on the seventh resolution of the Virginia
Plan, Gerry admonished the delegates to act more "like a band of brothers"
and less like "political negotiators," but most, including Gerry himself, disregarded the admonition. The resolution, which dealt with representation in the
lower house of the proposed legislature, consisted of two parts: first, that representation ought not to follow the one vote per state rule; and second, that it
ought to be in proportion to the whole number of free inhabitants, including
servants bound for a finite term, and three-fifths of all other persons. The convention adopted the first half of the resolution, but before any action could
be taken on the second, William Samuel Johnson and Oliver Ellsworth moved
for a postponement in order to take up the eighth resolution. Clearly, what the
Connecticut delegation wanted was to keep open the possibility of a compromise by treating the question of representation in the two houses of the National Legislature as a single issue. That the motion to postpone passed easily by
a vote of nine to two, with only Massachusetts and Delaware opposed, indicated that most delegates thought that the time had arrived for a showdown on
the rule of representation alone, that is, without the complication of the three-
fifths provision.[60]

Ellsworth opened the discussion of the eighth resolution by moving that
the rule of representation in the Senate "be the same with that established by
the Articles of Confederation." As Johnson had done earlier that morning,

59. Farrand, 1:466, 467.   60. Farrand, 1:467–68.

Ellsworth argued that the new National Legislature must be a reflection of the reality that "we were partly national; partly federal." He hoped, therefore, that his motion "would become a ground of compromise." Although he was "not in general a half-way man," he was taking the "middle ground" on this occasion because without a compromise the Philadelphia meeting "would not only be in vain but worse." Like Madison, Ellsworth believed that a failed convention might lead to the dissolution of the republic, possibly "cutting the body of America in two." Unlike the Virginian, he thought the large states would bear the responsibility for this failure due to their seemingly unshakeable determination to deprive the smaller states of an "equal voice in both branches" of the legislature.[61]

The next morning James Wilson responded to Ellsworth's claim that the only alternatives left were compromise or disunion. He hoped that Ellsworth was wrong and that the small states "would not abandon a Country to which they were bound by so many strong and endearing ties." Even the thought of such a "deplored event" was painful. Nevertheless, "if a separation must take place" because a "minority of the people of America refuse to coalesce with the majority on just and proper principles," then so be it. Separation "could never happen on better grounds." Rufus King, whose June 19 motion to re-report the resolutions of the Virginia Plan had sunk the New Jersey Plan, added his voice to the quarrel. While the "adherence to an equality of votes was fixed & unalterable" on one side, "there could not be less obstinacy on the other side." Under these conditions, the Union was "in fact cut asunder already, and it was in vain to shut our eyes against it." Gunning Bedford, the unapologetic champion of Delaware's interests, was not impressed by such bold talk coming from the large-state delegates. They were bluffing, for the "large states dare not dissolve the confederation." But even if it was not all hot air, the smaller states still had nothing to fear. Delaware and the other "small ones" could "find some foreign ally of more honor and good faith" than Virginia or Massachusetts or Pennsylvania, a foreign nation that would "take them by the hand and do them justice." King, literally, could not take this sitting down. "He could not sit down without taking some notice of the language of the honorable gentleman from Delaware." The "intemperance" of Bedford's rhetoric and the "vehemence" with which he made the "unprecedented" threat to turn away from "our common Country" and to "court the protection of some foreign hand" left King much "grieved." Bedford might be excused "on the score of passion," King declared, but as "for himself whatever might be his distress, he would never court relief from a foreign power."[62]

61. Farrand, 1:468–69.   62. Farrand, 1:482, 489, 492, 493.

We Are Now at a Full Stop

The convention adjourned after King had spoken, and the next day being Sunday the delegates got some relief from the grind of constitution making. The first order of business on Monday morning, July 2, was a vote on Ellsworth's motion allowing one vote for each state in the upper house of the National Legislature. Connecticut, New York, New Jersey, Delaware, and Maryland were for the motion. Virginia, Massachusetts, Pennsylvania, North Carolina, and South Carolina were opposed. Georgia was divided. The convention was deadlocked. A "pleasant" Sunday, cool and overcast with occasional showers, had given way to a hot Monday, with temperatures soaring into the mid-nineties in what turned out to be the warmest day in July. "We are now at a full stop," Connecticut's Sherman lamented.[63]

General Charles Cotesworth Pinckney of South Carolina conceded that "some compromise seemed to be necessary" to save the convention. Noting that the delegations were "exactly divided on the question," he proposed appointing a committee consisting of a representative from each state to come up with a compromise. Gouverneur Morris of Pennsylvania, Caleb Strong and Elbridge Gerry of Massachusetts, Hugh Williamson of North Carolina, and Roger Sherman of Connecticut all supported the proposal, albeit with a note of desperation. Williamson said unless concessions were made "on both sides, our business must soon be at an end." He hoped a "smaller body" of men might pursue a solution with "more coolness" than the convention as a whole. Sherman agreed the convention must not "break up without doing something" to try to save the Union, and a committee was "most likely to hit on some expedient." Gerry, too, said he was for the committee because "something must be done" before the "failure of the Union" left the states in such confusion that "we must have war."[64]

Others were resigned to the appointment of a committee, but with faint hope of its succeeding. John Lansing of New York "would not oppose" the motion, "though expecting little advantage from it." Lansing understood that "some conciliatory measure" had to be adopted to avert the fast approaching crisis, he later explained, but the positions of the large and small states had grown so rigid that "a dissolution of the Convention appeared unavoidable." Luther Martin, as if to prove Lansing's point, had "no objection" to the proposal but cautioned the members of the projected committee that "no modifications whatever could reconcile the Smaller States to the least diminution of their equal sovereignty." Edmund Randolph, who "did not expect much" from

---

63. James H. Hutson, ed., *Supplement to Max Farrand's Records of the Federal Convention of 1787* (New Haven, CT, 1987), 331; Farrand, 1:510, 511.
64. Farrand, 1:511, 514, 515, 519.

the committee was equally combative, using the occasion first to protest the "warmth exhibited in debate" and then in the next breath to attack the "warm & rash language of Mr. Bedford."[65]

Madison and Wilson opposed the proposal because the committee would operate "according to that very rule of voting which was opposed on one side." Experience had proven, Wilson observed, the "inutility of committees consisting of members from each state." The vast majority of the delegates, however, shared the sentiments of Gerry, Sherman, and others desperately seeking a way out of the morass, and Pinckney's motion passed by a wide margin, with only Wilson's Pennsylvania opposed. The delegates then proceeded to elect one member from each state to serve on the committee. Once that was done, the convention adjourned until July 5, in order to give the committee time enough to complete its work and to observe the upcoming anniversary of independence.[66]

The Grand Committee

Elbridge Gerry as the chairman of the select committee reported its recommendation to the convention on July 5: representation in the lower house would be proportional according to population; representation in the upper house would be equal by states. In essence, the committee had adopted the compromise suggested earlier by the Connecticut delegation, Sherman on June 11 and Johnson and Ellsworth on June 29. The one new element in the committee's recommendation was the stipulation that "all bills for raising or appropriating money" must originate in the lower house. Franklin, who was a member of the committee, was the inspiration for this clause. On June 30, two days before the convention came to a dead stop and talk of disunion and the quest for foreign allies jarred most delegates into accepting the idea of a select committee, Franklin proposed a solution. His "accommodating proposition" called for the states to have equal numbers of representatives in the second house of the National Legislature. On matters pertaining to the sovereignty of individual states, each state would have an equal voice; however, for "all appropriations & dispositions of money" the representatives would vote "in proportion to the sums which their respective states do actually contribute to the treasury." The larger states having presumably contributed more money to the general government would have more say in how that money was spent. Franklin had hoped that his proposal "might lie on the table for consideration," but, aside from Charles Cotesworth Pinckney saying he did not like it very much, few paid any attention to it at the time. Circumstances were different in the select committee. According to Yates, because the "grand committee"

65. Farrand, 3:336, 1:511, 514, 515, 519.   66. Farrand, 1:515, 516.

reflected the deep division within the convention itself, things looked bleak at first, as members wasted too much time engaging in "lengthy recapitulation" of arguments already familiar to all of them. With each side "equally tenacious," they could make no progress toward fulfilling the "salutary purpose" of their existence until, Yates said, he spoke of his "attachment to the national government on federal principles." Never shy about taking credit for himself, Yates claimed that his remarks moved Franklin then to offer the proposal that became "the basis of the . . . report of the committee."[67]

Nathaniel Gorham, the senior member of the Massachusetts delegation and presiding officer of the convention when it met as a committee of the whole, posed the obvious question after Gerry delivered the select committee's report. Why had the committee put forth two "mutually conditional" propositions? After all, the committee was formed when the convention had stalled over the eighth resolution of the modified Virginia Plan, which called for proportional representation in the second house of the National Legislature. Gerry's answer was as predictable as it was logical: the committee members were as divided "as the deputations from which . . . [they] were taken"; thus for the sake of finding some common "ground of accommodation," they had to forge a compromise. As with any compromise, it was a packaged deal. Large-state members "assented conditionally," so that if the "other side" did not accept the whole recommendation, those opposed to equal representation in the second house would not be "under any obligation to support the report."[68]

It was a hard sell for the large-state delegates. Insisting "the committee had exceeded their powers," Wilson proposed "a division of the question." Gouverneur Morris found both the form and the content of the proposal "objectionable." He could appreciate the "pledge to agree to the 2d. part if the 1st. should be agreed to," but he "conceived the whole aspect of it to be wrong." Madison added that he did "not regard the exclusive privilege of originating money bills as any concession on the side of the small states." If the senators of seven states favored a particular spending bill, they "might surely find some member from some of the same states in the lower branch who would originate it." North Carolina's Hugh Williamson said he was ready to discuss the committee's report "but thought the propositions contained in it, the most objectionable of any he had yet heard." Gerry grew more and more distressed as his large-state colleagues carried on in this vein. He had "assented to the Report," even though he shared many of their "very material objections to it," Gerry explained. "We were however in a peculiar situation." If each side refused to budge and, as a result, "no compromise" was reached, "a secession . . . would take place."

67. Farrand, 1:526, 488–89, 507, 511, 522–23.
68. Farrand, 1:526–27.

Distasteful as the compromise might be, therefore, the alternative was far worse. "If we do not come to some agreement among ourselves some foreign sword will probably do the work for us."[69]

A Defective Union Was Better Than None

The small-state delegates were at once more willing to accept the committee's report and less sympathetic to the supposed plight of the larger states. Bedford, whose comment about the small states seeking some foreign ally made him an easy mark for the opponents of equal representation, sounded a common refrain when he declared it essential that the separate identities of the states be protected under any proposal. In order to obtain this, the "smaller states have conceded as to the constitution of the first branch, and as to money bills." But if no "correspondent concessions" were forthcoming from the larger states "as to the 2d. branch," it was not "to be supposed they will ever accede to the plan." To those who opposed the compromise, Bedford asked that they contemplate "the consequence if nothing should be done!" Apparently the fear of disunion that moved Gerry also motivated Bedford. "The condition of the U. States requires that something should be immediately done," he advised. Given the wages of failure, even a "defective plan" of Union was "better" than none.[70]

Bedford spent no time detailing the disastrous consequences of disunion. Madison had done so the preceding Friday, and if the convention needed a refresher, Gouverneur Morris supplied it just before Bedford's speech. "This country must be united," Morris declared. In terms more graphic than Madison's, he described "scenes of horror" attending the warfare that would come in the wake of disunion, where the "stronger party" preyed upon "the weaker" and unity was achieved by the "sword" and maintained through the liberal use of "the Gallows & Halter." Madison subscribed to all of these fears and thus fully appreciated the risks of failure, but he refused to believe that the small states would secede. Would tiny Delaware choose to brave it alone? Despite the "decided tone of the gentlemen from that state," namely, Paterson, would New Jersey? If the "principal states" held firm in their commitment to the rule of representation put forth by the Virginia Plan, "all the other states would by degrees accede to it." Mason, who prior to the convention had singled out equal representation of the states as the most objectionable feature of the Confederation Congress, now disagreed with his junior colleague. "There must be some accommodation on this point," he said. Mason had been Virginia's representative on the select committee, and in a rare instance of concurrence with Bedford, Mason allowed that however objectionable the reported compromise might be, it was "preferable to an appeal to the world by the different sides."

69. Farrand, 1:527, 529, 532.   70. Farrand, 1:531–32.

A decidedly private man and dedicated father to his five children, Mason had never ventured out of Virginia until he traveled to Philadelphia for the convention at the age of sixty-two. Having left his beloved Gunston Hall in Fairfax County in May, it pained him "to remain absent from his private affairs" for so long; nevertheless, he informed his fellow delegates, he would rather "bury his bones in this city . . . than expose his country to the consequences of a dissolution of the convention without any thing being done."[71]

On July 7, when the convention took up the second part of the report from the select committee, which the official journal had begun routinely to refer to as the "Grand Committee," the debate was surprisingly brief. Gerry said he preferred to have equal representation in the Senate than to "have no accommodation" at all. The compromise might mean that the new frame of government would fall short of "a proper national plan," but if "generally acceptable," it was superior to a properly national one forced to operate "on discontented states." Wilson thought "conciliation was . . . misapplied in this instance," but regardless of whether it was or not, "firmness" in the cause of "justice and right" was a higher virtue than "a conciliating temper." Following this abbreviated exchange, the convention adopted the committee's recommendation, with six states for equal representation in the Senate, three opposed, and two divided. A deflated Madison excused the brevity of the discussion and the disappointing results of the polling with the comment that some delegates voted for the compromise knowing they would have another chance to voice their opinions when the "final question" on the whole report came before the convention. It seems far more likely, however, that there was not much new to be said on the matter of equal versus proportional representation, as evidenced by the speeches of Gerry and Wilson, and that many delegates had reconciled themselves to the necessity of concessions, as Mason had done.[72]

Also, by this point in the convention another issue, equally divisive and inseparably linked to the rule of representation, had begun to insinuate itself into the debate on voting in the upper house. The first part of the Grand Committee's report recommended that representation in the first house of the National Legislature be proportional, according to the whole number of free inhabitants, indentured servants included, and three-fifths of all other persons. Predictably, whenever the convention turned to this part of the compromise, sectional interests rather than size determined the lines of division. On July 13, as the delegates reconsidered the definition of an "equitable ratio of representation," Pennsylvania's Morris probably startled some large-state delegates with his

71. Farrand, 1:530, 528–29, 533; Jack P. Greene, "Character, Persona, and Authority: A Study of Alternative Styles of Political Leadership in Revolutionary Virginia," in Jack P. Greene, *Understanding the American Revolution: Issues and Actors* (Charlottesville, VA, 1995), 234–43.
72. Farrand, 1:538, 549, 551, 557.

declaration that southern insistence on counting slaves as inhabitants had caused him to have second thoughts about equal representation in the Senate. The persistence of the southern delegates indicated to him that they would not be satisfied until they had gained "a majority in the public councils" and effected "a transfer of power from the maritime to the interior & landed interest." If this was their intent, then he would be "obliged to vote for the vicious principle of equality in the 2d. branch in order to provide some defence for the N[orthern] states" against southern domination. [73]

Compromise and a Caucus

The vote to accept the whole report of the Grand Committee was the first item on the agenda for the convention on the morning of July 16, and the outcome was nearly identical to that of July 7. In the earlier and supposedly preliminary poll, six states had voted in favor of equal representation in the Senate; on July 16 five states did. The difference is explained by the departure of John Lansing and Robert Yates from Philadelphia, which meant that New York was no longer officially represented and therefore incapable of casting a vote, even when Hamilton was present, from July 10 onward. Contrary to the hope Madison had expressed on July 7, only one state, Georgia, switched its vote, moving from the ranks of the divided to join those opposed to the final report. The convention thus adopted the committee's recommendation, "including the equality of votes in the 2d. branch," by a vote of five to four, with one delegation, Massachusetts, still divided.[74]

The convention seemed poised now to return to the sixth resolution of the modified Virginia Plan, dealing with the enhanced powers of the National Legislature, which the delegates had decided unanimously to postpone on June 27 in order to move on to the proportional representation scheme proposed in the seventh and eighth resolutions. But the debate had barely begun before Edmund Randolph interrupted. All of the powers mentioned in the sixth resolution, including the power to veto state laws that contravened the Constitution or federal treaties, "were founded on the supposition that a proportional representation was to prevail in both branches of the Legislature." The decision instead to grant equal representation in the Senate had thus complicated "the business extremely." Claiming to have been taken aback by the stubborn persistence and sudden success of the smaller states in gaining an equal vote in the second house, Randolph asked for an adjournment so "that the large states might consider the steps proper to be taken in the present solemn crisis."[75]

73. Farrand, 1:604.   74. Farrand, 2:15–16, 3:588, 590.
75. Farrand, 2:17–18.

William Paterson, combative as ever, rose to the challenge. He did not like being told by the thirty-three-year-old governor of Virginia that the smaller states had been inflexibly obstinate and that they might usefully spend the time upon adjournment deliberating "on the means of conciliation." Paterson said he was prepared to second Randolph's motion "with all his heart," if the governor was calling "for an adjournment sine die," that is, if he were calling for an end to the convention. He was eager to return to New Jersey, knowing that the rule of secrecy had been rescinded and that his constituents might be "consulted." An alarmed Charles Cotesworth Pinckney asked for clarification from Randolph, "whether he meant an adjournment sine die, or only an adjournment for the day." If it was the former, then Pinckney "differed much from his idea" because he did not think, indeed it would be foolish for anyone to suppose, that the states would agree separately to meet again after consultations of the sort Paterson alluded to had transpired. Pinckney could not imagine ever being authorized to return to Philadelphia once he reported back to South Carolina.[76]

Randolph was not amused by the antics of the gentleman from New Jersey who had "so readily & strangely misinterpreted" his motion. Of course he meant an adjournment until tomorrow rather than permanently. He was possibly even more annoyed by the results of the first vote on his motion. The states divided evenly, five to five, so that Randolph's motion for a temporary adjournment was defeated, perhaps because some delegates had not been paying attention. Jacob Broom, the quiet farmer, toolmaker, and "plain good man" from Wilmington, for example, felt duty-bound to speak out against "an adjournment sine die." In any case, Randolph renewed his motion, and the second vote to adjourn for the day passed with seven states in favor, two opposed, and one divided. Massachusetts and South Carolina switched sides to allow the motion to carry. Both states may have done so because their delegates learned of a large-state caucus scheduled for the next morning.[77]

In defending his motion for a postponement, Randolph explained that the large-state delegates needed some time to ponder "such measures . . . as might be necessary" in response to the decision to allow equal representation in the upper house. On the morning of July 17, before the ten o'clock start of the convention, the larger states met to determine precisely what measures they might pursue to counter "the apparent inflexibility of the smaller states." How long they met is unknown. What is clear, however, is that the delegates were so divided that they failed to agree on "any specific proposition." Whereas one side argued that it made more sense to yield to the compromise than to jeopardize the convention itself, the other held that the "principal states," comprising

76. Farrand, 2:18.   77. Farrand, 2:18–19.

a "majority of the people," should stand together "in a firm opposition to the smaller states." Madison aligned himself with the latter; indeed the arguments of the caucus hard-liners, as he recounted them, were identical to the ones he had made on July 5, when the Grand Committee first presented its report. The smaller states would not dare to secede from the Union; they were bluffing. Unfortunately, Madison noted, the differences voiced by the caucus partici- pants took place before an audience of small-state observers and effectively confirmed their suspicion that they had "nothing to apprehend from a union of the larger." The time spent that morning in caucus was time "wasted," Madison lamented. An "imperfect & exceptionable" compromise, "decided by a bare ma- jority of states and by a minority of the people," would be allowed to stand.[78]

78. Farrand, 2:19–20.

CHAPTER TWO

A Union with Slaveholders

William Lloyd Garrison, the most influential abolitionist of the 1830s and 1840s, editor of the *Liberator* and mentor to Frederick Douglass, hated the Constitution. He hated the Constitution because he hated slavery. And he hated the framers of the Constitution because they were responsible for the "most bloody and heaven-daring arrangement ever made by men for the continuance" of slavery. They protected the slave trade for "at least twenty years," shored up the "slaveholding oligarchy . . . by allowing three-fifths of the slave population to be represented by their taskmasters," and denied the "panting fugitive from slavery" sanctuary anywhere by obligating "every citizen" of the United States to be a potential "slave-hunter and slave-catcher." The framers thus reinforced the practice of slavery, indeed encouraged it, in effect telling slave owners to "go on . . . from day to day, from month to month, from year to year, from generation to generation, plundering two millions of human beings of their liberty and the fruits of their toil—driving them into the fields like cattle—starving and lacerating their bodies—selling the husband from his wife, the wife from her husband, and children from their parents—spilling their blood. . . . Go on, in these practices— we do not wish nor mean to interfere, for . . . we like your company too well to offend you by denouncing your conduct." There was "much declamation about the sacredness of the compact which was formed between the free and slave states," Garrison declared, but all of it was utter nonsense, for the agreement reached in Philadelphia in 1787 condoned the "most atrocious villainy ever exhibited on earth." Rather than being a "sacred instrument," the Constitution, "*dripping as it is with human blood*," was a "covenant with death." What possessed the framers to draft a Constitution that aroused such "feelings of shame and indignation"?[1]

The Line of Discrimination between North and South

In October 1787, more than a month after the convention had adjourned sine die and the "injunction of secrecy [had been] taken off," James Madison made

1. William Lloyd Garrison, "On the Constitution and the Union," December 29, 1832, and "The American Union," January 10, 1845, in William E. Cain, ed., *William Lloyd Garrison and the Fight against Slavery* (Boston, 1995), 87–89, 114.

good on a promise to Thomas Jefferson, giving his friend "pretty full gratification" with regard to the proceedings of the Philadelphia meeting. When he came to the confrontation over representation, Madison did not bother to conceal his disappointment. The one issue that "created more embarrassment," that is, did more to impede the progress of the convention, "and a greater alarm . . . than all the rest put together," he wrote, was the insistence of the "little states . . . on retaining their equality in both branches" of the new legislature, lest "a complete abolition of the state governments should take place." Unable to convince these little states that their fears were unfounded, the large states settled for a compromise that was "very much to the dissatisfaction of several members."[2]

Madison's account was less than fair to the small states—they did not insist on equality of representation in both houses—and it was more than a little selective in singling out size as the most divisive issue the delegates had to overcome. Madison certainly knew better. Three months earlier on July 14, when the convention appeared to be on the verge of accepting the Grand Committee's compromise proposal, Charles Pinckney made a desperate attempt to salvage proportional representation in the Senate. The South Carolinian moved that seats in the second house of the legislature be allocated roughly in accordance with population, ranging from a low of one for Delaware to a high of five for Virginia. His motion touched off a new round of debate but, with one exception, no new arguments. Madison called the proposal "a reasonable compromise" and listed five major reasons for opposing equal representation in the Senate. The first four were recapitulations of earlier pronouncements on the impropriety of a system in which "Delaware had equal weight with Pennsylvania," but the fifth objected to "the perpetuity it would give to the preponderance of the Northern against the Southern" states. Currently, Madison reckoned, there were eight states in the North and five in the South. With the rule of proportional representation in place, the North "would still outnumber" the South "but not in the same degree," and given the projected growth and migration of the American population out of the North and into the South, "every day would tend towards an equilibrium." Madison's comment indicated that the sectional confrontation over slavery had already begun to displace the dispute over size. Although "scale was a serious consideration," Madison concluded, the "institution of slavery & its consequences formed the line of discrimination."[3]

2. Farrand, 2:650; James Madison to Thomas Jefferson, July 18, October 24, and November 1, 1787, *Republic of Letters*, 1:484, 503.
3. Farrand, 2:5, 9–10.

An Equitable Ratio

The second resolution of the Virginia Plan stipulated that representation in the proposed National Legislature "ought to be proportioned to the quotas" of revenue contributed by, "or to the number of free inhabitants" residing in, each state. Madison, knowing that the counting of free inhabitants only "might occasion debates," and wishing to avoid that confrontation for the moment in order to concentrate on the more fundamental question of whether the equal representation rule established under the Articles of Confederation should be altered, moved to strike that portion of the resolution. The problem with Madison's remedy, however, as Rufus King of Massachusetts pointed out on May 30, was that it left revenues contributed as the sole criterion for determining representation, which would be unsatisfactory because contributions might be "continually varying" and difficult to measure. After admitting the propriety of King's observation, Madison settled for the words "an equitable ratio of representation" as a substitute for the problematic phrases in second resolution. But Delaware's George Read, it will be recalled, asked for and succeeded in getting a postponement of the entire issue due in large part to his delegation's threat to abandon the Philadelphia meeting altogether.[4]

It was not until June 11 that the convention adopted the Madisonian substitute, supplemented by James Wilson's amendment defining an "equitable ratio of representation" as proportional "to the whole number of white & other free citizens & inhabitants[,] . . . including those bound to service for a term of years and three fifths of all other persons." Elbridge Gerry of Massachusetts, speaking "without respect to elegance or flower of diction," protested that property was "not the rule of representation" and therefore that slaves, "who were property in the South," ought not to be counted any more than the "cattle & horses of the North." But Gerry's objection generated no responses, primarily because it raised questions, at once familiar and disturbing, that dated back to July of 1776, a week after the Declaration of Independence, when the Continental Congress began debating the merits of the first draft of the Articles of Confederation. That draft, prepared by a committee chaired by John Dickinson, at the time representing Pennsylvania, included a revenue-raising provision with quotas based on "the number of inhabitants of every age, sex and quality" in each state. Slave state congressmen rejected the idea, contending "that negroes are property" indistinguishable from "cattle, horses, &c.," and consequently, as Maryland's Samuel Chase argued, should not be counted for purposes of taxation. Benjamin Harrison of Virginia suggested a compromise of counting a slave as one-half of a freeman, but Congress decided instead to

4. Farrand, 1:35–38.

avert the issue by making taxes proportional to the value of all improved lands in a given state.[5]

The immediate precedent for Wilson's definition of an "equitable ratio" was a revenue measure enacted by Congress in 1783. Desperate for funds to retire the public debt and to meet the demands of an increasingly restless cadre of Continental army officers encamped at Newburgh, New York, Congress proposed an impost coupled with a supplementary tax that was to be determined by each state's free and three-fifths of its slave population. By 1786 all of the states, except New York, had agreed to the terms of this impost and revenue proposal. But New York's steadfast refusal doomed the measure, for without unanimous consent it could not be implemented. Disappointed advocates of the impost began contemplating a more far-reaching solution to the Confederation's financial distress, which culminated in the call for a convention to meet in Annapolis in September. To Wilson and others familiar with the circumstances of the impost's failure, however, the one consolation was that New York's rejection had little to do with the three-fifths formula and everything to do with the insistence that its recently issued paper money be accepted by Congress as the equivalent of gold and silver for the purposes of meeting the state's revenue obligations. That the three-fifths motion of June 11 was made by a Pennsylvanian, Wilson, and seconded by a South Carolinian, Charles Pinckney, and passed by a vote of nine to two, with only Delaware and New Jersey in opposition, may also have encouraged the belief that, Gerry's protest notwithstanding, the formula for "apportioning quotas of revenue on the states" might be well received when applied to proportional representation.[6]

Madison was never lulled into such a false sense of complacency on questions related to slavery. On June 30, amid heated exchanges over the relative merits of equal versus proportional representation and loose talk by some of the smaller states about courting foreign allies, Madison tried to change the direction of the debate by resurrecting an issue he had scrupulously avoided a month earlier. As an alternative to the strictly proportional representation scheme that the smaller states found so objectionable, he suggested the convention might consider using the free population alone as the basis of representation in one house of the legislature, and all inhabitants, "counting the slaves as if free," in the second. "By this arrangement the southern scale would have the advantage in one house, and the northern in the other." It is difficult to imagine that Madison, who proclaimed openly that the American people were "constantly

5. Farrand, 1:196, 201, 3:88; Merrill D. Peterson, ed., *Thomas Jefferson: Writings* (New York, 1984), 25–27.

6. Farrand, 1:201; Roger H. Brown, *Redeeming the Republic: Federalists, Taxation, and the Origins of the Constitution* (Baltimore, MD, 1993), 23–24; Edmund Cody Burnett, *The Continental Congress* (New York, 1941), 570–71.

swarming . . . from the Northern & middle parts of the U.S. to the Southern & Western," seriously thought his proposal stood any chance of gaining the assent of the delegations from Pennsylvania and farther north. More probably, he wanted to draw attention away from an issue that was dangerously close to veering out of control by reminding the delegates of an "important truth," which was "that the states were divided into different interests not by their difference of size, but by other circumstances . . . principally from the effects of their having or not having slaves." In other words, Madison raised the specter of slavery and sectionalism in order to check the progress of extremism on either side of the large-state-small-state divide, in the same way that firefighters sometimes ignite backfires to contain rapidly spreading wildfires.[7]

Apportioning Seats in the First Congress

The July 5 report of the Grand Committee recommended a version of the compromise first suggested by Roger Sherman of Connecticut, allowing proportional representation in the first house of the National Legislature and equal representation in the second. But Sherman's proposal, relying on the phrasing in the original Virginia Plan, specified that the allocation of seats in the lower house be "according to the respective numbers of free inhabitants" residing in a given state. The Grand Committee chose to ignore that aspect of Sherman's compromise and to incorporate instead the convention's June 11 decision on Wilson's "equitable ratio." Each state would be allowed one representative "for every 40,000 inhabitants of the description reported in the 7th Resolution" of the modified Virginia Plan. This was a roundabout way of saying that representation would reflect the total number of free inhabitants and "three fifths of all other persons."[8]

For the next two days, the convention was preoccupied with questions pertaining to the weight of the concessions made to secure equal representation in the Senate. The vote of July 7 changed all of this. Once a majority of the delegations indicated their willingness to accept the committee's recommendations, attention was perforce drawn to the specifics of the seventh resolution. On July 9 the convention got a taste of what was coming. A committee of five charged with fixing "the number [of representatives] for each state in the first instance," that is, with apportioning seats for the first session of the new legislature, recommended a total of fifty-six representatives distributed unevenly across the thirteen states. Sherman immediately demanded to know "on what principles or calculations the report was founded," because as far as he could tell "it did not appear to correspond with any rule of numbers." Gouverneur Morris, who had chaired the Committee of Five and whose home state, Pennsylvania, was

<hr>

7. Farrand, 1:486–87, 585–86.   8. Farrand, 1:196, 236.

due to receive eight representatives, second only to Virginia's nine, confessed that the allocations were founded on "little more than a guess." George Read, the indefatigable guardian of Delaware's interests, asked why Georgia got two representatives to his state's one, when it had fewer inhabitants. Morris answered that the committee factored into its computations the "rapidity" with which Georgia's population was growing. But his answer practically invited an objection from William Paterson as being "too vague" to gain his approval. Besides, Paterson knew that New Jersey was much larger than Georgia—his colleague David Brearley had in his possession an enumeration mistakenly showing New Jersey to be five times larger—but was allotted only one more representative. In the face of such determined opposition, the convention decided to refer the matter to another committee, only this time to a committee of eleven, with one member from each state.[9]

The following morning, Rufus King presented the new committee's report, which proposed increasing the total number of representatives from fifty-six to sixty-five by adjusting the allotments of eight states. But this supposed remedy simply added fuel to the fire. As soon as King was done reading his report, South Carolina's John Rutledge, who was on the committee, moved to reverse the committee's decision with regard to New Hampshire by reducing its allocation of representatives by one. Rutledge may have selected New Hampshire as a target of convenience because that state's delegation still had not arrived in Philadelphia. But King rose to its defense. Repeating arguments he had probably aired in committee to garner the extra number for New Hampshire, King explained that approximately 120,000 people resided in New Hampshire and, given the "tolerable fertility" of its "extensive country," its population "may be expected to increase fast." King was not particularly interested in New Hampshire, but he was concerned about the fate of his region. The "Eastern states," that is, the states east of the Hudson River, were inhabited by "800,000 souls," King said, and yet were allowed one-third fewer representatives than the "four Southern states, having not more than 700,000 souls." The New England states would not sit idly by while "their Southern brethren" attempted to further this "gross inequality" by robbing New Hampshire of its due.[10]

General Charles Cotesworth Pinckney shot back that the new proposal was less favorable to the southern states than the old. Unless some corrections were forthcoming, said this South Carolina planter familiar with the drivers of slaves, the southern states would be reduced to "nothing more than overseers for the Northern states." Thus when the convention rejected Rutledge's motion to take a seat away from New Hampshire, Pinckney spearheaded a series of motions aimed at bolstering southern representation. First, he and Alexander

9. Farrand, 1:538, 540–42, 559–62. 10. Farrand, 1:566, 573.

Martin of North Carolina moved to increase that state's allotment from five to six representatives. Next, he and his colleague Pierce Butler moved that South Carolina's quota be increased from five to six. And finally, he teamed with William Houstoun of Georgia in moving for another representative for this neighboring state. All of the general's initiatives failed. North Carolina, South Carolina, and Georgia voted as a bloc for them, but the New England states plus Pennsylvania and Jersey were solidly opposed.[11]

Numbers and Sections

Pennsylvania's Gouverneur Morris "regretted the turn of the debate." The states, he said, had many champions, but who spoke for "America"? Morris's lament notwithstanding, the situation could hardly have been otherwise. The New Jersey and South Carolina delegations had precise, although not necessarily accurate, population estimates for all of the states, and it is unlikely that these were unavailable to others. Using these estimates, the delegates could assess the relative merits of the allotments for their states as well as their sections. It would certainly account for the alterations made by the Committee of Eleven. In all of these estimates, for example, Massachusetts had a population that equaled or exceeded Pennsylvania's; thus the committee granted it an additional representative to match the eight assigned to the latter under the original distribution by the Committee of Five. Similarly, Connecticut's numbers were larger than North Carolina's, even in Pinckney's enumeration and even with the inclusion of three-fifths of its slave population. Hence, the committee added another representative to Connecticut's initial four and left North Carolina's five unchanged. The supplement of two additional members to Maryland's initial allocation, making it the equal of New York with six representatives, was also a by-product of the population numbers possessed by the delegates. Again, it is important to note that these estimates were often inaccurate. They uniformly underestimated the size of North Carolina and, in at least a couple of instances, inflated Maryland's population. The point remains that the state delegations understandably pored over these numbers in search of apparent inequalities.[12]

Sectional complaints about the unfairness of the dispensations of the Committee of Eleven are somewhat more perplexing. That the delegates generally appreciated sectional differences and jealously defended their perceived interests is clear. How they defined these competing sections is problematic. Pinckney's insistence on July 10 that the recommended distribution of nine additional seats in the legislature worsened the South's position in the Union was

11. Farrand, 1:567–68.   12. Farrand, 1:190, 572–74, 3:253.

defensible only by excluding Maryland as southern state. Otherwise, the committee's work left the sections in the same situation as before. Under the first allocation of fifty-six seats, fourteen (25 percent) went to New England, seventeen (30 percent) to the mid-Atlantic states—Pennsylvania, Delaware, New York, and New Jersey—and twenty-five (45 percent) to the South. Of the nine seats added by the Committee of Eleven, three went to New England, two to the mid-Atlantic states, and four to the South. The addition of nine new members, in short, left the percentage of seats held by the South unchanged at 45 percent.[13]

Pinckney, in fact, did not rank Maryland among the states of "the South." While expressing his disapproval of the committee's report, Pinckney noted that he was nevertheless "glad" that Virginia had been granted an additional representative because "he considered her as a Southern State." He said nothing of the sort about Maryland's much improved situation. Paterson's abbreviated tabulation also excluded Maryland from the South, as he divided his totals according to "4 Eastern States," "4 Southern States," and "5 Middle States." Paterson's New Jersey colleague Jonathan Dayton joined the debate, protesting "that the line between the Northern & Southern interest had been improperly drawn." Pennsylvania, he said, was "the dividing state" between the sections, "there being six on each side of her." Confused, perhaps, and increasingly impatient, many delegates probably came to share Gouverneur Morris's misgivings about the direction the debate had taken. When South Carolina demanded of the Committee of Five a statement of the "principles on which they grounded their report," no other state endorsed the motion. At the end of the day on July 10, the convention voted to adopt the committee's report, with only South Carolina and Georgia opposed, and then adjourned until eleven o'clock the next morning.[14]

The Necessity of a Census

The noisy confrontation over distribution of seats among the states may have been prolonged by the apprehension that the initial allocation would prove to be permanent. As Edmund Randolph observed on July 10, the recommendation of the Committee of Five relied on the "discretion of the Legislature to regulate representation." Preferring to make periodic revisions compulsory, a "duty" rather than an option, Randolph moved to amend the committee's report by requiring a "census . . . to be taken within one year after its [National Legislature's] first meeting; and every _____ years thereafter." However, the convention chose to ignore Randolph's concerns and to postpone any

13. Farrand, 1:559, 566.   14. Farrand, 1:573, 570.

consideration of his motion because most members at that time were too nar-
rowly focused on the immediate apportionment of seats to pay much attention to provisions for subsequent dispensations. The vote to accept the committee's recommended allocation of sixty-five seats forced them to take a
longer view of the subject.[15]

When Randolph first made his motion, Morris "opposed it as fettering the
Legislature too much." Some delegates suspected "that if the Legislature are
left at liberty, they will never readjust the representation," Morris said, but he
did not share their suspicions because he believed that appropriate adjustments
would be made "unless the reasons against a revision of it [representation] were
very urgent and, therefore, "ought not to be done." On the morning of July 11,
upon the resumption of Randolph's motion, Roger Sherman voiced the same
objection to a "periodical census." Rather than "shackling" the legislature with
mandatory tasks, "we ought to choose wise & good men, and then confide
in them." But few were willing to follow Morris and Sherman. They shared
George Mason's reservations about trusting their representatives to do the
right thing. "From the nature of man we may be sure," Mason declared,
"that those who have power in their hands will not give it up while they can
retain it. On the contrary, we know they will always when they can rather
increase it."[16]

Mason's words of caution resonated with his listeners, as he knew they
would, because the belief that weak and naturally selfish men were incapable of
resisting the temptations of power was political orthodoxy for the Revolutionary generation. Like Mason, they were willing to accept the "conjectural ratio
which was to prevail in the outset," that is, the initial apportionment of sixty-
five seats, "but considered a Revision from time to time according to some permanent & precise standard as essential." Without it, as Randolph explained in
defense of his motion, the initial allotments, although founded on "mere conjecture," would persist. If that distribution "placed power in the hands of that
part of America" not entitled to it, "this power would not be voluntarily renounced." It was incumbent on the convention, therefore, "to secure its renun-
ciation when justice might so require, by some constitutional provisions." Contrary to the assertions of Morris and Sherman, legislators must not be left to
their own devices. "Fair representation," the lifeblood of the republic, required
"tying their hands in such a manner that they could not sacrifice their trust to
momentary considerations."[17]

15. Farrand, 1:557–59, 564, 567, 570–71.
16. Farrand, 1:571, 578.
17. Bernard Bailyn, *The Ideological Origins of the American Revolution* (Cambridge, MA, 1967), 55–61; Farrand, 1:578, 579–80.

This Peculiar Species of Property

Having moved beyond the supposed irregularities of the initial allocation of fifty-six or sixty-five representatives, some delegates thought it necessary to revisit the issue of an "equitable ratio." The convention had already voted to adopt the July 5 report of the Grand Committee, which reaffirmed the modified Virginia Plan's provision for counting three-fifths of the slave population in implementing the one-representative-per-forty-thousand-inhabitants recommendation. But the nature of the recent exchanges, especially the prioritizing of matters related to sectional standing, had elevated the importance of numbers. That these numbers would reflect the accounts of census takers rather than the conjectures of legislators heightened the sense that power would be even more directly proportional to population than many had bargained for at the outset.

The debate began in earnest when North Carolina's Hugh Williamson moved to amend Randolph's motion with a provision specifying that the proposed census must include the total number of "free white inhabitants and 3/5ths of those of other descriptions," and that "representation be regulated accordingly." Randolph readily endorsed Williamson's motion, considering it a friendly amendment to incorporate prior agreements. But Pierce Butler and General Pinckney were not satisfied with what Randolph and Williamson took to be a simple point of clarification. Insisting "that blacks be included in the rule of representation *equally* with the Whites," the two South Carolinians moved "that the words 'three fifths' be struck out." Their proposal opened the floodgates to pent-up resentments. Nathaniel Gorham, the highly regarded Boston merchant who presided over the convention whenever it met as a committee of the whole, reminded the delegates that three-fifths was the ratio "fixed by Congress as a rule of taxation" in 1783, and that "then it was urged by the delegates representing the states having slaves that the blacks were still more inferior to freemen." Now, when the same ratio was to be applied to the question of representation, "we are assured that they are equal to freemen."[18]

Gorham's suggestion that the southern delegates were hypocrites drew a sharp response from the usually good-humored Williamson, who proceeded to tell "Mr. Ghorum" that the imputation of hypocrisy cut both ways. "If the Southern States contended for the inferiority of blacks to whites when taxation was in view, the Eastern States [New England] on the same occasion contended for their equality." It was thus best to avoid "either extreme." He

18. Farrand, 3:87–88, 1:579–80.

himself had been consistent throughout, having approved of the three-fifths ratio for both taxation and representation. Mason also counseled moderation. He could not support the Butler-Pinckney motion, "notwithstanding it was favorable to Virginia" because he "thought it unjust." Slaves in the South were as valuable and productive as freemen in the North, Mason explained, but they were not "equal to freemen." Nor were they simply possessions. "Useful to the community" in numerous ways, including defense "in cases of emergency," they were rather a "peculiar species of property, over & above the other species of property common to all the states," and consequently "ought not to be excluded from the estimate of representation."[19]

The convention handily defeated the Butler-Pinckney motion, but South Carolina was not done. Rutledge moved that "wealth" be factored into the formula for determining the allocation of representatives. South Carolina's delegates believed their state's wealth would more than offset the loss of representation they would suffer as a result of having their slave population discounted by two-fifths. But Rutledge's motion also failed, principally because, as James Wilson observed, wealth was "an impracticable rule." Mason agreed, adding that the danger of relying on "something too indefinite & impracticable" was that it would be "a pretext for doing nothing." And doing nothing, Mason pointed out, reprising an argument he had made earlier when he spoke in favor of a census, was unacceptable because it would prolong the rule of "the states now containing a majority," namely, the New England states. Inaction meant that representation would not be adjusted when "the Southern & Western population should predominate, which must happen in a few years." Including wealth as a category of representation, therefore, would not increase the influence of the South as Rutledge anticipated; instead, it might ensure that "power would be in the hands of the minority."[20]

Returning to Williamson's original motion, the delegates approved without debate the clause for "taking a census of the *free* inhabitants" in each state. However, when the "next clause as to 3/5 of the negroes" came up, Rufus King rose immediately in opposition. He thought the inclusion of blacks "would excite great discontents among the states having no slaves." Harking back to his earlier comments about the underrepresentation of the New England states in the initial allotment of sixty-five seats, King said that he was not inclined to perpetuate that maldistribution by counting three-fifths of the slave population of the South. Roger Sherman and Nathaniel Gorham tried to mollify the discontent of those who felt as King did. Gorham, perhaps recalling the advice he had just received from Williamson, said he understood the "umbrage which

19. Farrand, 3:95, 1:581.   20. Farrand, 1:582, 583, 586.

might be taken by the people of the Eastern states," but the three-fifths ratio had gained the approval of all of New England in 1783 when taxation was at issue. Wilson, too, acknowledged that the three-fifths ratio would likely "disgust" his constituents in Pennsylvania. He himself, although he was responsible for the June 11 motion defining "an equitable ratio" as "three fifths of all other persons," was at a loss to explain "on what principle" it might be justified. If slaves were "citizens," then they ought to be counted "on an equality with white citizens." If they were "property," then other forms of property ought to be "admitted into the computation." These were "difficulties" that defied explanation, but they "must be overruled by the necessity of compromise." Wilson did not subscribe to Mason's "peculiar species of property" argument and understood the disgust of most Pennsylvanians, but he did wish with Williamson to avoid "either extreme."[21]

Gouverneur Morris did not share Wilson's sympathies. "Reduced to the dilemma of doing injustice to the Southern States or to human nature," he chose to "do it to the former." Others almost certainly agreed with Morris. Even among the Pennsylvania delegates, more sided with Morris than with Wilson. But six states voted against counting three-fifths of the slave population in the proposed census, South Carolina included. Surely, the South Carolinians found little they liked in Morris's phrasing of the convention's dilemma. Their opposition to the three-fifths clause is explained by their attachment to the Butler-Pinckney motion, which called for counting the whole of the slave population. In any case, having rejected the three-fifths ratio, the convention moved quickly in seriatim to three related questions. When should the first census be taken? How often should it be taken? Must representation be altered accordingly after every census? The convention decided all of these questions without dissent. The first census would be taken the first year after the National Legislature met, subsequent censuses would follow every fifteen years, and representation must reflect census results. Finally, the convention voted on "the whole resolution of Mr. Williamson as amended" and rejected it, unanimously.[22]

Thus ended what the constitutional historian Clinton Rossiter has identified as "the most awkward day of the summer." The delegates voted at last to undo everything they had done since eleven o'clock that morning. A most frustrating day to be sure, but it could not have ended differently. Having rejected both the proposal to count slaves and whites equally and the compromise of counting three-fifths of the slave population, the delegates were in a quandary. The awkwardness of their conduct accurately mirrored the

---

21 Farrand, 1:586–87.   22. Farrand, 1:588, 577.

confusion of wanting a census without knowing exactly who or what was to be counted.[23]

Taxation and Representation

The next morning Morris took the convention back to square one. Morris was never a firm supporter of a census in lieu of legislative discretion, and he "could not persuade himself that numbers [alone] would be a just rule at any time." Thus as soon as the delegates were called to order on July 12 he moved to allow the National Legislature to adjust representation as needed according to "wealth & number of inhabitants," with the "proviso that taxation shall be in proportion to representation." Mason recognized the "justice of the principle" espoused by Morris but wondered whether his juxtaposition of two variables, both in need of definition, might not prove so cumbersome that the legislature would be driven back to a "plan of requisitions." Wilson likewise "approved the principle, but could not see how it could be carried into execution." Charles Cotesworth Pinckney, with an eye on South Carolina's economy, asked specifically that exports be excluded from any computation of wealth. Morris met these objections by saying he was willing to limit "the rule to *direct* taxation," thus removing "*exports* & imports & consumption" from his equation.[24]

Morris's amended motion gained the unanimous consent of the convention. However, it left unsettled the issue that sank Williamson's motion a day earlier. What rule would apply when tabulating the "number of inhabitants" in each state? Mindful of the lingering effects of the previous afternoon's futility, Connecticut's Oliver Ellsworth moved "that the rule of contribution by direct taxation," and consequently the allocation of representatives, "be the number of white inhabitants, and three fifths of every other description in the several states." Randolph promptly offered a substitute motion because Ellsworth's proposal followed Morris's lead in leaving the legislature free to devise "some other rule that shall more accurately ascertain the wealth," and Randolph identified with those who perceived a "design" to exclude "slaves altogether." As before, he urged limiting the discretionary powers of the legislature through the use of periodic censuses, only this time he was more emphatic about the need to count "slaves in the ratio of representation." Although he understood the feeling that the existence of "such a species of property" was lamentable, "it did exist," and slave owners deserved the "express security" of having three-fifths of their slaves included permanently in the rule of representation. The "Legislature therefore ought not to be left at liberty" to tinker with definitions of wealth.[25]

23. Clinton Rossiter, *1787: The Grand Convention* (New York, 1966), 188.
24. Farrand, 1:591–92.
25. Farrand, 1:594.

Ellsworth, always adept at assessing the strengths of a potential adversary's arguments, withdrew his motion and seconded Randolph's. Wilson also approved of Randolph's motion but, anticipating resistance, suggested a way of rendering the compromise more palatable to northerners. Perhaps non–slave owners would take "less umbrage" over the "admission of slaves into the rule of representation, if it should be so expressed as to make them indirectly only an ingredient in the rule." Wilson's proposal amounted to a rearrangement of Randolph's motion so that the three-fifths ratio applied directly to the "rule of taxation" rather than to representation. Whereas Randolph prescribed "rating the blacks at 3/5 of their number" and then apportioning "representation accordingly," Wilson proposed affixing the three-fifths ratio to the "rule of taxation." By then linking representation to taxation, the desired "end would be equally attained." His modified motion thus called on census takers to make a tally of all the inhabitants in a given state "in the manner and according to the ratio recommended by Congress in their Resolution of April 18, 1783." The National Legislature "shall proportion the direct taxation accordingly," with the stipulation that representation will "always . . . be proportioned according to direct taxation." Described by one observer as a "fine genius[,] . . . well acquainted with Man, and . . . all the passions that influence him," Wilson was a master of indirection.[26]

The convention adopted Randolph's motion, "as varied by Mr. Wilson," by a vote of six to two. This favorable outcome was aided by Wilson's contribution, but it was also shaped by the threats frustrated delegates made during the confrontation over the rule appropriate for both taxation and representation. Wilson himself may have been motivated by the inflammatory exchanges that preceded his action. Pierce Butler fired the first shot when he questioned the three-fifths ratio, proclaiming Morris's motion to be acceptable as long as population totals included the "full number" of slaves. General Charles Cotesworth Pinckney, Butler's South Carolina compatriot, also "liked the idea" Morris was currently espousing but "was alarmed at what was said yesterday," referring to Morris's statement about doing injustice to the southern states, and "was now again alarmed" by talk of taxing "the fruit of the labor of her blacks." Charles Pinckney, General Pinckney's cousin, was even more insistent than his kinsman that slaves must be treated as "equal to whites in the ratio of representation." This was simply a matter of "justice," but it was "politic" as well because the northern states could take comfort in the fact that "taxation is to keep pace with representation." Finally, North Carolina's William R. Davie, declaring "it was high time now to speak out," broke his silence. Accusing "some gentlemen" of wanting to deny "the Southern States

26. Farrand, 3:89, 91, 1:595.

of any share of representation for their blacks," Davie warned his listeners "that N. Carolina would never confederate on any terms that did not rate them at least as 3/5. If the Eastern States meant therefore to exclude them altogether the business" of the Convention "was at an end." The fact that Davie was a moderate and usually "silent in the Convention" doubled the force of his announcement.[27]

To Rufus King, who apparently lumped Davie together with the South Carolinians, it all sounded like an ultimatum. Disclaiming any desire to retain an "unjust advantage whatever in one part of the Republic," King said he was not intimidated by southern threats of disunion unless "justice" was served. "If they threaten to separate now in case injury shall be done them," that is, merely in anticipation of injustices to be perpetrated by the North, "will their threats be less urgent" when they "shall be more numerous" than the northern states? If the minority of southern states succeeded in forcing concessions from their northern counterparts, "there will be no point of time at which they will not be able to say, do us justice or we will separate." King thought it best at present to meet the southern challenge, before the "force" of numbers "shall back their demands."[28]

Morris seemed to relish the flare-up occasioned by his comments and the ensuing motions. "It has been said that it is high time to speak out," Morris began, in an obvious reference to Davie, who sat a few feet to his right, and he "would candidly do so." He had come to Philadelphia for the sake of doing something "good for America," specifically "to form a compact" of union, and he hoped "that all would enter into such a compact." Some states, however, might choose not to do so, and that was their privilege because the compact was "voluntary." In that event, he was "ready to join with any states that would." Apparently resigned to a separation because Pennsylvanians, who had enacted the nation's first abolition law in 1780, would "never agree to a representation of Negroes," Morris said it was as futile for the northern states "to insist on what the Southern states will never agree to" as it was for "the latter to require what the other states can never admit." When he set his mind to it, Morris was a compelling orator, "conspicuous and flourishing," and as he worked up to his conclusion, he cast around the chamber his characteristic "glare," which commonly captivated "all who hear[d] him." But even his considerable powers of persuasion could not make converts to the cause of disunion. In fact, his speech, coupled with those of the Carolinians, had precisely the opposite effect. Only New Jersey and Delaware voted against Randolph's amended motion, and they were motivated more by their opposition to pro-

27. Farrand, 1:597, 596, 593, 3:96.   28. Farrand, 1:595–96.

portional representation in any form than by their hostility to the notion of counting slaves.[29]

Two-Headed Snakes

On July 13, the day after the convention had voted to adopt his motion, Randolph attempted to do a bit of housecleaning. The July 9 report of the Committee of Five came in two parts: the first recommended that fifty-six representatives constitute the lower house for initial session of the National Legislature; the second authorized the legislature periodically to adjust each state's allocation of representatives according to its wealth and population. The delegates, drawn to questions involving the fairness of the initial distribution, approved the second part of the report "without any debate." The adoption of the motion to count three-fifths of the slave population for purposes of taxation and representation may have obviated the need to revisit the vote taken on July 9, but Randolph wanted to minimize the chances of confusion by moving "to strike out 'wealth' and adjust the resolution to that requiring periodical revisions according to the number of whites & three-fifths of the blacks." If Randolph expected a speedy passage he was disappointed.[30]

Gouverneur Morris took advantage of the opportunity to repeat his opposition to the compromise. If slaves were "inhabitants," their "entire number" ought to be counted rather than "in the proportion of 3/5." If they were "property," then eliminating the word "wealth" would produce "the very inconsistency" the proposal "was meant to get rid of." Randolph's motion, in short, did nothing to remove the "incoherence" implicit in the three-fifths agreement. Warming up to the moment once again, Morris continued with comments that were designed to evoke a response from his audience. The "late turn" in the business of the convention, Morris said, specifically the distinction "set up & urged between the Northern & Southern states," had sent him "into deep meditation" and forced on him certain conclusions. Although he had never subscribed to the belief, indeed "had hitherto considered this doctrine as heretical," he now saw that the distinction "is persisted in, and that the Southern gentlemen" were willing to pursue any means necessary to gain "a majority in the public councils." The situation was no longer tolerable. It was high time for the delegates to decide whether "this distinction is fictitious or real: if fictitious let it be dismissed. . . . If it be real, instead of attempting to blend incompatible things, let us at once take a friendly leave of each other."[31]

29. Farrand, 1:593, 3:92.
30. Farrand, 1:599, 603.
31. Richard Beeman, *Plain, Honest Men: The Making of the American Constitution* (New York, 2009), 48–49; Farrand, 1:603–4.

During his tirade against the perpetrators of sectionalism, Morris mentioned the southern states' demand that "their peculiar objects" be protected, an obvious reference to Mason's description of slaves as a "peculiar species of property." The "demands for security" would be endless "if every particular interest is to be entitled to it," Morris declared. Pierce Butler replied that the Pennsylvanian may have misunderstood the claims of the South, for the only "security the Southern states want is that their negroes may not be taken from them, which some gentlemen within or without doors have a very good mind to do." At this point, Morris's Pennsylvania colleague James Wilson intervened to avert a prolonged and contentious debate over an issue he and others considered settled. "In 1783, after elaborate discussion of a measure of wealth, all were satisfied then as they are now that the rule of numbers does not differ much from the combined rule of numbers & wealth," Wilson explained. A few continued to express their disapproval of the principle adopted by the convention, but then, Wilson asked, "Why is not some better rule pointed out"? Congress could not "discover a better" rule and "no state . . . has suggested any other." Wilson's timely intervention was welcomed by the vast majority of delegates, and Randolph's motion carried by a vote of nine in favor, none opposed, and one delegation divided.[32]

The next day, Benjamin Franklin, whose home was two blocks from the Pennsylvania State House, was entertaining several members of the convention when a caller from Massachusetts arrived. The visitor was Manasseh Cutler, former Continental army chaplain and a director of the Ohio Company of land investors. In a jovial mood, Franklin took Cutler by the hand, introducing him to "several other gentlemen and two or three ladies." After wasting away several hours "most agreeably" in "free conversation," Franklin showed Cutler "a curiosity he had just received," a preserved specimen of a "snake with two heads." He imagined the creature "traveling among bushes, and one head should choose to go on one side, and the other head should prefer the other side, and that neither of the heads would consent to come back or give way to the other." Carried away by the fanciful predicament of the unfortunate creature, and "comparing the snake to America," Franklin was about to recount "a humorous matter that had that day taken placed in Convention" when he was cut short. Most of his guests that evening were fellow delegates, and "the secrecy of Convention matters was suggested to him, which stopped him." What specific episode struck Franklin as humorous is anyone's guess, and like Cutler, we can only lament being deprived "of the story he was going to tell." But the implications of Franklin's metaphor are beyond doubt: America was of two minds on vital issues linked to representation. Without compromises, the

32. Farrand, 1:604, 605, 606.

republic might end up as yet another historical specimen "preserved in a large vial" for inspection by the curious.[33]

Committee of Detail

As the convention moved toward confirming the three-fifths compromise, one argument made by its opponents gained momentum. Initially, it passed nearly unnoticed, as it appeared to be merely a supplementary argument to strengthen the objection to counting slaves in the rule of representation. On July 9 William Paterson opposed the recommendation of the Committee of Five by rattling off his reasons for wanting to exclude slaves from any calculation of representation based on "numbers." Slaves were "no free agents, have no personal liberty, no faculty of acquiring property, but on the contrary are themselves property, and like other property entirely at the will of the Master." Nowhere was a slave owner entitled to more votes "in proportion to the number of his slaves." Since slaves were "not represented in the states to which they belong, why should they be represented in the General Government"? The "true principle" of a representative assembly is expedience: it meets "in place of the inconvenient meeting of the people themselves." Were the people actually to meet, would slaves be allowed to participate? "They would not." Finally, at the end of this long list of objections, Paterson added that "he was also against such an indirect encouragement of the slave trade."[34]

What had been a mere appendage, almost an afterthought, eventually became the main focus of the argument over slavery and representation. The shift had its beginnings on July 23, when Elbridge Gerry moved that a select committee be appointed "to prepare & report a Constitution." Except for matters related to the tenure of the chief executive, the convention had tentatively settled most of the major questions associated with the proposed federal government, and Gerry thought it was time for the delegates to have a preliminary draft of the Constitution in their hands, summarizing the progress that had been made and serving as a guide to the work still needing to be done. The convention agreed to a five-member committee on July 24, and on July 26 the delegates voted to adjourn until August 6, so that the Committee of Detail, as it came to be known, would have the time to do its work.[35]

On the morning of the appointed day, William Jackson, the convention's secretary, received the committee's report, read it aloud once, and delivered copies of the document to the delegates. Some of the recipients wanted two days to examine the report, but a motion to that end failed, and the convention then adjourned to eleven o'clock the next morning. For over a month,

33. Farrand, 3:58–59.   34. Farrand, 1:561.
35. Farrand, 2:95, 106, 128.

from August 7 until September 12, when the Committee of Style submitted its draft of the finished Constitution, the twenty-three articles contained in the report of the Committee of Detail set the agenda for the convention. The report was the reference point for all ensuing discussions, doing essentially what the Virginia Plan had done for the first two months of the Philadelphia meeting.[36]

Given the confrontations leading up to the appointment of the Committee of Detail, the two articles dealing with the houses of Congress generated surprisingly little discussion. Article 4, Section 3, apportioning seats in the lower house, now formally called the House of Representatives, produced a mild response on August 8 because it engaged in a bit of indirection by avoiding any mention of counting "three-fifths of all other persons" and choosing instead to tie future allocations of representatives "to the provisions hereinafter made." But this was merely a clumsy attempt at linking taxation to representation and both of those to the three-fifths ratio, which appeared as Section 3 of Article 7. Thus when Hugh Williamson moved to substitute the words "according to the rule hereafter provided for direct taxation," the North Carolinian's motion passed without debate. Similarly, Article 5, Section 1, prescribing equal representation in the Senate, provoked no exchanges, except in relation to Article 4, Section 5, which gave the House control over money bills. And even here, the result was a minor blowup. Madison, who from the outset had challenged the fairness of the compromise that granted the House the exclusive privilege of initiating money legislation in exchange for equal representation in the Senate, was in favor of deleting this section of Article 4. The supposed advantage to one house would be a definite disadvantage to the republic when it became, as it surely must, a "source of injurious altercations between the two houses." Madison was joined by Oliver Ellsworth and George Read, both of whom agreed that the distinction "might be a dangerous source of contention." George Mason, on the other hand, disagreed with Madison, saying he was "unwilling to travel over this ground again." To do what Madison was suggesting would "unhinge the compromise of which it made a part." Franklin also "considered the two clauses, the originating of money bills, and the equality of votes in the Senate, as essentially connected by the compromise." Williamson even chided Connecticut's Ellsworth and Delaware's Read for "forsaking the condition on which they had received their equality." The reprimand may have had its desired effect on the Connecticut delegation, which voted to keep Section 5 as is, but seven states, including Delaware, New Jersey, Maryland, and Georgia, succeeded in removing it from the report.[37]

By far the most controversial part of the committee's report appeared under Article 7, which enumerated the powers granted to or withheld from the legis-

---

36. Farrand, 2:176.

37. Farrand, 2:178, 219, 224, 225, 233.

lature of the United States. Section 3, as noted above, stipulated that direct taxation be proportional to the number of inhabitants, servants included, "and three fifths of all other persons." Section 4 consisted of three interrelated clauses, the first of which withheld from Congress the power to tax exports, which was not unexpected given the concessions the convention made on July 12 in order to meet the objections the South Carolina delegation raised in conjunction with Morris's motion for making both taxation and representation proportional. Charles Cotesworth Pinckney, it will be recalled, had insisted that exports be excluded from any computation of taxes, and Morris complied by amending his motion so that it applied to direct taxes only. Section 4, however, went beyond the issue of exports. Its second clause prohibited Congress from imposing taxes on "the migration or importation of such persons as the several states shall think proper to admit," and its third clause protected "such migration or importation" in perpetuity. In other words, the new federal government would have no authority whatsoever to regulate the slave trade.[38]

What might account for this provocative action taken by the Committee of Detail? That John Rutledge chaired the committee partly explains it. Rutledge led the South Carolina delegation, and his wartime service as governor had earned him "a distinguished rank among the American Worthies." Georgia's William Pierce rated him an indifferent orator at best because Rutledge was "too rapid in his public speaking," but he admired the South Carolinian as "a man of abilities" and a "gentleman of distinction" who undoubtedly held his own in private exchanges. As a staunch defender of his state's interests, Rutledge was without superiors. On July 23, when Gerry moved to create the Committee of Detail, his motion carried without dissent. Charles Cotesworth Pinckney, however, thought it necessary to remind the delegates "that if the Committee should fail to insert some security to the Southern States against an emancipation of slaves, and taxes on exports, he should be bound by the duty to his state to vote against their report." Rutledge carried these same sentiments into the meetings he chaired.[39]

Importation of Slaves

The delegates did not get around to Article 7, Section 4, until August 21, but they had a preview of its disruptive potential on August 8. After the convention adopted Williamson's motion to include a clause linking representation to direct taxation in place of the vague reference to "provisions hereinafter made" in Article 4, Section 4, Rufus King demanded "to know what influence the vote just passed was meant to have on the succeeding part of the report,

38. Farrand, 2:183.   39. Farrand, 3:96, 2:95.

concerning the admission of slaves into the rule of representation." King had earlier voiced his opposition to using numbers as the basis of representation, "particularly so on account of the blacks" in the South, and "he could not reconcile his mind" now to the decision on Williamson's motion "if it was to prevent objections to the latter part." The very idea of counting slaves was abhorrent to him, "a most grating circumstance to his mind," but he had held his emotions in check, hoping his restraint would reap a just return. The "tenor" of the Rutledge committee's report "put an end to all these hopes." King could not understand the logic behind Section 4. The "hands of the legislature were absolutely tied" with regard to the importation of slaves. "Is this reasonable?" Convinced that the "people of the Northern States could never be reconciled" to the prohibition against regulating the slave trade, King was at a loss to explain it. "No candid man could undertake to justify it to them." If some concessions had been made, if "at least a time would have been limited for the importation of slaves," there might be room for accommodation of sorts. But to "agree to let them be imported without limitation & then be represented in the National Legislature" was beyond the pale.[40]

King, barely thirty-two years old, was a gifted orator, and the combination of a "handsome face," "strong expressive eyes," and "sweet high toned voice" made him "irresistible at times," but not on this occasion. Nathaniel Gorham and Oliver Ellsworth, both of whom were members of the Committee of Detail, ignored King's complaint. Sherman chose not "to make opposition," even though he "regarded the slave-trade as iniquitous," because the "point of representation having been settled after much difficulty & deliberation," he felt himself bound by it. Only Gouverneur Morris took up where King left off. In an appeal even more impassioned than his statement a month earlier about preferring to do injustice to the South rather than to human nature, Morris decried the implications of Section 4. "When fairly explained," what it amounted to was "that the inhabitant of Georgia and South Carolina who goes to the Coast of Africa, and in defiance of the most sacred laws of humanity tears away his fellow creatures from their dearest connections & damns them to the most cruel bondages, shall have more votes . . . than the Citizen of Pennsylvania or New Jersey who views with a laudable horror so nefarious a practice." Contrary to "every principle of right," the southern states were "not to be restrained from importing fresh supplies of wretched Africans[;] . . . nay they are to be encouraged to it by an assurance of having their votes in the National Government increased in proportion" to their imports. Morris was loath to "saddle posterity with such a Constitution."[41]

40. Farrand, 1:586, 2:220.   41. Farrand, 3:87, 2:220–21, 222–23.

The full-blown debate over the contested portions of Article 7 began with a proposal from Luther Martin of Maryland on the afternoon of August 21 to alter the second clause of Section 4 "so as to allow a prohibition or tax on the importation of slaves." Reiterating the contentions of King and Morris, Martin advocated such an alteration because the three-fifths ratio for representation amounted to "an encouragement to this traffic." Rutledge responded by repeating arguments he first aired in the Committee of Detail, which denied the premise of these assertions. He "did not see how the importation of slaves could be encouraged by this section," and recalling Morris's emotional address, which had singled out South Carolina and Georgia for condemnation, he declared that "humanity had nothing to do with this question." The driving principle of every nation was "interest alone," and "if the Northern States consult their interest, they will not oppose the increase of slaves which will increase the commodities of which they will become the carriers." Ultimately, however, what the northern delegations had to decide was whether their best interests would be served if the "Southern States shall or shall not be parties to the Union."[42]

Charles Pinckney stated the threat of disunion more bluntly. As his cousin Charles Cotesworth Pinckney had done with his warning a month earlier to prospective members of the Committee of Detail, Charles Pinckney told the convention that "South Carolina can never receive the plan [Constitution] if it prohibits the slave trade." The citizens of that state, and therefore their delegates, had "expressly & watchfully excepted that of meddling with the importation of negroes" as a precondition to every "proposed extension of the powers of Congress." Ellsworth, who had a hand in framing the report of the Committee of Detail, advised the delegates to leave well enough alone, to leave " the clause as it stands." His home state of Connecticut had passed an abolition law similar to Pennsylvania's in 1784, and Massachusetts and New Hampshire had pursued the same end through different means, and all of that was as it should be. "The morality or wisdom of slavery are considerations belonging to the states themselves," Ellsworth declared. In words certain to endear him to Rutledge, Pinckney, and other slaveholders, the onetime divinity student and future chief justice of the United States, whose habit of talking to himself unsettled friends and acquaintances alike, informed the convention that the "old confederation had not meddled with this point" and the "new one" should not either because "the states are the best judges of their particular interest."[43]

---

42. Farrand, 2:364.
43. Arthur Zilversmit, *The First Emancipation: The Abolition of Slavery in the North* (Chicago, 1967), 109–24, 128–31; Farrand, 2:364; Rossiter, *Grand Convention*, 93.

The next morning, as soon as the convention resumed its consideration of Article 7, Sherman pleaded with his colleagues to act with dispatch in dealing with the disputed clauses. Protracted discussions would only exacerbate sectional prejudices and incite more talk of disunion. Not wishing further to alienate the southern delegates, he came out in favor of "leaving the clause as it stands." The states "now possessed the right to import slaves," and the "public good did not require it to be taken from them." Disapproval of the slave trade notwithstanding, the interest of the Union dictated that there be "as few objections as possible to the proposed scheme of government." It was "best to leave the matter as we find it." Evidently misled by actions taken in Pennsylvania and the New England states, Sherman believed that "the abolition of slavery seemed to be going on in the U.S." without the intervention of the general government and that "the good sense of the several states would probably by degrees complete it."[44]

Let Us Not Intermeddle

The delegates simply could not follow Sherman's advice. There was too much at stake and there were too many political as well as moral issues to be addressed to allow a speedy resolution. And as Sherman feared, the exchanges became more heated as the confrontation over the importation of slaves dragged on for the rest of the day. George Mason, who spoke after Sherman, instigated the rhetorical escalation when he denounced the "infernal traffic" in slaves, which he said "originated in the avarice of British merchants" but was sustained by the "lust of gain" on the part of several states. Maryland and Virginia expressly prohibited slave imports, but their actions would be meaningless "if South Carolina & Georgia be at liberty to import." That states currently possessed the "right to import," as the Connecticut delegates had argued, was hardly decisive, for "this was the case with many other rights now to be properly given up." Mason would have been well advised to end his speech there, but he persisted, venturing into new and much more provocative territory with comments on the "evil of having slaves." This evil manifested itself first in security concerns. The safety of Virginians, for example, had been jeopardized during the Revolutionary War by the presence of slaves. Fortunately, the ineptitude of the British coupled with the "folly" of the "Tories" prevented them from making good use of this "dangerous instrument." But the evil extended into other areas of life as well, having nothing to do with foreign invasion or domestic insurrection. Southern society was menaced by an erosion of its moral fiber resulting from its reliance on slaves. Reflecting the influence of Thomas Jefferson, who contemporaneously assessed the "unhappy

44. Farrand, 2:369–70.

influence on the manners of our people produced by the existence of slavery among us" in his *Notes on the State of Virginia*, Mason noted that the institution had a "most pernicious effect on manners." It turned "every master" into a "petty tyrant," and taught poor whites to "despise" the sort of common labor "performed by slaves." Jefferson said he "tremble[d]" for his country, knowing "that God is just" and that "his justice cannot sleep forever." Similarly, Mason feared that because "nations cannot be rewarded or punished in the next world they must be in this." Provoked by their convenient accommodation of the evils of slavery, "providence punishes national sins, by national calamities."[45]

Ellsworth again rose in defense of the work of the Committee of Detail, this time homing in on Mason's observations about slavery's impact on morality. Having "never owned a slave" he could not "judge of the effects of slavery on character," he began, but if Mason was sincere about considering slavery "in a moral light," why stop with sanctions against the slave trade? Why not "go farther and free those already in the country"? Ellsworth may not have known that the master of Gunston Hall owned some three hundred slaves, making him one of the largest slaveholders in the country and easily the largest at the convention, but he knew that Virginia had more slaves than any other state, and he had a knack, as William Pierce observed, for "selecting such parts of his adversary's arguments as he finds make the strongest impression—in order to take off the force of them, so as to admit the power of his own." Ellsworth went on to summarize the situation of the United States: Virginia had no need for imported slaves and neither did Maryland; South Carolina and Georgia did; Connecticut had a law for "abolishing it"; and "abolition has already taken place in Massachusetts." Recalling the recommendation he had offered the afternoon before, Ellsworth advised, "Let us not intermeddle."[46]

The cousins Pinckney, owners of a combined one hundred and eighty slaves, and John Rutledge, whose two hundred and forty slaves placed him second only to Mason among the slaveholding delegates, likewise condemned all expressions of hostility toward slavery or the slave trade. Charles Pinckney, after saying he would vote to stop the practice and that South Carolinians "will probably of themselves stop importations," predicted nevertheless that any "attempt to take away the right" to import slaves "will produce serious objections." Charles Cotesworth Pinckney went further, declaring ratification an impossibility if the convention dared to meddle with the slave trade. Even if all of the members of the state's delegation were unequivocally supportive of the

45. Thomas Jefferson, *Notes on the State of Virginia*, ed. William Peden (New York, 1972), 162–63; Farrand, 2:370.

46. Farrand, 2:370–71, 3:89; Forrest McDonald, *We the People: The Economic Origins of the Constitution* (Chicago, 1958), 72.

Constitution and committed to using "their personal influence" to secure its adoption, they would still fail to win the "assent of their constituents" because South Carolina could not "do without slaves." As Ellsworth had pointed out, Virginia had "more slaves than she wants"; therefore, any stoppage of importations would redound to Virginia's benefit, as "her slaves" would "rise in value" on the domestic market. Virginia's gain, however, would be South Carolina's loss. Small wonder his constituents would refuse "to confederate on such unequal terms." A vote to remove Section 4 from Article 7 was, therefore, tantamount to an act of "exclusion of South Carolina from the Union." Rutledge endorsed his countrymen's sentiments, pronouncing the Constitution dead on arrival in South Carolina unless the "right to import slaves be untouched." Carolinians, he said, "will never be such fools as to give up so important an interest."[47]

Other southern delegates sided with the South Carolinians rather than with the Virginians. Abraham Baldwin of Georgia, the state most frequently mentioned in conjunction with South Carolina as the principal importers of slaves, declared the "evil" of engaging in the slave trade to be one of the "favorite prerogatives" of Georgians, and they would not surrender control over this prerogative to a distant central government. Say what you will, "Georgia was decided on this point." North Carolina's Hugh Williamson was equally firm. Although his state imposed a tax on each slave imported from Africa, he thought "it was wrong to force anything down" the throats of southerners. And "he thought the Southern States could not be members of the Union," if Section 4 were to be rejected by the convention.[48]

The opponents of Section 4 reacted as might be expected to these declarations. John Dickinson was astonished to hear such rant. "He could not believe that the Southern States would refuse to confederate on the account apprehended." Rufus King, who had previously indicated he would not be intimidated by threats of disunion, said he was convinced that the opposition of the Carolinas and Georgia would be met by the "great & equal opposition" of the remaining states. The "exemption of slaves from duty whilst every other import was subjected to it" constituted an unconscionable "inequality that could not fail to strike the commercial sagacity of the Northern & middle states." James Wilson, the fourth member of the Committee of Detail, agreed with King that the lone exemption granted to slave imports under Section 4 and defended by Baldwin, Rutledge, and the Pinckneys, was "in fact a bounty on that article," an encouragement to continue the enterprise, contrary to the protestations of the Carolinians and Georgians that external interference would be gratuitous

47. McDonald, *We the People*, 79–81; Farrand, 2:373.
48. Farrand, 2:372, 373.

because they were themselves "disposed to get rid of the importation of slaves in a short time."[49]

These Things May Form a Bargain

In the middle of these exchanges came a predictable motion from an unpredictable source. Gouverneur Morris moved that the "whole subject" be submitted to a select committee. Given the uncompromising tone of his earlier comments, especially his verbal assault on South Carolina and Georgia slave traders for violating "the most sacred laws of humanity" by tearing their "fellow creatures from their dearest connections," one would have expected the volatile Pennsylvanian to join King and Wilson. He had been an unabashed critic of Section 4 and its supporters. What might explain Morris's motion? William Pierce would have ascribed it to a character flaw. Morris, the Georgian said, was a "genius" who, despite his talent, learning, wit, and charm, could be "fickle and inconstant—never pursuing one train of thinking—nor ever regular." A more likely explanation, however, is that Morris, who had learned the art of political manipulation as an assistant to Robert Morris in the Office of Finance under the Confederation government, was not about to allow an opportunity for a negotiated advantage slip out of his hands. He suggested that the committee, which was to consist of one member from each state, be charged primarily with resolving the controversy over slave importations but also engage those "clauses relating to taxes on exports & to a navigation act. These things may form a bargain among the Northern & Southern States."[50]

The bargain Morris envisioned entailed concessions from both sides on the disputed clauses of Section 4 in combination with Section 6 of Article 7. "Clauses relating to taxes on exports" was a return to the first part of Section 4, which prohibited federal taxes from being imposed on state exports, while clauses relating "to a navigation act" was a reference to Section 6, which stipulated that "no navigation act shall be passed without the assent of two thirds of the members present in each House." The prohibition of federal export taxes was dear to southerners, as evidenced by South Carolina's insistence that only "direct" taxes be considered as part of Morris's July 12 motion tying taxation to representation. General Pinckney, it will be recalled, had then said he was "alarmed at what had been thrown out concerning the taxing of exports," and Morris had obliged the Carolinians by excluding both export and import duties from any formula for computing taxes. When the first clause of Section 4 came up for consideration, however, opponents of the prohibition made a more

49. Farrand, 2:372, 373.
50. E. James Ferguson, *The Power of the Purse: A History of American Public Finance, 1776–1790* (Chapel Hill, 1961), 117–45; Farrand, 3:92, 2:374.

compelling case for allowing the federal government to tax exports. As an issue limited to revenue raising and trade regulation, one unencumbered by the question of proportional representation, taxes on exports gained new supporters from the ranks of the nationalists.[51]

Morris himself emphasized two "general interest" reasons for authorizing export taxes. First, arguments to the contrary notwithstanding, such taxes would not be "partial & unjust" because commodities such as "tobacco, lumber, and livestock" would all be susceptible to export duties, and these were the chief exports of "different states." Furthermore, changes in the situation and economy of the country would mean that soon "skins, beaver & other peculiar raw materials" would join the list of taxable items, which would be "politic in view of encouraging American manufactures." Second, "local considerations ought not to impede" the good of the whole, Morris declared, expressing sentiments befitting a protégé of Robert Morris. The benefits that might accrue to the nation through federal regulation of trade far outweighed the harm that might be done to particular localities. "In time of war," for example, the inability of the federal government to institute an "embargo . . . may be of critical importance" to the fate of the nation.[52]

Madison, frustrated by the actions of individual states under the Confederation, especially with regard to selfish commercial policies that foiled all attempts to "counteract foreign plans" to foment interstate rivalries that might "break the Union," agreed with Morris. "We ought to be governed by national and permanent views," Madison said, and an essential component of such a vision was the "power over exports that a tax" provided. Again remembering the futility of the Confederation government's protests against the discriminatory trade practices of Great Britain in particular, he contended that "a proper regulation of exports" was necessary for "procuring equitable regulations from other nations." In extreme circumstances, "an embargo may be of absolute necessity, and can alone be effectuated by the General authority."[53]

Southerners who supported the prohibition established in the first clause of Section 4 were joined by those worried about extending the powers of the federal government too far. Elbridge Gerry "was strenuously opposed to the power over exports." Fearful that it might be used "to oppress the states," compelling them to bend to the arbitrary will of heavy-handed federal regulators, he cautioned the convention to be wary of surrendering any more power to the new central government without sufficient knowledge of how it would be "exercised." Mason was also opposed to extending the taxing power over exports, although

51. Farrand, 1:592.   52. Farrand, 2:360.
53. *PJM*, 8:431–32; Farrand, 2:361.

for distinctly sectional reasons. The "8 Northern states have an interest different from the five Southern states," and they have an advantage of "36 votes against 29" in the House of Representatives and "8 against 5" in the Senate. The maxim that "a majority when interested will oppress the minority" was applicable here and should therefore be the guiding principle of the five southern states, namely, Virginia, Maryland, North Carolina, South Carolina, and Georgia. The "impolicy" of taxing, let alone embargoing, tobacco should be obvious to all of his countrymen, Mason concluded, glancing in Madison's direction. "Other nations do raise it, and are capable of raising it as well as Virginia."[54]

Madison took his esteemed colleague's reservations to heart and proffered a compromise of sorts. "As a lesser evil than a total prohibition," he moved to amend the contested clause with the stipulation that the federal government could not tax state exports, "unless by consent of two thirds of the Legislature." Earlier in the afternoon, John Langdon of New Hampshire first floated the idea of a supermajority as a reassurance to those who "feared that the Northern states will oppress the trade of the Southern." Langdon's suggestion gained no traction among southern delegates and neither did Madison's motion, which went down to defeat with the help of all five of Mason's "southern states," Virginia included. Faced with such unyielding opposition, the convention was inclined to heed Ellsworth's advice on the disputed clause: "It is best as it stands." The deciding factor was the warning issued again by Hugh Williamson. North Carolina "would never agree to this power," he declared, and suspecting that other southern states shared the same determination, Williamson predicted that if the convention removed the prohibition against taxing exports, "it would destroy the last hope of an adoption of the plan" of union. On a vote of seven to four, the convention allowed the first clause of Section 4 to stand.[55]

Morris did not get his wish to revisit this issue as part of a larger "bargain," but the convention was receptive to his idea of appointing a select committee. Roger Sherman, whose appeal for dispatch was made in vain earlier that morning and who witnessed in Williamson's ultimatum the bitter fruits of that failure, supported the idea of turning to a committee for the resolution of the slavery clauses of Section 4. Answering the question posed by Rutledge on August 21, Sherman conceded that if the slave trade was the "sine qua non" of the South's attachment to the Union, then "it was better to let the Southern States import slaves than to part with them." Edmund Randolph, the fifth member of the Committee of Detail, finally chimed in after nearly two days of silence as

54. Farrand, 2:362–62.   55. Farrand, 2:359, 360, 363.

the debate swirled around him. Randolph "dwelt on the dilemma to which the Convention was exposed." If it allowed the clauses protecting the slave trade to stand, it would "revolt the Quakers, the Methodists, and many others in the states having no slaves." But if it insisted on changes, at least "two states might be lost to the Union." Treating the prohibition against taxing slave imports and the prohibition against impeding slave migration as a single issue, Randolph said "he could never agree to the clause as it stands"; indeed, he "would sooner risk the constitution." He was willing nevertheless to charge a select committee with trying to find "some middle ground."[56]

Committee of Eleven

By a vote of seven to three, the convention adopted the motion to refer the two remaining clauses of Section 4 to a committee consisting of eleven members. Immediately after the vote had been taken, Charles Pinckney moved to charge the committee with making a recommendation on Section 6 as well. Nathaniel Gorham objected. Declaring he "did not see the propriety" of the motion, the senior Massachusetts delegate demanded to know whether Pinckney "meant to require a greater proportion of votes." Was it his intention to seek a larger percentage than the two-thirds majority currently required under Section 6 in order for Congress to enact navigation laws? Gorham's uncharacteristically gruff response suggests that the issue of commercial regulations had been addressed in meetings of the Committee of Detail and that the two-thirds ratio had been arrived at after much wrangling. He "desired it to be remembered that the Eastern States" were already handicapped by the requirement of a supermajority and would not tolerate a furthering of their disadvantage. These states "had no motive to Union but a commercial one," Gorham warned. Moreover, "they were able to protect themselves" and therefore, absent the commercial incentive, "did not need the aid of the Southern States."[57]

James Wilson, probably aware that Pinckney and others were already engaged in striking a bargain on the disputed sections of Article 7, quickly intervened, reminding Gorham that the Committee of Eleven might vote "to reduce the proportion of votes required" for navigation laws. An increasingly alarmed Ellsworth, probably unaware of any bargain in the works, again pleaded with the convention to take "the plan as it is." The ongoing jockeying for advantage had resulted in a "widening of opinions" and assumed a most "threatening aspect." Unless the delegates found some "middle & moderate ground," the states would "fly into a variety of shapes & directions." Most would eventually

56. Farrand, 2:374.   57. Farrand, 2:374.

find refuge in "several confederations," but only after much chaos and confusion and "not without bloodshed."[58]

Ellsworth's alarm was grounded in the realization that the contest over trade regulation could be as divisive a sectional issue as the confrontation over the importation of slaves. Morris understood this, which is why he included Section 6 along with the slavery clauses of Section 4 in his contemplated bargain between the northern and southern states. Section 6 stipulated that navigation laws, unlike ordinary legislation, required the consent of two-thirds of both houses of Congress, and the "*staple* and *commercial states* were solicitous to *retain*" this restriction, Luther Martin explained, "lest their *commerce* should be placed too much under the power of the *eastern* states." George Mason, who seemed to bristle at every mention of trade regulation, was more solicitous than most. He believed that the two-thirds requirement alone prevented the northern states, temporarily in the majority, from establishing a monopoly of their shipping business, demanding "exorbitant freight," and compelling the purchase of "commodities at their own price." Even worse, if a "bare majority" were allowed to pass navigation acts, "a few rich merchants in Philadelphia, New York & Boston" would be perfectly positioned "to monopolize the staples of the Southern States & reduce their value perhaps 50 percent." The protection afforded under Section 6, in other words, was elemental, for it saved the "five Southern States" from being "ruined" by the "eight Northern and Eastern States."[59]

About mid-afternoon on August 22, Pinckney's motion to add a reconsideration of Section 6 to the charge of the Committee of Eleven passed overwhelmingly by a vote of nine to two. With this addition, the committee possessed the components needed to forge a compromise that hopefully might abort the threats of disunion coming from both sides of the sectional divide. The convention spent the next day almost routinely dealing with other questions raised by the recommendations of the Committee of Detail. It unanimously adopted the equivalent of the supremacy clause, declaring the Constitution, federal laws, and treaties of the United States to be "the supreme law[,] . . . anything in the Constitutions or laws of the several states to the contrary notwithstanding," and by large margins agreed to disallow bills of attainder, ex post facto laws, and federal officials from accepting salaries or titles from foreign states.[60]

Only Charles Pinckney's motion to give Congress the power to veto state laws it deemed to be harmful to the "general interests and harmony of the

---

58. Farrand, 2:375

59. Luther Martin, "The Genuine Information, Delivered to the Legislature of the State of Maryland" (1787), in Farrand, 3:210; Oliver Ellsworth, "The Landholder" (1787), in Farrand, 3:164; George Mason, "Objections to This Constitution of Government" (ca. September 16, 1787), *PGM*, 3:989, 992.

60. Farrand, 2:375, 380–94.

Union, provided that two thirds of the members of each House assent to the same," produced some heat. Madison endorsed the proposal, saying he "had been from the beginning a friend of the principle." But aside from James Wilson, who called it "the key-stone" to completing the "government we are raising," and New Hampshire's John Langdon, no one else spoke in support Pinckney's motion. George Mason wanted "to know how the power was to be exercised." Were all state laws to be scrutinized by Congress? "Is no road nor bridge to be established without the sanction of the General Legislature?" Gouverneur Morris "did not see the utility or practicability of the proposition." Hugh Williamson dismissed the motion as "a waste of time." And John Rutledge spared no vitriol in condemning his junior colleague's proposal. "Will any state ever agree to be bound hand & foot in this manner?" he demanded. If adopted, "this alone would damn and ought to damn the Constitution." Faced with such stiff opposition, Pinckney withdrew his motion.[61]

Slave Importation and Taxes

On August 24 William Livingston of New Jersey, on behalf the Committee of Eleven, delivered its report to the convention. The committee recommended substantially altering Section 4. Whereas the Committee of Detail protected the slave trade indefinitely, the Committee of Eleven prohibited federal interference only until 1800. And whereas the earlier report forbad federal taxes on slave imports, the new report authorized taxes "at a rate not exceeding the average of the duties laid on imports." The Committee of Eleven also recommended dropping Section 6 altogether. The convention sat on these recommendations for the rest of the day while resuming deliberations on two other sections of the report of the Committee of Detail, the first under Article 9 dealing with the convoluted process of resolving disputes between two or more states and the second under Article 10 prescribing the method of electing the president of the United States. The convention voted to expunge the former as an unwieldy and unnecessary relic of the Articles of Confederation and to keep intact the latter, allowing Congress to elect the president.[62]

When the convention took up the first part of the committee's report on August 25, Charles Cotesworth Pinckney moved to insert the year 1808 in lieu of the recommended 1800, extending the inviolability of the slave trade for another eight years. Gorham of Massachusetts seconded the motion, indicating that he and the South Carolinian represented others who had previously agreed to the extension. Only one delegate, James Madison, spoke against the motion. Madison thought that leaving the states at "liberty to import slaves" for twenty years was "more dishonorable to the national character than to say

61. Farrand, 2:390–91.   62. Farrand, 2:400–04.

nothing about it in the Constitution." He could not have spoken for more than a few minutes before the question was called, and the convention adopted the Pinckney-Gorham motion by a vote of seven to four.[63]

That a version of the bargain he envisioned had been realized gave Morris no small measure of satisfaction, but he wished for greater transparency, in part no doubt to deflect the criticism he anticipated arising in Pennsylvania in response to the slave clauses. Morris moved to change the wording of the clause. Rather than proclaiming that the "migration or importation of such persons as the several states now existing shall think proper to admit, shall not be prohibited prior to the year 1808," Morris suggested a more straightforward rendering: the "importation of slaves into North Carolina, South Carolina & Georgia shall not be prohibited &c." His proposed substitution "would be most fair" to all of the parties concerned, and besides, "he wished it to be known . . . that this part of the Constitution was a compliance with those states." There should be no mistaking who demanded these conditions or what they entailed. Roger Sherman and George Clymer, Pennsylvania's representative on the Committee of Eleven, concurred with Morris. Sherman "liked a description better than the terms" used in the committee's report, even if it was "not pleasing to some people." Mason, on the other hand, said he understood the complaint and "was not against using the term 'slaves' but against naming North Carolina, South Carolina & Georgia, lest it should give offense to the people of those states." North Carolina's Hugh Williamson, a former Presbyterian minister with roots in Pennsylvania, explained that although he was against slavery "both in opinion & practice," he supported the committee's report because it was better "from a view of all the circumstances, to let in South Carolina & Georgia on those terms, than to exclude them from the Union." Fully cognizant of the "circumstances" to which Williamson alluded and never fully committed to the "change of language" he proposed should it be "objected to by the members from those states," Morris withdrew his motion. The convention then adopted the first part of the committee's report, as amended by Pinckney's motion to extend the protection of slave imports to 1808, by a vote of seven to four.[64]

The second part of the committee's report, authorizing the imposition of federal taxes on imported slaves, sailed through the convention with equal ease. Indeed, only one member voiced a substantive reason for opposing such a tax, and that delegate was not a southerner, as might be expected, but Sherman of Connecticut, whose state would not be susceptible to the tax because it had already enacted a gradual abolition law. As he had done three days earlier, Sherman argued that an import tax on slaves made a bad situation worse by

63. Farrand, 2:415.   64. Farrand, 2:396, 415–16.

"acknowledging men to be property . . . [and] taxing them as such." While
Madison agreed with Sherman that it would be "wrong to admit in the Constitution the idea that there could be property in men," Gorham advised him
to view "the duty, not as implying that slaves are property, but as a discour-
agement to the importation of them." It was a familiar argument, dating
back to July 9, when William Paterson used it to oppose the counting of
slaves for purposes of representation; and to August 8, when Rufus King
and Morris resurrected it to oppose the three-fifths ratio; and most recently
to August 21, when Luther Martin referred to it in proposing a tax on slave
imports. But there was no need for the delegates to retrace their steps over
well-traveled ground. King and John Langdon, both of whom were on the
Committee of Eleven, simply reminded the convention of the bargain that
had been struck in committee, that they "considered this as the price of the
1st part." Charles Cotesworth Pinckney, also a member of the Committee of
Eleven, "admitted that it was so." After amending the clause to read "but a tax
or duty may be imposed on such importation not exceeding ten dollars for
each person," the convention adopted the second part of the committee report
on Section 4.[65]

And Navigation Laws

The third component of the bargain, the recommendation of the Committee
of Eleven to expunge Section 6 from the report of the Committee of Detail,
came before the convention on August 29. Charles Pinckney positioned himself to speak first and attempted to derail this part of the bargain by moving
to postpone further consideration of the committee report in favor of a substitute proposition. For laws regulating commerce, his motion required "the
assent of two thirds of the members of each House" of Congress. In essence
Pinckney was asking the convention to ignore the committee's recommendation and to keep Section 6 in the proposed Constitution. Without the check
afforded by the two-thirds rule, rival interests gaining a bare majority "would
be a source of oppressive regulations." Edmund Randolph viewed Pinckney's
motion favorably as an attempt to stanch the "accumulation of obnoxious
ingredients" in the new federal frame, a commendable effort to check the
"complete deformity of the system." Hugh Williamson, who served multiple
terms in Congress from 1782 to 1788 and therefore should have known better, argued for the motion, contending that the two-thirds rule never en-
cumbered the conduct of the Confederation's business. "No useful measure
he believed had been lost in Congress for want of nine votes." Predictably,

65. Farrand, 2:374, 416.

Mason proved to be Pinckney's most avid backer. Those behind the movement to remove the two-thirds barrier were hoping the southern states would be so foolish as to "deliver themselves bound hand & foot to the Eastern States," he declared.[66]

The opponents of Pinckney's motion argued that the supermajority required under Section 6 would prove "highly injurious" to the nation. Gouverneur Morris predicted it would hurt the domestic production of commercial vessels as well as the development of a navy because the shipping industry "stood in need of public patronage" in the form of preferential laws that would encourage "American bottoms & seamen" and discourage foreign competitors. Madison "went into a pretty full view of the subject" to refute the assertions made by Pinckney's supporters. The chief impact of navigation acts on the South would be "a temporary rise of freight," temporary because the growth in the number of American ships coupled with the "emigration of Northern seamen & merchants to the Southern States" would soon mitigate the negative repercussions of such laws. In conjunction with the "removal of the existing & injurious retaliations among the states on each other" and the advancement of "our retaliatory measures" to counter foreign laws that discriminated against American commerce, navigation acts would be a "national benefit." Roger Sherman and James Wilson contradicted the statement made by Williamson, whose term in the Confederation Congress had overlapped with theirs, regarding the two-thirds rule. The requirement of "more than a majority to decide questions was always embarrassing," always an impediment to conducting business, Sherman said. Wilson concurred. "Great inconveniences," he contended, "had been experienced in Congress from the Articles of Confederation requiring nine votes in certain cases." More incensed by Pinckney's motion than any of the others however, was Nathaniel Gorham. The widely admired Massachusetts delegate had not been his usual "agreeable and pleasing" self a week earlier in expressing his distaste for the two-thirds requirement, and he was not about to backtrack now that the Committee of Eleven had recommended the deletion of Section 6. If the new federal Union was "to be so fettered as to be unable to relieve the Eastern States," either by promoting domestic commerce or counteracting the prejudicial maritime laws of other nations, "what motive can they have to join in it." Although he "deprecated the consequences of disunion," Gorham thought the southern states "had the most reason to dread them."[67]

Ultimately, all of this venting and hand-wringing may have been good for the spleen and for play back home later, but the bargain struck in committee

66. Farrand, 2:449, 450, 451.　　　　67. Farrand, 2:451–52, 450, 453, 3:88.

and concluded over dinner at the Indian Queen tavern and other popular gathering places around the city was a done deal. General Charles Cotesworth Pinckney, who represented South Carolina on the Committee of Eleven, told his cousin and others that he knew "it was the true interest of the Southern States to have no regulation of commerce," but considering the "liberal conduct" of the New England states "towards the views of South Carolina," he thought it proper to accommodate their wish to drop Section 6. What the general meant by "liberal conduct," Madison explained, was the "permission to import slaves." South Carolina and the New England states had reached "an understanding on the two subjects of *navigation* and *slavery*[,] . . . which explains the vote" on Charles Pinckney's motion. And indeed, the motion to postpone the committee's recommendation in order to retain the two-thirds requirement for navigation laws was defeated by a vote of four to seven, with South Carolina alone among the southern states joining in the opposition.[68]

Following the defeat of Pinckney's motion, two votes were taken in rapid order. Neither generated any discussion and both passed without dissent. First came the vote for striking Section 6 from the proposed Constitution, and second, a vote for inserting a fugitive slave clause. The problem of runaway slaves was first raised by South Carolina's Pierce Butler the previous afternoon when the convention considered Article 15 of the report of the Committee of Eleven. Article 15 dealt with accused felons fleeing from one state to another. In such cases, authorities in the second state were obligated to apprehend and return the suspect "to the state having jurisdiction of the offense." Butler and Charles Pinckney moved to amend the article "to require fugitive slaves and servants to be delivered up like criminals." But upon the objections of James Wilson and Roger Sherman, whose constituents in Pennsylvania and Connecticut could be expected to complain loudly if public funds were used to bolster the plantation regimes of the South, Butler withdrew his motion. That Butler acted with such alacrity strongly suggests an awareness on his part of an impending bargain. Thus during the debate over navigation laws, he declared himself in favor of removing the two-thirds requirement because he was "desirous of conciliating the affections of the Eastern States." Having made the complementary concession of voting to strike Section 6, Butler moved straightaway to insert into the Constitution an early version of the fugitive slave clause: "If any person bound to service or labor in any of the United States shall escape into another state, he or she shall . . . be delivered up to the person justly claiming their service or labor." And he met no opposition.[69]

---

68. Farrand, 2:449–50, 453.   69. Farrand, 2:187–88, 443, 453–54.

It Was Done

In late November 1787, two months after the convention ended, Luther Martin delivered a lengthy summary of its proceedings to the Maryland legislature. When he got to the clause dealing with slave importations, Martin recounted the difficulties that necessitated the appointment of the Committee of Eleven. The Committee of Detail had recommended that "such importations should not be prohibited," but eight states rejected that recommendation, according to Martin, and only "Georgia, South Carolina, and, I think, North Carolina" voted for it. "We were then told by the delegates of the two first of those states, that their states would never agree to a system, which put it in the power of the general government to prevent the importation of slaves." Martin was mistaken about the vote to reject the committee's recommendation—the convention took no vote on whether importations should be allowed "without confining it to a particular period"—but he recalled quite accurately the response of the South Carolina delegates to his proposal to give the federal government the power to limit and tax slave importations. They uniformly condemned Martin's proposal and demanded an unimpeded license to import slaves as the price of union. His recollection of the bargaining that occurred in the Committee of Eleven, on which he "had the honor to be a member," was also on the mark. "I found the *eastern* states, notwithstanding their *aversion to slavery*, were willing to indulge the southern states with a temporary liberty to prosecute the *slave-trade*, provided the southern states would, in their turn, gratify them, by laying *no restriction on navigation acts.*" Once this foundation was laid, "a great majority agreed on a report, by which the general government was to be prohibited from preventing the importation of slaves for a limited time, and the restrictive clause relative to navigation acts was to be omitted."[70]

Like Martin, Charles Cotesworth Pinckney also served on the Committee of Eleven. Unlike the Marylander, however, he represented a state that depended on the importation of slaves from abroad. He was "thoroughly convinced," Pinckney said, that the climate and "swampy situation of our country obliges us to cultivate our lands with negroes." Why then would he have agreed to the clause that protected slave imports for twenty years and no more? In the South Carolina House of Representatives in January 1788, Pinckney answered his critics. He understood well the state's predicament, the extent of its reliance on the labor of slaves, so "that without them South Carolina would soon be a desert waste." But the Carolina delegates faced

70. Luther Martin, "Genuine Information," Farrand, 3:210–11.

a formidable coalition of selfishly motivated opponents; they "had to contend with the religious and political prejudices of the Eastern and Middle States, and with the interested and inconsistent opinion of Virginia, who was warmly opposed to our importing more slaves." Some of these enemies of "unlimited importation" described slaves as a "dangerous species of property" because they could be turned "against ourselves" by an invading force, and "as we were allowed a representation for them in the House of Representatives, our influence in government would be increased in proportion as we were less able to defend ourselves." A way to avert the looming and potentially destructive deadlock presented itself when the delegates from the "Eastern" states, or New England, offered to "restrain the religious and political prejudices" of their constituents if we could "show some period" when slave imports might end. Thus his reference to the "liberal conduct" of these eastern states, Pinckney explained, for the "Middle States and Virginia made us no such proposition; they were for an immediate and total prohibition." The "settlement" reached in the Committee of Eleven and secured by the vote of the convention guaranteed "an unlimited importation of negroes for twenty years." Nor was "it declared that the importation shall be then stopped; it may be continued." Moreover, with the fugitive slave clause, "we have obtained a right to recover our slaves in whatever part of America they may take refuge." In the end, considering all of the objections confronting them, Pinckney opined, "we have made the best terms for the security of this species of property it was in our power to make."[71]

George Mason, "steady and firm in his principles," was never reconciled to the bargain, never satisfied with the "best terms" argument of its proponents. For nearly two days after the vote on August 29, he sat in silence in the convention, which was unusual for him, before announcing "that he would sooner chop off his right hand than put it to the Constitution as it now stands." On Saturday, September 15, the penultimate day of the convention, as the delegates were on the verge of ordering the Constitution to be engrossed, he was still trying to undo the agreement. He moved to add a "further proviso" to the effect "that no law in nature of a navigation act be passed before the year 1808, without the consent of 2/3 of each branch of the Legislature." His motion failed on a vote of three to seven, with South Carolina again in the ranks of the opposition. Mason promptly declared his intent to stand against ratification in Virginia. That being the case, he would also not be signing the Constitution because "he could not sign here what he could not support there."

71. Charles Cotesworth Pinckney, "Speech in South Carolina House of Representatives," January 1788, in Farrand, 3:253–55.

To Thomas Jefferson five years later, he justified his refusal to be a signatory to the Constitution by dwelling on the bargain. As the document stood "till a fortnight before the convention rose," that is, up until two weeks before the convention adjourned sine die, Mason said, he was ready to "set his hand & heart to" the new frame of government. Then the question of "a vote of 2/3 in the legislature on particular subjects & expressly on that of navigation" came up for consideration, and "the 2 southernmost states," South Carolina and Georgia, sensing that Congress was anxious to suppress the importation of slaves, "struck up a bargain." If "the 3 New England states would join to admit slaves for some years, the 2 southernmost states would join in changing the clause which required 2/3 of the legislature" to enact navigation laws. "It was done."[72]

It Is Not Worth a Price Like This

William Lloyd Garrison, like Mason, rejected the "best terms" settlement between the northern and southern states, but for entirely different reasons. Mason wanted immediately to put a stop to the importation of slaves and to keep the two-thirds requirement for trade laws. He lost on both counts. Garrison demanded an end to slavery itself, not just to the slave trade, and he blamed the framers of the Constitution for failing to achieve that end. During the debate over slave importations, when Mason spoke in support of the proposal to prohibit such imports and waxed eloquent about the "evil of having slaves," Oliver Ellsworth asked him why he was stopping with sanctions against the slave trade; if he was serious about the immorality of slavery, why not "go farther and free those already in the country"? Ellsworth posed a rhetorical question to compel Mason to drop his line of argumentation. To Garrison, however, there was nothing rhetorical about the question. Indeed, contrary to Ellsworth's advice, he would have the federal government "intermeddle" in the affairs of the slave states and abolish a barbarism that should have ended a half century earlier. Only "an unblushing and monstrous coalition" of states, completing an "infamous bargain which they made between themselves," could choose to sacrifice "the bodies and souls of millions" upon the altar of politics. Garrison was "as uncompromising as justice" on this issue because by the 1830s he had concluded that if the preservation of the Union required "treading upon the necks, spilling the blood, and destroying the souls of millions," then it ought to be dissolved, for "it is not worth a price like this." Indeed, in the early 1840s he was openly advocating disunion, condemning the "accursed . . .

72. Thomas Jefferson, record of a conversation with George Mason on the Federal Convention, September 30, 1792, *PGM*, 3:1275–76; Farrand, 3:94, 2:479, 631, 632.

American Union" as a "frightful despotism" and calling for unity under the rallying cry, *"No Union with Slaveholders."*[73]

The framers of the Constitution and the Revolutionary generation as a whole were not as certain as Garrison about the price of union. Garrison's problem, as he saw it, was to answer the query, "How is the dissolution of the Union to be effected?" He needed to convince Americans who had more than a half century's worth of accumulated memories under the Constitution that disunion was preferable to union, that the much vaunted union of the states was "a snare" and "a curse," deserving "to be resisted, denounced and repudiated." For the framers, the problem was exactly the reverse. With the exception of Georgia, all of the states had autonomous colonial pasts that stretched back a century or more. Independence from Britain initially enhanced their sense of autonomy by severing their most important common bond. The time-tested status of the newly independent states was, therefore, separation from one another. By contrast, union was new, untested, and not to be taken for granted. That the Articles of Confederation established a "league of friendship" in which "each state retains its sovereignty, freedom and independence" was perfectly in accordance with custom and conventional wisdom.[74]

Even more important than the price of union, however, were the costs of disunion. For Garrison, there were none. After effecting a separation, the northern states would "frame a new government, free from the spirit of bondage," a new nation that paid no homage to "the will of the Slave Power." Garrison assumed that one union would replace the other; the Revolutionaries made no such assumption. Instead, they assumed that disunion would be followed by further fragmentation, intensified competition among the sovereign states, unchecked contention leading to armed confrontations, a precipitous decline of civilian rule and the corresponding elevation of military leaders as people willingly sacrificed liberty for security, and, lastly and inevitably, despotism. This was what led Madison to say he "tremble[d]" at the thought of the *"irregular experiments"* that would follow the dissolution of the Union, and what moved Jefferson to declare disunion to be the "most unfortunate of all consequences" that could possibly befall the American nation. For Garrison the choice was between an existing "Union with Slaveholders" and a better *"Union for freedom,"* and he implored his listeners to choose the latter. Who would not? For the delegates at Philadelphia in 1787 the choice was between a continuation of the Union with slaveholders or

73. William Lloyd Garrison, "On the Constitution," December 29, 1832, "To the Public," January 1, 1831, "The American Union," January 10, 1845, and "Disunion," January 15, 1855, in Cain, *Garrison*, 87, 72, 114, 142.

74. Garrison, "Disunion," 141–42.

unceasing conflicts ending in the extermination of freedom. The choice they made may be blameworthy, and Garrison may have been more morally deserving than any of them, but historical condemnations ought to be mediated by context.[75]

75. Garrison, "Disunion," 115, 142; Melvin Yazawa, "Republican Expectations: Revolutionary Ideology and the Compromise of 1790," in *A Republic for the Ages: The United States Capitol and the Political Culture of the Early Republic*, ed. Donald R. Kennon (Charlottesville, VA, 1999), 3–35; Melvin Yazawa, "Dionysian Rhetoric and Apollonian Solutions: The Politics of Union and Disunion in the Age of Federalism," in *Empire and Nation: The American Revolution in the Atlantic World*, ed. Eliga H. Gould and Peter S. Onuf (Baltimore, 2005), 178–96, 349–52.

PART TWO

RATIFICATION
Stacking the Deck

The congressional resolution of February 21, 1787, authorized a "Convention of delegates" to meet in Philadelphia for the "sole and express purpose of revising the Articles of Confederation." This resolution together with the commissions of several state delegations, it will be recalled, became a rallying point for the proponents of the New Jersey Plan presented by William Paterson. Unlike the Virginia Plan, they argued, Paterson's did not exceed the limits of the Convention's authority because it complied with the charge of revising rather than rejecting the Articles. It was not an unanticipated challenge. Indeed, according to Charles Pinckney, "the first question that naturally presented itself to the view of almost every member . . . was the formation of a new, or the amendment of the existing system." The convention chose the former because the delegates "saw and felt the necessity of establishing a government upon different principles." Pinckney's cousin, Charles Cotesworth Pinckney, was even more direct. "It had been alleged" that the delegates had exceeded their powers, but he "thought not." The South Carolina delegation, for example, had been commissioned to devise "all such alterations" as it thought necessary to render the general government capable of ensuring the "future good" of the republic. This meant that they were empowered "to propose anything which they imagined would strengthen the Union, and be for the advantage of our country; but they did not pretend to a right to determine finally upon anything." Pinckney's reasoning was modeled after the argument he heard James Wilson make in Philadelphia. The convention, Wilson had said in response to Paterson's supporters, was "authorized to *conclude nothing*, but . . . at liberty to *propose anything*." In other words, as James Madison explained, the powers the convention exercised were "advisory and recommendatory" rather than "real and final." Therefore, the Constitution as it stood on September 17, 1787, was "of no more consequence than the paper on which it is written." Power resided in the people. It was up to them to determine whether the Constitution became something more than a recommendation.[1]

1. Charles Pinckney, debate in the South Carolina Legislature, January 16, 1788, in Farrand, 3:248, 3:581–84; Charles Cotesworth Pinckney, speech in South Carolina House of Representatives, January, 1788, 3:252–53; 1:253; *Federalist* no. 40, 290–91.

Conventions Instead of State Legislatures

The proponents of the Constitution understood what Madison meant when he described the convention's powers as "recommendatory" only, and they accepted the fact that their work needed to be validated in the various states, but they were not about to leave Philadelphia without stacking the deck in favor of ratification. They began by prescribing state conventions as the proper venues for ratification. Article 21 of the report of the Committee of Detail recommended such conventions, but on August 31 Gouverneur Morris moved to alter it to allow "the states to pursue their own modes of ratification." Allowing the states to choose, however, was not a wide-open proposition. The delegates saw only two possible methods of addressing the question of ratification: conventions or the sitting state legislatures. Rufus King rose immediately in opposition to Morris's motion. To strike "conventions" from Article 21 "was equivalent to giving up the business altogether," he declared. "Conventions alone" would free the process from "all the obstacles" that plagued the state legislatures, "and if not positively required by the plan, its enemies will oppose that mode." James Madison endorsed these sentiments, explaining it was "best to require conventions" for one simple reason, namely, "that the powers given to the General Government being taken from the State Governments," their legislatures "would be more disinclined" to advance ratification "than conventions composed in part at least of other men." Morris's motion was defeated, with six states voting to keep the prescription for state conventions.[2]

Nine States Shall Be Sufficient

Although the Committee of Detail prescribed state conventions under Article 21, it did not specify how many states needed to ratify the new federal plan to make it operational. The committee left a blank, to be filled in by the convention, before the phrase "states shall be sufficient for organizing this Constitution." Marylanders Daniel Carroll and Luther Martin moved to fill in the blank with "thirteen," that is, to require the consent of all of the states. They were no doubt motivated by their recollection of the pivotal role Maryland had played as the last state to ratify the Articles of Confederation in 1781, having held up the process for two years in an effort to force those states with claims in the west to cede their lands to the general government. But the other delegates remembered the same drawn out process less fondly and roundly defeated Carroll's motion: "all no—except Maryland." Next Roger Sherman of Connecticut and Jonathan Dayton of New Jersey moved to insert the number "ten" into the blank space. James Wilson opposed the motion as conceding too

2. Farrand, 2:189, 475–77.

much to the smaller states and recommended instead Madison's earlier proposal to require at least seven states with a cumulative total of thirty-three members in the House of Representatives, which would amount to "the concurrence of a majority of both the states and the people." George Mason then declared himself in favor of "preserving ideas familiar to the people." Since the Articles of Confederation required "nine states . . . in all great cases . . . that number was on that account preferable." The convention agreed with Mason, defeating the Sherman motion by a vote of four in favor and seven opposed and adopting Mason's by a vote of eight to three. The second step the supporters of the Constitution took to advance the cause of ratification was thus to lower the bar for making the new federal government operational. Enshrined as Article 7 of the Constitution, it amounted to a strategic advantage as well because as more states ratified the Constitution, bringing the number ever closer to the required nine, momentum gathered on their side, while those opposed to ratification had to confront the nagging fear of their states being left out of the new Union.[3]

Congressional Approval?

The friends of the Constitution next concentrated on Article 22 of the report of the Committee of Detail and altered it to their advantage. That article called on the Convention to present its work to the "United States in Congress assembled for their approbation," which made it consistent with the February 21 congressional resolution authorizing the convention to revise the Articles of Confederation and then to submit the proposed revisions to Congress for its endorsement. On August 31 Morris and Charles Pinckney moved to expunge the words "for their approbation" from Article 22. Without any discussion, the motion carried on an eight to three vote. Buoyed by their success, Morris and Pinckney then moved further to amend Article 22 so that it instructed the states to act "as speedily as circumstances will permit" with respect to the calling of conventions, thereby preventing "enemies to the plan from giving it the go by." Morris expected his Pennsylvania constituents to be favorably impressed with the proposed Constitution "when it first appears." Its opponents would therefore aim to prolong the entire process of ratification, to make an ordeal of it, so that "by degrees" and through "intrigue" they might "turn the popular current against" the new federal plan. But with strong opposition coming from Luther Martin, who thought the motion was a cheap trick to secure ratification "by surprise," and Elbridge Gerry, who "enlarged" on Martin's idea and "represented the system as full of vices," the second Morris-Pinckney proposal went down to defeat, gaining the assent of only four states.[4]

3. Farrand, 2:189, 475, 477.   4. Farrand, 2:189, 478, 479.

Ten days later, on September 10, Gerry asked for a reconsideration of Articles 21 and 22, specifically with regard to the nine-state threshold for ratification and the dispensing of the requirement to secure congressional approval of the Convention's work. To bypass Congress was "improper," tantamount to "giving just umbrage to that body," Gerry declared, and to proceed to "an annulment of the confederation" with anything less than the unanimous consent of the states might prove "pernicious" in the extreme. Preying on the delegates' fears of the consequences of disunion, he added that "if nine states out of thirteen can dissolve the [current] compact, six out of nine will be just as able to dissolve the new one," and so forth until the predictable end. But no one took the bait to reopen the debate over the nine-state requirement. Most speakers focused instead on the prospect of congressional intervention, which they saw as the more immediate threat to ratification. Surprisingly, Alexander Hamilton "concurred with Mr. Gerry as to the indecorum of not requiring the approbation of Congress" and moved to postpone further consideration of the articles in question in order to take up an alternative proposal. Hamilton's alternative called for modifying Article 22 by reinstating its congressional approbation requirement while keeping the nine-state minimum established under the amended Article 21.[5]

Hamilton's proposal was seconded by Gerry but found no other supporters. Asking for the imprimatur of Congress "will defeat the plan altogether," Nathaniel Gorham explained, because its members will revisit the same issues and reiterate the same sort of arguments that the delegates in Philadelphia had already confronted and hopefully settled. Anyway, Pennsylvania's Thomas Fitzsimmons noted, irrespective of their personal preferences, how could the members of Congress endorse the Constitution when doing so would be "inconsistent with the Articles of Confederation under which they held their authority"? The most effective speech of the afternoon, however, was James Wilson's. For all of his erudition and expertise—"No man is more clear, copious, and comprehensive than Mr. Wilson," one admirer exclaimed—Wilson was a pragmatic politician who knew how to win. He had been opposed to a reconsideration in the first place, but now that it was under way, he "expressed in strong terms his disapprobation of the expedient proposed" by Hamilton. It would be "worse than folly" to submit the Constitution to Congress for its approval. Rhode Island had chosen not to participate in the convention at all; New York was not a participant after July 10, when John Lansing and Robert Yates left Philadelphia in a huff; Maryland was displeased with the Constitution because it departed from the rule of unanimity set under the Articles of Confederation; and "many individual deputies from other states have spoken

5. Farrand, 2:478, 559–62.

much against the plan." Given these circumstances, he asked, "can it be safe to make the assent of Congress necessary?" Having spent "four or five months in the laborious & arduous task of forming a government," were the supporters of the Constitution now going to throw "insuperable obstacles in the way of its success"? Rufus King closed with a terse summary of Wilson's argument, "If the approbation of Congress be made necessary, and they should not approve, the state legislatures will not propose the plan to conventions." In that unfortunate situation, "everything will go into confusion, and all our labor be lost."[6]

This combined opposition had its intended effect. After handily defeating Hamilton's motion to postpone, the convention unanimously adopted Article 21, thus keeping the nine-vote requirement for ratification. Hamilton promptly withdrew the remainder of his proposal, "observing that his purpose was defeated by the vote just given." Elbridge Gerry and North Carolina's Hugh Williamson were not so easily discouraged, however, and they moved to reinstate the phrase calling for congressional approbation under Article 22. But, as Hamilton had probably anticipated, the convention unanimously rejected the Gerry-Williamson motion.[7]

Take This or Nothing

The supporters of the Constitution managed yet another, a fourth and perhaps most consequential, way of advancing the cause of ratification. They succeeded in limiting the options open to the state ratifying conventions. State conventions had to choose between all or nothing, between adopting the Constitution in its entirety as it emerged from the Philadelphia Convention or rejecting it. There was no middle course. Edmund Randolph more than any other delegate objected to this up-or-down choice. On September 10, in the middle of the debate over Articles 21 and 22, Randolph "took this opportunity to state his objections to the system" as a whole. He listed a number of its perceived shortcomings—the role of the Senate as a court of impeachment, a weak presidential veto, inadequate representation in the House of Representatives, insufficient safeguards against a standing army, the absence of restraints on navigation acts, an unqualified power in the president to pardon treason, the ambiguity of the necessary and proper clause, indistinct boundaries between the general government and the states—before asking "what course" he should follow. He was in a quandary. He did not want to "impede the wishes" of the convention, but he also did not want to promote a plan of government "he verily believed would end in Tyranny." Others, surely, must be experiencing some of the same "embarrassments," must find themselves in the same predicament.

6. Farrand, 3:92, 2:562, 563.   7. Farrand, 2:563.

Randolph suggested what he believed to be the only way out of this bind, which was to grant to the several state ratifying conventions the "power to adopt, reject, or amend" the proposed Constitution, after which a second general convention could be held, "with full power to adopt or reject the alterations proposed by the state conventions."[8]

At the urging of George Mason, the convention voted to let Randolph's motion "lie on the table for a day or two," essentially choosing to await the report of a committee of five created on September 8. This new committee was supposed "to revise the style of and arrange the articles which had been agreed to" by the convention on August 7, more than a month earlier, when the delegates had begun their deliberations of the report submitted by the Committee of Detail. As we shall see momentarily, this so-called Committee of Style did more than merely revise and arrange previously adopted articles; it also instituted substantive changes. But it did not do so with regard to the issues Randolph raised. Hence, on September 15, Randolph, "expressing the pain he felt at differing from the body of the Convention, on the close of the great & awful subject of their labors"—the convention ended two days later—and anxious to find some accommodation that might "relieve him from his embarrassments," moved to authorize the state conventions to propose amendments that would be "finally decided on by another general Convention." Should his proposal be disregarded, Randolph said, it would be "impossible for him to put his name to the instrument."[9]

This time Mason endorsed Randolph's motion, contending "it was improper to say to the people, take this or nothing." And, like his fellow Virginian, he threatened not to sign the Constitution without the "expedient of another Convention." Elbridge Gerry declared he was also "determined . . . to withhold his name from the Constitution." Stating his specific objections, a few of which overlapped with Randolph's earlier enumeration, although his opposition to counting three-fifths of the slave population for purposes of representation was understandably not among Randolph's complaints, Gerry thought the best thing to do would be to "provide for a second general Convention."[10]

Charles Pinckney for one was not impressed by such arguments and "descanted on the consequences" of pursuing the course of action proposed by these three "members so respectable." To call for amendments prior to ratification would be foolish and possibly dangerous. Thirteen states "will never agree in their plans," and therefore their delegates to a second convention, meeting under the influence of these "discordant impressions," will be constantly at odds with one another. In the resulting "confusion & contrariety," the pull

8. Farrand, 2:563–64.	9. Farrand, 2:553, 564, 631.
10. Farrand, 2:632–33, 635–36.

toward "an ultimate decision by the Sword" might prove too powerful to resist. Pinckney said he was not without reservations of his own about the new federal plan—the "contemptible weakness" of the president and the power of a simple majority to regulate commerce being foremost in his mind—but considering the "danger of a general confusion," he preferred to "give the plan his support" rather than contend for a prospective revision that might be more to his liking but would almost certainly flirt with disunion. When Randolph's motion came up for a vote at the end of the day on September 15, "all the states answered—no." The vast majority of the delegates agreed with Pinckney that "Conventions are serious things, and ought not to be repeated." There would be no opportunity for the states to amend the document they received and no call for a second federal convention.[11]

We the People of the United States

The supporters of the Constitution thus succeeded in taking four strategically important steps to improve the chances of ratification: committing the decision to state conventions as opposed to state legislatures; empowering nine ratifying states to constitute the new United States; avoiding a congressional vote of approval or disapproval; and allowing only an unconditional adoption or rejection of the Constitution. The fifth step is known best as a philosophical statement of fundamental authority, but it too was intentionally strategic. The preamble to the Constitution famously declares that "we the people of the United States" ordained and established the new federal Union. But that declaration was a modification of a more prosaic preamble. In its initial iteration, as it appeared in the report of the Committee of Detail on August 6, the preamble read, "We the people of the States of New Hampshire, Massachusetts, Rhode Island," and so forth, until all thirteen states appeared as parties in establishing the Constitution. The convention adopted this version of the preamble without debate or dissent the next day, in large part because it was modeled after the opening statement of the Articles of Confederation and therefore familiar. The preamble remained in this form until the Committee of Style altered it sometime between September 10 and 12.[12]

There were practical reasons for the change initiated by the Committee of Style. In the first place, it was a bit awkward to list Rhode Island among the consenting states, given its conspicuous refusal to participate in the convention. Also, with the departures of John Lansing and Robert Yates on July 10, it would have been only slightly less awkward to rank New York among the consensual collaborators. And what would happen if one or two states chose ultimately not to ratify, a prospect that did not seem too farfetched in September

---

11. Farrand, 2:632–33.

12. Farrand, 2:177, 193, 196, 565, 585, 590.

1787? Would their names subsequently have to be deleted from the engrossed copy of the Constitution?

Far more important than these practical considerations, however, was the statement of principle that the Committee of Style, led by James Madison, Alexander Hamilton, and Gouverneur Morris, sought to make by distancing the Constitution from the Articles of Confederation. The Constitution was not an effort to perfect the "league of friendship" established under the Articles. Instead its champions sought to promote "a more perfect union" than before, and the preamble's "we the people of the United States" captured the essence of this intent. The words themselves were probably penned by Morris, but its central idea is more closely associated with Madison than anyone else. Troubled by what he identified as the particular "evils" of the Confederation government, evils that he traced to the derelictions of the sovereign people of the states, Madison sought a higher form of popular sovereignty to which he could appeal. As the historian Edmund S. Morgan has argued, Madison eventually located this superior authority in the people of the United States as a whole. The newly invented sovereignty of the American people "constituted a separate and superior entity" capable of trumping popular sovereignty at the state level. With the Constitution, and especially with the sacralization of its preamble, Madison's "crucial invention of a sovereign American people" was realized.[13]

The Unanimous Consent of the States Present

The final step taken by the supporters of the Constitution in the interest of ratification came on September 17, the last day of the convention. William Jackson, the secretary of the convention, began by reading aloud the entire text of the Constitution, which all eleven states had unanimously adopted at the close of business on September 15. The reading completed, Benjamin Franklin rose with a prepared speech in his hand, which, as on other occasions, his colleague James Wilson read for him. Franklin appealed for unanimity. He himself had objections to certain parts of the Constitution, but he was willing to endorse it because he was not certain he was right and others wrong, and therefore he was "not sure that it is not the best." Perfection cannot be expected from any assembly comprising, as it must, conflicting "prejudices . . . passions, . . . errors of opinion, . . . local interests, and . . . selfish views." In any case, because there were "salutary effects & great advantages" associated with a show of "real or apparent unanimity," the delegates should observe the rule of silence while "abroad." Of his own reservations, Franklin said, "within these walls they were

13. James Madison, "Vices of the Political System of the United States," April–June 1787, *PJM*, 9:348–57; Edmund S. Morgan, *Inventing the People: The Rise of Popular Sovereignty in England and America* (New York, 1988), 263–87, quotations at 267, 285.

born, and here they shall die." Following these words of "salutary caution," as Charles Pinckney described them, Franklin moved to "make manifest our unanimity" by having each member "put his name to this instrument." Preceding the signatures would be this proclamation drafted by Morris: "Done in Convention, by the unanimous consent of *the States* present the 17th of September &c.—In witness whereof we have hereunto subscribed our names."[14]

James McHenry was duly impressed by Franklin's speech, which he found to be "plain, insinuating, persuasive." The Marylander may have been, as William Pierce concluded, "a man of specious talents, with nothing of genius to improve them," but he was not alone in his admiration of Franklin's speech. Indeed, the supporters of the Constitution had asked Franklin to prepare the eleventh-hour appeal for unanimity and to make the final motion precisely because they hoped that the respect the elderly Pennsylvanian commanded might "gain the dissenting members." They did not rely solely on the "Doctor's fame" to carry the day, however, for the purposefully "ambiguous form" of the closing proclamation itself seemed to "better [the] chance of success."[15]

Morris's carefully drafted proclamation conveyed unanimity while coaxing dissenters to become signatories. The phrase "unanimous consent of the states present" was at once deceptively convincing without being truly deceitful. Rhode Island and New York did not consent, but they were not *present* on September 17. Similarly, George Mason, Edmund Randolph, and Elbridge Gerry did not consent, but their respective *states*, Virginia and Massachusetts, did. The salutary ambiguity of the closing sentences was a brilliant articulation of Franklin's "real or apparent unanimity." Thus when Randolph stated he would not sign the Constitution because he could not pledge his support of the new federal plan, Morris explained that "signing in the form proposed related only to the fact that the *States* present were unanimous." Randolph still refused, insisting that "signing in the proposed form" was the same thing as "signing the Constitution." But North Carolina's William Blount, whose character, according to one observer, was "strongly marked for integrity and honor," disagreed. Having earlier declared he would not sign, Blount was now "relieved by the form proposed and would without committing himself attest to the fact that the plan was the unanimous act of the States in Convention." Blount, and perhaps others, could sign without pledging "support of the plan." The states present were unanimously in agreement, and Blount, "in witness whereof," could attest to that fact without compromising his principles.[16]

Ten states voted for Franklin's motion; none was opposed. "The members then proceeded to sign the instrument." Mason, Randolph, and Gerry

14. Farrand, 2:641–43.
16. Farrand, 3:95, 2:643, 645, 646.

15. Farrand, 2:649, 643, 3:93.

"declined giving it the sanction of their names, [and] the Convention dissolved itself by an adjournment sine die." As the delegates left Philadelphia after four months of grueling work, the supporters of the Constitution could quiet some of their apprehensions about the struggle ahead, knowing that they had done much to improve the chances of ratification. The convention had proposed a new frame of government for the United States, but, as James Wilson explained, "it is to take its constitutional authenticity" from the endorsement of sovereign American people expressed through "their ratification, and their ratification alone." Without the approval of "we the people," the document drafted in Philadelphia was "no more than *tabula rasa*."[17]

17. Farrand, 2:647, 649; James Wilson, summation, December 11, 1787, in Bailyn, *Debate*, 1:836.

CHAPTER THREE

Massachusetts and the First Nine States

"The new constitution! the new constitution is the general cry this way. Much paper is spoiled on the subject, and many essays are written which perhaps are not read by either side," complained Henry Knox, the onetime Boston bookseller and self-taught artilleryman who became Washington's designated successor as commander in chief of the Continental army. James Madison was as aware as anyone of the hubbub that accompanied the question of ratification. "The Constitution proposed by the late convention engrosses almost the whole political attention of America," he informed Thomas Jefferson in December of 1787, and no one was more engrossed than Madison himself. Among his peers, Madison had a well-earned reputation for an unflagging attention to detail. His preparation for the Federal Convention had included a systematic analysis of the problems of the Confederation, which he distilled over a three-month period in the "Vices of the Political System of the United States." During the sessions of the Philadelphia meeting itself, Madison had impressed the other delegates as "the best informed man of any point in debate." After the convention, true to form, Madison was the most knowledgeable observer of the progress of ratification in the states. He kept in touch with Federalists in the closely contested states, relayed valuable information to them and to interested observers elsewhere, and assessed the chances of success under changing circumstances around the nation.[1]

Madison's Assessment

As the first conventions began to assemble or were already under way, Madison summarized the outlook in the various states. Pennsylvania was safely on the side of ratification, he thought, with the supporters of the Constitution outnumbering its opponents by a margin of two to one. The Constitution was also safe in Connecticut because "those who know" had reported that "a very great majority will adopt it in that state." In New Hampshire, "friends of the New Government" were "sanguine," believing that their state, along with

---

1. Henry Knox to John Sullivan, January 19, 1788, *DHRC*, 15:461, quoted in Bernard Bailyn, *The Ideological Origins of the American Revolution*, rev. ed. (Cambridge, MA, 1992), 327; James Madison to Thomas Jefferson, December 9, 1787, *Republic of Letters*, 1:508; Farrand, 3:94.

Delaware and New Jersey, would "pretty certainly be on the affirmative side." Correspondents in Georgia likewise "denote[d] a favorable disposition." The Maryland Antifederalists, however, Madison thought would be more "formidable" than "first conjectured" because John Francis Mercer, who with Luther Martin had bolted the Federal Convention before it adjourned, was now an "auxiliary" to the Constitution's opponents. "New York is much divided," Madison concluded, but "will hardly dissent from N. England."[2]

Madison's assessment, made less than three months after leaving Philadelphia, was remarkably accurate. Pennsylvania ratified the Constitution on December 12 by a vote of 46 to 23. Delaware, New Jersey, and Georgia, respectively on December 7 and 18, 1787, and January 2, 1788, all voted unanimously for ratification. Connecticut did have a "great majority" in favor of the Constitution and ratified it on January 9, 1788, by an overwhelming margin of 128 to 40. Madison's estimate of the strength of the opposition in Maryland proved not to be well founded and was based more on the performance of the state's delegation at the Federal Convention, especially the voluble Martin, than on reliable information. On April 28, after a relatively brief debate, Maryland became the seventh state to ratify the Constitution. Its easy victory on a vote of 63 to 11 had in fact been determined two weeks earlier by county elections that bound the vast majority of the delegates to vote for ratification. And the brevity of the sessions was no doubt assisted by Martin's sore throat which, as one experienced spectator noted, "saved a great deal of time & money to the state."[3]

Madison was also correct in his assessment of the situation in New York. That state was "much divided," and although Madison may have conflated "N. England" and Massachusetts, few contemporaries would have quarreled with his conclusion. Proponents and opponents of ratification did not look to Connecticut or New Hampshire, let alone Rhode Island, for encouragement. New York City merchant Samuel Blachley Webb was "Joyfull" over the news of Connecticut's ratification but found "a dampness is thrown on our spirits by the information that the convention of Massachusetts are much divided." To his contact in Boston, Webb wrote that Massachusetts was the key, for "every Federal man in this City looks up to your state for our political salvation." If "your state" should reject the Constitution, Webb told Joseph Barrell, "we are ruined." Melancton Smith, Antifederalist businessman and arch foe of Alexander Hamilton's, shared Webb's sense of the crucial importance of the pro-

2. James Madison to Thomas Jefferson, October 24, November 1, and December 9, 1787, *Republic of Letters*, 1:507, 508.

3. Farrand, 3:93; Robert Allen Rutland, *The Ordeal of the Constitution: Antifederalists and the Ratification Struggle of 1787–1788*, (1966; repr., Boston, 1983), 149–59; William Smith to O. H. Smith, April 28, 1788, quoted in Rutland, *Ordeal*, 157; Pauline Maier, *Ratification: The People Debate the Constitution, 1787–1788* (New York, 2010), 241–47.

ceedings in Massachusetts. "All sides are waiting here with anxious expectation for the determination of the Convention of Massachusetts," Smith recorded. Small wonder, then, that upon learning of the results in Massachusetts, New York Federalists "festivated" as they had not done over reports from any of the first five states. The "drinking & rioting in a good cause" continued throughout the day until nine o'clock at night. The jubilant Webb was surely not the only one "much afflicted with the Head Ache" the next morning.[4]

Zeal for Politics in Massachusetts

If the Constitution, as Madison wrote, absorbed the whole political attention of America, then from mid-January through the first week in February 1788, the nation's focus was on Boston, where the Massachusetts ratifying convention was meeting. Informed observers would have been struck by several distinctive features of the Massachusetts convention. First, it was the largest of the state conventions by far, with 364 delegates in attendance at one time or another. The number of delegates was so large that chamber of the house of representatives in the statehouse, where the convention met on January 9, became so overcrowded as to be "unwholesome." After a week of searching and one unsatisfactory move, the convention finally relocated to Long Lane Congregational Church on January 17. The church was large enough to accommodate the entire assembly, and with galleries capable of seating between six and eight hundred persons, the Reverend Jeremy Belknap thought it would be "convenient for spectators" as well.[5]

Belknap's concern for the comfort of spectators highlights a second distinctive feature of the Boston convention. The inhabitants of New England were "zealous upon politicks," and in early 1788 nothing could compete with the interest generated by the ratification proceedings. The galleries that Belknap thought were commodious proved incapable of handling the "immense number" of visitors who daily crowded into Long Lane Church. Demand was so great that would-be spectators learned to claim their seats at least an hour before the start of the morning's session. "Raw cold" or "severe cold" days did not discourage attendance, nor did snow "falling in great flakes and very fast." On days when the temperature was more moderate and roads were "full of water," making "traveling very bad," they still continued to come. From Rhode Island, George Benson braved a "very Disagreeable" two-day journey through a "heavy damp storm of snow" to be an observer in Boston. Ephraim Ward "expected" a rough trip from Providence and got more than he bargained for with

---

4. Samuel Blachley Webb to Joseph Barrell, January 13, 1788, *DHRC*, 5:1087; Melancton Smith to Abraham Yates Jr., January 28, 1788, 5:1091; *New York Journal*, February 15, 1788, *DHRC*, 7:1640; Samuel Blachley Webb to Joseph Barrell, February 17, 1788, *DHRC*, 7:1642.
5. Editors' note, *DHRC*, 6:1163–65.

the "extreme cold," but he would not be deterred. Benson, Ward, and "a number of the first characters from New Hampshire & Rhode Island" were more than willing to hazard an arduous winter trip simply to occupy a seat in the crowded galleries at least an hour before each session. And why not? "I looked upon it [as] the most important subject that had ever been canvassed since the civilization of America," Bossenger Foster Jr. exclaimed breathlessly to his uncle. The "exceedingly noxious & disagreeable" air in the overcrowded galleries eventually persuaded Foster that it was "unadvisable to attend the debates so often as inclination prompted." But his self-imposed absences were productive of "no small mortification."[6]

Those who did not troop over to Long Lane, renamed Federal Street shortly after ratification, could rely on the nearly complete newspaper coverage of the convention. A third characteristic of the Massachusetts ratifying convention, then, was the public's access to the deliberations of the delegates. Unlike the Federalist majority in Pennsylvania, which did its best to discourage public participation and to prevent the arguments made by the critics of the Constitution from being published in newspapers under its control, supporters of the Constitution in Massachusetts seemed to invite public discussion. About a dozen state newspapers printed or reprinted much of the convention's debates without discounting or denigrating the case made by the Antifederalists. In part, this openness was a reflection of the participatory politics to which most townsmen had grown accustomed. For over a century ordinary men had played a role in governing their communities through the institution of the town meeting. Why so many of them could participate, and how they voted with regard to the election of town officers are matters of scholarly dispute, and challenges to the use of the word "democracy" to describe the politics of colonial Massachusetts are certainly warranted. That they participated, however, and to an extent unrivaled in early modern British America, is beyond dispute. Their political awareness and organizational competence honed by the Revolution, townsmen were responsible for the rejection of the proposed 1778 state constitution and the acceptance of the 1780 version. Thus it was unsurprising that in 1787 the Massachusetts legislature called on the town meetings to elect the state's convention delegates. And townsmen responded with gusto. One reason the Massachusetts convention was so large was because most towns, whose allotments were based on the number of representatives they sent to the lower house of the legislature, chose to send their full complement of delegates.[7]

6. Dwight Foster to Rebecca Foster, January 16, 1788, *DHRC*, 7:1529; William Heath diary, 7:1523–25; George Benson to Nicholas Brown, January 29, 1788, *DHRC*, 7:1556; Ephraim Ward to Enos Hitchcock, March 2, 1788, *DHRC*, 7:1591; Henry Jackson to Henry Knox, January 20, 1788, *DHRC*, 7:1537; Dwight Foster to Andrew Craigie, February 24, 1788, *DHRC*, 7:1590.

7. Terry Bouton, *Taming Democracy: "The People," the Founders, and the Troubled Ending of the American Revolution* (New York, 2007), 180–84; Maier, *Ratification*, 99–101; Robert E.

Whether they crowded into the galleries of Long Lane Church or turned to the newspapers, which, according to one Bostonian, they "read more than the bible at this time," ordinary Massachusetts citizens were attentive to what people said about the Constitution. But custom alone cannot account for such political zeal. Town meetings in Connecticut, after all, were nearly as well established and participatory, although perhaps not as autonomous, as those of its larger neighbor, but press coverage there was extremely limited. Few Antifederalist essays appeared in print, and newspaper accounts of the state convention recorded only the speeches delivered by supporters of the Constitution. Connecticut's newspapers covered the Massachusetts convention better than their own. And the Connecticut convention apparently kept no journal of its proceedings. If Federalists in Massachusetts had enjoyed the same "great majority" as their counterparts in Connecticut, would they have placed the same restraints on the press? If the contest over ratification had been lopsided, would the galleries of Long Lane Church have been overcrowded? Perhaps not. The Massachusetts convention captured the attention of citizens in the state and around the nation because it was the first closely contested meeting between the supporters and opponents of the Constitution. The outcome of its deliberations was, as Madison observed, fraught with "greater uncertainty" than anywhere else, and its decision mattered everywhere.[8]

Procedural Rules

During its first two weeks, even as it searched for a more spacious meeting place, the convention made three important procedural decisions, two that affected the course of deliberations and advanced the cause of ratification and a third that provided more heat but proved to be less consequential. On January 14, the convention adopted a motion made by Caleb Strong, the Harvard-educated lawyer who had been a member of the Massachusetts delegation to the Federal Convention. Strong's motion called, first, for the delegates to enter into a "free conversation" on the Constitution "by paragraphs until every member shall have had opportunity fully to express his sentiments on the same" and second, to "consider and debate at large the question, whether this convention will adopt & ratify the proposed constitution." The motion was deceptively attractive, for who could object to a detailed discussion in which

Brown, *Middle-Class Democracy and the Revolution in Massachusetts, 1691–1780* (New York, 1969), 21–37; B. Katherine Brown, "The Controversy over the Franchise in Puritan Massachusetts, 1954 to 1974," *William and Mary Quarterly* 33.2 (1976): 212–41; Michael Zuckerman, "The Social Context of Democracy in Massachusetts," *WMQ* 25.4 (1968): 523–44.

8. Maier, *Ratification*, 141–53, 128–38, quotation at 142; Bruce C. Daniels, *The Connecticut Town: Growth and Development, 1635–1790* (Middletown, CT, 1979), 64–93; newspaper printings and reprintings of the debates of the Massachusetts Convention, *DHRC*, 6:1145–51; James Madison to Thomas Jefferson, December 9, 1787, *Republic of Letters*, 1:509.

every delegate had an opportunity to be heard? However, a long, drawn out, time-consuming paragraph-by-paragraph consideration was precisely what the supporters of ratification were seeking. In mid-January, although "no question" had ever divided the people of Massachusetts "in a more extraordinary manner," the outcome was too close to call. But most Federalists believed that time was on their side. If, as Rufus King assured Madison, the supporters of the Constitution were making the "most excellent" arguments, and if they enjoyed the advantage of a "superiority of talents," then over time they might legitimately hope to make converts of the truly undecided.[9]

Strong also called for the convention to act sequentially on the two parts of his motion: a paragraph-by-paragraph discussion was to be followed by the question to ratify, "before any vote" was taken "expressive of the sense of the convention, upon the whole or any part thereof." In other words, the convention would not vote after each discussion of a paragraph or paragraphs. Delegates would not be allowed to pick and choose among the various sections and clauses of the Constitution. Federalists were convinced, for good reason, that inviting selective opposition would hurt the chances of ratification by conjoining the opposition to discrete parts of the proposed federal plan. Strong's motion called on the convention to take one vote, at the conclusion of the paragraph-by-paragraph discussion, either to accept or reject the Constitution in its entirety.[10]

On January 15, the delegates adopted a second procedural motion that affected the conduct of business in Boston. According to this motion, if, during the discussion of a particular clause or paragraph, "any member conceives any other clause or paragraph of the Constitution to be connected with the one immediately under consideration," he shall have "full liberty to take up such other clause or paragraph." Introduced by Francis Dana, a Cambridge judge who had been elected as a delegate to the Federal Convention but did not attend due to poor health, the motion was an addendum to the previous day's motion. It further emphasized the idea that the delegates were engaged in a "conversation," a free-flowing exchange of ideas rather than a formal and systematic debate on the relative merits of each portion of the proposed Constitution. And its impact, as might be expected, was to stay the business of ratification. With this motion, the convention was set to pursue a paragraph by paragraph consideration of the federal plan, in which each member was guaranteed an opportunity to speak his mind, and during which any member might intro-

---

9. *DHRC*, 6:1182–83; Rufus King to James Madison, January 16 and 27, 1788, *PJM*, 10:376, 436.
10. *DHRC*, 6:1182.

duce any other clause he considered relevant. It was a recipe for conversation of the desultory variety.[11]

The third procedural matter dealt with the presence of Elbridge Gerry. As one of the three delegates who had refused to sign the Constitution on the last day of the Philadelphia Convention, Gerry had gained some renown or notoriety, as the case may be, among the opponents and supporters of the Constitution. To the latter, Gerry was a "Grumbletonian" who made a habit of "objecting to everything he did not propose." To Antifederalists in Massachusetts, however, his was the voice of reason. Gerry's explanation of his refusal to sign the Constitution—that it had "few if any federal features" but was "rather a system of national government"—officially tendered to the Massachusetts legislature on October 18, 1787, and widely circulated by the state's newspapers, emboldened the opponents of ratification while causing more than one Federalist to "*damn him—damn him.*" Unfortunately for Antifederalists hoping to capitalize on Gerry's reputation, he had not stood for election to the Boston convention, probably because he knew his chances of success were slim in Federalist Cambridge. Madison did little to conceal his delight upon learning "that Cambridge the residence of Mr. Gerry has left him out of the choice for the convention, and put in Mr. [Francis] Dana . . . and another gentleman [Stephen Dana], both of them firmly opposed to Mr. Gerry's politics."[12]

A Ruckus

Opponents of the Constitution, however, were not easily discouraged. On January 12 William Widgery of New Gloucester in Cumberland County, Maine, made a motion, seconded by Samuel Adams, to grant Gerry a seat in the convention, making him available to provide "Information &c., that *possibly* had escaped the memory of the other gentlemen of the General Convention," namely, Nathaniel Gorham, Rufus King, and Caleb Strong. In effect, Antifederalist Widgery wanted a counterpoint to Gorham, King, and Strong, all of whom had served as delegates to the Philadelphia Convention, gained election to the Boston convention, and expressed their support for the Constitution. Widgery's motion failed, but two days later, on January 14, he tried again. This time, Widgery moved only that Gerry be asked to attend the sessions in order to "answer any question of fact from time to time that the convention may want to ask respecting the passing of the Constitution." After "considerable

11. *DHRC*, 6:1187.

12. Letter to Thomas Jefferson [?], October 11, 1787, Farrand, 3:104; Gerry to the president of the Senate and speaker of the House of Representatives of Massachusetts, October 18, 1787, Farrand, 3:128–29; Maier, *Ratification*, 88; James Madison to George Washington, December 26, 1787, *PJM*, 10:345.

opposition" and a failed attempt by Federalists to limit Gerry to stating the "reasons which induced him to decline signing" the Constitution, Widgery's second motion carried. Several "friends of the Constitution" went along with the motion, King told Madison, in order to quiet the suspicions of its proponents, who were "not the most enlightened part of the convention," and also because they did not want to make this issue a "trial of strength" between the Federalists and Antifederalists.[13]

Gerry sat in the convention for two days without incident, quietly "biting the head of his cane." But on the afternoon of January 18, Abraham Fuller of Newton asked him why Massachusetts was allotted only eight representatives to Georgia's three, when the amount of money it was assessed in the last congressional requisition was thirteen times as large. As Gerry began to answer Fuller's inquiry, which at his request had been submitted to him in writing, Francis Dana moved that Gerry's response also be delivered in writing. A "long and desultory debate ensued" before the convention voted to adopt Dana's motion. Gerry presented his written reply to the convention the next morning, and his answer—that the initial allocation of sixty-five representatives was not based on a "fixed principle" but was rather the result of a "compromise"—caused scarcely a ripple among the delegates.[14]

After the delegates heard Gerry's report, they resumed their "conversation" without acrimony until they took up the question of equal representation in the Senate. Amid some confusion and more than a few objections, Caleb Strong mentioned that Gerry had served on the Committee of Eleven, indeed that he had chaired the Grand Committee that struck the compromise on representation in the new national legislature. The implication that he bore a great deal of the responsibility for the objectionable arrangement "roused *the very irritable* passions of Mr. *E. Gerry*." Thus agitated, Gerry began hurriedly to compose a response and, after about half an hour, informed William Cushing, the delegate from Scituate who was the convention's vice president, of his desire to "set the matter in its true light." But Dana, reminding the convention of the previous day's motion regarding Gerry, pointed out that it was improper for him to speak without a question being first "proposed to him *in writing*." When Gerry attempted to speak anyway, Theophilus Parsons interrupted, setting off "considerable conversation, which lasted until the convention adjourned."[15]

13. Winthrop Sargent to Henry Knox, January 12, 1788, *DHRC*, 7:1527–28; editors' note, *DHRC*, 7:1175–81; Rufus King to James Madison, January 16, 1788, *DHRC*, 7:1530.

14. Jeremy Belknap to Ebenezer Hazard, January 20, 1788, *DHRC*, 7:1534; *DHRC*, 6:1251, 1254, 1255.

15. "A Spectator," *Massachusetts Centinel*, February 2, 1788, *DHRC*, 6:1273; Jeremy Belknap to Ebenezer Hazard, January 20, 1788, *DHRC*, 7:1535; Jeremy Belknap, debate notes, January 19, 1788, *DHRC*, 6:1261; convention debates, *DHRC*, 6:1258.

Jeremy Belknap witnessed these proceedings and thought "Gerry was premature in *offering* his statement before he was called upon." More derisively, Belknap dwelled on the indignity to which Gerry was subjecting himself. Why would Gerry, jealously protective of his "fame" and personal independence, "sit there to be moved as a Machine only by the pull of *both* parties"? Gerry responded immediately to the taunt. The situation was a "humiliating condition" he endured contrary to his own "inclination," he told Cushing, who presided over the convention until January 30, only because the business of ratification was "of the highest importance to this country" and because he expected to "be treated with delicacy & candor." In this he was sorely disappointed, for "the honorable Judge Dana," motivated by "party virulence," would not allow him to "explain the matter" pertaining to his service on the Grand Committee. And when he protested the mischaracterization of his intention to submit a written response, he was criticized by others for attempting to enter into "their debates." The whole affair was demeaning in the extreme: "I confess to you sir, that the indelicacy & disingenuity of this procedure distressed my feelings beyond anything I had ever before experienced."[16]

Smarting under this perceived mistreatment, Gerry confronted Dana after the convention adjourned on January 19 and accused him of "injuring his reputation by partial information." Dana issued a "warm reply," which drew "some very high words," resulting in a "warm altercation" that required the intervention of other "gentlemen" hoping to avert "the utmost confusion." Following the fracas, Gerry submitted to Cushing "A State of Facts" in which he attempted to set the record straight, as he saw it, by recounting the proceedings of the Federal Convention with regard to the compromise that granted equal representation in the Senate in exchange for situating the exclusive power to initiate money bills in the "democratical" lower house. This compromise was necessitated, he pointed out, by the "firm determination" of the smaller states "to threaten a dissolution of the Convention" and to suffer all of the ill effects that entailed rather than relinquish a right to equal representation. But Gerry's statement of the "facts" itself became a subject of dispute when Cushing attempted to read it to the convention on the afternoon of January 22. Boston's Christopher Gore objected not to the content of the statement but to its infringement on the rules of the convention, which limited participation to duly elected members. After all, as Joseph Bradley Varnum had argued earlier, bending the rules for Gerry amounted to "a violation of the right of election of the inhabitants of Cambridge, who had not thought fit to send him as their

16. Jeremy Belknap, debate notes, *DHRC*, 6:1261; George Athan Billias, *Elbridge Gerry: Founding Father and Republican Statesman* (New York, 1976), 138–39; Elbridge Gerry to William Cushing, January 21, 1788, *DHRC*, 6:1265; Elbridge Gerry to William Cushing, *DHRC*, 6:1266.

delegate." Dana, who sulked for days after the altercation, interrupted to say a few words in support of Gore's objection and then walked out, vowing not to return until the convention "justified his conduct." The convention ultimately agreed to hear Gerry's account and then dropped the matter altogether. Gerry himself was not present to see any of this. Stung by erroneous statements that "tended to his injury" and by the convention's refusal to grant him "leave to *speak*" in his own defense, he did not return to the convention after January 19.[17]

Free Conversation

The convention began its consideration of the Constitution on January 14 by commencing what one newspaper described as a *"tedious* but interesting" discussion. Article 1, Section 1, vesting legislative powers in Congress, generated only a "short conversation" before the convention moved on to Section 2, Paragraph 1, which stipulated that members of the House of Representatives were to serve two-year terms. Opponents of the Constitution questioned the wisdom of biennial elections, contending that "the security of the people lay in frequent elections" and that annual elections had been customary in Massachusetts "ever since its settlement." Supporters of ratification conceded that annual elections might be best for single state legislatures, but the "great affairs of thirteen states" required longer terms in order to ensure that members of Congress were acquainted with the "extensive and weighty matters" of the nation. What some observers may have found tedious, or perhaps interesting, about this discussion was the disruption caused by Gilbert Dench, the Antifederalist delegate from Hopkinton. In the middle of the exchange between the proponents and opponents of Section 2, Paragraph 1, Dench interrupted, wishing "to know how representation was secured—as by the 4th section, Congress were empowered to make or alter the . . . times, places, and manner of holding elections." He continued in this vein until Theophilus Parsons called him to order, reminding Dench that the "subject of the debate was *the expediency of biennial elections*" and that he must therefore wait until Section 4 came up for consideration.[18]

Dench's interruption and the desire to encourage "free conversation" may have inspired Dana to offer his January 15 procedural motion, which invited members to enter into a discussion other clauses or paragraphs in any way

---

17. Jeremy Belknap to Ebenezer Hazard, January 20, 1788, *DHRC*, 7:1535; Rufus King to James Madison, January 20, 1788, *DHRC*, 7:1540; Elbridge Gerry, "A State of Facts," *DHRC*, 6:1268; "A Spectator," *Massachusetts Centinel*, February 2, 1788, *DHRC*, 6:1274; Henry Jackson to Henry Knox, January 23, 1788, *DHRC*, 7:1546; editors' note, *DHRC*, 6:1180; Elbridge Gerry to William Cushing, January 21, 1788, 6:1267.

18. *DHRC*, 6:1184–86.

connected to the one under consideration. Taking advantage of Dana's motion, Dench insisted that a full consideration of Section 2, Paragraph 1, required the convention "to recur to the 4th section." He could not get over the difficulty posed by that section, for if Congress was empowered to dictate the times, places, and manner of holding elections, then it was "immaterial whether [elections were] biennial or annual." When Dench was called to order, perhaps by Dana himself, "much debate was had thereon," until "a worthy member," former governor James Bowdoin, defended Dench by pointing out that the "motion made by the Hon. Mr. Dana, passed, which put an end to the conversation."[19]

At the outset of business on January 16, the convention voted "to pass on to the next paragraph." But Dench was not done. He asked "to add something on the paragraph last debated" and repeated his contention that as long as Congress was in control, the "rights of election are insecure." Gorham, clearly exasperated by the persistence of the delegate from Hopkinton, said he could not see any connection between the objection Dench was raising and the length of congressional terms. And if none existed, Dench was out of order and should refrain from stating his reservations about Section 4 until they came to it. Rufus King, somewhat more patiently, explained that the "controlling power of Congress" did not "extend to altering biennial elections." The provisions of Section 4 were therefore not relevant to the paragraph under consideration because: "1. Time of election does not mean the term for which the representatives are chosen; 2. Nor the place where elections are held; nor 3. The manner of holding elections." John Taylor, however, defended Dench and shared his fears. "Congress may make such regulations as to deprive the people of the right of electing," said the delegate from Worcester County, where Shays's rebels had many sympathizers in 1786 and distrust of a strong central government still ran rampant in 1788. For example, argued Taylor, by choosing to hold federal elections in some remote location "where the people cannot attend," Congress may effectively deprive them of their right to vote. Theodore Sedgwick, from far-western Berkshire County but a staunch Federalist nevertheless, took exception to Taylor's rendering of Section 4, arguing his comment "supposes the power will be used to the worst possible purposes." In so doing, Taylor undermined the basis of all governments, for none can exist where the people "contemplate only the possible abuse of power."[20]

Samuel Thompson, from Lincoln County, Maine, was unconvinced by such arguments. A vocal critic of the Constitution, Thompson insisted that, given the chance, Congress would abuse its power. "Men are as wicked now as

19. *DHRC*, 6:1189–93; Theophilus Parsons, debate notes, 6:1198.
20. Theophilus Parsons, debate notes, *DHRC*, 6:1210–11.

ever," he declared. What, in the present construction of its authority, prevented Congress from "order[ing] us to go to South Carolina" for federal elections? In any case, because the convention had "now got to the fourth paragraph," Thompson advised, "we had as good thump it about and see what is in it." Samuel Adams, still uncommitted on ratification, responded with a call to order. The convention had "gone from the point in debate," he protested, as the convention prepared to adjourn for the morning. Why were the delegates "now on the fourth section, which is a very different subject" from the provisions contained in the first paragraph of Section 2? Adams's challenge resonated with others, and the first order of business in the afternoon session was a reconsideration of the convention's earlier decision on Dana's motion. Nevertheless, after a reading of the second paragraph and a "desultory conversation on the mode" of proceeding, "it was *again* agreed, that in the debate on any paragraph, gentlemen might discuss any other part he [*sic*] might suppose had relation to that under consideration."[21]

Section 4: Times, Places, and Manner of Holding Elections

So it was settled. The delegates moved on to Section 4, Paragraph 1, thumping it about all afternoon on January 16 and again the next morning. The division between the proponents and opponents of Section 4 remained unchanged, with the former repeating variations of Sedgwick's earlier argument on the necessity of delegating power and the latter insisting, as Thompson had done, that Congress would abuse any power left unchecked. Led by Parsons, who took an impressive set of notes on the proceedings of the convention, and the trio of Nathaniel Gorham, Caleb Strong, and Rufus King, still fresh from their service at the Federal Convention, the supporters of Section 4 explained that it was essential both for "preserving the union" and for "securing to the people their equal rights of election." If, for example, said Strong, a state should refuse to enact any regulations pertaining to such elections, hoping the "general government will thereby be dissolved," then Congress was empowered by this paragraph to intervene. Parsons defended Section 4 in a long speech that "considered the subject very fully," the *Massachusetts Centinel* reported. According to Parsons, the Constitution created the two houses of Congress with entirely "different constituents" so that each might act as a check on the other. Whereas the Senate represented the states, the House's constituents were the people themselves. If the state legislatures, which elected the members of the Senate, were "vested absolutely" with the powers defined in Section 4, they would "very soon" institute regulations aimed at extending their control over the elections of the people's representatives. The two houses would end up serving the

21. *DHRC*, 6:1212, 1213.

same master. As a final superintending authority over elections must therefore reside somewhere, "there was much less danger in trusting these powers in Congress than in the state legislatures," because the latter already controlled senatorial elections, and Section 4 explicitly prohibited Congress from interfering with the "places of choosing Senators."[22]

Those opposed to granting Congress the power to alter state electoral regulations were adamant about the dangers posed by Section 4. "If we give up this section," warned Abraham White, an Antifederalist spokesman from Norton, "there is nothing left." Phanuel Bishop, a former Shaysite from Rehoboth, challenged Strong's interpretation of the paragraph in question. If it was intended merely to compel "refractory states" to do their duty, "why was it not so mentioned?" The insertion of a qualifying phrase before the grant of power would have sufficed. Section 4 would then have read: "The times, places and manner of holding elections for Senators and Representatives shall be prescribed in each State by the legislature thereof; but *if any State shall refuse or neglect so to do,* Congress may, &c." Such a qualification "would admit of no prevarication," but it was not included in Section 4, perhaps because the supporters of the Constitution intended for the "liberties of the yeomanry of this country" to be "sported with." William Widgery, who had sponsored the motion to have Elbridge Gerry in attendance, shared Bishop's distrust of power. Section 4 "ought to have had the provision in it mentioned by Mr. Bishop," Widgery said, because rulers "ought never to have a power which they could abuse." White agreed, saying the people "ought to be jealous of rulers" and that "he would not trust 'a flock of Moseses.'"[23]

In the afternoon session of January 17, the convention "reverted to" Paragraph 2, Section 2, pertaining to the minimum age requirement, twenty-five, and citizenship status, seven years as a citizen, for membership in the House of Representatives. In other words, the convention resumed its paragraph-by-paragraph "conversation" on the Constitution. Interestingly enough, on January 21, when the convention turned to Section 4 "in its order," there was little enthusiasm among the delegates to pick up where they had left off four days earlier. No one protested when Fisher Ames rose first to remind the delegates that they should forbear going over ground "already well trodden." And the convention entertained only a perfunctory debate on the subject. The *Massachusetts Centinel,* which for all practical purposes was the newspaper of record for the convention, provided some coverage of the brief exchange between the opposing sides that morning, but Parsons's notes simply record at one point, "Mr. Parsons. Dr. Taylor. Mr. Parsons, in reply," without bothering to enter

22. Convention debates, *DHRC,* 6:1215, 1217–18.
23. *DHRC,* 6:1219, 1214, 1215, 1218.

into specifics. The conversation about congressional control of federal elections, at once tedious and interesting, was over.[24]

Representation and Taxation at Three-Fifths

The third paragraph of Section 2 generated little debate, which is surprising in view of the fact that it contains the infamous three-fifths clause. The delegates spent most of the afternoon of January 17 and the morning of January 18 debating the provisions of Paragraph 3, splitting their time equally in addressing three issues: the adequacy of the initial distribution of sixty-five representatives, the relative benefits of taxation being proportional to population, and the necessity of the three-fifths compromise on slavery. John Taylor took up the first of these. Recalling the grievances of western Massachusetts agrarians that went largely unanswered because they were underrepresented in the state legislature at the time of Shays's Rebellion, Taylor thought it impossible for the "whole union" to be represented by sixty-five men. The number was clearly "too small," a reduction by "30 percent" of the ninety-one entitled to serve under the Articles of Confederation. Francis Dana objected, accusing Taylor of being disingenuous: "The gentleman has not made a fair calculation." To be sure, under the Articles, each of the thirteen states was entitled to send seven representatives to Congress, and Taylor arrived at his total of ninety-one by assuming that all did. However, in reality few sent more than five. For example, Massachusetts "at no time" either "had or wished to have more than four" members present in the Confederation Congress. But even supposing Taylor's ninety-one to be accurate, the proposed Constitution called for two senators from each state, and by adding these twenty-six to the sixty-five, the outcome is "that in this respect there is no difference."[25]

The benefit of having both taxes and representation based on population came up for discussion in conjunction with the three-fifths ratio, as it should, for "by this rule is representation and taxation to be apportioned," explained Rufus King. To King, Gorham, and Dana, this provision in Paragraph 3 was a vast improvement over the existing system. For money to meet all expenses incurred for the common defense or general welfare, the Confederation Congress was forced to rely on voluntary returns from the states, which were "very imperfect." Furthermore, because quotas were based on surveyed lands and improvements thereon, the requisitions were unfair to New England. Paragraph 3 apportioned taxes and representatives according to the whole number of free persons and three-fifths of all other persons, and the Federal Convention adopted this provision because, King declared, "it was the language of all America." To those who might be tempted to carp over the compromise of

24. *DHRC*, 6:1277–79, 1282.   25. *DHRC*, 6:1237–38.

counting only three-fifths of the slave population in the calculation of taxes, King offered "to make the idea of *taxation by numbers* more intelligible," explaining in his "sweet high toned voice" that "five Negro children of South-Carolina are to pay as much tax as the three governors of New Hampshire, Massachusetts, and Connecticut."[26]

King's clarification was too clever by half for Samuel Nasson. The York County Antifederalist called on the "honorable Mr. King" to show the "other side" of the "good rule," namely, that Massachusetts "will pay as great a tax for three children in the cradle, as any of the southern states will for five hearty working Negro men." Nasson and his compatriots seemingly ignored King's admonition that taxation and representation went "hand in hand." Samuel Thompson, the Lincoln County Antifederalist who even after ratification continued "roaring about like the old Dragon" out of the book of Revelation, challenged the Federalists' assertion that the new system was an improvement over the old. Claiming New Englanders "have more children than the luxurious inhabitants of the southern states" and would therefore contribute a higher share of the taxes, Thompson insisted that the new "rule is unequal." William Widgery also did not like the new system of computing taxes because "apprentices are not freemen," but he "blunder[ed] about" in making this point. Francis Shurtliff, no stranger to politics, having served in the state legislature for a half dozen years as a representative from Plympton, likewise blundered about as he attempted to illustrate his "difficulty" with the third paragraph. Losing sight of the relationship between taxation and representation, Shurtliff began to complain about the unfairness of the "number of representatives first chosen" because "our negroes are free, but those of other states are not," but either he stopped short in mid-sentence or Parsons did not bother recording the rest of his convoluted objection. And poor William Jones, the Antifederalist delegate from Lincoln County, Maine, desired to be heard on Paragraph 3 but spoke so softly that Parsons "could not hear him" and consequently left no record of what he said.[27]

What the convention did not discuss directly was the provision for counting three-fifths of the slave population for purposes of representation. The majority of the delegates were familiar with the so-called equitable ratio, but their "conversation" focused more on its application to taxes than to the apportionment of seats in the House of Representatives. When the latter came up, almost in passing, Thomas Dawes Jr. gave a brief response to the question of why slaves should "not be wholly represented." The Massachusetts Declaration of Rights as well as "ideas of natural justice" would lead one to consider

26. *DHRC*, 6:1236, 1237; Farrand, 3:87.
27. *DHRC*, 6:1239, 1240–41; Jeremiah Hill to George Thatcher, February 14, 1788, 7:1696–97.

"those blacks as *free men*" deserving of representation "as though they were all white inhabitants," said Dawes, a Boston judge familiar with the 1781–83 Quok Walker cases, in which William Cushing, as chief justice of the Supreme Judicial Court of Massachusetts, instructed the jury that slavery was inconsistent with the state constitution. For those discomfited by the compromise with slaveholders, however, Dawes thought they might "do well to connect the passage in dispute with another article in the Constitution," Paragraph 1, Section 9, which "permits Congress, in the year 1808, wholly to prohibit the importation of slaves." Slavery was not destroyed "in a moment," but it "received a mortal wound." In view of the "prejudices" of the southern states, "what could the Convention do more?" Dawes's appeal cleverly turned the three-fifths question into one dealing with moral principle rather than political advantage.[28]

Powers of Congress: Section 8

Over the next two days of business, from Saturday morning, January 19, until the following Monday afternoon, the convention virtually sprinted through Sections 3 to 7, often skipping over whole paragraphs, including those that dealt with the organization and responsibilities of the Senate, the minimum age and citizenship requirements of senators, and the process through which a bill becomes a law. Aside from the debate on the tenure of senators and the ensuing brouhaha between Gerry and Dana that nearly ended in fisticuffs, these sections provoked only limited discussion. Indeed, Section 5, covering matters of housekeeping and membership, and Section 6, on compensation, took up only a small portion of Monday's afternoon session as the delegates hurried on to Section 8 and the "powers of congress."[29]

Supporters of the Constitution anticipated a lively "conversation" on Section 8, beginning with Paragraph 1, which empowered Congress "to lay and collect taxes, duties, imposts, and excises." Rufus King opened by declaring that he did not possess "any particular knowledge" on the subject, a disclaimer that conveniently doubled as a reminder of his service in the Federal Convention, and then proceeded to offer a lengthy defense of this paragraph. Recounting the "melancholy" history of the Confederation, when a few states "shamefully neglected to pay their quotas" even during the war, King demanded to know "what faith is to be put in requisitions." States such as Massachusetts, which paid its quota, could find no justice or redress of grievances under the Articles of Confederation. Some might object that the grant of compulsory "power is too great," but if the want of power to "compel the delinquent states to pay"

28. Convention debates, *DHRC*, 6:1244–45, 1247.
29. *DHRC*, 6:1254–65, 1276–85.

was the principal "defect in the old confederation," what alternative remedy would they propose? "I know of none." Still others were troubled over the prospect of Congress possessing both the "power of the purse and the sword." But, King asked in response, was it conceivable that "any government can exist—or give security to the people which is not possessed of this power?"[30]

Other Federalists repeated the arguments King had articulated and emphasized two fundamental themes: first, the present configuration of the Union under the Articles was not working and could not be made to work; and second, the powers enumerated in Section 8, beginning with the power to tax, constituted the proper remedy for the defects of the Confederation. Thomas Dawes was certain that Americans had "suffered . . . for want of such authority in the federal head." The Articles, by denying Congress the power to raise money through taxes or to control commerce through duties and imposts, set up limitations that were "contrary to the policy of every nation on earth." Roxbury's Increase Sumner argued that the "design of uniting under one government," which was the promotion of "national dignity" and "safety," required the delegation of powers "by which alone those objects can be attained." To be sure, as some "gentlemen" had argued, such powers may be abused, but the "same may be said of any other delegated power." As long as the appropriate checks were in place, as they were in the proposed Constitution, added Christopher Gore, a Federalist lawyer from Boston, the people could rest assured that it was "not only safe but indispensably necessary to our peace and dignity, to vest the Congress with the powers described in this section." The people were right to demand that their federal government secure the "peace, dignity, and happiness of America," Gore observed, but in so doing they must also accept a basic maxim: "Where we demand an object, we must afford the means necessary to its attainment."[31]

According to the supporters of Section 8, the danger posed by their opponents was that while conjuring up some "imaginary evils" they were losing sight of a very real one. The weaknesses of the Confederation must tempt "our enemies to make war upon us," Gore warned, and ongoing warfare would require "large sums of money." Some states, as had been the case during the War of Independence, would be "slow and uncertain" in meeting their quotas. This time, however, the compliant states would resort to coercion "by arms," and thereupon unleash "all the horrors of a civil war." Given the "situation we are in," Boston merchant and banker William Phillips Sr. agreed, "we are verging towards destruction." Whereas Samuel Thompson, jealous of any delegation of power to a central government, had once lamented, "'O! my country' from an apprehension that the constitution should be adopted," Phillips said he

30. *DHRC*, 6:1285–87.   31. *DHRC*, 6:1287–88, 1300, 1311.

would "cry out '*O! my country*' if it is not adopted." He saw "nothing but destruction and inevitable ruin" in the wake of a rejection of the Constitution.[32]

Former governor James Bowdoin shared these concerns about "how inadequate to the purposes of the union the confederation has been." Having experienced firsthand the futility of Congress's effort to raise the funds necessary for sending federal troops into western Massachusetts to put down Shays's Rebellion, Bowdoin was adamant that the weaknesses of the Confederation government be remedied. The Shaysites had precipitated "a state of general confusion," and only his uncompromising response—"Every man ought to show his colors and take his side: No neutral characters should be allowed"— and the successes of a privately funded army had saved the state from the "horrors of anarchy." Knowing this, it should be evident to "every gentleman" that the American people could not rely on ad hoc measures to secure their "dearbought, blood-purchased liberty and independence." The new Congress must be empowered to "deliver us from evils, which unless remedied, must end in national ruin." Contrary to the assertions made by its opponents, the "investiture of such power" in Congress to lay taxes, pay debts, regulate commerce, declare war, raise armies, and so forth "is the most cogent reason for accepting the Constitution."[33]

Bowdoin's speech struck one admirer as further proof of the former governor's status as "really a great Man," but Jonathan Smith, a self-described "plain man" representing his "brother plough-joggers," delivered the speech that, according to Lincoln County delegate Dummer Sewall, "exceeded all" for its dramatic impact. Smith, from Berkshire County, one of the strongholds of Shays's rebels, said he knew from personal experience "the worth of good government by the want of it." The Shaysites "brought on a state of *anarchy*" in the western counties, distracting many into taking up "arms against government." Antifederalists interrupted Smith twice, the second time with a call to order, demanding to know "what the history of last winter [had] to do with the Constitution," but he found allies among "several gentlemen," including Samuel Adams, who said he was in order and to "go on in his way." "I am going," the Berkshire farmer declared, because the episode was too "dreadful" to be dismissed by the persnickety objections of a few. Smith proceeded to describe unsettling scenes sure to evoke empathy: muskets aimed at the breasts of innocents; threats to burn the houses of citizens suspected of siding with the government; wanton robberies and property damage committed without remorse or remedy; children stolen away from schools while their mothers

32. *DHRC*, 6:1298, 1300–2.
33. David P. Szatmary, *Shays' Rebellion: The Making of an Agrarian Insurrection* (Amherst, MA, 1980), 70, 73; *DHRC*, 6:1317–20.

wailed, "What shall I do for my child!" Only those who had witnessed such anarchy close up could understand why he and his "good neighbors" would have been "glad to catch at anything that looked like a government for protection." In order to escape the "black cloud" of chaos and its attendant insecurities, they were ready to flock to any standard that might guarantee stability, "even if it had been a *monarch*, and that monarch might have proved a tyrant." Imagine his excitement, then, upon hearing that the Constitution might fulfill his wish for good government. "I got a copy of it and read it over and over." Satisfied, finally, that it presented "a cure" for the disorders westerners had recently lived through, Smith "was pleased" to endorse the Constitution and urged others to do the same. "There is a time to sow and a time to reap," said the uncommon plain man paraphrasing the biblical passage in Ecclesiastes. "We sowed our seed when we sent men to the federal convention, now is the harvest, now is the time to reap the fruit of our labor." But the opportunity was not open-ended, Smith cautioned, "and if we don't do it now I am afraid we never shall have another opportunity."[34]

Those who had interrupted Smith's speech, of course, were not so willing to reap what others had sown. Martin Kingsley, the delegate who had called Smith to order, did not subscribe to Smith's description of the actions of the armed agrarian protestors in western Massachusetts nor to the solution proposed under Section 8. "Power is not dangerous, if the people have proper checks," explained Kingsley, a Shaysite sympathizer from Worcester County. The Articles of Confederation provided three essential checks on the wielders of power: annual elections, rotation of office, and removal through recall. The Constitution included none of these. With them, "federal rulers . . . are the servants of the people"; without them, they become "masters and not servants." The power "to lay and collect all taxes, duties, imposts and excises; raise armies, fit out navies . . . &c.," problematic by their very nature, proved invariably dangerous when lodged in the hands of "designing and interested men" capable of perpetuating their tenure indefinitely. Smith was dismissive of "those gentlemen who are so very suspicious," believing that "honest men" would be chosen to serve in new Congress, but the Antifederalists thought he was foolish to reject the virtue of jealousy. Samuel Willard, a Worcester physician and former Shaysite leader, delved into histories of Sparta, Athens, and Rome "to prove that where power had been trusted to men . . . they had always abused it."[35]

William Symmes Jr., of Andover, was similarly distrustful of power unchecked and the reassurance "that these are imaginary evils." Experience had shown that "all governments have degenerated, and consequently have abused

34. *DHRC*, 6:1330n17, 1344, 1346–48.   35. *DHRC*, 6:1297, 1291, 1302.

the powers reposed in them, and why we should imagine better of the proposed Congress than of the myriads of public bodies who have gone before them, I cannot at present conceive." As a young man serving in his first representative body, Symmes claimed to be a bit intimidated in rising to address so august an assembly of delegates. As a young lawyer who had studied under Theophilus Parsons, he was also more than a little mortified to have to take a position in opposition of his mentor. But he would be dishonoring his constituents were he to remain silent in the face of the unmistakable threat posed by the "absolute decree" of power contained in Section 8. "I hold to this maxim, that power was never given . . . but it was exercised, nor ever exercised but it was finally abused." With "unbounded permission" to lay taxes, "provide for the common defense and general welfare," "pay the debts, &c.," Congress "shall become tyrannical." Of this he was certain. Section 8 was the "cement of the fabrick," the "key-stone," the "magick talisman," the "very sinews of the Constitution," and its disposition by the convention would determine the fate of the nation.[36]

Conversation by Paragraphs Reconsidered

After spending nearly four full days on Section 8, two things had become apparent: first, the "conversation" on the Constitution could be extended ad nauseam; and second, the delegates strayed almost at will from the paragraph-by-paragraph format. On the morning of January 23, John Taylor first called attention to this, commenting that the "consideration of the 8th section had taken up a great deal of time" because some "gentlemen had repeated the same arguments over and over again." Rising immediately after former governor Bowdoin had finished his lengthy address, Taylor announced that the "Hon. Gentleman last speaking had gone into the matter at large," and that he hoped "other gentlemen would take the same liberty." In other words, although the convention had originally intended to consider the Constitution "by paragraphs," it should now proceed instead with "observations . . . on the system at large." The morning session adjourned without any action being taken on Taylor's proposal, so Samuel Nasson opened the afternoon session with a motion for "reconsidering a former vote to discuss the Constitution by paragraphs." When his motion "met with a warm opposition," Nasson agreed to withdraw his motion, with the tacit understanding that he would introduce it again the following morning. But on January 24, upon Nasson's renewing his call for dispensing with the paragraph-by-paragraph format, Samuel Adams, who, despite his "difficulties and doubts respecting some parts of the proposed Consti-

36. *DHRC*, 6:1307–11.

tution" had thus far "chosen to be an auditor than an objector," came out against the motion. He was "desirous to have a full investigation of the subject," Adams said, in order to help him and other undecideds make up their minds.[37]

Adams's opposition pretty much doomed Nasson's motion, and the convention disposed of it quickly with a negative vote that elicited a "small buzz of congratulation" from a few of the spectators in the gallery. Boston's Samuel Stillman described the attempt to speed up the proceedings as an act of desperation on the part of Antifederalists, who had come to realize that the paragraph-by-paragraph examination of the Constitution was unleashing a "blaze of evidence" that greatly increased the chances of ratification. The problem with Stillman's assessment is twofold. First, the rules adopted by the convention at the outset allowed delegates to bring up any paragraph they deemed to be connected to the one immediately under consideration. And prompted by objections to Gilbert Dench's insistence on discussing Section 4, Paragraph 1, while Section 2, Paragraph 1, was being examined, the convention twice reaffirmed this rule for promoting proper "conversation." Indeed, Samuel Thompson, the Lincoln County Antifederalist, argued that Nasson's motion was intended to encourage more not less participation, "to have the whole subject at large open to discussion, so that everybody might speak to it" without being "called to order." It is possible Thompson was simply being coy, but he himself had been called to order by Samuel Adams for suggesting, in the wake of Dench's leap to Section 4, that it might be time to "thump it about and see what is in it." Thompson then was in the same situation as his hypothetical "member" who rises and begins to speak but is interrupted by a call to order, "and this puts him out."[38]

The second problem with Stillman's inference regarding the desperation of the Antifederalists is that the contest between the supporters and opponents of ratification was still a toss-up. Madison informed Washington on January 20 that the "intelligence from Massachusetts begins to be very ominous to the Constitution." On January 23, the day Nasson made his motion, Rufus King, who stood with those warmly opposed the change, reported to Madison, "Our prospects are gloomy." Four days later, King repeated to Madison that the convention was seemingly evenly divided and that therefore "we were doubtful whether we exceeded them or they us in numbers." Receiving such reports, Madison may have suspected that King, whom he had gotten to know in Philadelphia through their work on the Committee of Eleven and the Committee of Style,

37. *DHRC*, 6:1323–24, 1333–35.
38. *DHRC*, 6:1336; George Benson to Nicholas Brown, January 29, 1788, *DHRC*, 7:1556–57.

was predisposed to "give a greater activity to his fears than to his hopes," but his was not the only guarded assessment. Nathaniel Gorham, another influential ally of Madison's in the Federal Convention and a "man of very good sense," was able to reassure the Virginian that the delegates gathered in Boston were well informed, and yet he remained "in doubt" as to whether they would approve the Constitution.[39]

A Scheme and Hancock's Infirmities

If Federalists found any reason to be encouraged around this time, it was not because of the "blaze of evidence" they were marshaling in favor of ratification. Rather, as King told Madison, they had by January 23 hatched a "scheme [that] may gain a few members" in support of the Constitution. "We are now thinking of amendments to be submitted not as a condition of our assent & ratification," King explained, "but as the opinion of the convention subjoined to their ratification." Gorham was an active participant in this scheme. In his account to Madison, Gorham included a survey of the parties arrayed against the Constitution. Three of these were "unhappily" beyond salvation, consisting of delegates representing debtors in favor of paper money, former Shaysites and their sympathizers, and residents of Maine who wished to be separated from Massachusetts. Their ranks were temporarily bolstered, however, Gorham explained, by members acting on behalf of "honest doubting people" still waiting to be won over. Amendments proposed, not as a "condition of ratification—but recommendatory only," might prove attractive to these honest people and "take off some of the opposition."[40]

The lynchpin of this scheme was John Hancock. Hancock, who had defeated the incumbent James Bowdoin in the spring gubernatorial election, was the most popular politician in Massachusetts and acceptable to moderate Federalists and Antifederalists alike. On January 9, the scheduled first day of business, the convention almost routinely chose the governor as its president, even though, as John Quincy Adams noted, "his infirmities are such as will probably prevent him frequently from attending." A chronic and severe case of gout did in fact keep Hancock from presiding over any session until January 30, when, an hour into the morning's discussion of the judiciary and the right to a trial by jury, his carefully choreographed entrance onto the floor of the

39. James Madison to George Washington, January 20, 1788, *PJM*, 10:399; Rufus King to James Madison, January 23, 1788, *PJM*, 10 :411; Rufus King to James Madison, January 27, 1788, *PJM*, 10:437; James Madison to George Washington, February 1, 1788, *PJM*, 10:455; Nathaniel Gorham to James Madison, January 27, 1788, *PJM*, 10:435; Farrand, 3:87.

40. Rufus King to James Madison, January 23, 1788, *PJM*, 10:411; Nathaniel Gorham to James Madison, January 27, 1788, *PJM*, 10:435–36.

convention—carried by his attendants and limping into his chair—interrupted the proceedings and "diffused much pleasure in the gallery & below."[41]

Hancock's attendance that morning was not simply a happy occurrence. Many Federalists had by this time concluded that the governor's endorsement of the Constitution would be determinative. If Hancock "appears openly in favor of the Federal System," Boston's Thomas Russell wrote his friend John Langdon in New Hampshire, "there will be I dare say a handsome majority in favor of the question." But Hancock had not committed himself one way or the other on the Constitution, and, according to one knowledgeable commentator, his "sentiments respecting the Constitution were known to be equivocal, and suspected to be averse." Eager to gain Hancock's support, Federalist leaders, including King, Gorham, Parsons, and Dana, met in caucus and appointed as their emissary Samuel West, a Congregational pastor and delegate from Bristol County who "understood the temper of Hancock" better than anyone else and "could manage his occasional caprices and waywardness with more address." West pleaded with the governor to "complete the glorious work which you commenced by signing, as President of Congress, the Declaration of Independence." The fate of the nation depends "on you, and you alone." The alternatives were as simple as they were stark: with his help the Constitution and therefore the nation were saved; without it, the Constitution would be lost and the nation "ruined." By answering the call of "all good men and true patriots," the Hancock "name will be immortal, and will be blessed by unborn millions." It was heady stuff and sure to appeal to Hancock's overweening vanity.[42]

Hancock, however, was not moved by vanity alone. An ambitious politician, he appreciated the impact his actions could have on his standing with the public. Some critics went so far as to suggest that Hancock's prolonged absence was due not to illness primarily but to a personal political predicament: he had reservations about the Constitution, but his Boston constituents were for ratification. By staying away from the convention he supposedly hoped to avoid addressing the question until the outcome was more certain and the risk to his reputation less pronounced. Rufus King repeated this charge on at least three different occasions, saying he expected Hancock's health to improve "as soon as the majority is exhibited on either side." Be that as it may, by the end of the first week of January Hancock had begun to express his qualified support for the Constitution. Theophilus Parsons was aware of this, having been

41. John Quincy Adams diary excerpt, January 10, 1788, *DHRC*, 7:1526; George Benson to Nicholas Brown, January 30, 1788, *DHRC*, 7:1558.

42. Thomas Russell to John Langdon, January 30, 1788, *DHRC*, 7:1562; Francis Baylies, eulogy for Benjamin Russell, March 10, 1845, *DHRC*, 7:1778, 1780–81.

informed by Fisher Ames that the governor "declares openly for the amendments" proposed by some of the more conciliatory partisans in other contested states. Thus when West met with Hancock, he came armed not merely with flattery but with a set of amendments drafted by Parsons.[43]

The Amendments Proposed by His Excellency

Federalist leaders couched their appeal in terms the shrewd new governor was sure to appreciate. They promised Hancock the "universal support of Bowdoin's friends," that is, acceptance by the disgruntled corps of Massachusetts voters still loyal to the former governor after the recently contested election. Furthermore, they predicted, he would be "the only fair candidate for President," should George Washington be disqualified in the event of Virginia's failure to ratify the Constitution. Mixing hard-nosed bargaining and blarney in equal doses, they gained his endorsement of their scheme. Jeremy Belknap had a slightly different take on what transpired. According to Belknap, the "Feds in concert" developed the recommendatory amendments and got Hancock to deliver "the product" because they thought it "would be better received" coming from him "than from any other person." In this rendering, the Federalist caucus manipulated Hancock to their advantage. But even Belknap viewed the governor as an "ostensible Puppet," ostensible because he pulled his own strings. Hancock presented their amendments in exchange for the caucus members' pledge to "help his popularity" by securing the support of Bowdoin's friends and thereby "ensure his election the next year."[44]

The Federalist caucus next approached Samuel Adams, "the old Patriot" who had remained uncharacteristically silent throughout the convention, and got him to agree to "come out in favor of the Constitution." All of this maneuvering was completed in secrecy, wrote Tristram Dalton, the Essex County leader, and was therefore "scarcely known out of our caucus, wherein we work as hard as in convention." With Hancock and Adams on the same side, their side, the members of the caucus were more optimistic about the final outcome. But when "all that is dear is at stake," complacency was out of the question. Dalton, King, Parsons, and their fellow conspirators were "not idle by Night or Day." Dalton confessed a willingness to "sacrifice everything but moral Hon-

---

43. Rufus King to George Thatcher, January 20, 1788, *DHRC*, 7:1541; Rufus King to Horatio Gates, January 20, 1788, *DHRC*, 7:1539; Rufus King to Henry Knox, January 27, 1788, *DHRC*, 7:1553; Michael Allen Gillespie, "Massachusetts: Creating Consensus," in *Ratifying the Constitution*, ed., Michael Allen Gillespie and Michael Lienesch (Lawrence, Kansas, 1989), 152, 154; Fisher Ames to Theophilus Parsons, January 8, 1788, in W. B. Allen, ed., *Works of Fisher Ames*, 2 vols. (Indianapolis, 1983), 1:557; Baylies, eulogy, *DHRC*, 7:1779.

44. Rufus King to Henry Knox, February 3, 1788, and Jeremy Belknap to Ebenezer Hazard, February 3, 1788, *DHRC*, 7:1572, 1566.

esty to carry our point." Still, "never—never were men more anxious than we are," he acknowledged.[45]

Shortly before the morning session adjourned on January 31, "the conversation on the Constitution by paragraphs being ended," Parsons rose immediately to move "that this convention do assent to and ratify this Constitution." Roxbury delegate General William Heath then asked, as if on cue, whether there was some way of winning the support those delegates who were generally in favor of ratification but objected to "particular parts" of the proposed plan. "I think there is," Parsons answered, and he then recommended that the convention ratify the Constitution unconditionally but that it also instruct the first members of Congress to propose such amendments as appeared to be necessary "for an efficient federal government." Governor Hancock next rose, again as if on cue, and announced his intention, with the permission of the convention, "to hazard a proposition" at the start of the afternoon session. Everyone sensed that something was afoot. Hundreds of spectators "were so anxious" to keep their seats in the galleries that they sat through the two-hour break between the morning and afternoon sessions "and sent home & had their dinners brought them."[46]

When the delegates reconvened at three o'clock, the galleries were "uncommonly crowded" with spectators. As Hancock took his seat, he made his "painful indisposition" evident to all, and his apparent fragility, coupled with "the ardent expectation of persons of every description, and the uncertainty prevailing as to the nature of the proposition to be made," rendered the "scene as interesting and affecting as possible." Amid the "most profound silence," Hancock first dispelled the uncertainty with a proposal that the Constitution be ratified with "amendments to be perfected by the first Congress upon the new system." He then read aloud nine recommendatory amendments, which "gave a shock to the *Antis* and caused an agreeable surprise in some of the *Feds*." Samuel Adams "seconded warmly" and moved that the governor's propositions be debated before the convention took any action on Parsons's motion. "This plan," Dalton confidentially told his brother-in-law, Newburyport merchant Stephen Hooper, would hopefully "cause a party to leave the Antis." If it did, if the plan succeeded in splitting the ranks of the Antifederalists, then, Nathaniel Gorham remarked, "I presume we shall have a small majority." Rufus King was more cautious and refused "to predict the issue," but he too was encouraged enough to believe "our wishes will be gratified."[47]

45. Tristram Dalton to Michael Hodge, January 30, 1788, and Tristram Dalton to Stephen Hooper, January 31, 1788, *DHRC*, 7:1560, 1563.

46. Convention debates, *DHRC*, 6:1377–79; Henry Jackson to Henry Knox, February 3, 1788, *DHRC*, 7:1570.

47. *Massachusetts Gazette*, February 1, 1788, and *Massachusetts Centinel*, February 2, 1788, *DHRC*, 6:1387; Tristram Dalton to Stephen Hooper, January 31, 1788, *DHRC*, 7:1563; Tristram

The nine amendments "proposed to the Convention by His Excellency" were almost certain to placate some of the opponents of ratification. The bulk of these, as might be expected given the length of time the convention spent on Article 1, modified the powers granted to Congress. The first paragraph of Section 4, which had generated so much dissent, would be amended, as Phanuel Bishop and William Widgery had suggested, to limit congressional interference in the election of senators and representatives to those instances in which a state was negligent. Similarly, the federal government's power to lay and collect taxes would be amended to take effect only when funds raised through tariffs and excise taxes were insufficient. To Antifederalists who were suspicious of all grants of power, believing they were susceptible to abuses that threatened the dissolution of the state governments, the first of the proposed amendments was a reassuring declaration that "all powers not expressly delegated by the aforesaid Constitution are reserved to the several states."[48]

These recommendatory amendments could not satisfy unreconstructed Shaysites like Bishop and Samuel Willard, whom Nathaniel Gorham had dismissed as irreconcilable, but they might convert "honest doubting people." James Bowdoin said he fully expected Hancock's amendments to do just that by quieting "the apprehensions of some very respectable and worthy gentlemen." Samuel Adams was bolder, predicting that the governor's "conciliatory proposition" would reap benefits "to this commonwealth and to the United States." Five states had already ratified the Constitution, but others had not, and "a proposal of this sort coming from Massachusetts, from her importance, will have its weight." As it turned out, Adams was correct to assume that the actions taken in Boston would be felt in states where conventions had not yet met. Federalists in Virginia, New York, New Hampshire, and South Carolina adopted the idea of recommendatory amendments and found it strategically useful in getting the Constitution ratified in their states.[49]

The Antis Are Very Skittish

Antifederalists who sought a "total rejection" of the Constitution "grew warm & passionate" in their opposition to the recommendatory amendments. Outmaneuvered by their opponents, they cried foul and "insinuated" that the amendments had been "artfully introduced to lead to a decision which would not otherwise be had." Some tried to make the best of a bad situation by lecturing the Federalists: "You have told us of the perfections of the Constitution—

Dalton to ——, February 3, 1788, *DHRC*, 7:1568–69; Nathaniel Gorham to Henry Knox, January 30, 1788, *DHRC*, 7:1561; Rufus King to James Madison, January 30, 1788, *DHRC*, 7:1561.
    48. Convention journal, *DHRC*, 6:1381–82.
    49. *DHRC*, 6:1381; Veit, 14–28.

now you acknowledge defects & want amendments *yourselves*." But they "perverted the idea of the proposed amendments," George Benson reported to Nicholas Brown in Rhode Island, by contending that the Constitution "could not be adopted unless the amendments were absolutely inserted in the Resolve of Ratification & made Conditional of it &c. &c." Others continued to insist they were in the majority, although it had shrunk to "a majority of 10," which led an incredulous Gorham to exclaim, "I shall be more mortified if they are right in their conjecture than I have ever been in my life."[50]

The most effective point Antifederalists made against the recommendatory amendments was a variation of the one articulated by John Taylor on January 31. Shortly after Samuel Adams had endorsed Hancock's proposition, the Worcester County doctor objected, saying he had examined "the several authorities which provided for the meeting of conventions, but did not see in any of them any power given to propose amendments." Instead, the Federal Convention had presented the state conventions with a simple choice: "We must take the whole—or reject the whole." To this objection, Federalists offered two responses. First, as Essex County's George Cabot explained, the authority for their amendments was not to be found in any of the documents Taylor had consulted but rather in Article 5 of the Constitution. Hancock's proposal did not call for amendments as a precondition to ratification. Rufus King and others had already made abundantly clear that Massachusetts would be voting to "take the whole," while recommending that certain alterations be considered by the first Congress meeting under the authority of the Constitution itself. Second, as Boston's Charles Jarvis explained, the power to accept or reject the Constitution implied a "discretionary" authority to decide the manner in which that power was to be exercised. But more importantly, said Jarvis, whom a critic later dubbed "Mr. Changeling" because he shed his earlier Antifederalist leanings in order to join Hancock, the authority under which the delegates met was derived from the "right of the people" and not from the Federal Convention or the state legislature. The convention, comprising "the fullest representation of the people ever known," was therefore not answerable to either of those bodies, Fisher Ames agreed, but solely to the "whole people of Massachusetts."[51]

On February 2 the convention agreed unanimously to submit Hancock's proposal to a committee of twenty-five "to examine if any other amendments

50. *Massachusetts Gazette*, February 1, 1788, *DHRC*, 6:1387; Jeremy Belknap, debate notes, January 31, 1788, *DHRC*, 6:1386; convention debates, February 4, *DHRC*, 6:1425; Jeremy Belknap to Ebenezer Hazard, February 3, 1788, *DHRC*, 7:1566; George Benson to Nicholas Brown, February 3, 1788, *DHRC*, 7:1567; Nathaniel Gorham to Henry Knox, February 3, 1788, *DHRC*, 7:1570.

51. Convention debates, *DHRC*, 6:1385, 1401, 1386, 1424, 1444; the writings of Laco, 1789, 7:1771, 1773, 1774.

of consequence were advisable & to report." The selection of two delegates from each county, one a Federalist and the other an Antifederalist, was supposed to convey impartiality, but, of course, twenty-five cannot be evenly divided. Martha's Vineyard in Dukes County, with only two convention delegates, both Federalists, had only one member on the select committee. The *"Antis* are afraid & very skittish, for they fear they may be led into a *trap*," Henry Jackson noted, before belittling them as "so damnable stupid." Such disparagement notwithstanding, the opponents of the Constitution had good reason to be suspicious. To claim, as Christopher Gore did, that the Committee of Twenty-Five was "nearly [evenly] divided on the great question" was tantamount to saying, as George Benson explained, that "in this committee the *Federals have a singular advantage.*"[52]

The Report of the Committee of Twenty-Five

Working through the Sabbath, the Committee of Twenty-Five submitted its recommendations to the convention on Monday, February 4. Not unexpectedly, given the composition of the committee, the report added no other amendments to the nine Hancock had proposed. It did complete the governor's proposal by filling in details that he had left out, first by prescribing that the one per thirty thousand ratio apply only until the total number of representatives reached two hundred and next by limiting the Supreme Court's jurisdiction to cases in which the dispute between citizens of different states exceeded $3000. The committee also altered Hancock's fourth amendment so that Congress' power to lay direct taxes would affect only those states that refused to pay their proportionate share of a requisition for funds. However, as Henry Jackson observed, these changes did not amount to much, and the committee's amendments were "nearly the same as recommended by his Excellency."[53]

The consensus among Federalists now was that Massachusetts was in a "promising situation for the adoption of the Constitution," Henry Van Schaack informed his brothers, Peter and David, in New York. The actions taken by Hancock "had an amazing influence over a great number of wavering members." Tristram Dalton voiced the same sentiment. Since the beginning of the convention "the balance of power" had been "each day vibrating, as the mercury in a thermometer," he wrote, but Hancock's declaration of support for the Constitution, the "plausibility of his plan," and the composition of the Com-

52. George Benson to Nicholas Brown, February 3, 1788, *DHRC*, 7:1568; Henry Jackson to Henry Knox, February 3, 1788, *DHRC*, 6:1410–12; *DHRC*, 7:1571; Nathaniel Gore to George Thatcher, February 3, 1788, and George Benson to Nicholas Brown, February 3, 1788, *DHRC*, 7:1569.

53. Report of the Committee of Twenty-Five, February 4, 1788, *DHRC*, 6:1413–14; Henry Jackson to Henry Knox, February 3, 1788, *DHRC*, 6:7:1581.

mittee of Twenty-Five boded well for a "large majority" in favor of ratification. Nathaniel Gorham would not go so far as to predict an easy win, but his own sources indicated a margin of victory of about fifteen votes. Christopher Gore likewise thought there was "a fair probability of an adoption" of the Constitution. Even Rufus King, the most cautious of the caucus members, was "encouraged to think our success is probable."[54]

On February 5, after an abbreviated discussion, the convention scheduled a vote on the report of the Committee of Twenty-Five at eleven o'clock the next morning. Everyone realized that a vote to accept the report would be the equivalent of a vote to ratify the Constitution because the committee's recommendatory amendments concluded, as had Hancock's proposal, with Congress being given "due notice of the assent & ratification of the said Constitution by the convention." Sensing that "the Fed party" would be "too strong for them," Antifederalists sought an indefinite postponement, Joseph Savage observed. Gilbert Dench moved that the convention adjourn "to a future day," explaining that the people ought to be consulted on the subject of recommendatory amendments before a final vote was taken. But Federalists agreed with Henry Jackson that Dench's motion was a ploy adopted by "the *Antis*" once they "discovered their weakness." Antifederalists, "alarmed" by the turn of events and apprehensive "of their being in the minority," were doing their utmost "to suspend the prosecution of the business to a future day," spectator George Benson recorded, and therefore "the Yeas & Nays will not be called before Wednesday or Thursday," February 6 or 7. Rhode Islander Benson, who was "so fortunate as to tarry in the same [boarding]house" in Boston as Federalist leader Theodore Sedgwick, was confident, however, that the delay could not reverse the outcome because there was "a small but decided majority in favor of the Constitution."[55]

A Majority of Nineteen

On the afternoon of February 5, by a vote of 214 to 115, the delegates rejected Dench's motion to adjourn, which put "a damper upon the opposition" and occasioned the *Massachusetts Centinel* to "felicitate the public" under the headline an "Auspicious Omen." The next morning, February 6, "4 a clock P.M. was assigned to take the *great Question*" regarding the report of the Committee of Twenty-Five. Henry Jackson, who had occupied a seat in the gallery since 9:00

54. Henry Van Schaack to Peter Van Schaack, February 4, 1788, *DHRC*, 7:1575; Tristram Dalton to ———, February 3, 1788, *DHRC*, 7:1569; Nathaniel Gorham to Henry Knox, February 3, 1788, *DHRC*, 7:1570; Nathaniel Gore to George Thatcher, February 3, 1788, *DHRC*, 7:1569; Rufus King to Henry Knox, February 3, 1788, *DHRC*, 7:1571.

55. *DHRC*, 6:1382, 1414; Joseph Savage to George Thatcher, February 1, 1788, *DHRC*, 7:1565; Dummer Sewall journal, *DHRC*, 7:1520; Henry Jackson to Henry Knox, February 6, 1788, *DHRC*, 7:1581; Georg Benson to Nicholas Brown, *DHRC*, 7:1567–68.

a.m., an hour before the start of the morning's session, dared not vacate his position for lunch, sending a boy to fetch some *"ginger bread & cheese"* from a shop nearby. Others did the same, and "the galleries remained full the whole time of the adjournment of the convention from 1 to 3" o'clock. At the appointed hour, according to Dummer Sewall, "anxiety sat on every brow," and the "very much crowded" spectators sat in such "profound silence" as Secretary George Richards Minot began recording the votes of the delegates that, William Widgery noted, "you might have heard a copper fall on the gallery floor." By 5:00 p.m. it was over.[56]

Twenty-one-year-old Bessenger Foster Jr., who in six months would begin his legal studies in the office of Theophilus Parsons, was "chagrined to find at the decision of the Question, so small a majority in favor of its adoption," but the more experienced Rufus King reported to Madison that the nineteen-vote margin of victory, with 187 in favor of ratification and 168 opposed, was "extremely respectable." Indeed, Boston merchant Joseph Barrell told New Yorker Samuel Blachley Webb, the "majority [of] 19" in Massachusetts "is equal to a Unanimous Vote in any other state," especially considering the presence in the opposition of "at least 80 Shays men & some more as bad as you or I ever wish any men to be." John Quincy Adams was not quite so willing to overlook the slight Federalist majority, but he too found some comfort in the observation that "satisfaction" among the residents of Boston "is almost universal." As soon as the news of the vote "was declared outdoors, the whole of the bells in Town were set a ringing & a general Joy & Congratulation took place throughout the Town," Henry Jackson confirmed. In an instant, it seemed, a crowd of thousands gathered before the statehouse and shouted "three *Huzza's* to *Heaven* which made all nature tremble."[57]

If Bostonians were united after the vote on the *"Grand Question,"* friends of the Constitution had Hancock and leading Antifederalists to thank for this. Just before Secretary Minot took the roll of yeas and nays, Hancock, as president of the convention, rose to address the delegates, begging leave "to close the business with a few words." He began by asking for their indulgence because he had nothing new to add to the "ideas appertaining to the system," a subject that after four weeks of paragraph-by-paragraph debate was under-

56. Benjamin Lincoln to Washington, February 6, 1788, *DHRC*, 7:1582; *Massachusetts Centinel*, February 6, 1788, *DHRC*, 6:1452; Jeremy Belknap, debate notes, February 6, 1788, 6:1490; Henry Jackson to Henry Knox, February 6, 1788, *DHRC*, 7:1580; Dummer Sewall journal, February 6, 1788, *DHRC*, 6:1520; William Widgery to George Thatcher, February 9, 1788, *DHRC*, 7:1690.

57. Bessenger Foster Jr., to Andrew Craigie, February 24, 1788, *DHRC*, 7:1590; Rufus King to James Madison, February 6, 1788, *PJM*, 10:475; Joseph Barrell to Samuel Blachley Webb, February 6, 1788, *DHRC*, 7:1602; John Quincy Adams Diary, *DHRC*, 7:1607; Henry Jackson to Henry Knox, February 6, 1788, *DHRC*, 7:1580.

standably "quite exhausted." But Hancock had a "request" to make that he hoped might save them from the potentially ruinous "discordance" they all dreaded. "Let the question be decided as it may, there can be no triumph on the one side or chagrin on the other," Hancock advised. Once the results became known, "every good man, every one who loves his country," should consciously avoid "extraordinary marks of joy," that is, refrain from gloating, and instead "lament the want of unanimity." Such cultivation of "a spirit of conciliation" will go a long way toward relieving any "uneasiness" among the people of Massachusetts, who possessed "great intelligence in public business" and subscribed to the "first principle of society, that of being governed by the voice of the majority."[58]

Hancock's appeal, delivered with a reminder of his poor health, seemed to have its desired effect. Upon learning that the motion to ratify had carried "by a majority of nineteen," Abraham White, who earlier had declared "he would not trust 'a flock of Moseses'" with the kind of power surrendered to federal authorities, rose immediately to state that although he had voted against the Constitution, "yet, as a majority had seen fit to adopt it, he should use his utmost exertions to induce his constituents to live in peace under, and cheerfully submit to it." William Widgery, Elbridge Gerry's champion, followed with a pledge to tell his constituents "he had been overruled . . . by a majority of wise and understanding men" and that "he hoped . . . no person would wish for or suggest the measure of a PROTEST." Others began lining up to proclaim their newfound allegiance to the Constitution. Josiah Whitney, Daniel Cooley, and John Taylor announced their determination to convince their constituents of the propriety of ratification, the once contentious Taylor going so far as to say he wanted "to infuse a spirit of harmony and love among the people." Other Antifederalists were awaiting their chance to speak when the convention adjourned for the day.[59]

When the delegates reconvened at ten the next morning, February 7, their main order of business was "completing their pay rolls, &tc., &tc.," in preparation for dissolving the convention. Still, "a number of the principal leaders of the Antis begged to have an opportunity to speak a few words." Samuel Nasson, who by late January had grown testy over the "conversation" by paragraphs, said he "fought like a good soldier" against the Constitution, but having been "conquered" he would support it as the "foundation of Law." Benjamin Randall, one of only five who opposed ratification in the thirty-nine-member Suffolk County delegation, "fought like a good soldier, but, as he was beat, he should set down contented." Middlesex County Antifederalist Benjamin

---

58. Winthrop Sargent to Henry Knox, February 3, 1788, *DHRC*, 7:1574; *DHRC*, 6:1475–76.
59. Convention debates, *DHRC*, 6:1487–88.

Sawin stated that because ratification was given a "fair trial" in convention, "he should support the Constitution as cheerfully and as heartily as though he had voted on the other side of the question." Reporting on these speeches, the *Massachusetts Centinel*, in an article reprinted at least twenty-eight times, praised the "open, manly and honorable conduct of the gentlemen who composed the minority." Their behavior would bring "everlasting honor" to the state and "convince the world that her sons know rightly how to prize the great principle of republicanism—that of submitting to the decision of a majority." New York physician John Howard could not "suppress the satisfaction" he felt after the convention had adjourned because, as a native of Bridgewater, Massachusetts, he was "charmed with the behavior of the minority."[60]

The Gentlemen of the Minority

George Washington was not surprised by the decision of the Massachusetts convention, but he found the "conciliatory behavior of the minority" in the aftermath "more pleasing and satisfactory" than anything he had anticipated. Washington had earlier been informed by Benjamin Lincoln, a Hingham delegate who had served under his command during the Revolutionary War, that Massachusetts Federalists had chosen not to "bear down the opposition" as their Pennsylvania counterparts had done. There, two months earlier, Federalists had won handily, but an Antifederalist minority, aggrieved over the heavy-handed tactics of the majority, issued a dissenting report sharply critical of the "violence and outrage," undue haste, and "suspicious secrecy" that together challenged the legality of all proceedings from the calling of the convention to its conclusion. Washington was not unfamiliar with the Pennsylvania protest, and on the eve of the vote in Boston, he was fearful lest a negative result should encourage opponents of the Constitution "to blow the Trumpet of discord more loudly." Even an "acceptance by a bare majority, tho' preferable to rejection," he thought, was to be "deprecated" for essentially the same reason. The "conciliating behavior of the minority" was thus "extremely pleasing" to Washington because it negated an otherwise disappointing margin of victory and would "strike a damp on the hopes which opponents in other states might otherwise have formed from the smallness of the majority."[61]

---

60. Henry Jackson to Henry Knox, February 10, 1788, *DHRC*, 7:1585; *DHRC*, 6:1492–93; Samuel Nasson to George Thatcher, February 8, 1788, *DHRC*, 7:1649; *Massachusetts Centinel*, February 9, 1788, 6:1494, 1496–97n1; *DHRC*, 7:1648n1; John Howard to George Thatcher, February 27, 1788, *DHRC*, 7:1653.

61. Georg Washington to Benjamin Lincoln, February 29, 1788, *DHRC*, 7:1653; Maier, *Ratification*, 99–122; Bouton, *Taming Democracy*, 180–82; Cecelia M. Kenyon, ed., *The Antifederalists* (Indianapolis, 1966), 27–60; George Washington to James Madison, February 5, 1788, *PJM*, 10:468–69; George Washington to Benjamin Lincoln, February 29, 1788, *DHRC*, 7:1653.

The contrast between the actions of the two minorities could not have been more compelling. The *Massachusetts Centinel* commended the "gentlemen" of the minority for pursuing a course of action "very different from that of the turbulent opposers of the Constitution in Pennsylvania, who, not content with their declamatory and odious protest against its adoption, are now endeavoring to involve their country in all the horrors of a civil war by exciting tumult and insurrection." The *Centinel* was a bit too smug in its reporting, but it accurately reflected the prevailing hope of the friends of the Constitution that the acquiescence of the minority in Massachusetts might serve as a salutary counterpoint to the protest of the Antifederalist minority in Pennsylvania. Indeed, many Pennsylvanians wished it would. After singling out for praise the "patriotic, temperate, and manly conduct of the minority," the *Pennsylvania Gazette* went on to compliment the former combatants in Massachusetts for their goodwill toward one another and to call for the "same harmony" to prevail in Pennsylvania. Similarly, in a piece reprinted a dozen times in seven states, the *Pennsylvania Mercury* advised its readers to compare the actions of the minorities in both states. Whereas one accepted defeat graciously, acknowledging "they were outvoted" and earnestly recommending "*union* and *submission*," the other became "*incendiaries*" and "strove to spread dissension and to raise rebellion amongst their constituents." Elsewhere, the *Virginia Gazette* had high praise for the "genuine republican principles" held by the minority delegates in the Massachusetts convention who, "almost to a man," were determined to support the Constitution and to "exert their influence with their constituents" to do the same. Madison himself, concerned about "very disagreeably large" minority faction, found the "temper of it is some atonement." Reassurances from Rufus King that Massachusetts Antifederalists, leaders and ordinary members alike, "in general are in good humor and will countenance no irregular opposition there or elsewhere" reinforced his hope that the Pennsylvania example had been effectively blunted.[62]

Adoption or Anarchy

In the days leading up to the vote in Boston, Washington was worried because the stakes were high and the outcome there "remained problematical." A rejection by Massachusetts would be felt "not only in New York, but in all those [states] which are to follow." In the ensuing chaos, the Confederation would disintegrate. Its ability to govern, already "*suspended by a Thread*," would be completely compromised, Washington told Charles Carter, an in-law of his

62. *Massachusetts Centinel*, February 7, 1788, *DHRC*, 6:1494; Convention debates, February 6, 1788, *DHRC*, 6:1487; *Pennsylvania Gazette*, February 20, 1788, *DHRC*, 7:1652n2; *Pennsylvania Mercury*, February 21, 1788, *DHRC*, 7:1652, 1653n1; *Winchester Virginia Gazette*, March 19, 1788, *DHRC*, 7:1655; Madison to Washington, February 15, 1788, *PJM* 10:510.

niece Betty Lewis, and thus there could be "*no Alternative* between the *Adoption*" of the Constitution "and *Anarchy*." Fisher Ames issued the same warning to the convention on February 5. "If we reject" the Constitution, "we are exposed to the risk of . . . being torn with factions, and at last divided into distinct confederacies." In view of the probable consequences of a rejection, therefore, the supposed alternative to ratification was, Ames declared, "too absurd to need any further discussion." The next day, the Reverend Samuel Stillman of Boston, Andover's William Symmes Jr., and finally Governor Hancock all expressed the same sentiment shortly before the convention voted. Stillman, who confessed earlier to having "some doubts" regarding the Constitution but whom a detractor dismissed as a "vociferous brawler" for the Federalists, announced, "I am ready, Sir, to submit my life, my liberty, my family, my property, and . . . the interest of my constituents, to this general government." He was ready to do so, he said, because he was convinced by the "best information" collected from "gentlemen of observation and of undoubted veracity . . . that the rejection of this Constitution will be followed with anarchy and confusion." Symmes, the young lawyer who had spoken eloquently against the powers granted to Congress under Section 8, said he would break from his two fellow Andover delegates and vote for the Constitution. Although he still "thought it had great defects," Symmes "expected the worst consequences to follow a *total* rejection of it." The "national distress" due to the "weakness of the present Confederation" coupled with the "danger of instant disunion" were the Constitution to be rejected had convinced him to abandon what he now perceived to be "a *deadly* opposition." Hancock closed with a simple declaration that the Constitution, accompanied by the amendments he had proposed to address its "defects," was "indispensably necessary to save our country from ruin."[63]

Elbridge Gerry's response to the vote in Massachusetts is instructive. Embittered, he "left the convention in dudgeon," vowing never to return, after his noisy dustup with Francis Dana on January 19. Gerry kept his promise to stay away, but he continued to monitor the proceedings at Boston from his quarters "close at Cambridge" and as late as three days before the final vote was still directing the actions of "his Adherents." Nevertheless, once the results were known, he openly declared his support for the Constitution. The *Pennsylvania Gazette*, in an article reprinted in Virginia and New York, reported that the "Honorable Elbridge Gerry," formerly an avowed opponent of the Constitution, "now declares, since it has received the sanction of the majority of the people, that he will firmly support it." The *Virginia Gazette* likewise announced its "highest

63. George Washington to James Madison, February 5, 1788, *PJM*, 10:469; Maier, *Ratification*, 127; *DHRC*, 6:1446; George Benson to Nicholas Brown, January 29, 1788, *DHRC*, 7:1557; *DHRC*, 7:1522n13; *DHRC*, 6:1456, 1460, 1474.

satisfaction" with the results of the Massachusetts convention and with Gerry's statement that "he will steadily support" the Constitution.[64]

Federalists in Pennsylvania, Virginia, and New York had much to gain by Gerry's conversion, but what was in it for Gerry? He still doubted the constitutionality of dissolving the Confederation without the consent of all thirteen states, objected to the absence of a bill of rights, believed the Constitution comprised "few, if any, *federal* features, but is rather a system of *national* government," and questioned the propriety of recommendatory amendments. And yet, Gerry, like the young Symmes, never entertained a "*mortal* hatred" of the Constitution. Instead, he shared with Washington a mortal fear of the consequences of a rejection. The Articles of Confederation were incapable of meeting the exigencies of governing the nation and preserving the Union; therefore, if the Constitution were to be rejected, "anarchy may ensue." Gerry believed that "proper amendments" were necessary to render the new plan of government perfectly safe for the "preservation of liberties," but he did not press the issue to the point of endangering the Constitution itself. "Gerry is crest-fallen but acquiesces," commented Jeremy Belknap, who attended most of the sessions of the convention as a keen if not entirely impartial spectator. More importantly, according to the *Hampshire Chronicle*, Gerry considered it the "duty of every honest man in the community" to acquiesce. Between total rejection and total acceptance, Gerry chose the latter because it "blended virtue and vice, errors and excellence," whereas the former would be an unmitigated disaster with social instability trending toward civil war. Six months earlier, as a member of the Massachusetts delegation to the Federal Convention in 1787, Gerry was "laborious" on matters he opposed, but no one gainsaid William Pierce's characterization of him as a person who "cherishes as his first virtue, a love for his country."[65]

---

64. Benjamin Lincoln to George Washington, January 27, 1788, *DHRC*, 7:1555; Rufus King to Henry Knox, February 3, 1788, *DHRC*, 7:1571; Belknap to Ebenezer Hazard, February 10, 1788, *DHRC*, 7:1695; *Hampshire Chronicle*, February 13, 1788, *DHRC*, 7:1695; *Pennsylvania Gazette*, February 27, 1788, *DHRC*, 7:1695–96; *Richmond Virginia Gazette*, February 28, 1788; *DHRC*, 7:1696.

65. *DHRC*, 6:1474; Billias, *Elbridge Gerry*, 207–8; Veit, 90; *Hampshire Chronicle*, February 13, 1788, *DHRC*, 7:1695; Farrand, *Records*, 3:88.

CHAPTER FOUR

Virginia Matters

In early February 1788, Thomas Jefferson proposed a strategy for ratifying the Constitution that he thought would "have all its good, and cure its principal defect." To James Madison, he wrote, "I sincerely wish that the 9 first conventions may receive, and the 4 last reject it. The former will secure it finally, while the latter will oblige them to offer a declaration of rights in order to complete the union." Jefferson repeated this same proposal to others at greater length and with seemingly greater conviction. "I wish with all my soul that the nine first conventions may accept the new constitution, because it will secure to us the good it contains," he told Alexander Donald, a Richmond tobacco merchant and sometime correspondent, "but I equally wish, that the four latest conventions, which ever they be, may refuse to accede to it, till a declaration of rights be annexed." Their refusal would "command the offer of such a declaration, and thus give the whole fabric perhaps as much perfection as any one of that kind ever had." In Paris, serving as the American minister to France, Jefferson informed the secretary to the American legation in London, William S. Smith, that if he were in America, he "would advocate" the Constitution "warmly till nine should have adopted and then as warmly take the other side to convince the remaining four that they ought not to come into it till the declaration of rights is annexed to it."[1]

Jefferson soon abandoned his own scheme, convinced perhaps by Madison's opposition to the idea of a declaration of rights, especially as a precondition to ratification, but more likely because he realized it jeopardized the Constitution itself. At the time Jefferson first made his proposal, five states had already ratified the Constitution. Delaware, New Jersey, and Georgia had done so unanimously, and Pennsylvania and Connecticut had ratified by margins of two to one and three to one, respectively. And Jefferson was "glad to hear that the new

1. Thomas Jefferson to James Madison, February 6, 1788, *Republic of Letters*, 1:529–30; Thomas Jefferson to Alexander Donald, February 7, 1788, in Merrill D. Peterson, ed., *Thomas Jefferson: Writings* (New York, 1984), 919; Thomas Jefferson to William S. Smith, February 2, 1788, in Dumas Malone, *Jefferson and the Rights of Man*, vol. 2 of *Jefferson and His Time* (Boston, 1951), 171.

constitution is received with favor" because its advantages over the Articles of Confederation were "great and important." The contest in Massachusetts revealed, however, that ratification would not be easily accomplished and that the strategy he proposed actually played into the hands of the most ardent Antifederalists. In the Virginia convention, Patrick Henry reminded the delegates of the "opinion of Mr. Jefferson our common friend." Jefferson's advice, Henry said, was for nine states to ratify and for four to reject the unamended Constitution. If, as "the most authentic accounts" predicted, New Hampshire became the ninth state, "where then will four states be found to reject, if we adopt it?" And if Virginia ratified under these circumstances, Henry warned, "the counsel of this enlightened and worthy countryman of ours will be thrown away." Of greater importance to Henry was a more pragmatic consideration. If Virginia adopted the Constitution unconditionally, "what states will be left, of sufficient respectability and importance, to secure amendments by their rejection?" In other words, Jefferson's plan whereby the nonratifying states would command the ratifying states to make concessions would be undermined completely. Indeed, Henry added, with "Massachusetts the great Northern state, Pennsylvania the great Middle state, and Virginia the great Southern state" in the balance on one side, all of the remaining states "will not have sufficient weight to have the government altered."[2]

Madison protested the reference to Jefferson and Henry's blatant attempt to capitalize on the "name of this distinguished character." Knowing that the "delicacy of his feelings" would be "wounded" by the unwarranted appeal to his authority, Madison lamented, "I wish his name had never been mentioned." Most of the delegates in the convention knew that Madison and Jefferson had been best friends since 1776 (they would continue to be close for the next fifty years, until Jefferson died in 1826), so when Madison said, "I am in some measure acquainted with his sentiments on this subject," they understood that to be an understatement. Madison went on to suggest that "were that Gentleman now on this floor, he would be *for* the adoption of this Constitution." But out of respect for "personal delicacy" and because he thought it was "not right" to disclose what had been conveyed to him in private, Madison said he would not pursue the matter any further. Later, he recounted the episode to Jefferson. Patrick Henry and George Mason had "endeavored to turn the influence of your name even against parts" of the Constitution "of which I knew you approved," Madison wrote, using a secret code the two friends shared. "In this

2. Thomas Jefferson to James Madison, February 6, 1788, *Republic of Letters*, 1:529; Thomas Jefferson to Alexander Donald, February 7, 1788, in Peterson, *Jefferson Writings*, 919; Bailyn, *Debate*, 2:674.

situation I thought it due to truth as well as that it would be most agreeable to yourself and accordingly took the liberty to state some of your opinions on the favorable side."[3]

Madison knew that by the time of the Virginia convention, Jefferson had renounced his earlier proposal for securing amendments to the Constitution and therefore that Henry and Mason were wrong to mention him in that context. Nevertheless, they were correct in their emphasis on the role the "great" states played in the process of ratification. "This state," Henry said of Virginia, "has weight and importance." Why should Virginians forsake their "station in America" and defer instead to the "more weak and less respectable" states whose demands "may be overborne by the example of so many adopting states?" Fisher Ames, the prominent Massachusetts Federalist, did not have much in common with Henry, but on this particular point there was hardly any daylight between them. The problem with Jefferson's proposal, Ames explained, was that it could not possibly achieve its desired end of uniting thirteen states under an amended Constitution. "Suppose the four largest states, viz.: Virginia, Pennsylvania, Massachusetts, and New York had rejected the Constitution and insisted upon all the amendments which their conventions required." Could these four "brow-beat" the other nine into accepting their alterations without producing a "schism" in the Union? Alternatively, "had the four smallest states in the Union withheld their consent in order to obtain amendments, is it likely the others would have regarded their idle threats?" Ames's rhetorical questions probably evoked the same response as Henry's distinction between the actions of states that had "weight" and those that did not. Contrary to what Jefferson's suggestion implied, the states were not equal, and therefore the last four could not be "which ever" were left after the first nine had ratified, not if they hoped to "command" any changes to the Constitution.[4]

The Most Mighty State in the Union

What Virginia did mattered. No one believed this more strongly than the Virginians themselves, and not without reason. Among the leaders of Revolutionary America, few could compete with George Washington, Thomas Jefferson, James Madison, and Patrick Henry. Indeed, notables from other states routinely deferred to the Virginians. The Continental Congress, Patrick Henry noted, "looked to Virginia" for a commander of the American Army; the Philadelphia Convention followed the agenda put forth in the Virginia Plan; fed-

3. James Madison to Thomas Jefferson, July 24 and 26, 1788, *Republic of Letters*, 1:542; Bailyn, *Debate*, 2:689.
4. Bailyn, *Debate*, 2:674–75; W. B. Allen, ed., *Works of Fisher Ames*, 2 vols. (Indianapolis, 1983), 2:969–70.

eral delegates representing twelve states unanimously elected Washington to preside over them; Georgian William Pierce, who studied his fellow delegates in action, observed that Madison "took the lead" in managing "every great question" that came before the convention; Madison, Mason, and Edmund Randolph ranked among the top ten delegates in the frequency of their participation at Philadelphia; and Federalists and Antifederalists alike uniformly assumed that if the Constitution was ratified, Washington would be the new nation's first president.[5]

When delegates to the state convention gathered in Richmond on June 2, many thought that Virginia might be the pivotal ninth to ratify, making it the state that confirmed the existence of a new Union under the Constitution. It did not turn out that way, as New Hampshire became the ninth state, ratifying the Constitution on June 21 while the Virginia convention was still wending its way toward a decision. In the larger scheme of things, however, as Henry and Ames pointed out, what Virginia did one way or the other was far more important than when. "The example of Virginia is a powerful thing," Henry declared. Therefore, ninth, tenth, or never, its decision on whether to ratify would affect all of the other states. As it should, for Virginia was the "most mighty state in the Union," Henry announced. "Does not Virginia surpass every state in the Union, in number of inhabitants, extent of territory, felicity of position, and affluence and wealth?" More than a few heads nodded in agreement when Henry asked, "Do I not speak the truth?"[6]

The progress of business in the Virginia convention reflected this common realization that whatever the 170 delegates decided in Richmond would have repercussions far beyond the borders of their state. Thus although the convention adopted at the outset Mason's motion to go through the document "clause by clause" to ensure a free and full examination of the Constitution, the debates took on a helter-skelter quality as speakers leaped from one point to the next without regard to article, section, or paragraph. Conducting business in this manner was highly "irregular" and "contrary to our resolution," Edmund Randolph protested on June 5, after Henry, the most frequent violator of the clause-by-clause rule, had spoken for hours on a multitude of topics, only a few of which were remotely related to the clauses assigned for discussion that day, namely, the first two sections of Article 1. If the convention allowed speakers to proceed in this random fashion, "it will take us six months to decide this question." Henry realized, even before Randolph voiced his objection, that he had "fatigued" the other delegates with his "multifarious" discussion "in so general

5. Farrand, 3:94; Jack P. Greene, "The Constitution of 1787 and the Question of Southern Distinctiveness," in Jack P. Greene, *Imperatives, Behaviors, and Identities: Essays in Early American Cultural History* (Charlottesville, VA, 1992), 342.

6. Bailyn, *Debate*, 2:675, 628.

a manner." But he could not help himself. The subject was too important to be bound by rules, and though he had taxed their patience, he had not covered "one hundred thousandth part" of what he wanted to say. Mason likewise ignored his own rule, explaining that on "so important a subject as this, it is impossible, in the nature of things, to avoid arguing more at large" rather than clause by clause.[7]

For nearly two weeks, the convention routinely opened each morning's session with "the 1st and 2d sections still under consideration," and the delegates just as routinely wandered freely over the entire text of the Constitution. Randolph continued to object that a "variety of points are promiscuously debated" without regard to the convention's rule. Equally frustrated, Madison bemoaned the departure from "the resolution we have taken," pleading with his fellow delegates to refrain from "mere sports of fancy" bearing no relevance at all to the clause under consideration. Despite their protests, however, Randolph and Madison were soon ignoring the rule themselves. As Randolph explained with an apology, "the relation of a variety of matters renders it now unavoidable." Madison, speaking after Henry on June 12, said he too was "sorry" to have to deviate from the rule, but the "utmost latitude" taken by the opponents of the Constitution made it "necessary that those who favor the government should answer them." As he took the "liberty to answer some observations which have been irregularly made," Madison continued to express his wish for the convention to return to the rule "as soon as possible" so that it might "take up the subject regularly." William Grayson, a veteran lawyer accustomed to tightly reasoned arguments, bluntly justified his "desultory" remarks by citing the "bad example which has been set me, and the necessity I am under of following my opponents through all their various recesses." The vast majority of the delegates thus adopted Mason's justification for his meanderings: "As gentlemen have indulged themselves in entering at large into the subject, I hope to be permitted to follow them."[8]

Big Questions and a Testy Exchange

Instead of plodding clause by clause over well-trodden ground, Virginians soared freely over the entire terrain mapped out by the Constitution in search of telltale features to help them answer the larger questions pertaining to ratification. Why did the Philadelphia Convention abandon the Articles of Confederation? Were amendments needed to render the Constitution safe? If they were, when should the state ask for them? Would the Union be in jeopardy if Virginia refused to ratify? Would Virginia be in jeopardy outside of the Union? Specific clauses in the document were useful ultimately in the service of these

---

7. Elliot, 3:64, 262.   8. *PJM*, 11:107, 129; Elliot, 3:273.

questions. They were illustrative, and therefore the order of their presentation was not particularly relevant. Patrick Henry set the precedent for ignoring the convention's rule with his surprisingly brief opening remarks to the convention on June 4. Ignoring the contents of the first and second sections of Article 1, Henry asked, "Why are we brought hither to decide on this great national question?" Until the late meeting of the Federal Convention, the "minds of our citizens were at perfect repose," Henry said, but now they "are exceedingly uneasy and disquieted." This regrettable situation he traced to the proposed Constitution, which threatened to annihilate the several state governments, the very "soul of a confederation," and to replace them with "one great consolidated National Government." That this new plan was the handiwork of Federal Convention delegates charged solely to amend the Articles of Confederation was doubly disturbing. Why did they willfully disregard their commissions and cobble together such a dangerous innovation? "And for what?" With liberty and the life of the republic at risk, Henry said he would have demanded an explanation even from Washington, "that illustrious man who saved us by his valor," had he been present in Richmond.[9]

Washington was at home in Mount Vernon, having chosen not to participate in the state convention, but, as Henry observed, "there are other Gentlemen here, who can give us that reason." Henry might just as well have pointed directly at Edmund Randolph when he intoned "other Gentlemen." Randolph had played a prominent role at Philadelphia. He introduced the Virginia Plan, was the moving force behind the mandatory census, contributed to the three-fifths compromise, and was one of the five members of the Committee of Detail, which prepared the preliminary draft of the Constitution. More conspicuously, however, during the final week of the Federal Convention, Randolph tried twice to get a motion passed that would have allowed the states to adopt, reject, or amend the proposed Constitution. Without such a proposition, Randolph said, it would "be impossible" for him "to put his name to the instrument." George Mason, who seconded Randolph's motion, and Elbridge Gerry, who spoke in support of it, likewise threatened not to sign the Constitution unless Randolph's motion carried. It did not, and all three, true to their word, withheld their signatures on the final day of business. Gerry, as we have seen, then went on to lead the Massachusetts Antifederalists, even though he was not a delegate to the Boston convention. And Mason was second only to Henry in opposing ratification in the Richmond convention. The problem for Randolph was that he seemed to have experienced a change of heart. He had a lot of explaining to do, and he knew it.[10]

9. Bailyn, *Debate*, 2:595–97.   10. Farrand, 2:631–33, 649.

Randolph took the floor immediately after Henry was done. Famous for his protest in Philadelphia, many expected him to take his place next to Henry and Mason at the head of the Antifederalist camp. He did not. Neither would he "apologize to any individual within these walls," he declared defiantly, nor "to the convention as a body, or even to my fellow citizens at large." He was not a "candidate for popularity," could not be tempted by the allure of "honors and emoluments," and cared not that he might be "upbraided" for his views. The only concern he had and continued to have was to oppose "any scheme" that could lead to "a dissolution of the Union." This was a constant with him. He had refused to sign the engrossed document in Philadelphia, Randolph explained, because the choice presented by the convention "wholly to adopt or wholly to reject" seemed too "hard an alternative to the citizens of America." He was afraid the people might refuse to ratify the Constitution, regardless of its merits, if the "chance for amendments was cut off." He believed the "Union would have been irredeemably lost" in that event, and with it the security and happiness of the American people.[11]

What had changed? Why was Randolph willing now wholly to adopt the unamended Constitution? "As with me," he answered, "the only question has ever been between previous and subsequent amendments," that is, whether amendments should be proposed as a condition of ratification or submitted after ratification as recommendations to be taken up by the first Congress under the terms described in Article 5 of the Constitution. Earlier, he might have favored previous amendments, but the "postponement of this convention to so late a day has extinguished" that option. Eight states had already adopted the Constitution unconditionally, and they would balk at the idea of revisiting their decision in order to accommodate Virginia. Hence, the insistence on previous amendments at this late stage portended an "inevitable ruin to the Union," and, Randolph announced, he would sooner "assent to the lopping of this limb (meaning his arm)" than condone the "dissolution of the Union."[12]

Madison, listening intently, was delighted by what he heard. Later that evening, in a letter to Washington, with whom he had been working to gain Randolph's endorsement of the Constitution, Madison was pleased to report that the "Governor has declared the day of previous amendments past, and thrown himself fully into the federal scale." To Randolph, Madison wrote appreciatively, "had your duty led you to throw your influence into the opposite scale," it would have given the opponents of ratification a "decided and unalterable preponderancy." For the same reason, Antifederalists were predictably as angry at Randolph as Madison and the Federalists were "elated" by him. Mason started to refer to Randolph as "young Arnold," equating him with

---

11. Bailyn, *Debate*, 2:598–99.   12. Bailyn, *Debate*, 2:600.

Benedict Arnold for his betrayal of the cause. Henry was more persistent and clever with his insults. The custom of using the adjective "honorable" was anything but formulaic in the context of his utterances about Randolph. The "system once execrated by the Honorable member must now be adopted." The "Honorable Gentleman" must account for his "very strange" behavior, must explain how it came to pass that what was once the "object of his execration should now receive his encomiums." Randolph had once "magnanimously and nobly" withheld his signature from a Constitution known to be defective. What could possibly explain the "alteration" brought about in the honorable gentleman in just "a few months"? The honorable gentleman was pursuing a course of action inconsistent with "that noble and disinterested conduct which he displayed on a former occasion." And in his most biting blow, Henry, re-coiling at Randolph's suggestion that he had misrepresented some facts, said he was surprised the "Honorable member" would dare accuse him of "want of candor" when "what he has given the public," namely, his report of October 1787, following his return from Philadelphia, was completely at odds with "what has happened since."[13]

Randolph, the sitting governor of the state and patriarch of one of the first families of Virginia, was not accustomed to such abuse. To be attacked so per-sonally "in the most illiberal manner" went far beyond the limits of "parlia-mentary decency" and the "least shadow of friendship." Looking at Henry, he added for emphasis, "if our friendship must fall, *let it fall, like Lucifer, never to rise again!*" That he and Henry had never been close did not matter in the larger context of the politics of honor. "I disdain his aspersions and his insinu-ations," Randolph exclaimed, alluding to developing rumors that he had been swayed by promises of a federal appointment in a Washington administration. "The highest honors have no allurements to charm me. . . . Give me peace—I ask no more." Randolph said he did not wish to dignify Henry's remarks with a response, but "severe charges" had been made and he was determined to de-fend himself. "It is a right I am entitled to, and shall have," the governor de-clared. Henry should know, however, "that it is not to answer him," for he was immaterial, "but to satisfy his respectable audience, that I now get up." Ran-dolph proceeded to read from his October 1787 letter, the very one Henry had singled out, in order to "prove the consistency of his present opinion with his former conduct." Henry interrupted the reading to say "he was sorry if he of-fended the honorable gentleman without intending it," but his apology did little to calm the situation and instead set the stage for a testy exchange.

13. James Madison to George Washington, June 4, 1788, *PJM*, 11:77; James Madison to Ed-mund Randolph, January 10, 1788, *PJM*, 10:354; George Mason to John Mason, December 18, 1788, *PGM*, 3:1136, 1140n; Bailyn, *Debate*, 2:624; Elliot, 3:159; Edmund Randolph to the speaker of the Virginia House of Delegates, October 10, 1787, Farrand, 3:123–27.

Addressing the convention at large, Randolph claimed, without acknowledging Henry's presence, that "were it not for the concession of the gentleman," he would have made "some men's hair stand on end by the disclosure of certain facts." Henry jumped to his feet and demanded of Randolph that "if he had anything to say against him, he would disclose it." But Randolph ignored Henry, concluded his reading, and "then threw down the letter on the clerk's table, and declared that it might lie there for the *inspection of the curious and malicious.*"[14]

Demosthenes in a Divided Convention

Randolph never made clear precisely what he was referring to when he said he was in possession of certain facts that would make "men's hair stand on end." There had been talk for some months, however, of Henry's lukewarm commitment to the Union. From Edward Carrington, with whom he had served in the Confederation Congress, Madison heard "it is said" that Henry was determined to have his amendments or, failing that, to commit to an independent Virginia in pursuit of its own "foreign alliances." George Nicholas, who in 1781 had joined Henry in calling for an investigation of Jefferson's conduct as the wartime governor of Virginia but had since switched his allegiances, warned Madison that his former ally was "avowedly an enemy to the union." His "real sentiments" were "industriously concealed," however, because Henry knew that as long as he spoke "only of amendments, such of the friends to the union as object to particular parts of the Constitution" might continue to "adhere to him, which they would not do a moment, if they could be convinced of his real design." John Blair Smith of Prince Edward County, bemoaning the onus his county bore for sending Henry to Richmond, similarly warned Madison of the "poison" Henry had been spreading among the "people in this quarter," specifically the "idea of Virginia standing independent of the other states, or forming a partial confederacy or a foreign alliance." But Madison was familiar with "facts" such as these; indeed he had disseminated a few of them himself. As early as June 1787, with the Federal Convention barely a week into its consideration of the Virginia Plan, Madison informed Jefferson, again in a coded message, that Henry was "hostile to the object of the convention" because what he truly desired was "a partition or total dissolution of the confederacy." In December, when Henry's outspoken support for alterations to the Constitution made ratification in upcoming state convention problematic, Madison claimed that Henry's call for amendments was a cover for his real aim, which was "a partition of the Union into several Confederacies." He repeated this "fact" to Randolph in January 1788: "I have for some

14. Elliot, 3:189, 187–88.

time considered him as driving at a Southern Confederacy" apart from the Union. Despite his noisy proclamations, therefore, Madison wrote, Henry's advocacy of amendments must be understood to be "subservient to his real designs."[15]

Raising questions about Henry's "real" motives was especially important to friends of the Constitution because the delegates in Richmond were nearly evenly divided, both in talent and in numbers, between supporters and opponents of ratification, thus leaving the outcome of the convention very much in doubt until the end. "Matters are not going so well in this state as the friends of America could wish," Pennsylvania Federalist Gouverneur Morris, visiting Richmond on business, informed Alexander Hamilton. On June 4, Madison told Rufus King that Federalists held a "small" majority but conceded the Constitution "may possibly be yet defeated." A week later, on June 11, following a session during which he was forced to "beg Gentlemen" not to engage in "vague discourses" in lieu of the "clause under consideration," Madison wrote Tench Coxe to complain about the "slow progress" of the convention. Madison informed the Philadelphia merchant, whose essay "An American" highlighting the "miserable and hopeless alternatives" to ratification he had read with "pleasure & approbation," that because the "parties are pretty nicely balanced," each side was making "great exertions" to win favor with the "undecided few." For the advocates of ratification, however, the return on their investment was disappointing. After two weeks of "full debate" and "in defiance of great exertions," Henry "Light-Horse Harry" Lee reported, Federalists may have gained a "majority, but very small indeed."[16]

It was precisely this situation that made Henry as much a danger to the Federalists as a source of hope to the Antifederalists. "It seems probable," Madison reported to Jefferson after studying the election returns of the various counties, "that a majority of the members elect are friends to the Constitution." But since this numerical advantage was "not absolutely certain," Madison found it somewhat reassuring to add that the "superiority of abilities at least seems to lie on that side." For proof, Madison listed twenty "characters of most note," including Edmund Pendleton, George Wythe, and John Marshall, as "for the Constitution," and only half that number of notables in opposition.

15. Edward Carrington to James Madison, January 18, 1788, *PJM*, 10:383; George Nicholas to James Madison, April 5, 1788, *PJM*, 2:9; John Blair Smith to James Madison, June 12, 1788, *PJM*, 2:120; James Madison to Thomas Jefferson, June 6, 1787, *Republic of Letters*, 1:479; James Madison to Thomas Jefferson, December 9, 1787, *Republic of Letters*, 1:509; James Madison to Edmund Randolph, January 10, 1788, *PJM*, 10:355.

16. Gouverneur Morris to Alexander Hamilton, June 13, 1788; *PAH*, 5:7;; James Madison to Rufus King, June 4, 1788, *PJM*, 11:76; James Madison to Tench Coxe, June 11, 1788, *PJM*, 11:102; "An American," *DHRC*, 9:841; Tench Coxe to James Madison, December 28, 1787, *PJM*, 10:348; James Madison to Tench Coxe, January 3, 1788, *PJM*, 10:349; Henry Lee to Alexander Hamilton, June 16, 1788, *PAH*, 5:10.

Heading the list of opponents, however, was Henry, and Henry's reputation for powerful and persuasive oratory posed a threat to whatever superiority the Federalists possessed or claimed to possess. "Virginians speak in raptures" about Henry, John Adams observed at the First Continental Congress in 1774, considering him the "Demosthenes of the Age." Jefferson, who neither cared much for Henry personally nor thought much of his legal expertise, admired and perhaps even envied this in Henry, calling him "the greatest orator that ever lived." Madison agreed. Months before delegates to the Richmond convention had been elected but anticipating a close contest over ratification, he fretted because "much will depend on Mr. Henry."[17]

Pray for His Death

Easily distracted and uncharacteristically listless when confronted with mundane issues, Henry was transformed into a different person and commanded the attention of his audience with "bold and splendid eloquence" in the face of "general grievances." Spencer Roane, who in 1786 married Henry's daughter Anne, could not explain his father-in-law's oratorical prowess, except to say that as Henry spoke, "the tones of his voice, to say nothing of his matter and gesture, were insinuated into the feeling of his hearers, in a manner that baffled all descriptions." But baffling or not, no one doubted Henry's ability to sway the affections of his listeners, and in a closely contested convention where methodical rules of engagement gave way to sweeping declarations, Henry was in his element. As "Light-Horse Harry" Lee noted, Henry was a mediocre talent when it came to "solid argument and strong reasoning," but he had few equals at "throwing those bolts" that swayed men's opinions. George Lee Tuberville, whose service in the House of Delegates in 1785–86 overlapped Henry's second stint as governor, gratuitously reminded Madison, six months before the Richmond convention, of "the force of this wonderful man's oratory" on a captive audience. Gouverneur Morris, the Philadelphia merchant who frequented the Richmond convention's sessions as a spectator, described Henry as "warm and powerful in declamation." Henry, he said, was the perfect exemplar of the "power of speech to stir men's blood."[18]

For Henry's opponents, the problem of how best to handle him did not yield to easy answers. What could friends of the Constitution do, Tuberville

17. James Madison to Thomas Jefferson, April 22, 1788, *Republic of Letters*, 1:534; L. H. Butterfield, ed., *Diary and Autobiography of John Adams*, 4 vols. (Cambridge, Mass., 1961), 2:113; James Madison to George Washington, October 18, 1787, *PJM*, 10:197.

18. Pauline Maier, *Ratification: The People Debate the Constitution, 1787–1788* (New York, 2010), 230; Richard Beeman, *Patrick Henry: A Biography* (New York, 1974), 25; Bailyn, *Debate*, 2:637; George Lee Tuberville to James Madison, December 11, 1787, *PJM*, 10:318; Gouverneur Morris to Alexander Hamilton, June 13, 1788, *PAH*, 5:7.

lamented, to counterbalance the force Henry "erroneously or injudiciously" projected? Morris hoped the "weight of argument" would be strong enough "wholly to destroy even on weak minds the effects of his eloquence" but admitted it might not be, for Henry was a master of "certain dark modes of operating on the minds of members which like contagious diseases" could not be properly diagnosed, let alone remedied. The search for an answer to Henry's influence brought out the worst in Jefferson. Henry, he said, was "all tongue and without head or heart," so there could be no reasoning with him. In 1784, as he and Madison discussed the necessity of revising the Virginia constitution, Jefferson wrote in a coded message that "while Mr. Henry lives," the chances of being saddled with a "another bad constitution" were too great to warrant proceeding with a convention. Therefore, there was only one recourse left. "What we have to do I think is devoutly to pray for his death." Jefferson's prayers went unanswered for another fifteen years, leaving the friends of the Constitution in search of a more immediate way of neutralizing, as John Blair Smith put it, Henry's "gross & scandalous misrepresentations of the new Constitution."[19]

The Bugbear of Disunion

Capitalizing on rumors and allegations about Henry and his supposed disaffection for the Union, Edward Carrington recommended to Madison what he perceived to be the effective mode of moving against him. In February 1788, a month before the several counties began electing delegates to the Richmond convention, Carrington was journeying through the Virginia backcountry and relayed to Madison the highlight of his experiences in Cumberland, Powhatan, and Chesterfield Counties. Although the residents there were "within the neighborhood of Mr. Henry" and "much disposed to be his blind followers," Carrington wrote, he felt compelled to make the case for ratification, satisfied that if he could "work a change in even a single man," it would be well worth the effort. His primary emphasis was "preserving the Union." Carrington hoped to convince his otherwise hostile listeners that Henry's numerous objections to the Constitution notwithstanding, he had not "even once specified the amendments" he wanted, and therefore it was fair to conclude that his talk of constitutional alterations was a cover for his real intention, which was a "dismemberment of the Union." This manner of proceeding "must, at a certain stage, separate the members from Mr. Henry." Indeed, it had already worked in selected instances. William Ronald from Powhatan County had objections

19. George Lee Tuberville to James Madison, December 11, 1787, *PJM*, 10:318; Gouverneur Morris to Alexander Hamilton, *PAH*, 5:7; Beeman, *Patrick Henry*, 132, 133; Thomas Jefferson to James Madison, December 8, 1784, *Republic of Letters*, 1:353–54; John Blair Smith to James Madison, June 12, 1788, *PJM*, 11:120.

"that would be taken for absolute" under ordinary circumstances, but he became "alarmed at the probable extent of Mr. Henry's views" and professed "a determination to do nothing which may . . . endanger the Union." Judge William Fleming, another candidate from Powhatan County, declared himself "earnestly for amendments" but thought "the Union ought in no degree to be hazarded."[20]

Neither Carrington nor the other accusers were clear about what Henry sought, whether it was an independent Virginia or a southern confederation, but Henry's own vacillations and his utterances on separate occasions lent credence to their allegations. In his lengthy June 5 speech, during which his "mind hurried on, from subject to subject" in a disjointed effort to limn the "dreadful oppression" pending the establishment of the new federal government, Henry proclaimed his affection for the Union, but in a manner not likely to quiet suspicions. "The first thing I have at heart is American liberty," he declared, and "the second thing is American union." Responding to Randolph's contention that since eight states had unconditionally ratified the Constitution it was too late for Virginia to require prior amendments without jeopardizing the Union, Henry was dismissive. That whole argument, he said, was a "bugbear," a bogeyman conjured up to frighten Virginians "into an inconsiderate adoption." Even if nine or all twelve of the other states agreed to operate under the terms of the new frame of government, it still would not matter, for Virginia could "refuse to join with those states," and by entering into an "amicable alliance" with them, it would suffer no ill effects. What exactly was the dreaded "consequence" then, Henry shrugged, "if we are disunited?"[21]

On June 9, Henry tried to backtrack a little in order to convince even the most skeptical of his critics that he was, as he had earlier declared, "a lover of the American Union." True friends of the Union, he said, would not "attempt to force" the Constitution "down men's throats, and call it union." Rather they would demonstrate their regard for the objections of "so respectable a body of men discontented in every state" and not insist on unconditional ratification. The way, then, to guarantee the unity of which he was "so fond," Henry said in response to Randolph's earlier tirade, would be for Virginia to propose changes to the Constitution. If the consequences of disunion were as dreadful as Randolph suggested, and "if disunion will really result from Virginia's proposing amendments," would not the ratifying states willingly "admit us, if not on such terms as we prescribe, yet on advantageous terms?" Assuming that Randolph was correct, "is not union as essential to their happiness as to ours?" Moments later, however, Henry further fanned the flames of Federalist suspi-

20. Edward Carrington to James Madison, February 10, 1788, *PJM*, 10:494.
21. Elliot, 3:57, 61–63.

cions by challenging Randolph's argument that the formation of "separate confederacies will ruin us." Quite possibly true, he conceded, but in comparison to the "absolute despotism" of a consolidated government, "small confederacies are little evils." If necessary, Virginia and North Carolina "could exist separated from the rest of America." The prospect was far from "desirable," but these two nonratifying states could be "joined together," conduct themselves as a separate confederation, and not be "swallowed up" by the United States.[22]

Dictatorial Demands or Humble Request?

At the very least, Henry's comments about the viability or desirability of "small confederacies" indicated that he, like most others, accepted the passing of the Confederation. Upon learning that the Massachusetts convention had ratified the Constitution, revelers in Boston set fire to a "leaky" longboat labeled the "Old Confederation," which had been condemned by a jury of carpenters as too "rotten" to be of "any further service." The eight ratifying states had similarly relegated the Articles of Confederation to the proverbial ash heap of history, and despite his protestations, Henry knew this to be true. He might "see great jeopardy in this new government" and speak approvingly of "our present one," but there was no hope of resurrecting the Union under the Articles. The only avenue open to Henry and all other opponents of ratification, therefore, was to try through well-placed amendments to remove the imperfections of the new government and thereby to render it as safe as the old.[23]

Supporters of unconditional ratification readily admitted that the Constitution was imperfect. "The warmest friends and the best supporters the Constitution has," Washington asserted, "do not contend that it is free from imperfections." The expectation of "perfection in any institute devised by man was as vain as the search for the philosopher's stone," declared Edmund Pendleton, the unanimously elected president of the convention. "In vain you will seek, from India to the pole, for a perfect constitution," emphasized James Innes, the state's attorney general and lone delegate from Williamsburg. An exasperated Zachariah Johnston scolded Henry and his cohorts for teasing "every word and syllable" of the text in a "strained" search for ambiguities or omissions. "This Constitution may have defects," he conceded, for there "can be no human institution without defects." In some place "out of this world" the situation might be different, said the self-described planter of the "middle rank," but the "annals of mankind do not show us one example of a perfect Constitution."[24]

22. Elliot, 3:57, 159, 161.
23. William Heath diary, February 8, 1788, *DHRC*, 7:1623; *Massachusetts Centinel*, February 13, 1788, *DHRC*, 7:1623–24; Elliot, 3:54.
24. Elliot, 3:303, 637; Bailyn, *Debate*, 2:754, 755.

Given this temporal reality, changes were inevitable. The question separating Federalists and Antifederalists, then, was not whether but when amendments should be proposed. As Madison predicted more than a month before the convention began, this would be the overriding issue in Richmond. By this time, the debate over specifics had already commenced, especially with the circulation in late 1787 of Mason's "Objections to this Constitution," described by Washington as part of a concerted effort to "alarm the people" and dismissed by Tuberville as foremost among all publications that "pretend to analyze this system," but, Madison wrote, the "preliminary question will be whether previous alterations shall be insisted on or not." Virginia could prescribe alterations as a condition of ratification, or it could ratify now and ask for amendments later.[25]

Madison much preferred the latter, unconditional ratification, as did every other Federalist of note. Like Randolph, he believed that an insistence on prior amendments would endanger both the "Constitution and the Union." On April 22, six weeks before he traveled to Richmond for the convention, Madison wrote Jefferson, "It is not to be expected that the states which have ratified will reconsider their determinations, and submit to the alterations prescribed by Virginia." Two months later, on June 24, in his last major address to the convention, Madison made the same point. Appealing to the good sense Virginians had demonstrated in the past, he asked the assembled delegates whether they thought the nine states that had adopted the Constitution after "freely and fully" considering the subject "will, upon the demand of a single state, agree that they acted wrong"? Absolutely not, answered James Innes, whom Madison identified as one of the "characters of most note" among the Federalists. "States are but an aggregate of individuals. Would not an individual spurn such a requisition?" Even discounting the likelihood that the ratifying states held sincerely to a belief in the soundness of their "most solemn deliberations," Innes argued, pride would cause them to resist such a demand. "We are as free, sister Virginia, and as independent, as you are; we do not like to be dictated to by you." Francis Corbin, whose "purest American principles" and "warmest" attachment to Virginia were, according to Randolph, unaffected by his Loyalist parents or his ten years of study in England, also bridled at the suggestion that Virginia could make demands of the ratifying states. "Had we adopted" the Constitution, "would we recede" from that decision just to "please the caprice of any other state? Pride, sir, revolts at the idea." In all of this, Federalists were merely stating what Randolph had said repeatedly. If

25. George Washington to James Madison, October 10, 1787, *PJM*, 10:190; James Madison to Thomas Jefferson, April 22, 1788, *Republic of Letters*, 1:534.

Virginia demanded that its amendments be adopted prior to ratification, contrary to the rules prescribed by the Federal Convention and acceded to by at least eight other states, the "spirit of Virginia would be dictatorial. Virginia dictates to eight states."[26]

Henry had heard all of these arguments before, beginning with Randolph's exculpatory speech on June 6, and remained unimpressed. How anyone could suggest that a call for prior amendments was "dictatorial" was a mystery to him. The Constitution is a compact, and "in a compact there are two parties—one accepting and the other proposing," explained Henry patiently, drawing on more than a quarter century of legal experience dealing with litigious creditors and debtors in ordinary civil suits. Only a fool, an absolute "lunatic," would "enter into a compact first, and afterwards settle the terms." It was an "insult [to] your judgments," therefore, for anyone to suggest "that you are first to sign and seal" the agreement and afterward bargain to amend it. The "absurdity" of such advice left him speechless. "I am at a loss what to say," he said, before continuing. Virginia, as "a party" contemplating entering into a compact with the eight or nine ratifying states, was proposing certain conditions, which they in turn were free to accept or reject. The "language" in question conveyed a "proposition" and was nearly identical in tone and intent to that used in recent communications. "We proposed that convention which met at Annapolis. It was not called dictatorial. We proposed that at Philadelphia. Was Virginia thought dictatorial?" On the contrary, Virginia's overtures on those occasions "met with a favorable reception." Before signing a compact that would bind Virginians in perpetuity, "have we not a right to say, Hear our propositions!" The poor, those in the "meanest occupations of human life," properly claimed such a right. "Why, sir, your slaves have a right to make their humble requests."[27]

Shall We Stand by Ourselves?

Henry was being more than a little disingenuous on June 24 in thus describing his take on prior amendments. Edward Carrington offered a contrasting and not entirely inaccurate description of Henry's disposition. "His language is, that the other states cannot do without us," Carrington explained, "and therefore we can dictate to them what terms we please." And in fact, beginning with his June 5 monologue, Henry conveyed an attitude in keeping with his assessment of Virginia as the "most mighty state in the union." That eight states had ratified the Constitution did not impress him, he said, because the "adopting

---

26. James Madison to Thomas Jefferson, April 22, 1788, *Republic of Letters*, 1:534; Elliot, 3:636, 113, 192; Edmund Randolph to James Madison, September 13, 1783, *PJM*, 7:316–17.
    27. Elliot, 3:174, 176, 588, 591, 596.

states can hardly stand on their own legs," let alone stand up to Virginia. Some
of them were already experiencing the "heart-burnings" usually associated
with buyer's remorse, and all would be overjoyed, given the enviable record of
Virginia's past contributions, "to be in confederacy with us." On June 24, the
penultimate day of debate, Henry persisted in the same vein, first saying he
would "make no comparison" between Virginia and the ratifying states but
then commenting that the "states which have adopted will not make a respectable appearance without us." William Grayson was even more demonstrative
in expressing this same arrogance. In an animated harangue delivered before a
receptive audience in his own Prince William County, Grayson held aloft a
snuffbox so tiny that the "point of finger and thumb" could only be "inserted
with difficulty" and announced, "You may think it of consequence that some
other states have accepted of the new Constitution." But "what are they?" An
insignificant coalition with the "paltry state of Pennsylvania & the still more
paltry estate of Delaware" as anchors. "When compared to Virginia they are
no more than this snuff box is to the size of a Man."[28]

Washington took a dim view of such pronouncements. To his nephew
Bushrod Washington, a delegate from Westmoreland County, he wrote, "I am
sorry . . . that Virginians entertain *too* high an opinion of the importance of
their country." Although Virginia "stands first in the Union," it cannot stand
apart from the other states, and therefore "it is not . . . more the interest of any
one of them to confederate, than it is the one in which we live." Edmund Pendleton also expressed dismay at the thought of alienating the ratifying states by
conveying the impression that "Virginia is too *important*" for them "to risk
separation by refusing her *reasonable* propositions." But no one spoke more often
or more forcefully about Virginia and the Union than Edmund Randolph. Posing the "hard question" of "whether Virginia, as contradistinguished from the
other states, can exist without the union," he answered simply, "she cannot."
Virginia was paramount among the states, and therefore "our rejection must
dissolve the Union," but the dissolution of the Union "will destroy our political
happiness" as well.[29]

Although his "respect for Virginia" was surpassed by "no man," Randolph
scoffed at the suggestion that the state was strong enough to thrive on its
own. To be sure, Virginia was preeminent, but "in the Union." Outside of the
Union, it was a different story. Alone, Virginia would be a tempting target for
France, Spain, and Britain. Without a navy, which would be too expensive to

28. Edward Carrington to James Madison, January 18, 1788, *PJM*, 10:383; Elliot, 3:62–63,
624–25; Maier, *Ratification*, 236; Hugh Williamson to John Grant, June 3, 1788, *DHRC*, 9:603–
4; John Vaughan to John Dickinson, c. April 19, 1788, *DHRC*, 9: 606–9.
29. George Van Cleve, *Slaveholders' Union: Slavery, Politics, and the Constitution in the Early
American Republic* (Chicago, 2010), 111; *DHRC*, 10:1624; Elliot, 3:67–68, 71.

build and maintain in readiness, and with a coastline offering easy "access of foes by sea," it was nearly impossible to defend the state "against invasions." Also, at its continental borders, Virginia would confront rival states no longer bound to it by the emotional ties of union. The "history of every part of the world" reveals that countries thus situated deteriorated rapidly into a "perpetual scene of bloodshed and slaughter." Within its borders, the state faced two more dire threats. "Cruel savages, your natural enemies," would wreak havoc in the west, where Virginians were "scattered thinly over so extensive a country." And the large population of slaves living in their midst was even more frightening. "Their number amounts to 236,000; that of whites only to 352,000." Those who were most familiar with the subject "think there is a cause of alarm in this case," Randolph opined in a classic bit of understatement. "I beg gentlemen to consider these things" before attaching conditions to the vote on ratification. "Shall we stand by ourselves and be severed from the Union?"[30]

Not a Virginian but an American Government

The day after Randolph's speech, Bushrod Washington reported to his famous uncle that "Mr. Henry's confidence in the power and greatness of Virginia, which he said she might rest upon though dismembered from her sister states was very well exposed" by the governor. Washington may have been glad to get the news, but he knew that Henry's confidence, though exposed, could not be shaken. More than any other Virginian, more than Washington or Jefferson or Madison, Henry thought of Virginia first. Almost invariably, his objections to the Constitution were coupled with a certain smug appeal to state pride. "Virginia has certain scruples" that prevented it from mindlessly joining the eight ratifying states. The "spirit of domestic peace" was best preserved by consulting the "humble genius of Virginia." The same "genius of Virginia" that triumphed over the British would now "lead us to happiness." Virginia's interests could not be protected whenever "the Representatives from Massachusetts, New Hampshire, Connecticut, &c. were against us." The "two petty states of Rhode Island and Delaware, which together are infinitely inferior to this state . . . have double her weight" in the Senate. "Virginia is now to lose her preeminence." And most revealingly with respect to the proposed Constitution: "This government is not a Virginian, but an American government."[31]

This Virginia-first perspective was at the root of Henry's drawn out exchanges regarding the Federalist claim that necessity was the mother of the

30. Elliot, 3:189, 72–73, 75, 77, 79, 68.
31. Bushrod Washington to George Washington, June 7, 1788, *DHRC*, 10:1581; Elliot, 3:61, 161, 162, 596, 55.

convention. He rejected the very suggestion that the feebleness of the Confederation government, or its utter "imbecility" in the face of domestic disturbances, as Pendleton put it, was behind the creation of an entirely new federal structure. Not turmoil or insecurity but "a general peace, and a universal tranquility prevailed in this country" until the meeting of the Philadelphia Convention, asserted Henry. "Our situation, sir," was nothing short of idyllic. "Go to the poor man, and ask him what he does. He will inform you that he enjoys the fruits of his labor, under his own fig-tree, with his wife and children around him, in peace and security. Go to every other member of society, you will find the same tranquil ease and content." In other words, the alarms sounded by the proponents of the Constitution were not activated by "real, actual, existing danger." Rather, they were triggered by "imaginary" fears, not the sort that "we may see and touch."[32]

Pendleton could not believe he was hearing such blather coming from such a "worthy friend." Was the public mind really "at ease" before the Federal Convention met in 1787? If it was, it must have been in an "unaccountable stupor." The Confederation was rife with "political diseases": commerce was "decayed," finances were "deranged," revenue requisitions were ignored, public and private credit was "destroyed," foreign relations were "ineffectual," and prescriptions for improvement were "interrupted." These and numerous other crippling "national evils" too clearly proved that the old Confederation was "totally inadequate." In fact, if a government's sole reason for being was to promote the "happiness and security of the people," then the system set up by the Articles was the equivalent of "no government at all." And if the public appeared now to be unsettled, it was not because of the proposed Constitution. The delegates in Philadelphia concocted a "remedy" for a preexisting condition. Only the most "inactive" mind agitated by "mistaken apprehensions" would prefer the "repose" of the Confederation to the promise of the Constitution.[33]

Henry, it would seem, was clueless, although his mind was neither inactive nor in a stupor. How could he paint such a rosy picture, if he was fully aware of the nation's afflictions and the need to treat them? The answer is that Henry was first and foremost a Virginia patriot. He never tired of extolling the sacrifices and accomplishments of his "country," but his country, as Richard Beeman, one of Henry's ablest biographers, has said, "was Virginia, not America." His references to "this country" and "our situation," applied to Virginia and Virginians, not to America and Americans. "Where is the danger? I see none," he asked and answered. To be sure, "disorders have arisen in other parts of America, but here, Sir, no dangers, no insurrection or tumult, has happened." Shaysites

---

32. Elliot, 3:38, 54, 48; Bailyn, *Debate,* 2:681, 595, 597.
33. Elliot, 3:35, 36, 38.

had defied the dominion of laws in western Massachusetts, but "has there been a single tumult in Virginia?" When Francis Corbin, who said his regard for Henry was second to none, nevertheless challenged his portrayal of pre-1787 tranquility by describing the appearance of "ruin and decay everywhere," Henry was unforgiving. "Why did it please the gentleman" from Middlesex County "to bestow such epithets on our country?" That Corbin was describing the "distresses" of "the country" rather than "our country" did not seem to register with Henry. "I consider such epithets to be the most illiberal and unwarrantable aspersions on our laws." Henry's poor man in perfect repose was resting under a Virginia fig tree.[34]

Henry concluded his June 5 address with a reference to this Virginia-first attitude. "When I speak, I speak the language of thousands," he declared. But claiming to be the voice of thousands in a nation of three and a half million would be a modest boast, and while Henry possessed many admirable qualities, modesty was not high among them. Accuracy was, however, especially when it came to calculations based on population. He opposed the amendment procedure described under Article 5 of the Constitution, for example, because it required the assent of three-fourths of the state legislatures for validation. Henry found it unacceptable that the "four smallest states," collectively comprising less than "one tenth part of the population of the United States, may obstruct the most salutary and necessary amendments." He was wrong to couple size and shared interests, but Henry's population estimate was on the mark. With a combined total of approximately 350,000 inhabitants, New Hampshire, Rhode Island, Delaware, and Georgia accounted for about 10 percent of the American people. In short, Henry knew his numbers. When he said he spoke for "thousands," he meant Virginians only, and that was more than enough for him.[35]

Wythe versus Henry

On Saturday, June 21, the convention ended its haphazard clause-by-clause consideration of the new federal plan by briefly discussing the paragraph in Section 3 of Article 4 pertaining to the admission of new states and then reading through the "remainder of the Constitution." The next day, Madison informed Rufus King, who was "extremely obliged" to receive any word on the proceedings in Virginia, that the work of the Richmond convention was approaching its end. King had conveyed in no uncertain terms the "real anxiety experienced in Massachusetts concerning your decision," and Madison tried to

34. Beeman, *Patrick Henry*, 156–57; Richard Beeman, *Plain, Honest Men: The Making of the American Constitution* (New York, 2009), 396; Bailyn, *Debate*, 2:597; Elliot, 3:48, 104–5, 163.
35. Elliot, 3:63.

alleviate some of the distress by reporting that his "calculations promise us a majority of 3 or 4, possibly 5 or 6." And yet the projected margin of victory was "so small" and the task of evaluating "so great a number of opinions" so problematic that Madison said he "dare not" predict the outcome of the final vote. Questioning the depth of Henry's commitment to the Union undoubtedly helped the forces of ratification because, as Madison noted, there were "too many moderate and respectable characters" even among the generality of Antifederalists to allow talk of "secession" to gain much traction beyond Henry's immediate circle. But additional incentives needed to be factored into an appeal to the broad spectrum of undecideds. And given the ubiquity of references to the subject, either directly during prolonged exchanges or by implication in nearly every debate, the prospect of amendments would have to loom large in such an appeal.[36]

When the delegates reconvened on Tuesday morning, June 24, George Wythe, who was described by a contemporary as "confessedly one of the most learned legal characters of the present age" and who in 1760 had refused to sign Patrick Henry's license to practice law in Virginia, took the floor first. In a voice "so very low that his speech could not be fully comprehended," Wythe read a motion calling for an unconditional ratification of the Constitution. He briefly described the defects of the Confederation government and the resulting "misfortunes suffered by the people." Wythe conceded that the proposed Constitution was itself not free of "imperfections," but he advocated a wait-and-see approach, as "experience was the best guide" when it came to the "propriety of amendments." If experience revealed specific changes were necessary, they "would be easily obtained *after ratification*" in the manner stipulated under Article 5 of the Constitution. In an obvious attempt to capture some undecided votes, Wythe's motion included a general statement of the principle: first, because the people were the source of all power vested in the government, they were entitled to revoke such grants to offset any injury or oppression; and second, the people reserved to themselves all powers not expressly delegated. Additionally, the preamble to Wythe's motion mentioned liberty of conscience, freedom of the press, and trial by jury as three inviolable rights of the people.[37]

Henry was sitting close enough to Wythe to hear what the learned lawyer was proposing, and he did not like what he was hearing. Labeling Wythe's call for ratification "premature," Henry said the importance of the subject demanded the "most mature deliberation" on the part of the delegates. They should not be hurried into voting, certainly not by one who "admits that the new system is defective." After restating his objections to what he perceived to

---

36. Rufus King to James Madison, May 25, 1788, *PJM*, 11:57; James Madison to Rufus King, June 22, 1788, *PJM*, 11: 167.
37. Farrand 3:94; Elliot, 3:586–87.

be the lunacy of the ratify now and ask for amendments later argument, ridiculing Wythe's singling out of only "three great rights" for protection, and challenging the notion that amendments were easily obtained under Article 5, Henry countered with a proposal of his own. Comprising a declaration of rights and some twenty "amendments to the most exceptionable parts of the Constitution," Henry's alternative resolution was the most recent incarnation of a proposal drafted on or before June 9 by an Antifederalist committee under Mason's direction. Unlike Wythe's motion, Henry said his proposal protected all of the "unalienable rights" governments were instituted to secure. Henry concluded with a hope that "his resolution would be adopted," but his closing appeal came with a warning that if the convention adopted Wythe's resolution instead of his, he was prepared to "go home" and "act as I think my duty requires."[38]

Randolph rose next, somewhat reluctantly and "perhaps" for the "last time," he said, and quickly launched into a criticism of Henry for his "sad reverse" to a threat to "secede." Henry interrupted to deny "having said anything of secession." He meant only that "he would have no hand in subsequent amendments" and therefore intended to return home because he "would have no business here" if the convention voted to ratify unconditionally. But Randolph, who had asked to be corrected if he managed somehow to "misrecite" Henry, ignored the clarification coming from this "honorable gentleman." Saying simply, "I see . . . I am not mistaken in my thoughts," Randolph continued with his "remarks on the subject of secession." Henry's proposal for prior amendments was "but another name" for rejecting the Constitution, he reasoned, and a rejection "will throw Virginia out of the Union." In other words, Virginia will have effectively seceded from the ratifying states, and the "dogs of war will break loose" in the wake of this disruption of the Union.[39]

A "violent storm" cut short Henry's second speech of the afternoon. Years later, unabashed Henry admirers would claim that the storm "shook the whole building," as though the "celestial beings" whom he had summoned to his side with an oration unsurpassed "in any age or country in the world" were announcing their arrival. In truth, Henry's second speech was mediocre in comparison to most of his earlier efforts, or indeed, somewhat pedestrian even when judged by the standards applied to mere mortals. And if the "spirits" had come to do "his bidding," what their interruption accomplished instead was to speed up the convention's business, contrary to Henry's call for more time for mature deliberation. After the storm had passed, George Nicholas rose immediately and moved that the final question be taken at 9:00 a.m. the next morning.

38. Elliot, 3:587, 593; *PGM*, 3:1115–18.
39. Elliot, 3:586–87, 588, 591, 593, 597, 603.

William Ronald opposed the motion, but not because he agreed with Henry that it was premature. He only "wished amendments to be prepared by a committee before the question should be put," for without such a list of proposed amendments, he would have to "vote against this Constitution." Three things were soon apparent about Ronald's objection to Wythe's motion. First, although he had seen both Wythe's preamble and Henry's specific formulation of amendments, he refused to declare himself "for or against" either of them. Second, although formally undecided, Ronald indicated that he wanted to vote for the Constitution. If the absence of amendments forced him to vote otherwise, it would be "much against my inclination," he said. Third, Ronald seemed not to care whether the amendments he demanded were made "previous or subsequent" to ratification, preferring to leave that decision to the majority of the committee of the whole. In short, Ronald, from Antifederalist Powhatan County in Mr. Henry's neighborhood, was precisely the sort of moderate Madison had alluded to earlier.[40]

Hand in Hand with Massachusetts

Fortunately for Madison and the other proponents of ratification, there was a ready-made means of winning over men like Ronald. As early as June 7, when the convention was supposed to be focusing on the first two sections of Article 1 but found it impossible to avoid prolonging the debate over the merits and methods of amending the Constitution, Francis Corbin proposed a solution that he thought might satisfy those seeking a respectable middle ground between conditional and unconditional ratification. "My idea is that we should go hand in hand with Massachusetts," said the Middlesex County Federalist whose affection for Virginia was beyond reproach. Ratify the Constitution "first, and then propose amendments," as Massachusetts had done. The combination of these two states, "the two most populous, wealthy, and powerful states in the Union," would be irresistible. With Massachusetts "commanding the north" and Virginia "the south," the chances of "carrying any amendments" in the first federal Congress were better than good. Would any state be so bold as to reject their recommendations? "Would any gentleman turn a deaf ear to their solicitations?"[41]

Madison was well acquainted with the actions taken in Massachusetts and ultimately approved of them, but not without some misgivings. Although he was glad to learn that the recommendatory amendments introduced by John Hancock had served to "brighten" the prospects of ratification in a closely

40. William Wirt, *Sketches of the Life and Character of Patrick Henry* (Philadelphia, 1817), quoted in *DHRC*, 10:1511; Elliot, 3:625–26.
41. Elliot, 3:113.

contested convention, Madison wished they could have been "dispensed with." Hancock's amendments were a "blemish," a stain on the document crafted in Philadelphia, he told Washington in February, after the Boston convention had voted for ratification. Two considerations, however, had persuaded him to endorse such a course of action: the amendments were cast in the "least offensive form" and, in the end, were "the means of saving the Constitution from all risk in Massachusetts." Four months later, anticipating a close vote in Richmond, Madison told Rufus King, the Newburyport delegate who had been his principal informant in matters relating to the Boston convention, that Virginia Federalists were contemplating following the Massachusetts example. They were thinking, Madison wrote, clearly aware of the resolution Wythe was preparing, of prefacing their motion to ratify "with a declaration of a few obvious truths which cannot affect the validity of the act, and to follow it with a recommendation of a few amendments to be pursued in the constitutional mode" specified under Article 5. "This expedient is necessary to conciliate some individuals who are in general well affected," for example, Powhatan's William Ronald, "but have certain scruples drawn from their own reflections, or from the temper of their constituents." It was also "judged prudent" to make a show of "so exemplary a fairness on our part, (and even in some points to give way to unreasonable pretensions)" in order to court favor with the few remaining undecideds while countering a preconceived plan by Henry and other Antifederalists to "bring forward a bill of rights with sundry other amendments as conditions of ratification." To Alexander Hamilton on June 22, Madison offered the same rationale, adding that reservations about recommendatory amendments notwithstanding, "expedients are rendered prudent by the nice balance of numbers" in the Richmond convention.[42]

A More Perfect Constitution

On June 25, George Nicholas opened the morning session, as he had indicated he would, with a motion to vote on Wythe's resolution. There was no need for more debate. The new plan of government "being now fully discussed," he said, any further postponement of the final question would serve no purpose except to promote the "cause of those who wish to destroy the Constitution." Antifederalist John Tyler of Charles City rose in response and moved that the delegates be given the opportunity to vote on Henry's alternative proposal. The debate that followed seemed to validate Nicholas's assertion that "no more time" should be spent airing familiar arguments. Patrick Henry had nothing new to say but at least he said it well. Wythe's proposal was simply a ploy "to

42. James Madison to George Washington, February 8 and 15, 1788, *PJM*, 10:482, 510; James Madison to Rufus King, June 22, 1788, *PJM*, 11:166; James Madison to Alexander Hamilton, June 22, 1788, *PJM*, 11:167.

lull our apprehensions," he warned. One look at the amendments contained in his motion should be sufficient to convince an impartial observer that "they mean nothing serious." Wythe presented pabulum to please the palate of the unsuspecting while leaving "many essential and vital rights" unprotected. From this it was possible to infer the real intent of his amendments, which was "to defeat every attempt to amend." His motion deserved to be rejected, therefore, as merely the final manifestation of the tortured reasoning of those making the "ridiculous" case for subsequent amendments. "I speak in plain, direct language," Henry apologized half-heartedly, because "it is extorted from me."[43]

Of the remaining speakers on this last day of debate, James Innes probably created the greatest stir. Innes first chided the proponents of prior amendments for their inconsistency. Reprising Henry's opening objection, in which he accused the delegates to the Federal Convention of having exceeded the explicit terms of their commissions when they abandoned the Articles of Confederation without consulting their constituents, Innes demanded to know what authority allowed them now to propose a conditional ratification of the Constitution. The people had sent them to Richmond "to adopt or reject" the new plan. "Have we more latitude on this subject?" Have the people been "consulted" with regard to "amendments as the previous condition of our adoption?" Have they been given an "opportunity of considering previous amendments?" If the response to any of these questions was no, the convention would "transcend and violate the commission of the people" by approving Henry's motion. The same could not be said of Wythe's proposed amendments because, Innes explained in response to John Tyler's query, "being only recommendatory in their nature, [they] could be reviewed by the people before they would become a part of the system."[44]

Innes made a deeper impression on the minds of the undecideds when he went on to condemn the "spirit of jealousy" directed against "our *northern brethren*" by many Antifederalists. Insisting that the sections had separate and incompatible interests, the Virginia-firsters in particular warned that the temporary majority held by northerners would allow them to monopolize trade, surrender navigation rights on the Mississippi River, and, most fearfully, abolish slavery and "fetter and manacle the hands of the southern people." Such dire predictions, however, flew in the face of past experience. "It was not a Virginian, Carolinian, or Pennsylvanian, but the glorious name of an American," declared Innes, that "enabled us to triumph over our enemies." Furthermore, if "our existence as a nation depends on our union," what would possess northerners to "adopt measures" that would "produce discontents, and terminate in

43. Elliot, 3:627, 649–50.   44. Elliot, 3:6, 632–33; Bailyn, *Debate*, 2:597.

a dissolution of a union as necessary to their happiness as to ours?" Would not the logic of self-interest alone move them to promote the "great principles of reciprocal friendship and mutual amity . . . so as to conciliate all parts of the Union?" To suppose otherwise "would be to suppose them to be not only destitute of honor and probity, but void of reason—not only bad, but mad men."[45]

Innes concluded by simply and concisely defining the alternatives open to the delegates. They had to choose between adopting or rejecting the Constitution. Previous amendments "are equal to a rejection," which would be highly "imprudent, destructive, and calamitous." Because they portended nothing less than the disruption of the Union, Innes pronounced conditional amendments to be "the greatest of evils." Recommendatory amendments, on the other hand, signified adoption with an expectation that the first federal Congress consider certain alterations in accordance with the provisions set in Article 5. There were no guarantees, of course, but there was no invitation to disunion either. "Let us try it; experience is the best test," advised Innes. To be sure, the Constitution was not perfect, but it was "more perfect" than any other plan that "can be obtained at this time."[46]

A Small Majority and the Wythe Committee

Patrick Henry was impressed by Innes's performance. "Great eloquence," he exclaimed, "eloquence splendid, magnificent and sufficient to shake the human mind!" How many minds were shaken is unknown, but in a nearly evenly divided convention just one conversion among the "undecided few" would have been important. On the eve of the convention vote on June 25, Madison informed his brother Ambrose that the "final question is likely to be decided by a very small majority." Although the "friends of the government seem to be in the best spirits," neither side could afford to be complacent. A slight miscalculation of the numbers or mere "accidents" could affect the outcome. Thus Madison took some satisfaction in the fact that "two members on that side," Notley Conn of Bourbon County and Thomas Pierce of Isle of Wight County, had left Richmond "with a purpose of returning" in time to vote but were "still absent."[47]

Despite his uneasiness, Madison hoped the final vote would support the "best reason" for optimism. He would not be disappointed. Late in the afternoon on June 25, the committee of the whole presented a modified version of Wythe's motion to the convention, recommending ratification with "whatsoever

---

45. Elliot, 3:633–34.
46. Elliot, 3:637.
47. Robert Allen Rutland, *The Ordeal of the Constitution: The Antifederalists and the Ratification Struggle of 1787–1788* (1966; repr., Boston: Northeastern University Press, 1983), 249; James Madison to Ambrose Madison, June 24, 1788, *PJM*, 11:170–71.

amendments may be deemed necessary" to be forwarded to the first Congress. Henry's followers moved quickly to amend the motion, essentially gutting the original and replacing it with a call for amendments "previous to the ratification of the new Constitution." Following established procedures, the question on the amended motion came up first. It failed by a margin of eight votes, with eighty delegates in favor of it and eighty-eight opposed. The convention next took up the original motion and adopted it on a vote of eighty-nine to seventy-nine. The roll call on the second question was nearly the exact opposite of the first. Of the 168 delegates present for both, only David Patteson from Chesterfield County in Henry country, switched sides, having voted for the amended motion and, after its defeat, voting for the motion to ratify.[48]

Before adjourning on June 25, the convention created a committee of twenty to draft the recommendatory amendments to accompany the convention's official notice of ratification to the Confederation Congress. Probably anticipating some difficulties, it appointed eleven Federalists, led by Wythe as chair and including Madison, Randolph, John Marshall, and Innes as members. Among the nine Antifederalists, however, sat Henry and Mason, and it was soon apparent that the committee would bend to their will "in order to relieve," as the first resolution of the motion to ratify put it, "the apprehensions of those who may be solicitous for amendments." This became evident to all after Wythe submitted the committee's report to the convention on June 27.[49]

The Wythe committee's recommended amendments, according to David Robertson, the "short hand gentleman" responsible for recording the proceedings of the convention, "were nearly the same as those" contained in Henry's June 24 motion. The first twenty constituted a declaration of rights and, like Henry's defeated proposal, were based almost entirely on the document prepared earlier by Mason's Antifederalist committee. Thirteen items in the Wythe report were identical to those in Mason's declaration. The remaining seven also tracked closely to the original, with deletions of certain passages or phrases principally altering the scope of the rights protected. For example, the June 9 declaration stipulated that "no particular religious sect or society of Christians ought to be favored or established by law in preference to others." The Wythe committee deleted the words "of Christians" from that sentence, thus extending the "free exercise of religion" to other believers.[50]

This declaration of rights could, if adopted by two-thirds of both houses of Congress and ratified by three-fourths of the states, be attached to the proposed Constitution without altering either its substance or arrangement. By contrast, the second group of twenty amendments dealt with specific provisions and

48. Elliot, 3:653–55.
50. DHRC, 9:819–21, 10:1551–53.

49. Elliot, 3:653, 656; DHRC, 10:1514.

clauses in the Constitution itself and thus entailed changes that would have affected the structure and operation of the federal government. But even here, the Wythe committee relied heavily on Henry's motion and work done by the Mason committee. Nine of the twenty structural amendments came directly from these Antifederalist proposals. That all eleven of the new recommendations drew their inspiration from the convention debates hardly comes as a surprise. That nearly all of them catered to the concerns raised by the Antifederalists and reflected their preferred remedies may be more surprising. Why would Federalists, who were in the majority on the committee, have agreed to forward recommendatory amendments that limited the federal government's taxing powers, modified its control over state militias, curtailed its legislative authority over a federal district that would be the seat of the government of the United States, and minimized its supervision of the times, places, and manner of electing senators and representatives? What could have persuaded them to go along with recommendations to require the consent of two-thirds of both houses of Congress to enact commercial legislation or three-fourths of all members of Congress to conclude treaties affecting the navigation of American rivers?[51]

Compromise

James Madison clearly disliked the "recommendatory alterations." He had dismissed as "improper and inadmissible" similar structural amendments contained in Henry's June 24 motion. The Constitution, he declared, was "infinitely more safe in its present form, than it would be after introducing into it that long train of alterations." And a declaration of rights, he consistently argued, was "unnecessary and dangerous." Unnecessary because the "general government had no power but what was given it," and dangerous because rights not enumerated would appear to be unprotected. Madison repeated these sentiments to Hamilton on June 27, shortly after the Wythe committee had presented its report to the convention. He found many of the committee's recommendations "highly objectionable," Madison wrote, and none more so than the proposal to allow the federal government to "lay direct taxes" only in those states that failed to meet their revenue quotas. But "it was impossible to prevent this error," Madison apologized, sensing that Hamilton, who warned that "too much facility in the business of amendment-making" threatened to leave the Constitution "wounded in some of its vital parts," might otherwise be sorely disappointed to learn that he had a hand in drafting the amendments that came from the Wythe committee.[52]

---

51. *DHRC*, 9:821–23, 10:1553–56.
52. *PJM*, 11:174, 175; Elliot, 3:626; James Madison to Alexander Hamilton, June 27, 1788, *PJM*, 11:181; Alexander Hamilton to James Madison, July 8, 1788, *PJM*, 11:186.

What made these recommendatory amendments impossible to prevent for Madison and most other Federalists was the conviction on their part that some of the "flaming opposers of the Federal System" were planning to continue to oppose the Constitution long after the convention adjourned sine die. Led by Mason, they had spearheaded a meeting of the minority after the June 25 vote, "ostensibly to prepare an address to reconcile the minds of their constituents to the new plan of government." The real purpose of the meeting, however, was to secure the attendees' approval of a "fiery, irritating manifesto" read by Mason, which aimed to exacerbate existing divisions within the state. Madison was aware of many of these events transpiring between June 25 and June 27, that is, simultaneously with the meetings of the Wythe committee. He knew that the leaders of the minority were preparing "an address to the people." He knew that the "announced" purpose of the address was to encourage an acceptance of the "result of the convention." But he also knew that there was enough "ill will to the Constitution" still percolating through the ranks of "the leaders on that side" to move them to countenance "every peaceable effort to disgrace & destroy it." Thus he suspected that the address they would present at the impending gathering of the minority would be more combative than conciliatory. This would explain why he reported to Washington that "highly objectionable" alterations resembling those proposed by Henry in his June 24 motion "could not be parried" in the Wythe committee without inflaming the hostility of an influential cadre of Antifederalists.[53]

The concessions made by Madison and the Federalist majority on the Wythe committee did the trick. Wythe submitted the recommendatory amendments on June 27, including a closing statement enjoining Virginia's representatives in Congress "to exert all their influence and use all reasonable and legal methods to obtain a RATIFICATION of the foregoing alterations" and to ensure that all laws "passed in the mean time" conformed to the "spirit of these amendments as far as the said Constitution will admit." Later that evening, the "very full meeting" of the minority refused to endorse Mason's manifesto. Benjamin Harrison, one of the nine Antifederalists on the Wythe committee, reportedly took the lead in opposing Mason's address. Harrison, who two days earlier had condemned the motion to ratify with recommendatory amendments as "unwarrantable, precipitate, and dangerously impolitic," now advised against "taking any farther steps in the business" of upending the Constitution. John Tyler, another Antifederalist member of the committee, had broken his silence before the vote on June 25 in order "to hand down to posterity" his opposition to a system whose predicted pattern of operation caused him to "tremble" for his country. But

53. *Virginia Independent Chronicle,* July 9, 1788 DHRC, 10:1560–61; *Massachusetts Centinel,* July 26, 1788, DHRC, 10:1561; James Madison to Alexander Hamilton, June 27, 1788, *PJM,* 11:181–82; James Madison to George Washington, June 27, 1788, *PJM,* 11:182.

he "so successfully" endorsed Harrison's "opinion" on the evening of June 27 that Mason was forced "prudently and with temper" to withdraw his address.[54]

Henry himself, according to an account written at least three years after the event, resisted the call of the "*discontents*." Although he accepted their invitation "to take the chair" of the minority assembly, he did so only to waylay a concerted "plan of resistance to the operations of the Federal Government." Addressing the audience with his "accustomed animation," Henry explained that he had done his level best "in opposing the Constitution, in the *proper place*." Regrettably, the convention went against him in the end, but since the question was "fully discussed" and fairly "settled," he felt compelled to support the new government and urged all "true and faithful republicans" to do the same and to "go home!" Because this account was based on the recollections of an avowed admirer of "the venerated patriot," it may have exaggerated the "impressive arguments of Mr. Henry." Madison, by contrast, identified Henry as one of the leaders of the conspiracy that attempted "to induce the minority to sign" the inflammatory document Mason read before the gathering on June 27. But Henry's last words to the convention did in fact resemble those of the anecdotal account. "If I shall be in the minority," he announced June 25, "I shall have those painful sensations which arise from a conviction of *being overpowered in a good cause*. Yet I will be a peaceable citizen" and "patiently wait" while seeking to render the new federal government "compatible with the safety, liberty, and happiness of the people" by addressing its defects "in a constitutional way."[55]

Madison was skeptical, altering crucial parts of Henry's message in the retelling, so that in his letter to Hamilton, "peaceable citizen" became "quiet citizen" and "patiently wait" became "wait with impatience." Nevertheless, even Madison had Henry declaring his intention to seek changes "in a *constitutional way*." It is not inconceivable, therefore, that he would have opposed a churlish minority address, if for no other reason than the belief that it would alienate the "general moderation of the party," which it did. According to one spectator at the minority assembly, "a number of that respectable body immediately withdrew" after Mason delivered his fiery message, while "others for some time either remained in silence, or, in general terms recommended temper and moderation." Henry was a more skillful practitioner of the art of politics than Mason or the other leaders of the discontented. He knew exactly what he needed to do to salvage the situation. He accepted a seat on the Wythe committee on June 25, a day after announcing "he would have no hand in

54. *DHRC*, 10:1556, 1560–61; Elliot, 3:626, 637, 629.
55. *DHRC*, 10:1561–62; James Madison to Thomas Jefferson, July 24, 1788, *PJM*, 11:196–97; Elliot, 3:652.

subsequent amendments." In committee he pushed for the amendments he had presented with his June 24 motion, knowing that his chances of success were greatly improved by Mason's nearly transparent maneuvering for a meeting of the minority. After the convention adopted the Wythe report, he returned home to act as "duty requires." Since the report instructed Virginia's congressional delegation to ensure that all federal legislation conformed to the "spirit of these amendments," Henry felt justified in impeding the progress of the new government until the sort of alterations recommended by the committee were ratified. Madison had won the war but the compromise left Henry free to contest the terms of the peace.[56]

56. James Madison to Alexander Hamilton, June 27, 1788, *PJM*, 11:182; James Madison to Alexander Hamilton, July 24, 1788, *PJM*, 11: 197; Elliot, 3:597, 593; *DHRC*, 10:1556; Beeman, *Patrick Henry*, 167.

CHAPTER FIVE

New York Joins the Union

Opponents of ratification in New York were deeply interested in the proceedings at Richmond. As early as May 8, nearly a month before the opening of the Virginia convention, George Clinton, the decidedly Antifederalist governor of New York, wrote to Virginia governor Edmund Randolph to suggest that their respective state conventions "hold a Communication" during debates over the proposed "great change of government." Clinton assumed, based on Randolph's refusal to sign the document in Philadelphia, that his Virginia counterpart shared his misgivings about the Constitution. He "received a shock," therefore, upon learning that Randolph was a leading supporter of ratification and that his letter was not seen by the delegates in Richmond until June 26, the day after they had voted to ratify. Randolph's inaction, however, did not materially impede opposition efforts at coordination. John Lamb, chairman of the Federal Republican Committee of New York, contacted Patrick Henry, George Mason, and William Grayson in late May, about two weeks after Clinton had sent his letter to Randolph, seeking "to form an union with our friends." On behalf of their own "Committee of Opposition," all three Virginians responded positively to this overture of "our northern Friends," especially because it invited, as Mason wrote, "a free correspondence on the subject of amendments." With his return letter, Mason accordingly enclosed a copy of the alterations to the Constitution that his Antifederalist committee was in the process of completing—the same set of proposed amendments that would form the basis of Henry's June 24 motion.[1]

By the time Lamb received the responses of the Virginians, the New York ratifying convention had begun its deliberations in Poughkeepsie, and Lamb made a point of circulating Mason's letter and enclosure among the delegates "who are in sentiment with him." The chairman of the convention's Antifederalist committee, Robert Yates, saw the documents and wrote to Mason, informing him that his members were "happy to find that your sentiments with respect to the amendments correspond so nearly with ours." Yates, it will be

1. *DHRC*, 9:791–92; Edward Carrington to James Madison, June 17, 1788, *PJM*, 11:149; William Grayson to John Lamb, June 9, 1788, *DHRC*, 9:816; Patrick Henry to John Lamb, June 9, 1788, *DHRC*, 9:817; and George Mason to John Lamb, June 9, 1788, *DHRC*, 9:818–23.

recalled, was one of the two New York delegates—John Lansing was the other—who had left Philadelphia in "disgust" in early July 1787, after it became clear that the Federal Convention had decided irreversibly to abandon rather than to augment the Articles of Confederation. Not surprisingly, he found the Constitution unacceptable "without previous amendments." Nevertheless, Yates would not be pursuing a more formal policy of cooperation between the opponents of ratification at the two conventions because, he explained on June 21, the decision in Virginia was too "doubtful" and the outcome in New York was a foregone conclusion.[2]

Yates was of course correct about the situation at Richmond. He knew from Henry's letter to Lamb that the "numbers in convention appear equal on both sides; so that the majority which way soever it goes will be small." Mason's letter added that although there was a "general concurrence" on the necessity of amendments, the delegates were "so equally divided with respect to the time and manner of obtaining them, that it cannot now be ascertained whether the majority will be on our side or not." Grayson described a state of affairs "suspended by a hair," making it impossible, he told Lamb, to predict "on which side the scale will turn." Yates's reluctance to establish formal lines of communication with Virginia, however, involved more than the doubtful outcome of the deliberations in Richmond. Although the New York delegates had been in Poughkeepsie a mere four days at the time of his letter, Yates thought it likely they would quickly settle the question of ratification, so quickly that it would be pointless to correspond with the Virginians. "We will complete our determinations before we could avail ourselves of your advice," Yates told Mason. Why was he so casually dismissive?[3]

Going on Very Deliberately

The confidence Yates exuded was a reflection of the impressive Antifederalist majority in the Poughkeepsie convention. Unlike their colleagues in Virginia and Massachusetts, or any other state for that matter, opponents of the Constitution in New York possessed what appeared to be an insurmountable numerical advantage. Forty-six of the sixty-five convention delegates were Antifederalists. And because organized partisan activities, including the identification of political affiliation as "Federalist" or "Antifederalist" by candidates standing for election as delegates, was more pronounced in New York than anywhere else, this Antifederalist majority seemed solid. A disappointed Hamilton reported to Madison that the election results were "beyond expectation favorable to the

2. Robert Yates to George Mason, June 21, 1788, *PGM*, 3:1111–12.
3. Patrick Henry to John Lamb, June 9, 1788, *DHRC*, 9:817; George Mason to John Lamb, June 9, 1788 *DHRC*, 9:818; William Grayson to John Lamb, June 9, 1788, *DHRC*, 9: 816; Robert Yates to George Mason, June 21, 1788, *PGM*, 3:1111.

Antifederal party" and that they consequently enjoyed a commanding "majority of two-thirds in the convention." On its first day of business, the convention elected Governor Clinton as its president. According to Hamilton, Clinton's opposition to the Constitution was so "inflexibly obstinate" that it was immune to "reason." And yet the vote for Clinton was unanimous. The next day, as if to prove a point, the Antifederalist majority flexed its muscles again. When Federalists expressed a desire to have Richard Morris, the chief justice of the state supreme court, serve as chairman of the committee of the whole, they were told that Henry Oothoudt, Albany County judge and member of the county's Antifederal committee, was the choice of the majority. The Federalist delegates "acquiesced without opposition," John Lansing noted, and Oothoudt was "unanimously elected" to preside over the convention whenever it sat as a committee. In this case, as in the earlier election of Clinton, the Federalists were forced to submit because they knew, Lansing observed smugly, that "opposition would be vain."[4]

Lansing's gloating may have been mean spirited, but the nineteen Federalists in the New York convention were in trouble and desperately needed outside help. Their only hope of success was to delay the final vote on ratification until Virginia had decided. As Hamilton told Madison on June 25, the second week of the proceedings at Poughkeepsie and the second day devoted to the first two paragraphs of Article 1, Section 3, on the election of senators, "We are going on very deliberately in the discussion" of the Constitution in anticipation of the outcome at Richmond primarily because "our chance of success here is infinitely slender, and none at all if you go wrong." New Hampshire voted to ratify on June 21, and most New Yorkers knew this by the time of Hamilton's letter, but staunch Antifederalists were not inclined to make any concessions as a result of the actions taken at Concord. "The news of the adoption of New Hampshire does not seem to make an impression [and] I expect it will not," declared Chairman Oothoudt. "The Federalists here plume themselves much on the accession of New Hampshire," Abraham G. Lansing observed more derisively, and "we congratulate them" in the hope that "they can now give the new system an experiment without interfering in the politics of the state of New York." But even Lansing, one of the leaders of a very active group of Antifederalists in Albany County, recognized that an affirmative decision in "Virginia will have a more serious affect . . . upon the spirits and determinations of our friends."[5]

4. Alexander Hamilton to James Madison, May 19 and June 8, 1788, *PJM*, 11:53, 99; John Lansing Jr., to Abraham Yates Jr., June 19, 1788, *DHRC*, 22:1702.

5. Alexander Hamilton to James Madison, June 25, 1788, *PJM*, 11:179; Henry Oothoudt to Abraham Yates Jr., June 27, 1788, *DHRC*, 23:2355; Abraham G. Lansing to Abraham Yates Jr., June 29, 1788, *DHRC*, 21:1235.

If Federalists were in a bind because, as Hamilton acknowledged in his letter to Madison, "our only chance of success depends on you," it made sense for them to play for time in Poughkeepsie and "take the chance of events." What appears less commonsensical is the willingness of the Antifederalists to play along. They had much to lose and little or nothing to gain by waiting on Virginia. With a better than two to one advantage, New York Antifederalists did not need the assistance of a negative vote at Richmond. A positive vote there, however, would hurt their cause. John Lansing appreciated the risks. "I apprehend some injury from a long delay," which might diminish "our numbers," he worried. So why would they endorse Robert R. Livingston's motion for the convention to discuss the Constitution and every proposed amendment "clause by clause, through all its parts," before it proceeded to the final question on ratification? Livingston, chancellor of the state, or the chief judge of the state's court of equity, was one of the principal leaders of the Federalists. He made his motion after delivering a "speech of considerable length," one that consumed most of the June 19 session, and then pleading for the privilege of hearing "every member . . . coming forward with his sentiments." Clearly capable of holding his own with the best of those "going on very deliberately," Livingston offered a motion that was a proven recipe for a stall, and yet it passed "without opposition."[6]

In part, the majority's endorsement of the Livingston motion was due simply to the hubris of some of its leaders, an instance of the same overweening confidence that inspired the convention's Antifederalist committee to spurn the suggestion of extended discussions with the Virginia Committee of Opposition. "We yielded to a proposal made by our opponents" because, Robert Yates explained to Mason, "fully relying on the steadiness of our friends, we see no danger in this mode" of proceeding. And the anticipated benefit in the aftermath of the convention's refusal to ratify would not be inconsiderable, for Livingston's motion would prevent the defeated Federalists "from charging us with precipitation." But there was a more compelling reason for the majority's conciliatory gesture. Antifederalist leaders discovered that many rank-and-file partisans were, as Hamilton put it, "somewhat squeamish" about an outright rejection of the Constitution. Although a "considerable majority of the convention are undoubtedly Antifederal," explained William Duer, the New York merchant and speculator who had written in support of ratification under the pseudonym "Philo-Publius," its constituent members by and large wished for "amendments previous to the adoption of the government." To be sure, Governor Clinton and his more "violent" allies "would, if they could find support, go

6. Alexander Hamilton to James Madison, June 27 and June 21, 1788, *PJM*, 11:183, 165; Abraham G. Lansing to Abraham Yates Jr., June 19, 1788, *DHRC*, 22:1702; convention proceedings, *DHRC*, 22:1688, 1695, 1699, 1701.

further," but they could not and therefore would not. Besides, there was no need for the Clintonians to force the issue on those "minor partisans" who, according to Hamilton, "have their scruples and an air of moderation." A confrontation would be gratuitous, for as Randolph and the Virginia Federalists had convincingly argued, setting amendments as a precondition to ratification was tantamount to a rejection.[7]

Revisiting Publius

On June 20, Melancton Smith, a former confidant of Governor Clinton's who helped to set up the Antifederalist committee of New York City, proposed to amend the third paragraph of Article 1, Section 2, in order to fix the number of representatives at one for every twenty thousand inhabitants. The third paragraph's stipulation that House membership "shall never exceed one to every thirty thousand" was so imprecise as to invite a self-serving Congress, at its own discretion, to reduce the number well below the presumed maximum. But even the supposedly prescribed level of representation was insufficient, for one person could not adequately represent thirty thousand persons. Hamilton rose to address Smith's proposal, saying that the provision in question stood "on a better footing" than Smith imagined. Although there were no "direct words" to prohibit Congress from doing what he was projecting, that is, reducing the number of representatives to below the one per thirty thousand ratio, the "true and genuine construction" of Paragraph 3 "gives Congress no power whatever" to do so. "One representative for every thirty thousand inhabitants is fixed as the standard." As to Smith's further objection that the standard itself was defective because it resulted in too few representatives, "I confess it is difficult for me to say what number may be said to be sufficiently large." There may be a consensus, especially among Antifederalists, that the "number ought to be large," but how large "is a matter of opinion, and opinions are vastly different upon the subject." For proof, one needed only to look at the various state legislatures. The lower house in Massachusetts contained about three hundred members; South Carolina, not quite one hundred; New York, sixty-five. "Let the gentlemen produce their criterion" for the proper size of the lower house of Congress, therefore, and it would still not quiet all dissent.[8]

The Smith-Hamilton exchange dominated the first day of the clause-by-clause examination of the Constitution, taking up two and a half hours of the four-hour session on June 20, and these two principals continued to command

7. Robert Yates to George Mason, June 21, 1788, *DHRC*, 22:1799; Linda Grant De Pauw, *The Eleventh Pillar: New York State and the Federal Constitution* (Ithaca, NY, 1966), 107–8; William Duer to James Madison, June 23, 1788, *PJM*, 11:169; Alexander Hamilton to James Madison, June 19, 1788, *PJM*, 11:156.
8. Convention proceedings, *DHRC*, 22:1718, 1715–16, 1720, 1728–29.

the bulk of the convention's time day after day for the next two weeks. Together, Smith and Hamilton were responsible for more than one half of the speeches delivered during this period. As each in turn asked for the indulgence of the members while he answered the charges and misrepresentations coming from the other or his allies, the business of the convention almost ground to a halt, probably to Hamilton's delight. On the eve of the first full day of debate, he had predicted that a "full discussion" under the rules adopted by the delegates would keep them in Poughkeepsie for "at least a fortnight." On June 21, after a second day of deliberations, he passed on to Madison the "only good information I can give you," which is that "we shall be sometime together."[9]

George Clinton was understandably not quite as pleased with the slow and repetitious pace of the proceedings. "The most that has been said by the new government men has been only a second edition of Publius," the governor complained. This, of course, was a reference to *The Federalist* essays, which ran in New York newspapers for seven months, from October 1787 through May 1788. And Hamilton, who had conceived of the project with John Jay in early October, recruited Madison after Jay took ill, and written fifty-one of the eighty-five essays himself did borrow freely from them. His answer to Smith's objection concerning the inadequacy of representation in the House, for example, revisited *Federalist* no. 55, in which Madison argued that there was no "point on which the policy of the several states is more at variance." Hamilton selected Massachusetts, South Carolina, and New York to illustrate his case. Madison had mentioned the disparities of all three and extended the comparison to include Delaware, Pennsylvania, Rhode Island, and Georgia. To Smith's opposition to the three-fifths compromise, his contention that "he could not see any rule by which slaves are to be included in the ratio of representation" since they neither voted nor governed themselves, Hamilton again repeated arguments first articulated in *The Federalist*. In no. 54, Madison created a fictional "Southern brethren" who explained that slaves were not merely property. They were persons, but peculiarly so in that they were subjected to "restraints," were "vendible," and were liable to be "chastised" in accordance with the "capricious will of another." Accordingly, they were "debased by servitude below the equal level of free inhabitants" by an arbitrary "two-fifths." Furthermore, this fictional southerner went on, in every state "a certain proportion of inhabitants" were denied the privilege of voting, and yet they were counted as whole persons in the apportionment of representatives. Hamilton reprised these arguments on June 20, noting that slaves were by no means to be "considered

9. De Pauw, *Eleventh Pillar*, 198; Alexander Hamilton to James Madison, June 19 and 21, 1788, *PJM*, 11:156, 165. The *New York Independent Journal* for June 25, 1788 (*DHRC*, 22:1742) and the *New York Journal* for July 27, 1788 (*DHRC*, 22:17421743) describe Hamilton as having spoken for an hour and a half and Smith for an hour.

altogether as property—They are men, though degraded to the condition of slavery." Proceeding without the benefit of the cover afforded Madison by his fictional southerner, Hamilton went on to observe that "you have a great number of people in your state, which are not represented at all" because, having no vote, they have "no voice in your government." But these residents "will be included in the enumeration—not two fifths—nor three fifths, but the whole." Small wonder that Clinton criticized "the little Great Man," Hamilton, for "repeating over parts of Publius to us." Charles Tillinghast, the New York Antifederalist who took possession of the letters Lamb received from Henry, Mason; and Grayson in June and delivered them to Clinton, seconded the governor's criticism. "Mr. Hamilton," he declared, deserves little credit "*for retailing, in convention, Publius.*"[10]

The Relevance and Irrelevance of *The Federalist*

Readers today, long accustomed to the truism that *The Federalist* is, as the historian Jacob E. Cooke puts it, properly situated beside the Declaration of Independence and the Constitution as one of the "three historic documents of major importance" produced by the United States, are perhaps startled to discover it being dismissed so casually. However, there was "no aura of sanctity" around the essays in 1787–1788, and many contemporaries refused to follow its advice. As Bernard Bailyn has shown, the "near-religious veneration for a series of political arguments" developed slowly over time, and the further removed in time, the greater the veneration has become. Antifederalists at Poughkeepsie were familiar with *The Federalist*, but they were not particularly impressed by its arguments nor persuaded to change their vote on ratification because of it. Most would not have gone as far as Samuel Bryan, the Philadelphia Antifederalist who, under the pseudonym "Centinel," characterized some of its main assertions as having emanated from a "deranged brain" and all of its essays as being needlessly "long-winded." But they likely shared his feeling of embattled "fatigue" on encountering Publius's attempt "to force conviction by a torrent of misplaced words." Melancton Smith, the unofficial leader of the Antifederalists whose "prepossessing plainness" and "amiable disposition" were occasionally overshadowed by outbursts of haughtiness, said of Hamilton that "he speaks frequently, very long and very vehemently—has, like Publius, much to say not very applicable to the subject."[11]

10. George Clinton to John Lamb, June 21, 1788, *DHRC*, 22:1798; Charles Tillinghast to John Lamb, June 21, 1788, *DHRC*, 22:1796; convention proceedings, *DHRC*, 22:1715, 1728; *Federalist* no. 55,375; *Federalist* no. 54, 370–72; George Clinton to John Lamb, June 28, 1788, *DHRC*, 23:2357.
11. Jacob E. Cooke, ed., *The Federalist* (Middletown, Conn., 1961), ix; Bernard Bailyn, *To Begin the World Anew: The Genius and Ambiguities of the American Founders* (New York, 2003), 104, 126; De Pauw, *Eleventh Pillar*, 116, 199; Pauline Maier, *Ratification: The People Debate the*

These commentators were exceptional in that they had read more than a few of the essays themselves. *The Federalist* achieved its widest circulation in New York City, the Federalist stronghold, where it was preaching to the choir. Outside of the city, where it might reach readers conflicted or undecided about ratification, it was unevenly distributed. Between October 27, 1787, when the first essay appeared, and August 31, 1788, about three months after the publication of the last number, sixteen newspapers out of eighty-nine that were published outside of New York City had reprinted portions of *The Federalist*. Twelve of these sixteen were out-of-state newspapers, and half of them reprinted one essay only, which was not, as modern readers might expect, *Federalist* no. 10. Madison's examination of the stabilizing impact of countervailing factions in a large republic is celebrated by modern readers, but in 1787–88 only one newspaper outside New York State reprinted it. None of the newspapers outside of New York City carried all eighty-five essays. Bryan's hometown paper the *Pennsylvania Gazette*, which reprinted eighteen essays, led all others, and the *Albany Gazette* in upstate New York was a distant second at twelve. Antifederalist pamphlets by the "Federal Farmer" and "Columbian Patriot" had a wider out-of-state distribution. In short, as the historian Elaine F. Crane has concluded, Publius "did not reach an audience of any significant size in 1787–88."[12]

The publication of the essays in two bound volumes, beginning with the first thirty-six in March 1788 and the remainder in late May, no doubt increased their availability but not their influence on ratification. We know that James Kent, a spectator at nearly every session of the convention and an ardent admirer of Hamilton's, received "a large number" of the volumes "for gratuitous distribution" in Poughkeepsie and that he and a friend circulated them according to their best "judgements." However, it seems unlikely that Kent, who memorized whole passages of *The Federalist* and thought it superior to the works of "Aristotle, Cicero, Machiavel, Montesquieu, Milton, Locke, or Burke," would have given any of the precious volumes to unappreciative Antifederalists sneering at the "dry trash of Publius in 150 numbers." In any case, *The Federalist* was poorly designed to win converts. The pieces were, according to one contemporary critic, "of no value whatever to well-informed people, and . . . too learned and too long for the ignorant." Even Kent reserved his highest praise for *The Federalist's* explication of "the principles of free government" rather than its refutation of Antifederalist arguments. Revealingly,

Constitution, 1787–1788 (New York, 2010), 85; Melancton Smith to Nathan Dane, June 28, 1788, *DHRC*, 22:2015–16.

    12. Elaine F. Crane, "Publius in the Provinces: Where Was *The Federalist* Reprinted Outside New York City?" *William and Mary Quarterly* 21.4 (1964): 589–93, quotation at 591; De Pauw, *Eleventh Pillar*, 113.

Publius did not address the absence of a bill of rights, the principal objection of many Antifederalists, until May 28, that is, not until the eight-fourth of the eighty-five essays. By then, eight state conventions had already ratified the Constitution.[13]

Game Changer

If *The Federalist* did not accomplish "more toward insuring the adoption of the Constitution than anything else that was said or done" in 1788, as the nineteenth-century historian John Fiske argued, what did? The answer is, Virginia. News of the action taken at Richmond on June 25 reached New York City by special courier at 3:00 a.m. on July 2. Amid joyous bell ringing, William Smith Livingston, a Federalist lawyer who graduated from the College of New Jersey, now Princeton, in 1772, a year after Madison, set out immediately for Poughkeepsie with glad tidings for supporters of the Constitution. "Changing horses several times" in order to keep a steady pace, Livingston traveled eighty miles in about nine hours, arriving in Poughkeepsie shortly after noon and going directly to the courthouse where the convention was meeting. The delegates in Poughkeepsie had heard of New Hampshire's ratification a day earlier and were anticipating a decision from Virginia. Livingston's hurried entrance thus "occasioned such a buzz" among the delegates that Governor Clinton, who was then speaking in support of an amendment to require two-thirds consent of both houses for Congress to borrow money on credit, could barely be heard. But it mattered little whether the delegates could hear him because the news from Virginia made the specifics of the governor's statement inconsequential. Indeed, much of what had transpired in Poughkeepsie prior to July 2 was rendered moot by Virginia's ratification.[14]

A few Antifederalists insisted that nothing had changed. De Witt Clinton, the precocious eighteen-year-old nephew of the governor and, under the pseudonym "A Countryman," an influential critic of the Constitution in his own right, said that the news Livingston conveyed made "no impressions" on the Antifederalist members of the convention. Nathaniel Lawrence, an Antifederalist delegate from Queens County, was a little less certain, saying only that the "information from Virginia seems to have no effect on *Us.*" But the Richmond decision was a game changer. Lawrence himself recognized this. To John Lamb, he reported that the "other party," meaning the Federalists, apparently changed "their plan of defense" in the wake of the news. Until July 2, they "disputed every inch of ground" in the clause-by-clause examination of the

13. De Pauw, *Eleventh Pillar*, 112–13, 115, 117; Maier, *Ratification*, 84.
14. *New York Journal*, July 8, 1788, *DHRC*, 22: 2080; De Pauw, *Eleventh Pillar*, 214–16.

Constitution, but from July 3 onward "they have quietly suffered us to propose our amendments without a word in opposition." New York City delegate Isaac Roosevelt confirmed the adoption of a new strategy by the Federalists: "We now permit our opponents to go on with their objections and propose their amendments without interruption."[15]

Although the Clintonians continued to wish that, as Ulster County's Cornelius C. Schoonmaker put it, "our deliberations will not in the least be affected or changed" by the knowledge that Virginia had ratified, they wished in vain. If nothing else, Federalists managed to control the pace of the proceedings in Poughkeepsie. Using the Livingston motion to maximum effect, they managed to bog down the business of the convention until July 2. After learning of the Virginia decision, they promptly abandoned the strategy of disputing "every inch," and proceedings speeded up. Between the morning of June 20, the first day of substantive debate, and midday July 2, when Livingston interrupted Clinton's speech, the delegates had moved in fits and starts from Article 1, Section 1, to Article 1, Section 8, Paragraph 2. On July 3 they progressed quickly through the rest of Section 8, and by noon on July 7 they had completed their examination of the remaining five articles of the Constitution. The alacrity with which the convention completed its clause-by-clause analysis "was owing to the Federalists taking no notice of the *string* of amendments that were offered," the *New York Daily Advertiser* reported. Given the time-consuming exchanges that characterized the pre-July 2 debates, this "silence of the Federalists seemed to confound the opposition," who soon had exhausted "all the amendments they could *then* think of."[16]

The Antifederalists were in disarray and needed time to regroup. After July 7 they "met frequently" in caucus, where the effort to devise a plan for their amendments was productive of "much warm debate." What became visible in these heated sessions were the previously concealed fault lines dividing the members of the majority. Opponents of the Constitution outnumbered its supporters by more than two to one; however, it was not true, as one member of the New York Antifederalist Society would have it, that "unanimity and harmony reigns among the Anties." Governor Clinton and his adherents continued to argue "for rejecting the Constitution," the *Daily Advertiser* discovered, "but the majority, more moderate, insisted on an adoption with certain conditions." As Hamilton observed in a brief note to Madison, unlike the governor, "who

15. De Witt Clinton to Charles Tillinghast, July 3, 1788, *DHRC*, 22:2082; Nathaniel Lawrence to John Lamb, July 3, 1788, *DHRC*, 21:1261; Isaac Roosevelt to Richard Varick, July 5, 1788, *DHRC*, 23:2364.

16. Cornelius C. Schoonmaker to Peter Van Gaasbeek, July 2, 1788, *DHRC*, 22:2083; *New York Daily Advertiser*, July 8, 1788, *DHRC*, 22:2094.

wishes to establish *Clintonism* on the basis of *Antifederalism*," some of the other opponents of ratification appeared "to be desirous of a retreat" in the face of developing "*circumstances*."[17]

An Informal Committee and an Impasse

On July 8 Hamilton expected "some definitive proposition" regarding the amendments "to be brought forward" by the Antifederalists. But the convention "met, and adjourned, without doing business" that day because, as Robert Yates explained, the majority party "had not yet determined in what shape" the amendments they had proposed "should be brought forward." On July 9 the convention again met and adjourned "in order to give further time to the Anti-Federalists to arrange their plan for the amendments." Finally, on July 10, John Lansing brought a proposal before the convention. His plan called for arranging under three headings the potentially confusing array of more than fifty possible amendments introduced by the Antifederalists: "1st. Explanatory, 2d. Conditional, and 3d. Recommendatory." Explanatory amendments were primarily individual liberties ordinarily guaranteed by a bill of rights. These included such standards as freedom of the press and religion, the right to petition and peaceably to assemble, protection from unreasonable searches and seizures, and safeguards against general warrants and the quartering soldiers in private homes. Conditional and recommendatory amendments, however, were difficult to differentiate from one another, and Lansing's plan seemed to brush over the latter. Reporting separately on the proceedings of the July 10 session, both the *New York Daily Advertiser* and the *New York Journal* first described explanatory amendments and then listed a few conditional amendments, but neither bothered to mention any that might qualify as recommendatory alterations to the Constitution. And that was because proposals such as limiting the power of Congress to lay direct taxes, setting term limits for senators and the president, or requiring two-thirds consent of both houses for a declaration of war could be either. "Conditional" or "recommendatory" were alternatives rather than categories of amendments. The convention might adopt the structural changes in Lansing's submission as a condition of ratification or as recommendations to be brought before the first Congress but not both.[18]

After reading aloud the fifty-odd amendments in his proposal, Lansing advised the convention to adjourn and allow an informally appointed "committee

---

17. *New York Daily Advertiser*, July 16, 1788, *DHRC*, 22:2113–14; John M. Hughes to John Lamb, June 18, 1788, *DHRC*, 21:1202; Alexander Hamilton to James Madison, c. July 2, 1788, *PJM*, 11:185.

18. Alexander Hamilton to James Madison, July 8, 1788, *PJM*, 11:187; convention proceedings, *DHRC*, 22:2117, 2118, 2119–27; *New York Daily Advertiser*, July 15, 1788; *DHRC*, 22:2127–28, and *New York Journal*, July 17, 1788, *DHRC*, 22:2129.

of both parties" to arrive at such an accommodation of them "as to bring the business to a quick and friendly decision." The convention took Lansing's advice and adjourned, but when the informal committee met, John Jay, the New York City Federalist, "declared that the word *conditional* should be erased before there could be any discussion on the merits of the amendments." In other words, Jay and the other six Federalist members of the committee wanted to limit discussion to a bill of rights and recommendatory amendments to be submitted to the first Congress. Antifederalists, determined to keep conditional ratification on the table, refused "to give up that point," and after an hour of debate the committee, which had equal numbers of Federalists and Antifederalists, "dissolved without effecting anything." So much for a "quick" or "friendly" resolution, but all was not lost. Although most of the committee's opponents were "quite violent" in their objections to Jay's proposition, Dutchess County's Melancton Smith, dubbed "the Anti champion" by one newspaper, reportedly "discovered a disposition somewhat moderate."[19]

Jay's Motion and Smith's Substitute

In convention on the morning of July 11, Jay read a statement prepared on behalf of the Federalist members of the informal committee. Accusing the Antifederalists on the committee of "adhering rigidly to the principle of a conditional adoption," which was patently "inadmissible and absurd," Jay informed the convention that "no plan of conciliation had been formed" to accommodate the proposed amendments. He therefore took it upon himself to propose such a plan by moving that the convention ratify the Constitution with a proviso that "doubtful" clauses be "explained" and that "whatever amendments may be deemed useful, or expedient, ought to be recommended." Jay's motion, endorsed by fellow New York City delegates Robert R. Livingston and state supreme court chief justice Richard Morris, removed conditional amendments from consideration and thus accomplished exactly what the Federalists had promoted in committee. Jay explained that adopting only "certain parts" of the Constitution, a proposition the Antifederalists undoubtedly supported in the informal committee, would be the equivalent of a conditional ratification and would be deemed "not admissible" by the ten states that had ratified unconditionally. If the Poughkeepsie convention chose to pursue that course of action, he warned, New York "must of necessity remain out of the Union." The question before the delegates, therefore, may be "reduced to this point—the advantages in one scale and disadvantages in another" of being a member of the Union under the new Constitution.[20]

19. *Poughkeepsie Country Journal*, July 1, 1788, *DHRC*, 23:2360; *New York Daily Advertiser*, July 15, 1788, *DHRC*, 22:2128; *New York Journal*, July 17, 1788, *DHRC*, 22: 2129.
20. *New York Daily Advertiser*, July 16, 1788, *DHRC*, 22:2148; convention proceedings, *DHRC*, 22:2130–31.

Jay succeeded in changing the focus of the convention. There was little to be gained in debating the relative merits and demerits of the Constitution, as these had already been "fully discussed" in the conventions of "10 different states." The delegates at Poughkeepsie should ponder instead another set of questions. Were New Yorkers capable of sustaining a solitary existence, "standing upon our own ground unconnected . . . with our neighbors"? Was New York united internally? "Are all parts of the state happy and easy in their situation"? Earlier, Hamilton had indicated to Madison that in the event of a rejection of the Constitution, Federalists were contemplating a "separation of the southern district," where their concentrations were substantial, "from the other part of the state." Massachusetts newspapers on multiple occasions reprinted a New York correspondent's claim that the "southern district of this state will apply to the new Congress to be taken into the federal government" should the Poughkeepsie convention refuse to ratify. Jay played upon this rumor of secession when he asked the delegates to decide for themselves whether interested "neighbors" might subsequently make peace with "that part of the state." On a more immediately material level, Jay thought the delegates ought to consider the importance of having Congress continuing to meet in New York. "The sittings of Congress is worth 100,000 [dollars] a year," he estimated, and almost certainly more if their impact on commerce and commercial traffic was factored into the equation. Could the state afford to reject the Constitution, then, in view of the heavy toll it would take on interstate peace, internal harmony, and economic prosperity? "These are not threats—This is prudence." A deliberate and impartial assessment of the pros and cons must lead to this one conclusion, Jay said: that "it would [be] most happy for this state to continue in [the] union."[21]

George Clinton was vehement in opposing Jay's proposal and unmoved by his explanation. The convention must not be swayed by such "specious reasoning" geared toward "an unconditional adoption of an imperfect government." The Constitution ought to be ratified after "suitable amendments calculated to abridge and limit the powers" of the federal government were incorporated into it, and not one second sooner. The flaws in the system as it stood were too dangerous to be allowed to continue even temporarily, the governor cautioned, "for history does not furnish a single instance of a government once established, voluntarily yielding up its powers to secure the rights and liberties of the people." Smith, unveiling before the convention his newfound "disposition somewhat moderate," was less unyielding than Clinton but also opposed Jay's motion because, he said, it went "too far." Reflecting the tone of the exchanges

21. Alexander Hamilton to James Madison, June 8, 1788, *PJM*, 11:99; *Massachusetts Centinel*, July 16, 1788, *DHRC*, 23:2371; convention proceedings, *DHRC*, 22:2132–33.

that took place during the meeting of the informal committee on which they both served, Smith argued that mediation was impossible "if nothing can be done but *adopt* or *reject* the Constitution." For the sake of "accommodation," Smith proposed a substitute motion calling for ratification but also the disallowance of certain provisions of Article 1, Sections 4 and 8, from taking effect until a second federal convention met to consider amending the Constitution. Specifically, he wanted to curtail the federal government's power to supervise the elections of senators and representatives, deploy the state militia outside New York, and levy direct taxes in lieu of revenue requisitions.[22]

For much of the next week, the delegates debated the two motions to no avail. "We are now where we were 3 or 4 days ago," Montgomery County Antifederalist William Harper complained on July 15. This was because, as Columbia County's Matthew Adgate observed, hardly anything new could now be said to add to or detract from either proposition, and so "the question & arguments [are] repeated" over and over again. As if to confirm this observation, after admitting "it would be vain in me to attempt to offer any new arguments" to the question before the convention because "it is fairly exhausted," Governor Clinton proceeded on July 17 to repeat points he had previously made, some stretching back nearly three weeks. Harper's protest and Adgate's observation were thus justified, and the patience of others was undeniably being taxed by the tedium of repetition. "Our business here goes on heavily," Jay wrote his wife, Sarah, and "many of the members impatient to return" home. But there could be no resolution without concessions, and concessions seemed not to be in the offing. Abraham Bancker was not alone in dismissing Smith's motion as simply a cleverly disguised version of conditional adoption. It was, said the Richmond County Federalist, nothing more than a "gilded rejection" of the Constitution by pretended supporters. On the other side, De Witt Clinton, wholly in agreement with his uncle that Jay's proposal was dangerous, declared Smith's to be the "ne plus ultra of anti concession," or the most that Clintonians would be willing to concede. Bancker certainly understood the sentiment: "This, say they, is our *Ultimatum*. We go not a step beyond it." All the while, more than a few Antifederalists probably shared John Williams's predicament. Representing upstate Washington and Clinton Counties, where opponents of the Constitution ruled, Williams believed well-placed amendments were necessary to render the new federal system safe, but he also believed the "consequences of disunion dreadful." The dilemma virtually immobilized him: "cannot vote for a rejection—& cannot vote for an unconditional adoption." On

22. George Clinton, remarks, July 11, 1788, *DHRC*, 22:2147; convention proceedings, *DHRC*, 22:2135.

the verge of desperation, Williams clung to the hope that "some middle line" might yet be found.[23]

Congress Moves Forward

While the delegates were thus stalled in their consideration of rival propositions, the Confederation Congress was moving ahead with the transition to a new federal government. Meeting in New York City, Congress learned of Virginia's ratification on the morning of July 2, a few hours before the news reached Poughkeepsie. In compliance with the provision in Article 7, which stipulates that adoption by nine states "shall be sufficient for the establishment of this Constitution," Congress appointed a committee to prepare an act "for putting the said Constitution into operation." A week later, on July 9, the committee submitted a draft ordinance scheduling the first Wednesday in December 1788 for the appointment of presidential electors by the ten ratifying states, the first Wednesday in January 1789 for the election of the president, and the first Wednesday in February 1789 for the inauguration of the federal government under the Constitution. The new Union was set to begin with or without New York. De Witt Clinton was unfazed by the prospect, saying Jay and other Federalists were needlessly fretting about gaining admission after the fact. He had "no doubt" that the ten-state Union would be glad to receive New York as a member at any time, even with the state's conditional amendments.[24]

Melancton Smith was not as cocksure as the young Clinton. Shortly after Congress appointed its preparatory committee on July 2, Smith heard from Nathan Dane, the moderate Massachusetts Antifederalist whom he had befriended in the mid-1780s when both were elected to multiple terms in the Confederation Congress. Dane, in fact, was still a congressman, so he wrote with the knowledge of an insider when he informed Smith that a day "must soon be fixed, when all proceedings under the Confederation shall cease." In a long letter written with the "candor and frankness" each had come to expect of the other, Dane described the "peculiar situation of our government at this time." All of his observations stemmed from this one overriding truth: "The Constitution of the United States is now established." After a few states had adopted the new system, "the ground was materially changed," and now, with

23. Convention proceedings, *DHRC*, 23:2179, 2173; George Clinton, remarks, July 17, 1788, *DHRC*, 23:2222; George Clinton, remarks, June 27, 1788, 22:1972–73; John Jay to Sarah Jay, July 16, 1788, *DHRC*, 23:2370; Abraham Bancker to Evert Bancker, July 12, 1788, *DHRC*, 22:2149; De Witt Clinton to Charles Tillinghast, July 12, 1788, *DHRC*, 22: 2150; convention proceedings, July 17, 1788, *DHRC*, 23:2198.
24. Editors' note, *DHRC*, 21:1251; De Witt Clinton to Charles Tillinghast, July 12, 1788, *DHRC*, 22:2150.

ten states ratifying, it had "totally shifted." The only course of action now open to a nonratifying state such as New York was "either to accede with recommending certain alterations, or to make them a condition of her accession." If the state were to choose the latter, it isolated itself outside the Union because the ten ratifying states would never yield to New York "dictating" the terms of its admission. Some commentators were characterizing this prospective separation as a temporary inconvenience to be subsequently remedied in the spirit of mutual accommodation, but these unreflecting souls were foolishly sanguine. Dane thought it "almost an absolute certainty" that an estrangement, should one transpire, would be "forever." To make matters worse, the "ratifying and non ratifying states will immediately have opposite interests, which, in the nature of things, they will pursue." As a result, "counteracting laws" will displace earlier "affections and friendship for each other," so that a separation would become at once more permanent and less amicable. "And if we reason from experience and from the character of men, we must conclude it is at least highly probable that they will have recourse to arms." The disaffected states may not wish it, may even try to avoid it, but "a thousand accidents may give rise to hostilities," indeed, to a "civil war" whose outcome will be decided "by the longest sword."[25]

Clearly the better alternative, the only rational choice, was for New York to "accede" to the Constitution and join those states that considered it a "tolerable basis" for a perpetual union. The Constitution was admittedly "imperfect" without amendments, but it could be amended under the terms set forth in Article 5. And if New York ratified with recommendatory amendments, as Massachusetts, South Carolina, New Hampshire, and Virginia had done, the chances of the system being improved were greatly increased. Additionally, the state would " immediately have a voice in the federal councils" and could thereby exercise "all her influence" in the passage of "some of the most important laws" enacted by the first Congress. Dane had heard arguments similar to these coming from Massachusetts Federalists some five months earlier, and he found them persuasive enough to repeat to Antifederalists in New York, North Carolina, and Rhode Island. "I confess, I feel no impropriety in urging the three [nonratifying] states to accede" to an unconditional ratification. By so doing, they would join a collective effort to correct the "defective parts of the system" and make "the best of the Constitution now established." On the other hand, if they insisted on prior amendments, they would place themselves outside of the Union and recklessly tempt the forces of "anarchy, corruption, faction, and oppression."[26]

25. Nathan Dane to Melancton Smith, July 3, 1788, *DHRC*, 21:1254–55, 1258.
26. Nathan Dane to Melancton Smith, July 3, 1788, *DHRC*, 21:1256–59.

Melancton Smith's Second Motion

"I entirely accord with you in opinion," Smith wrote in response to Dane's letter, "and shall if necessary avow them." But Dane already suspected as much and knew that Smith needed encouragement more than convincing. Two weeks earlier, before the news of Virginia's ratification broke, Smith had written Dane to keep him posted on the proceedings at Poughkeepsie. His greatest "fear," Smith said, was the absence of "a sufficient degree of moderation in some of our most influential men." He himself preferred to ratify the Constitution with a recommendation for "substantial amendments" than to "adopt it conditionally with unimportant ones." However, he did "not find these endeavors sufficiently seconded" among the Antifederalists. Claiming for himself the "principal labor of managing the controversy," Smith said that he hoped to gain support for an intermediate proposal to make the "condition a subsequent one, that is, to take place in one or two years after adoption, or the ratification to become void." This idea that New York could vote to ratify the Constitution with the stipulation that it retained the right to reverse its decision unless certain conditions were met within a specified period became the basis of a new motion Smith was beginning to contemplate.[27]

On July 15 Smith modified his existing proposal in the hope that it might bridge the gap between the Clintonians and the proponents of unconditional ratification. He first changed his July 11 motion from a substitute for Jay's to an "amended" version of the same. He next listed more than two dozen amendments, including all of the bill of rights protections but none of the structural changes contained in John Lansing's much longer July 10 enumeration. Smith then called for the Constitution to be ratified "on the express condition that the rights aforesaid . . . will as soon as possible be submitted to the consideration" of a second federal convention. As an incentive to speedy action, Smith further proposed that until such a convention met the new federal government would exercise only limited control over the deployment of the New York militia, the elections of senators and representatives, and the levying of direct taxes. Smith expected a fight. "My task is arduous and disagreeable," he wrote Dane, and therefore will require "time & great industry" to complete. But even he underestimated the effort it would take, and the commitment he would have to make "to bring our party to accord."[28]

James Duane, the Federalist mayor of New York and erstwhile Hamilton patron, began the contest on July 17 when he moved for a postponement of

27. Melancton Smith to Nathan Dane, c. July 15, 1788, *DHRC*, 23:2369; Melancton Smith to Nathan Dane, June 28, 1788, *DHRC*, 22:2015.
28. Convention proceedings, July 15 and 17, 1788, *DHRC*, 23:2177–78, 2200–3; Melancton Smith to Nathan Dane, c. July 15, 1788, *DHRC*, 23:2369.

Smith's motion in favor of the "form of ratification" Hamilton had broached two days earlier. Hamilton had introduced his proposal in hopes of breaking the week-long stalemate between supporters of the rival plans of Jay and Smith. Comprising a section of explanatory amendments, mainly bill of rights protections, and another section of structural alterations that were "to be recommended" to Congress, it generated little opposition because Hamilton chose not to offer his proposal as a formal motion. None other than Lansing himself said he wished for such a motion because he found "many good ideas" in Hamilton's amendments and did "not wish to reject them entirely." But Duane's motion to postpone revealed just how few Antifederalists were willing to entertain Hamilton's form of ratification. De Witt Clinton denounced it as "a bait" to lure in unsuspecting Antifederalists. Notwithstanding his earlier praise, Lansing voted against the motion. Among the Antifederalists, only Queens County's Samuel Jones, who had emerged as a moderate voice during the aborted meeting of the informal committee, voted in the affirmative. Duane's motion lost by a wide margin, with twenty votes for and forty-one against the postponement.[29]

Melancton Smith was one of the forty-one. It soon became clear, however, that he was no longer committed to his earlier motion. He had assured Dane that when the time came for him openly to avow his support for unconditional ratification, he would do so. That time had come. As soon as the voting on Duane's motion was over, Smith rose to address the convention. He once believed that the ratifying states would accept the mode of adoption he had proposed for New York, Smith announced, but he was "mistaken." He wished, therefore, to "withdraw" his first motion, which Duane had asked to be postponed, because there was "little reason to expect that we shall be received on these terms." Thus if the delegates at Poughkeepsie insisted on the condition he had set, namely, the suspension of certain powers granted under the Constitution until a second federal convention met, New York would be left outside of the new Union that was already taking shape as Congress prepared the presidential election timetable for the ratifying states. "I stand on ticklish ground," Smith admitted, suspecting that his new motion would "not please either side of the house." Some former Antifederalist allies, especially, might be disappointed and "charge me with leaving the ground I have been striving to maintain." And truth be told, "I have shifted the ground" in order to occupy "a better position," one better suited than the old to "secure an admission into the union & procure a consideration of amendments."[30]

29. Forrest McDonald, *Alexander Hamilton: A Biography* (New York, 1979), 51, 66; convention proceedings, *DHRC*, 23:2179, 2205–08, 2210; De Witt Clinton journal, July 15, 1788, 23:2183; *New York Daily Advertiser*, July 15, 1788, *DHRC*, 22:2128.

30. Convention proceedings, *DHRC*, 23:2211–13.

What was Smith's new ground? His motion began with a statement of the reasons why a majority of the delegates at Poughkeepsie was reluctant to adopt the Constitution unamended: rulers wielded too much power at their own discretion; the federal government could willy-nilly encroach upon state authority; Congress exercised nearly unlimited power over the sources of revenue; there were too few representatives; federal judicial powers were too extensive and indefinite; Congress controlled the times, places, and manner of electing senators and representatives; and legislative, executive, and judicial powers were inadequately separated. "For these and various other reasons, this convention would be induced not to accede to this Constitution, did not other weighty considerations interpose," most importantly, a "regard to the common good of the Union." But after expressing the "firmest confidence that an opportunity will be speedily given" to consider constitutional amendments addressing the aforementioned concerns and pledging "with the utmost cheerfulness to abide by the result of such deliberations," Smith ended his motion on a cautionary note. New York claimed "a right to recede and withdraw from the said Constitution, in case such opportunity" to amend "be not given within _____ years."[31]

Some Detest Smith as Much as Hamilton

Most Federalists probably understood the withdrawal clause in Smith's new motion to be a form of conditional ratification and as such unacceptable. They were content, however, just to sit back and allow Antifederalist opponents express their disapproval of Smith and his proposal. The morning session on July 18 began awkwardly with "a long silence" after Smith read his "proposition of yesterday." The majority "party seemed embarrassed," Jay reported to Washington, initially "fearful to divide among themselves." Still, it was more than apparent that "many of them [were] very averse to the new plan." When Zephaniah Platt, the Dutchess County Antifederalist who had seconded Smith's motion, broke the silence with a plea to the "gentlemen opposed" not to react hastily to a proposal that had a distinct advantage over its predecessor in that it "obviated the objections which were brought against the first," he provoked negative responses only. John Lansing said that he did not "see the advantage" and that therefore the proposal did not meet with his "approbation." John Williams, reflecting the sentiments of the solidly Antifederalist delegation from Washington and Clinton Counties, responded simply that he did "not approve." De Witt Clinton suggested that Lansing and the others, including his uncle, the governor, were obliged to speak "against Smith's 2d proposal . . . in order to keep in with the violent members." By the end of the morning session, according to Jay, Smith had learned that some members of

31. Convention proceedings, July 17, 1788, *DHRC*, 23:2214–15.

his "own party were not pleased" with him. The younger Clinton put it more directly: "Some detest Smith as much as Hamilton."[32]

Antifederalists, discombobulated by Smith's action, met in caucus on the night of July 18 and again at eight o'clock the next morning in search of a united response. At one end of the spectrum, moderate Antifederalists supported Smith. If his motion were to be defeated, wrote De Witt Clinton, who was privy to much backstage information, these moderates were likely to "vote with the Feds. for unconditional adoption, and allege this as an excuse." Queens County's Samuel Jones said he needed no excuse. "We must join the union sooner or later and we might as well now," he argued, "and trust to future amendments." At the other end of the Antifederalist spectrum, the "more violent members" continued to be "much enraged" by the new motion "and its author." Some "ungenerously suppose," Clinton observed, that Smith "designed" his motion with defeat to be followed by unconditional ratification in mind. Many Antifederalists thus found themselves caught between a rock and a hard place, or as the classically schooled Clinton put it, between the "Scylla and Charybdis" of a "non-conditional adoption & a disunion of the opposition."[33]

Lansing's Motion

Fresh from their morning caucus, Antifederalists were ready with their newly devised plan when the July 19 session opened. Speaking for the majority, Lansing moved that the convention postpone consideration of all previous motions and take up instead a new resolution of ratification with amendments. This new proposal combined many of the amendments described in Lansing's July 10 report and the exemptions contained in Smith's first motion. Although it did not employ the terms "explanatory" and "conditional" to describe the proposed amendments, the new plan arranged them accordingly. It listed nearly two dozen amendments that fit under the former category and more than thirty under the latter. Conventional bill of rights guarantees—freedom of religion and the press, the right to assemble and to bear arms, due process and speedy trials, habeas corpus protection, security against double jeopardy and excessive bail—and some explanatory provisions—most importantly, a declaration that all power derived from the people and could be "re-assumed" by them—appear in the first section of Lansing's motion, which concludes with a statement of "confidence" that a second federal convention would consider them "as soon as possible." Until then, and here Lansing resurrected the conditions Smith had

32. John Jay to George Washington, July 18, 1788, *DHRC*, 23:2227; convention proceedings, 23:2231–32; De Witt Clinton journal, July 18, 1788, *DHRC*, 23:2232.

33. De Witt Clinton to Charles Tillinghast, July 19, 1788, *DHRC*, 23:2230; De Witt Clinton Journal, July 18, 1788, *DHRC*, 23:2232.

introduced on July 11 and repeated on July 15, Congress was prohibited from unilaterally deploying the New York militia out of state, interfering with the times, places, and manner of electing senators and representatives, or disregarding the requisition system of raising a revenue.[34]

The second part of Lansing's motion called for changes to the structure and operation of the Constitution itself. Congress would be prohibited from borrowing money on credit without the consent of two-thirds of the Senate and House of Representatives. A two-thirds majority of both houses would also be required for a declaration of war. No one could serve as a senator for more than six years in a twelve-year period. No president would be eligible for a third term. The writ of habeas corpus could not be suspended for longer than six months. And so forth. These were based on Lansing's July 10 enumeration, which had been modified by subsequent discussions in the committee of the whole and the Antifederalist caucus. Lansing's motion enjoined New York's congressional delegation to "use all reasonable means to obtain a ratification" of these amendments in compliance with the terms specified under Article 5 of the Constitution. This did not pose any particular problems, amounting to nothing more than an instruction to the state's representatives. The motion intruded on the privileges of the federal government and the other states, however, when it required all laws enacted "in the meantime, to conform to the spirit of the said amendments."[35] What would happen if New York's congressmen and senators determined that laws being passed did not conform to the spirit of these amendments?

For Federalists, Lansing's motion was worse than the "gilded rejection" Smith had proposed. It imposed the same condition and then buttressed it with an additional requirement pertaining to an extended list of structural amendments. But they put up scant resistance as the convention proceeded to adopt the Lansing motion by a vote of forty-one in the affirmative and eighteen in the negative. The voting over, the delegates began systematically to consider in turn each paragraph of Lansing's proposal. Making minor alterations, they moved rapidly through the first section and completed their deliberations within a few hours. Before adjournment, Governor Clinton proposed the appointment of a committee "for the purpose of arranging the amendments agreed to" and perhaps addressing "other matters not considered." The convention agreed, creating an informal committee of four, "two on each side, consisting of Mr. M. Smith and Mr. Yates on one, and Mr. Duane and Mr. Harison on the other." Federalists were so accommodating that the *Poughkeepsie Country Journal*

---

34. Convention proceedings, *DHRC*, 23:2234–37.
35. Convention proceedings, *DHRC*, 23:2237–42.

was able to summarize the day's business, dismissively but not altogether incorrectly, with one line: "Nothing very material has transpired in Convention."[36]

The delegates reconvened on Monday, July 21, at 11:00 a.m., an hour later than the usual starting time, and seemed to pick up where they left off on Saturday. Although the order of the day was a consideration of the second part of the Lansing motion, which called for structural changes to the Constitution and might therefore be more open to Federalist objections, the paragraph-by-paragraph examination progressed nearly as quickly as the review of the first part. One after the other, the proposed amendments were read by the secretary, came up for a vote, and passed by large margins with little or no debate. Restrictions on the collection of excise taxes, a return to the requisition system of revenue raising, limits on a senator's years of service, and the requirement of a two-thirds majority for borrowing on credit and for appropriating money for a standing army "were all carried by the entire voice of the opposition," the *New York Daily Advertiser* reported. The outcomes were never in doubt, with the "Anti's on one side, and all the Federalists on the other." Dirck Wynkoop, Governor Clinton's colleague from Ulster County, speaking in a voice "so low and so thick" that the "greater part of his reasoning" was lost on his listeners, tried nevertheless to emphasize this point in order to "expose the futility of the arguments urged against" Lansing's amendments.[37]

This apparent domination of the proceedings by the Antifederalists continued on July 22. The two-term limit on the presidency, jurisdictional restrictions on the lower federal courts, imposition of state taxes on residents of the federal capital—these and other proposed amendments passed easily. Only the amendment requiring a two-thirds vote in Congress for a declaration of war engendered a division in the majority party. The proposal passed, but with Melancton Smith and six other Antifederalists breaking ranks, the final vote of thirty-two in the affirmative and twenty-five in the negative was closer than usual. Still, as the *Daily Advertiser* informed its readers, there was "very little debate on any of them." Why? Perhaps Wynkoop was right and Federalists had come to understand the futility of further resistance.[38]

There is a more likely explanation, however. On the morning of July 21, before the first of Lansing's structural amendments came up for consideration, the delegates "waived for the present the question whether any of them should be conditional or not." This was a crucial decision because it suspended the question that most concerned the supporters of ratification. For Federalists

36. Convention proceedings, *DHRC*, 23:2242–50; *Poughkeepsie Country Journal*, July 22, 1788, *DHRC*, 23:2254.

37. Convention proceedings, *DHRC*, 23:2255–61; *New York Daily Advertiser*, July 25, 1788, *DHRC*, 23:2264.

38. Convention proceedings, *DHRC*, 23:2264–74; *New York Daily Advertiser*, July 25, 1788, *DHRC*, 23:2276.

and many moderate Antifederalists, the issue was never the substance of the amendments themselves. The Constitution had to be adopted or rejected, period. As John Jay declared, the convention "had no possible decisive power but to adopt or reject absolutely." The substance of an amendment was immaterial. Any amendment, good, bad, or indifferent, put forth as a condition of ratification was the same as a rejection because "the future Congress would have no authority to receive us into the union on such terms." Therefore, while Antifederalists racked up victory after victory on the convention floor, more consequential decisions were being made elsewhere.[39]

In Full Confidence

The morning session of July 23 opened with a report from the informal committee of four. Hamilton and James Duane, a member of the committee, argued that the convention proceed with the report, which included a draft of a notice of ratification to be submitted to Congress. Governor Clinton objected, demanding to know what was properly "the business of the Informal committee." That it had exceeded its authority was clear to Clinton, for the decision on "adoption or form of it was not committed to them—therefore [the convention] must not be bound by it." Richard Morris insisted that "if the report must be received & entered into the minutes—the whole must be gone through." But Samuel Jones, in the role of a conciliator wishing to end the confrontation before it escalated, pointed out that a "report of an informal committee never comes on the minutes." Acting on that understanding, Lansing moved to take up instead the form of ratification contained in Smith's first plan, which Smith had proposed as a substitute and then as an amendment to Jay's July 11 motion.[40]

The delegates voted to proceed as Lansing wanted, but the work done in the informal committee and the lobbying that occurred outside of the convention hall were soon apparent. Smith's first plan, it will be recalled, predicated New York's ratification "on the express condition" that a second federal convention meet "as soon as possible" for the purpose of considering the explanatory amendments submitted by the state. When the convention took up the introduction to that ratification form, however, Smith moved to expunge the conditional clause from his original motion and to insert in its stead one in which the key phrase "on the express condition" was replaced with "in confidence," thereby transforming what had been a prerequisite into a mere expression of hopeful expectation. With no debate, Smith's motion passed on a surprisingly lopsided vote of forty for the substitution and nineteen against. Twenty-two

---

39. *New York Daily Advertiser*, July 25 and July 16, 1788, *DHRC*, 23:2262, 22:2165.
40. Convention proceedings, *DHRC*, 23:2277–78.

Antifederalists, including not only Smith and Zephaniah Platt but also Lansing, Robert Yates, and Governor Clinton, voted with the Federalists for the motion. Their motives are not easily deciphered. But Smith and Yates were the two Antifederalist members on the informal committee of four, and Smith's motion may have reflected the substance of the draft that had caused a minor commotion earlier that morning. Lansing and Clinton, as De Witt Clinton had intimated a week earlier, were already having trouble keeping in with the "violent" partisans. The majority of the twenty-two, however, seemed simply to have accepted the argument that conditional ratification amounted to a rejection of the Constitution. Cornelius Schoonmaker, who voted against the motion despite the fact that three of his fellow Ulster County delegates, including the governor, voted for it, complained that "some of the members in the convention (in whom we have had great confidence)" proved to be unreliable. Contrary to their better judgment, they went along with the Federalist contention that if New York insisted on conditions, it would be left out of the government now being "put into operation" and that "great difficulties and embarrassments" would follow.[41]

The convention proceeded next to the incentive clause in Smith's plan, which stipulated that New York was ratifying the Constitution "upon the condition" that until a second federal convention met, Congress's power to deploy the state militia, supervise the elections of senators and representatives, and levy direct taxes would be severely limited. Samuel Jones, who a week earlier had voiced his willingness to ratify now and "trust to future amendments," moved to modify the clause by inserting the "words *in full confidence*" in place of the phrase "*upon condition*." Smith rose immediately to endorse the motion and gave his reasons for abandoning the position he once occupied. He still believed the Constitution to be "radically defective" and in need of corrective amendments. How best to achieve this end was not a static proposition, however, and he had been forced to "quit his first ground" after "Virginia came in." Previously, he thought amendments might be promoted as a condition of ratification, but he no longer did. William Harper protested, claiming he did not "understand the reasoning." But Zephaniah Platt cut short further declamations by criticizing the "fashionable" practice of calling on a "Gentleman to give reasons for his actions." He had heard all of this before, as had every other delegate in regular attendance. Having "made up his mind," Platt was ready for the question. He intended to vote for the motion, and nothing said at this late stage could possibly make him change his vote.[42]

41. Convention proceedings, July 23, 1788, *DHRC*, 23:2278–79; Cornelius C. Schoonmaker to Peter Van Gaasbeek, July 25, 1788, *DHRC*, 23:2298.

41. Convention proceedings, July 23, 1788, *DHRC*, 23:2278–79; Cornelius C. Schoonmaker to Peter Van Gaasbeek, July 25, 1788, *DHRC*, 23:2298.

42. Convention proceedings, *DHRC*, 23:2279–80, *New York Independent Journal*, July 28, 1788, *DHRC*, 23:2283.

Jones's motion carried on a vote of thirty-one in favor and twenty-nine opposed. Ten Antifederalists who had supported the first motion opposed the second, including Governor Clinton, Lansing, and Yates. Twelve, led by Smith, Jones, and Platt, voted for the substitution. After the vote, a crestfallen Schoonmaker wrote to Peter Van Gaasbeek, the Kingston merchant who had coordinated the election of Ulster County's Antifederalist delegation to Poughkeepsie, informing him that the "changing of these words in the restrictive part of our proposed adoption will essentially alter the force of the restriction." Abraham Bancker, who coined the phrase "gilded rejection" to describe Smith's first motion, was pleasantly surprised by the outcome and a bit more expansive than Schoonmaker about the meaning of the substitution. "Conditions appear to be laid aside" by this vote, he wrote, "and I expect will in some respect decide the final Question." John Jay was similarly hopeful and circumspect. The vote for "striking out the words *on Condition* and substituting the words *in full confidence*" signifies that "this state will adopt unconditionally," he told Washington, "if nothing new should occur." He had reason to be cautious because he suspected leaders on the other side "mean to rally their forces and endeavor to regain that ground" lost by a margin of two votes.[43]

A Reservation to Recede

Lansing did indeed try on July 24 to recover some of the lost ground. Having consulted with a number of his colleagues since the successive setbacks of the previous afternoon, he introduced a motion calling for the state's ratification form to include an escape clause. New York would ratify the Constitution but reserved the "right to recede and withdraw itself" from the Union if, "after the expiration of ____ years," a second federal convention still had not taken the state's amendments under consideration. Lansing explained that this provisional clause should pose no additional problems and would "not affect our union," if there really was, as Federalists kept assuring the delegates, "so strong an interest to bring about a convention." Lansing's new motion touched off the only extended debate of the week leading up to the final vote. The opponents of unconditional ratification quickly lined up behind Lansing. Dirck Wynkoop, an unshakable defender of the now-removed provisos, reminded the delegates that they were there not to decide for themselves but to represent the wishes of those who sent them to Poughkeepsie. "We should not forget from whence we came." At the outset, "2/3 were against an unconditional adoption," and although some of them have "cooled down," their constituents "will not be satisfied" by their behavior. Matthew Adgate remonstrated against the Federalist

43. Cornelius C. Schoonmaker to Peter Van Gaasbeek; Abraham Bancker to Peter Van Gaasbeek; and John Jay to George Washington, July 23, 1788, *DHRC*, 23:2285–86.

practice of saying "much of unanimity" but implying "this only means that we should totally adopt." The champions of unconditional ratification "ought to think of the parts of the state that are opposed to the Constitution." A real commitment to the goal of unanimity should convince the Federalists that "they ought to give up something too."[44]

Jay was the first to rise in opposition to Lansing's motion, and the degree of frustration he felt after more than a month of deliberations was reflected in the harshness of his tone. He was tired of the Antifederalists' habit of "giving with one hand and taking back with the other." Their latest proposal was yet another example of this, comprising "two clauses contradictory—one comes in [while] the other provides to come out." And the worst of it was that none of their fancy footwork mattered because, as Federalists had pointed out on numerous occasions, a reservation in any form "*is a condition*." It will be rejected by "our sister states," and New York will have to deal with the "consequences among ourselves" of being left out of the Union. Instead of coming to the same dead end by another route, New York should propose recommendatory amendments, as Massachusetts, South Carolina, New Hampshire, and Virginia had done. "Nothing can possibly prevent a convention" in the face of such a coalition. Moreover, contrary to Adgate's assertion, the friends of the Constitution would thereby be giving up something. Under this plan, "one side will be pleased—because they have carried all their amendments—the other because we have adopted such measures as will bring us into the union." Whereas Lansing's motion placed Federalists and Antifederalists "on opposite sides," this alternative would bring them together as "one people all pledged for amendments."[45]

Alexander Hamilton posed a series of questions for Lansing and his supporters. "Is it not of importance that we join—unanimously to procure a convention?" If the ten states that have ratified the Constitution "do not accept us—will they not sooner have a new convention than accept us"? With the "interest of some states against us," should New York adopt a measure by which the rest "are driven away by us"? Was the reserve clause "worth the jeopardy by which it must be obtained"? "Should we risk so much—on so little"? Hamilton then played his trump card. Two weeks earlier, on July 8, after the clause-by-clause examination of the Constitution had been completed and the convention was awaiting a report from Lansing on its proposed amendments, Hamilton had written Madison with an inquiry. He had "good reason to believe" that Antifederalists were considering three alternatives: "*conditions precedent*," elsewhere described as conditional ratification because adoption came after specific conditions had been met, that is, after prescribed changes had been

44. Convention proceedings, *DHRC*, 23:2290, 2292, 2293.
45. Convention proceedings, *DHRC*, 23:2290–91.

instituted; "conditions *subsequent*," or ratification on the condition that if desired amendments "are not adopted within a limited time, the state shall be at liberty to *withdraw* from the Union"; and lastly, "*recommendatory amendments*," otherwise known as unconditional ratification in line with the precedent set by Massachusetts. Anxious about the fate of the Constitution in a convention dominated by its opponents, Hamilton asked for Madison's opinion on the second option. "Let me know your idea of the possibility of our being *received* on that plan. You will understand," he thought it worth emphasizing, "that the only qualification will be *the reservation* of a right to recede in case our amendments have not been decided upon in one of the modes pointed out in the Constitution within a certain number of years—perhaps five or seven." Hopefully, this might be a middle ground between conditional and unconditional ratification. With this reservation, New York would probably ratify the Constitution, and Hamilton did "not fear any further consequences" because the first Congress would, he presumed, "recommend certain amendments."[46]

Hamilton may have been disappointed but could not have been greatly surprised by the Virginian's answer. Madison told him pointedly that the second alternative was unacceptable. The "idea of reserving a right to withdraw" was not a new one. It had come up at the Richmond convention, where it was "considered as a conditional ratification which was itself considered as worse than a rejection." It most assuredly did not stake out a middle ground, for there was none. Ratification must be unqualified, "*in toto* and *for ever*." An adoption "for a limited time would be as defective as an adoption of some Articles only" and would not gain New York entry into the new Union. Hamilton carried this "letter from a Gentleman of high public distinction" with him on July 24, and when he gained the floor read it to the convention. Having gotten the advice of "men of character," he was passing it along to his colleagues at Poughkeepsie. A reservation to withdraw violated the most fundamental premise of the Constitution in that it ran counter to the very concept of a "perpetual compact between the different states." If they adopted Lansing's motion, New York would not be admitted into the Union and the delegates would "vitiate the business" that had consumed so much of their time since mid-June. As a nonmember, New York would not be represented in the new Congress and could not introduce its long list of proposed amendments.[47]

Thank God We Have Now Got the Constitution

When the convention resumed its deliberations on July 25, Melancton Smith, who had kept to himself throughout the previous day's debate, rose to address

46. Alexander Hamilton to James Madison, July 8 and 19, 1788, *PJM*, 11:187, 188.
47. James Madison to Alexander Hamilton, July 20, 1788, *PJM*, 11:189; *New York Independent Journal*, *DHRC*, 23:2298; convention proceedings, *DHRC*, 23:2291.

the delegates. Interest in what he had to say was great, for everyone knew that Lansing had modeled his reserve clause after the one Smith had included in his July 17 motion to ratify. Everyone also knew that Smith had withdrawn his first motion in order to advance this second. Was he now about to disavow his second? Yes. Smith said he had offered this provision "as a Middle Ground," hoping "both sides of the house would be pleased with it." But rather than bringing them together, the clause made the "breach worse." Furthermore, realizing that the "plan will not answer the end" of getting New York into the new Union, he had to "be against it." Although this was one of his shortest speeches of the entire convention, Smith's announcement should not be discounted. The final vote on Lansing's motion was close, with twenty-eight in favor of it and thirty-one opposed, and Smith's recantation may have been the difference. Two delegates who voted earlier to keep the phrases "on the express condition" and "upon condition" in the form of ratification switched sides in casting their votes against Lansing. One of these, Jonathan Akin, was a colleague of Smith's from Dutchess County.[48]

Antifederalists were upset because the defeat of John Lansing's motion meant that there would be no conditions attached to the ratification of the Constitution by New York. Before the final vote in the committee of the whole, Thomas Tredwell, who was particularly offended by what he saw as the Constitution's "unwarrantable donations of power" to Congress, moved that the paragraph introducing the Declaration of Rights and explanatory amendments be reconsidered. "As it stands," argued the Suffolk County Antifederalist, "not a single right . . . remains." The paragraph in question was the one in which the phrase "on the express condition" had been replaced by "in confidence." Tredwell moved to drop the latter in favor of the word "*declaring*," so that rather than expressing confidence that fundamental rights would not be violated, the convention declared they could not be. Samuel Jones wished "to know what greater security we have under one word than another." Tredwell answered that the protection "is greater in one case than the other." Smith, whose motion had effected the initial substitution, disagreed, insisting that the sentence "as it stands . . . perfectly secures you as much as any other words possibly can." But there was little appetite among the rest of the delegates for a prolonged debate on semantics. As Jay put it, the proposed change did not make him "very anxious," and if others believed as Tredwell did that the revised wording offered a greater degree of protection, he was willing to indulge them.[49]

Tredwell's motion passed easily on a vote of thirty-seven to twenty-one, with all of the Antifederalists, save Melancton Smith and Samuel Jones, acting

48. Convention proceedings, *DHRC*, 23:2300, 2279, 2281, 2301.
49. *New York Daily Advertiser*, July 25, 1788, *DHRC*, 23:2262; convention proceedings, *DHRC*, 23:2301–04.

as one. But this unity was fleeting. On the final question, which came immediately after the vote on Tredwell's motion, the party again divided along the same lines as before. A dozen Antifederalists, led by Smith and Jones, joined the Federalists in approving an unconditional form of ratification on a vote of thirty-one to twenty-eight. On a subsequent motion by James Duane, the committee of the whole resolved unanimously that a circular letter be prepared "pressing in the most earnest manner" the necessity of a federal convention for the purpose of considering amendments, and appointed Jay, Lansing, and Smith to prepare the draft. The delegates also agreed, without debate, to "sundry amendments to be recommended" to the first federal Congress. The business of the convention was moving swiftly to a conclusion because the preceding vote of committee of the whole meant, as Philip Schuyler, Hamilton's father-in-law, observed, that New York would ratify the Constitution "with a bill of rights annexed, explanatory and recommendatory amendments but no conditional ones." The only task remaining before the convention "is to engross the Ratification," one Federalist spectator remarked. "Thank God we have now got the Constitution."[50]

They Beat Us with Our Own Weapons

At nine o'clock the next morning, July 26, the convention received the engrossed copies of the Declaration of Rights, form of ratification, and explanatory and recommendatory amendments. It also accepted the circular letter prepared by the committee of three and ordered a dozen engrossed copies of the same. The delegates then moved on to the final question and ratified the Constitution by a vote of thirty in favor and twenty-seven opposed. The margin was narrow but the outcome anticlimactic. Successive decisions on July 23 to remove the conditional phrases from the form of ratification, in combination with the affirmative vote in the committee of the whole the previous evening, made the final outcome unsurprising. Indeed, contemporary accounts mentioned July 25 rather than July 26 as the day New York ratified the Constitution. That the same core of twelve moderate Antifederalists, ten of whom came from Dutchess, Queens, and Suffolk Counties, voted with the Federalists to constitute a majority made the two decisions virtually indistinguishable. New York thus formally and unconditionally ratified the Constitution, even though Antifederalists had outnumbered Federalists by more than two to one at the outset of the convention. The intractable Cornelius Schoonmaker, stung by the defeat his party had suffered at the hands of the Federalists, was nevertheless impressed by their tactics. "The Federalists have outmaneuvered us," he

50. Convention proceedings, *DHRC*, 23:2203–9, 2311, 2313–17; Philip Schuyler to Peter Van Schaack, July 25, 1788, *DHRC*, 23:2376–77; *Independent Journal*, July 28, 1788, *DHRC*, 23:2320, 2318.

told Peter Van Gaasbeek, knowing that the Ulster County campaign strategist could at least appreciate shrewd political manipulation. By advocating explanatory amendments, including a declaration of rights, and affixing a long list of recommendatory amendments to the form of ratification, the Federalists "beat us from our own ground with our own weapons."[51]

De Witt Clinton was more disposed to find fault within the ranks of the Antifederalists than to credit the Federalists. To be sure, the opponents of the Constitution never formed a homogeneous party, but some lukewarm members had exacerbated nascent differences, thus creating opportunities for the Federalists to exploit where none had existed. For this, "I must impute the principal blame to Jones and Smith." The latter, especially, visited "so much among the Feds. that he . . . raised jealousies against him." Federalist merchant Seth Johnson, who heaped "much praise" on Smith for doing what he "thought necessary for the tranquillity & advantage of the state," confirmed that Smith's turnabouts "has been displeasing to many of the anti's." Abraham G. Lansing, the Albany County Antifederalist leader, was among the displeased. To Abraham Yates Jr., a onetime shoemaker and lawyer who helped draft the state constitution in 1777, Lansing wrote, "M. Smith is . . . charged with some improper steps." Although he told Yates, a self-described "Suspitious Man," he could not "give credit to what is alleged," if the allegations were true, then Smith had "injured the cause of our Country more than any Federalist."[52]

Smith offered no closing statement to justify his actions. He was a member of the committee that composed the convention's circular letter, however, and his draft of the same reiterated his motivation for doing what he did. Smith "considered the preservation of the Union as essential to the public prosperity, safety and happiness," and he did not want to undermine the system for governing that Union by demanding "amendments previous to its going into operation." And yet, "a large majority of the convention as well as of their constituents" continued to believe that "material alterations" had "to be made in the system in order to secure the liberties of the people." Therefore, ratification came with the "fullest confidence that the united councils of the people of the U.S. will effect such amendments and alterations" as soon as possible. None of this made its way into the final draft of the circular letter because the committee went with Jay's version, as amended by Lansing. But the sentiments Smith expressed were not his alone, and indeed, Jay's letter referred more affirmatively to the same "invincible reluctance to separating from our sister

51. Convention proceedings, *DHRC*, 23:2321–23; Cornelius C. Schoonmaker to Peter Van Gaasbeek, July 25, 1788, *DHRC*, 23:2299.

52. De Witt Clinton journal, July 18, 1788, *DHRC*, 23:2232; Seth Johnson to Andrew Craigie, July 27, 1788, *DHRC*, 23:2429; De Pauw, *Eleventh Pillar*, 28–30; Abraham G. Lansing to Abraham Yates, Jr., July 20, 1788, *DHRC*, 21:1330.

states" as the reason for the convention's vote to ratify "without stipulating for previous amendments."[53]

Zephaniah Platt, who voted consistently with Melancton Smith and was subjected to some of the same criticism, felt compelled to explain himself to William Smith, an "old friend" from Suffolk County. Smith was an associate of Schoonmaker's, and Platt wrote to him two days after the convention had adjourned. He imagined Smith was "surprised at first blush" to learn that the "Constitution is adopted and that I voted for its adoption." That he had done so was "true but not from a conviction that the Constitution was a good one." Platt said that Virginia's decision to ratify had forced a "choice of evils" on the delegates at Poughkeepsie. With the new government about to "go into operation," the best chance for New York to get the amendments it wanted was for the state to ratify unconditionally and to join the other states in pushing for another "convention as soon as possible." Alternatively, the worst thing for the "interest and peace of our state" would have been for New York to be left out of the new Union. "I beg you not to decide too hastily," Platt pleaded, saving his best for last. For "further particulars, I refer you to the Gentlemen of your own County who were in Convention," he advised, knowing that Smith's son, John, had been a delegate from Suffolk County and had voted, along with the rest of the delegation, for ratification.[54]

I Endeavor to Believe That It Is Best

Platt was confident that John Smith and the other Antifederalists who voted for ratification accepted some version of his explanation. Speaking for the group, Platt said that they had considered "all sides of the question & their probable consequences" before making their choice between "evils." They knew the new constitutional Union would soon be operational, especially after Virginia's adoption, regardless of whether New York ratified or not. They also knew that a separate confederation in alliance with North Carolina and Rhode Island was economically and geographically impractical if not impossible. And they realized that on its own New York would be exposed to external enemies and the "Terrors of *Disunion*." Henry Knox, the Massachusetts Federalist and sometime resident of New York City as the Confederation's secretary at war, was familiar enough with circulating rumors of secession to tell Washington that moderate Antifederalists voted for ratification because they feared "a perseverance in opposition would most probably terminate in Civil War."[55]

53. New York Convention, circular letter to the executives of the states, July 26, 1788, *DHRC*, 23: 2335–36; Melancton Smith, draft of New York circular letter, *DHRC*, 23:2337–39; John Jay: draft of New York circular letter, *DHRC*, 23:2339–40.
54. Zephaniah Platt to William Smith, July 28, 1788, *DHRC*, 23:2432–33.
55. John Vaughan to John Dickinson, July 26, 1788, *DHRC*, 21:1345; Henry Knox to George Washington, July 28, 1788, *DHRC*, 23:2432.

Other outside observers heard the same rumors and often came to the same conclusion. Aaron Burr, who declined to be a candidate for a seat in the convention but remained an interested spectator throughout, thought the action taken at Poughkeepsie was "the only one which could have preserved peace" in New York. Morgan Lewis, who failed to gain election as a delegate from New York City, wrote that the once formidable Antifederalist majority was defeated by an "apprehension of a separation of the southern part of the state." In New York, where he was serving as Spain's minister plenipotentiary to the United States, Don Diego de Gardoqui reported to his superiors that many feared the "division of the state" was a real possibility "because this city is in favor of the new government." John Brown Cutting, in London to complete his legal studies, learned that the "inhabitants of the City of New York, of Long, Staten and York [Manhattan] Islands . . . talk loudly of beseeching the new Congress for a dismemberment" from the rest of the state. Rhode Island lawyer William Ellery, a signer of both the Declaration of Independence and the Articles of Confederation, went so far as to wonder what the new Congress would do if the "federal counties should withdraw from the jurisdiction of the state" and ask for protection. "Would they give them protection?— Would they erect them into a new state; or divide them between Connecticut and New Jersey?" Even the redoubtable Abraham G. Lansing, arrested as an Antifederalist ringleader after a Fourth of July donnybrook involving "swords, bayonets, stones, &c." resulted in injuries to both sides, was somewhat reconciled to the decision by his concern over probable consequences. New York's ratification was "unconditional in every acceptation of the words," he told Abraham Yates Jr., a favorite target of the Hamiltonians, but "upon the whole I believe or *endeavor* to believe that it is best." If conditions had been attached to the decision and that decision then been rejected by the ten ratifying states, "yourself and our friends would have incurred blame & censure if any serious commotions had ensued." It was far better to stand "firmly united" and to "trust we shall be able to send such members" to Congress "as will assist in bringing about the reformation we wish." Lansing's concessions may not have measured up to manor lord Robert Livingston Jr.'s expectation that "all opposers would be quiet & settle their minds & be composed," but it was close enough.[56]

56. Aaron Burr to Richard Oliver, July 29, 1788, *DHRC*, 23:2433; Morgan Lewis to Tench Coxe, July 29, 1788, *DHRC*, 23:2434; Don Diego de Gardoqui to Conde de Floridablanca, July 25, 1788, *DHRC*, 21:1341; John Brown Cutting to Thomas Jefferson, August 30, 1788, *DHRC*, 21:1353; William Ellery to Benjamin Huntington, July 28, 1788, *DHRC*, 21:1348; Litchfield, Connecticut, *Weekly Monitor*, July 7, 1788, *DHRC*, 21:1265; *New York Packet*, July 15, 1788, *DHRC*, 21: 1273; Abraham G. Lansing to Robert Yates, August 3, 1788, *DHRC*, 23:2443–44; Robert R. Livingston to James Duane, August 8, 1788, *DHRC*, 23:2448.

Eleven-Gun Salutes and Midnight Heroes

Sometime around July 15, as the delegates at Poughkeepsie were quarreling over the arrangement of their proposed amendments and "what to do with them," Melancton Smith wrote to Massachusetts congressman Nathan Dane, begging his friend to "use your influence to defer the organization of the new government until we decide." By this time, as we have seen, the Confederation Congress had already received a committee report recommending the first Wednesday in December 1788 for the appointment of presidential electors, the first Wednesday in January 1789 for the election of the president, and the first Wednesday in February 1789 for the new federal government to begin its operations. Smith asked for a delay in the implementation of this timetable, explaining that the extra days might allow the convention time to "become of one mind" with regard to joining the Union. But Dane did not have to respond to Smith's request because Congress decided on its own on July 14 to take no action on the committee's recommendations. Apparently, supporters of the Constitution in Congress were not only willing to wait on New York but hoping to effect a positive outcome there by dangling the prospect of the federal capital being located in New York City. On July 28, two days after the final vote at Poughkeepsie, Congress resumed its consideration of the committee report and decided to push its recommended dates back a month.[57]

As Congress busied itself with the transition from the old to the new Union, the exhausted delegates at Poughkeepsie began to head home. In New York City, where "a general joy" prevailed and even "those who were of different sentiments drank freely of the *Federal Bowl*," Hamilton, Jay, Duane, and others in the delegation were greeted upon their arrival on July 28 "with a salute of eleven guns as they passed the battery" at Fort George near the southern tip of Manhattan and later "by the discharge of eleven guns at the dwelling house of each member, attended with repeated huzzas from a large concourse of people." For Hamilton, the honor that day paled in comparison to one he received in absentia a week earlier. On July 23 Federalists celebrated the ratification of the Constitution by ten states with a grand parade, decked out with multicolored banners and sashes, comprising seventy-six organized groups of assorted craftsmen and artisans, merchants, farmers, college students, clergymen, militiamen, and "strangers." A sky-blue ten-foot-by-eleven-foot flag depicting, among other things, Adam and Eve "naked, excepting fig leaves for aprons," Washington "nearly in full stature," and the "federal eagle . . . soaring towards the sun,"

57. Melancton Smith to Nathan Dane, c. July 15, 1788, *DHRC*, 23:2369; editors' note, *DHRC*, 21:1251.

garnered its share of attention, as did the giant loaf of bread, a "federal loaf" ten feet long, twenty-seven inches wide, and eight inches high, "with the names in full length of the ten states." But the centerpiece of the entire procession was a miniature thirty-two-gun frigate, twenty-seven feet long and ten feet wide, "everything complete and in proportion, both in hull and rigging," manned by more than thirty seamen, and named after the only signer of the Constitution from New York, Alexander Hamilton. Drawn by ten horses, the *Hamilton* fired a thirteen-gun salute at 10:00 a.m. to begin the marching, another as it passed by members of the Confederation Congress meeting in New York, yet another when it came within sight of the Spanish frigate *Pinzon* moored in the harbor, and a final one to end the festivities at 5:30 p.m. "amidst the acclamations of thousands."[58]

No eleven-gun salutes marked Melancton Smith's return from Poughkeepsie. No crowds gathered before his house shouting "repeated huzzas" in appreciation of his "unremitted and toilsome exertions." No newspaper reported that he had "completed the important business" of the convention to the "entire satisfaction" of his constituents. And no correspondent told him that his neighbors viewed his conduct with "perfect approbation." Home for Smith was New York City. Although he was a delegate from Dutchess County, where he had spent most of his adulthood and had substantial landholdings, Smith had resided in the city since 1784. He was, in effect, the ninth member of its delegation and the only Antifederalist. His vote to ratify the Constitution might thus have spared him a visit from the "midnight heroes" who gathered in front of George Clinton's home, hissing "a halter for the governor," and who ransacked printer Thomas Greenleaf's office because his publications had "insulted the Federalists." But his affirmative vote also marked a break with his former political allies, and the Clintonians never forgave him for that. Smith failed to gain the nomination for a seat in the new Senate or House of Representatives. He served a single term in the state legislature in 1791, was defeated the following year, and never held public office again.[59]

58. *New York Independent Journal*, July 28 and 30, 1788, *DHRC*, 23:2402, 2404; *New York Packet*, July 29, 1788, *DHRC*, 23: 2405; *New York Daily Advertiser*, August 2, 1788, *DHRC*, 21:1633–35, 1645–46.

59. *New York Packet*, July 29, 1788 *DHRC*, 23:2402; *New York Independent Journal*, July 28 and 30, 1788, *DHRC*, 23:2404, 2405; *Philadelphia Independent Gazetteer*, August 7, 1788; *DHRC*, 23:2411; *North American Magazine*, August 1, 1788, *DHRC*, 23: 2407.

CHAPTER SIX

North Carolina, the Bill of Rights, and the Madisonian Exchange

On the night of July 26, Hugh Williamson and John Swann, both in New York City as members of North Carolina's delegation to the Continental Congress, learned of the "rather unexpected" decision at Poughkeepsie. They considered the vote to ratify without previous amendments so momentous that news of the "event" could not be left solely to one "Captain Clark" who was setting sail for Edenton early the next morning. "Water passages" were too "uncertain," they explained in their letter to Governor Samuel Johnston, and time was of the essence, so they were entrusting the delivery of "this intelligence" to special couriers. What made the report out of New York so urgent to these North Carolinians was the meeting of their own convention, which was about to end its first week of deliberations. As supporters of the Constitution, both men knew that chances of its ratification in their home state were slim without the assistance of a positive outcome at "Pokepsie." The North Carolina convention, like that in New York, had a two to one Antifederalist majority. Unlike its northern counterpart, however, the Hillsborough meeting at full capacity would have nearly three hundred members. The defection of a dozen opponents would not swing the vote one way or the other.[1]

Federalists elsewhere shared the hope that the action taken at Poughkeepsie would have a beneficial impact on North Carolina. In Dutchess County, New York, a "sociable and harmonious" crowd spent the day celebrating "with the utmost cheerfulness" the adoption of the Constitution. After dinner, to the sound of cannons discharging in the background, "a number of gentlemen" concluded the festivities by drinking eleven toasts. An additional "volunteer" toast followed: "May North Carolina speedily become the Twelfth Pillar in the Federal Edifice." The Reverend Jeremy Belknap, whose Congregational church on Long Lane had been the setting for the Massachusetts convention, was "extremely happy" to hear of New York's ratification and expected "every southerly wind" to bring "like good news from North Carolina." George Washington received John Jay's letter of notification with "peculiar pleasure" and congratulated him on the successful completion of the work at Poughkeepsie.

1. Hugh Williamson and John Swann to Samuel Johnston, July 27, 1788, *DHRC*, 23:2430.

Given the composition of that state's convention and the "decided temper of the leaders in the opposition," Washington said, he had anticipated being disappointed. But now, as a result of this "great work," he entertained the hope that "North Carolina will not spend much time in deciding on this question."[2]

One-Sided Debate

The North Carolina convention, which began on July 21 and met continuously for fourteen days, saw the Federalist minority on the defensive from the outset. After routine matters of organization had been resolved but before the debates could actually begin, Halifax County's Willie Jones, the artful and determined leader of the Antifederalists, moved that a vote for or against the Constitution "be immediately put." Ratification had been up for national consideration for so long, and the delegates gathered at Hillsborough had been given "such ample opportunity" to review the issue in the intervening ten months since the Constitutional Convention had adjourned, declared Jones, who had refused to attend the 1787 meeting in Philadelphia, that "every one of them was prepared to give his vote . . . upon the question." Thomas Person, who served as a brigadier general during the Revolutionary War but now had the temerity to denounce George Washington as "a damned rascal and traitor to his country for putting his hand to such an infamous paper as the new Constitution," seconded Jones's motion, saying he was "sorry" for any man who had come to Hillsborough so uninformed as to be undecided. But Federalist lawyer James Iredell retorted he felt sorry for any delegate so close-minded that no amount of reasoning could penetrate his thick skull. Iredell, who quickly emerged as the state's most effective spokesman for ratification, said he was "greatly astonished" by Jones's motion. How was it possible, "without the least deliberation," even to conceive of rendering a decision on "a question which is perhaps the greatest that ever was submitted to any body of men"? His "repugnance to a hasty decision" was matched only by "the magnitude of the subject."[3]

To placate Iredell, Jones readily agreed to withdraw his motion. With opponents of ratification outnumbering proponents by a comfortable margin, he could afford to be generous. Jones was willing to play the game of appeasement for a while, within the parameters he defined. Accustomed to having his way, the transplanted Virginian with an Eton education, persuaded his allies to sit on their hands for most of the convention as a way of expediting the "para-

2. *Poughkeepsie Country Journal*, August 7, 1788, *DHRC*, 23:2415–16; Jeremy Belknap to Ebenezer Hazard, August 2, 1788, *DHRC*, 23:2420; George Washington to John Jay, August 3, 1788, *DHRC*, 23: 2446.

3. Elliot, *Debates*, 4:4; Louise Irby Trenholme, *The Ratification of the Federal Constitution in North Carolina* (New York, 1932), 66, 107.

graph by paragraph" consideration of the Constitution demanded by Iredell. At the end of the first full day of "debate," with the of the opponents of the Constitution remaining passively aggressive, thereby forcing its supporters to state both sides of an issue, William Shepperd commented on the oddity of the situation. It was passing strange, he said, "for a man to make objections and answer them himself." Archibald Maclaine, the prickly Federalist lawyer from Wilmington, responded that there was nothing else to be done when "gentlemen pass by in silence such parts as they vehemently decry out of doors." Unable to resist the temptation of having fun at the expense of the often abrasive Maclaine, Willie Jones suggested "let[ting] one of them . . . make objections and another answer them."[4]

After a week of such deliberations, during which a few Antifederalists participated in some of the discussions, while others, like Timothy Bloodworth, the tough-talking politician and sometime preacher, farmer, wheelwright, watchmaker, blacksmith, and self-educated doctor from New Hanover County, allowed "many words . . . in at one ear, and out the other," Jones was ready to end the charade. His opportunity to do so came on July 30, when Governor Samuel Johnston addressed the assembly in a voice so low that he could not be heard by all of the delegates. Johnston, the unanimous choice for president of the convention, moved that North Carolina ratify the Constitution and "at the same time propose amendments, to take place in one of the modes prescribed" under Article 5. If this motion were approved, North Carolina would take its place alongside Massachusetts and the four other states that had submitted amendments "subsequent to the ratification . . . and not previous to it." Jones listened to the ensuing exchanges, he said "with patience" for the better part of the day and then "moved that the previous question might be put." Moving the previous question is a parliamentary maneuver to cut off debate and to bring the motion on the floor up for an immediate vote; it is not itself open to debate. But the convention did not strictly abide by the rules of parliamentary procedure, and Jones shared the blame for this. In making his motion, Jones added a few "other remarks," explaining that if his motion carried he intended to introduce a resolution, "which he had in his hand," calling "for certain amendments to be made previous to the adoption" of the Constitution.[5]

The Question! The Question!

Most Federalists and probably many Antifederalists were taken aback by Jones's action. Iredell pleaded with Jones to withdraw his motion, claiming that it was unseemly of him to try to force the delegates to vote "precipitately"

---

4. Elliot, *Debates*, 4:29–30.　　　　　　5. Elliot, *Debates*, 4:143, 201, 216.

on an issue of such "great importance." Governor Johnston bemoaned the resort to "maneuvers and contrivance" aimed at impeding a fair and full examination of his original motion. Jones's intention was to impose an "improper system on the people," the governor declared, and that was "unworthy of any man." Fearing perhaps that the convention was rapidly trending toward incivility, Samuel Spencer, a moderate Antifederalist from Anson County whose tenure as a superior court judge briefly overlapped with Iredell's, endorsed a recommendation to postpone a vote on Jones's motion until the next day. But Thomas Person would have none of it. What would be the benefit of "putting it off till tomorrow"? The "other party," Person said, "had all the debating to themselves, and would probably have it again, if they insisted on further argument." William R. Davie, who with Hugh Williamson had a hand in drafting the Constitution at Philadelphia, resented the tenor of Person's remarks. He blamed the "gentleman from Granville"—convention rules stipulated that "no member . . . be referred to in debate by name"—for engaging in "ungenerous insinuations" and thus inflaming "the minds of his countrymen." Davie then ungenerously insinuated that the opponents of the Constitution had failed to "act openly and aboveboard."[6]

Jones protested his innocence, swearing that he "had not intended to take the house by surprise." It was true that "he had his motion ready" and his resolution "in hand," but he "waited for some time" in deference to the "gentleman from Edenton" (Iredell) and the "gentleman from Halifax" (Davie) before he moved the previous question. How anyone could claim that he had interrupted a full discussion of Johnston's motion was a mystery to him. "Gentlemen's arguments" had been made and "listened to attentively," Bloodworth excepted, but "no person had changed his opinion" as a result of the debates. "It was unnecessary, then, to argue it again." The time had arrived for the delegates to decide "whether they should ratify" the Constitution "unconditionally or not."[7]

Other Antifederalists stood with Jones. "There was a great cry for the question" after Jones finished speaking, so when Iredell rose again to address the delegates, he was greeted with outbursts of "The question! the question!" Iredell, shouting "I desire to be heard," pleaded with James Kenan, the chairman of the committee of the whole, to have order restored. Once the din had subsided, Iredell apologized for "troubling the house much oftener than I wished," but the regrettable fact that "so few gentlemen take a share in our debates" was forcing him to "beg leave now to make a few observations." Iredell then proceeded to review some familiar arguments. The newly established federal gov-

6. Elliot, *Debates*, 4:217–18.   7. Elliot, *Debates*, 4:217, 218.

ernment was "perfectly safe," he explained, because it was authorized to exercise "particularly enumerated and defined" powers and "no others." As such, the entire text of the Constitution was a guarantee, offering better protection against unwarranted governmental encroachments than "the strongest negative clause that could be framed." That ten states had already adopted the new federal plan was proof that a "great . . . majority of the American people" accepted this assessment, Iredell argued, not knowing that an eleventh state, New York, had ratified the Constitution four days earlier. The climax of his speech came, as it usually did in Federalist speeches, with a look at the probable consequences of an insistence on amendments prior to adoption. Conditional ratification was an impossibility. To make prior amendments a requirement would be tanta-mount to a rejection of the Constitution. North Carolina would then be out-side of the Union, and "we cannot exist by ourselves."[8]

Immediately upon Iredell's returning to his seat, calls for the question re-sumed. Without further objection, Jones's motion passed by a vote of 183 to 84, well above the mandatory two-thirds majority. The next day the convention opened with a consideration of Jones's resolution. Proper parliamentary proce-dure required a decision on Johnston's motion first, but the delegates behaved as though the previous day's vote had obviated the need officially to reject the governor's motion for ratification with recommendatory amendments. The only issues still in contention were whether North Carolina would insist on amendments prior to ratifying the Constitution, and if so, which ones. Again, Jones was ready with an answer. His two-part resolution called for amend-ments prior to ratification and provided an extensive list of proposed changes to correct the "most ambiguous and exceptionable parts of the said Constitu-tion." Jones offered to read his lengthy resolution aloud in convention, "if gentlemen thought proper."[9]

North Carolina as a Foreign Power

That the delegates consented to a reading at that time is unlikely, but they were familiar with the contents of Jones's proposal by the next morning, when Governor Johnston took up where Iredell had left off the previous afternoon. If the convention adopted the first part of Jones's resolution, North Carolina "shall be entirely out of the Union." The substance of the proposed amend-ments themselves was therefore irrelevant. "To whom are we to refer these amendments?" The new Congress? Perhaps, but with no representatives in that body, how would North Carolina accomplish this? The state would have to "appoint ambassadors to the United States of America, to represent what

8. Elliot, *Debates*, 4:219, 220, 222.   9. Elliot, *Debates*, 4:216.

scruples" it had "in regard to their Constitution." For its part, the United States would come to regard North Carolina "as a foreign power." This was the stuff of nightmares: "ambassadors" to the United States, "their" Constitution, "foreign" power. Johnston knew exactly what he was doing. He wanted North Carolinians to "pause" before deciding on "so awful a question," and if scaring them was the only way to keep them from making a hasty decision, so be it.[10]

Jones refused to be frightened: "It is objected we shall be out of the Union. So I wish it to be." Unlike Johnston, Jones was certain that the state would be better positioned to bargain over amendments if it made them a precondition of ratification. He also found foolish the notion that North Carolina would be reduced to a "foreign power" sending "ambassadors to Congress." The state could enter the Union whenever it chose to do so, and the other states would welcome its entry. To be sure, Federalists seemed to think otherwise, but they were wrong. Iredell, for example, was wrong on two interrelated counts when he argued that a refusal "to accede for the present" might come to haunt North Carolinians later because the other states "at their pleasure" may subsequently choose to impose onerous terms for admission. First, Iredell was mistaken in his assessment of the relative strengths of the Union and the state. He had asked rhetorically "whether ten states can do longer without one, or one without ten," when in reality neither could do well without the other. Jones's confidence relative to North Carolina's situation within the Union was grounded in an appreciation of basic geography. North Carolina was huge. In 1790 it had a total population of about 430,000 persons, including more than 100,000 slaves, making it the fourth most populous state at the time, just ahead of New York. Size may not always matter, but in this case it did. In 1788 North Carolina comprised some ninety-five thousand square miles. With a western district that later became the state of Tennessee, it stretched nearly nine hundred miles from the Atlantic to the Mississippi River, effectively cutting off South Carolina and Georgia from the rest of the Union. It was almost inconceivable that the newly formed federal government could long survive without North Carolina. "Virginia, our next neighbor," had already acknowledged that North Carolina's strategic location made it "of the greatest importance to her." Alone, Virginia, which in Iredell's own estimation was such a "powerful and respectable state" that her initial reluctance to ratify had raised "serious alarm," wielded enormous authority in Congress. But Virginia would not be alone. "South Carolina and Georgia are deeply interested in our being admitted." Separated from Virginia by at least a hundred miles in most locations, South Carolina,

10. Elliot, *Debates*, 4:223.

much less Georgia, "cannot exist without North Carolina." These geographic considerations, guaranteed that the state ran "no risk of being excluded from the Union when we think proper to come in."[11]

Underlying Iredell's first error was a second. The gentleman from Edenton seemed to think that the ratifying states would be resentful, that they would interpret North Carolina's action as an attempt to "dictate to the whole Union" the terms of its admission. Nothing could be further from the truth. North Carolina was not dictating anything, least of all arbitrary terms of "copartnership." Virginia would respond favorably to North Carolina's proposed amendments because "she wishes the same alterations." And this was not simply happenstance, Jones explained, because in composing his resolution he copied "word for word, the Virginia amendments." Rather than demanding burdensome concessions for admission, therefore, Virginia, finding common cause, "will do every thing she can to bring us into the Union." George Mason, who served prominently on the committee that drafted Virginia's recommendatory amendments, confirmed that the constitutional changes listed in Jones's resolution were "almost the same" as those "proposed by Virginia." Indeed Jones copied all twenty of the individual liberties that the Virginia convention protected under the heading "Declaration of Rights." He also took word for word all twenty items included in Virginia's "Amendments to the Body of the Constitution." The only reason Jones's proposal was "almost the same" rather than identical to Virginia's recommendations was because Jones attached six additional structural amendments to his resolution. The first four of these limited the power of Congress with respect to declaring a state to be in rebellion, creating mercantile monopolies, interfering in the redemption of paper money, and introducing foreign troops on American soil, the fifth extended the prohibition of duties on interstate commerce, and the sixth addressed the potential for conflict between existing federal laws and treaties. None of these would, in Jones's view, detract from his anticipated alliance between Virginia and North Carolina.[12]

Neither Entirely in Nor Wholly Out

Davie attempted one last maneuver to prolong the convention by asking that all forty-six amendments in Jones's resolution be "considered one by one." Most delegates, however, considered the "whole collectively" to be "very proper." The question finally being put, Jones's resolution "was agreed to by a

11. Elliot, *Debates*, 4:231, 232, 226.

12. Elliot, *Debates*, 4:226, 243–47; George Mason to John Mason, December 18, 1788, *PGM*, 3:1135; Veit, 17–21.

great majority of the committee" of the whole. The committee then adjourned, and chairman James Kenan delivered its report to the convention president, Governor Johnston. The next morning, August 1, Iredell opened the business of the convention with a motion to postpone consideration of the committee's report and to take up instead a resolution stating that "amendments should be proposed subsequent to the ratification on the part of this state, and not previous to it." He knew full well that his call to reverse the committee's decision would be "instantly rejected," Iredell said, and therefore his resolution was intended to serve no purpose other than to place on record the equivalent of a minority report for the sake of full disclosure to concerned constituents. Not unexpectedly, Iredell's motion touched off one last "warm altercation." Jones and his supporters blasted the resolution as "improper," "unprecedented," "irregular," and indicative of the minority's "great contempt of the voice of the majority." Iredell's backers accused the majority of "tyrannical" behavior—of "arbitrary" actions, "suppress[ion]" of dissent, bad faith, and an unwillingness to deal "fairly and liberally" with the minority.[13]

Having vented their frustration, the delegates were spent. Iredell conceded, "It is useless to contend any longer against a majority that is irresistible." On August 1, the convention defeated Iredell's motion by a vote of 184 to 84. On August 2, it adopted the committee's report, the equivalent of Jones's resolution, by the nearly identical margin of 184 to 83. "Those who voted yesterday *against* the amendment [Iredell's motion], voted for concurring with the report of the committee," the clerk of the convention recorded, and "those who voted *in favor* of the amendment, now voted *against* a concurrence with the report." On separate motions made by the victorious Jones, the convention then unanimously adopted two resolutions before adjourning sine die. First, it declared that North Carolina had decided "neither to ratify nor reject the Constitution." Iredell earlier had argued that "a refusal to adopt" as opposed to "a rejection" was a distinction without a difference. Jones begged to differ, and he sought now to position North Carolina so that it was neither entirely in nor wholly out of the Union. His resolution advised the state legislature to collect an impost on imported goods whenever Congress enacted such a law for the ten ratifying states, and that all "money arising therefrom" be appropriated "to the use of Congress." The second motion passed in the convention's closing moments urged Governor Johnston to transmit to Congress and the executives of the twelve other states copies of North Carolina's resolution regarding amendments along with copies of the previous resolution on imposts. Apparently, Jones was hedging his earlier bet that he would "forfeit . . . [his] life" if Congress withheld from North Carolina its share of any duties collected on future imports.[14]

13. Elliot, *Debates*, 4:240, 241, 242, 247.   14. Elliot, *Debates*, 4:231, 250–51, 225.

The First Congress

News of New York's ratification, conveyed with such dispatch to the North Carolina convention, had little or no effect on the delegates at Hillsborough. But the urgency felt by Williamson and Swann pertained not only to the business of the state convention but also to the affairs of Congress. The members of the Confederation Congress, they told Governor Johnston, "are extremely desirous to fix the time and place where and when proceedings shall commence under the new Government. Hitherto they have been restrained, partly we conceive, from a regard to the feelings of our state." Williamson and Swann were probably flattering the governor and the delegates at Hillsborough by suggesting that Congress was hesitating because of North Carolina's indecision. As we have seen, Congress decided to postpone consideration of a timetable for electing the president and commencing the operations of the new federal government in deference to New York, especially because of the prospect of keeping the federal capital in New York City. Hence on July 28, two days after New York had voted to adopt the Constitution but while North Carolina was still amusing itself with a one-sided debate, Congress set the revised timetable in motion.[15]

As scheduled, the members of the First Congress took their seats in Federal Hall in New York on the first Wednesday in March 1789. Only eleven states were represented because North Carolina and Rhode Island were officially not a part of the new federal Union. Of these two nonratifying states, North Carolina was far more important to contemporaries. Richard Platt, who chaired the committee that had arranged the grand federal procession in New York City to celebrate the adoption of the Constitution, hoped "soon [to] hear of North Carolina's accession." As for Rhode Island, however, "'tis of very little moment whether she comes in or not." The "animated" crowd that gathered in Plymouth, Massachusetts, "to indulge the pleasing impulses of joy together" in honor of New York's ratification, saw some benefit in Rhode Island's remaining out of the Union. "Accompanied with proper discharges of cannon" and "repeated cheers," the celebrants drank a toast to Rhode Island: "May the conduct of her majority exhibit the last sad example to the world of political depravity and error." Comte de Moustier, the French minister plenipotentiary to the United States, who had been an interested observer of American politics since his arrival in January 1788, had expected New York to ratify the Constitution because the state "will not want to break away from the union alone." North Carolina "will follow the example of Virginia." Accordingly, only one

15. Hugh Williamson and John Swann to Samuel Johnston, July 27, 1788, *DHRC*, 23:2430.

state would be left out, which was inconsequential, Moustier reported to the foreign minister in Paris, "for Rhode Island is counted as nothing." George Washington was a bit more diplomatic than the French diplomat, but even he dismissed Rhode Island as too inconstant for reliable "calculation." While he hoped for a positive result in North Carolina, he refused to "hazard an opinion" on Rhode Island, "lest he might be suspected of participating in its phrensy." To Connecticut representative Jonathan Trumbull, Washington wrote that the "infamy" of Rhode Island's conduct was so well known that "there is no state or description of men but would blush to be involved in a connection with the . . . Junto of that Anarchy."[16]

North Carolinians were, in fact, mortified to be coupled with Rhode Island. Williamson, who had befriended both Madison and Hamilton at the Constitutional Convention, commented sarcastically that North Carolina had "thrown herself out of the Union, but . . . happily . . . the large, upright, and respectable State of Rhode Island is her associate." His one wish was that the alliance not signify "that the delegates from North Carolina should profess a particular affection for the delegates from Rhode Island." James Iredell, whose reputation for tempered rhetoric made him one of the most respected lawyers in North Carolina, condemned "the peculiar obstinacy of Rhode Island" and could barely contain his contempt for "that little state." Despite her obvious "weakness, she uniformly opposed every regulation for the benefit and honor of the Union at large," Iredell observed, probably remembering in particular the contest over the Impost of 1781, when Rhode Island alone had succeeded in blocking an attempt by the Confederation Congress to raise some badly needed funds through the imposition of a 5 percent tax on imported goods. Even Thomas Paine could not persuade Rhode Islanders to accept a measure that twelve other states had adopted. But now eleven states had ratified the Constitution, having concluded that the "happiness of all America ought not to be sacrificed to the caprice and obstinacy" of Rhode Island. North Carolina should join them, Iredell advised, and reject any suggestion of an association with "so inconsiderable a part."[17]

16. Richard Platt to Winthrop Sargent, August 8, 1788, *DHRC*, 21:1351; *Massachusetts Centinel*, August 2, 1788, *DHRC*, 23:2423; Comte de Moustier to Comte de Montmorin, July 2, 1788, *DHRC*, 21:1248; George Washington to John Jay, August 3, 1788, *DHRC*, 23:2446; George Washington to Benjamin Lincoln, June 29, 1788, and George Washington to Jonathan Trumbull, July 20, 1788, in W. B. Allen, ed., *George Washington: A Collection* (Indianapolis, 1988), 404, 412.

17. Hugh Williamson to James Iredell, August 23, 1788, in Edmund C. Burnett, ed., *Letters of Members of the Continental Congress*, 8 vols. (Washington, DC, 1921–36), 8:784–85; Merrill Jensen, *The New Nation: A History of the United States during the Confederation, 1781–1789* (New York, 1950), 64–65; Elliot, *Debates*, 4:228–29.

Madison and the Bill of Rights

Madison, who on at least two occasions had confidently predicted that North Carolina would follow the example set by Virginia, must have been disappointed with the outcome of the Hillsborough convention. But he was inclined to be more sympathetic to the plight of the two nonratifying states than either Washington or Williamson. "Notwithstanding the ratification of this system of government by eleven of the thirteen United States," he declared, there remained "many, respectable for their talents [and] their patriotism," who remained "dissatisfied with it." What inspired these patriots was the "jealousy they have for their liberty, which, though mistaken in its object, is laudable in its motive." This observation applied "in a particular manner to those two states who have not thought fit to throw themselves into the bosom of the confederacy." Madison urged Congress "to take those steps which would be prudent and requisite at this juncture" to ensure that a "re-union should take place as soon as possible."[18]

Madison made these remarks in defense of the constitutional amendments he introduced in Congress on June 8. The "prudent" steps he recommended became the basis of the Bill of Rights and the subject of ongoing speculation regarding his motivation. Madison had been an outspoken opponent of a federal bill of rights. In the Constitutional Convention, he was instrumental in defeating George Mason's last-minute appeal for a bill of rights. Siding with Roger Sherman, who argued that federal guarantees of fundamental liberties were unnecessary because "State Declarations of Rights . . . being in force are sufficient," Madison's opposition all but ensured that the vote against the Mason-inspired motion would be unanimous. During the struggle over ratification, Madison even more insistently argued that a bill of rights was not only unnecessary but dangerous. Unnecessary because, as Hamilton explained in *Federalist* no. 84, the Constitution granted only certain enumerated powers to the federal government; powers not explicitly delegated could not be assumed. An "injudicious zeal" to single out for protection some individual liberties in a separate bill of rights, however, might render ambiguous this major premise of a government founded on delegated powers and thereby afford ambitious and unscrupulous men the opportunity to usurp power under the "plausible pretense" that rights not included in such a bill were left unprotected.[19]

What might explain his change of heart? What convinced Madison that a bill of rights was "requisite at this juncture"? The answer may lie in the

18. *Congressional Register*, June 8, 1789, Veit, 78.
19. Farrand, 2:587–88; *Federalist* no. 84, 535.

ordinary politics of the period. "It was my misfortune," Madison explained to Jefferson, "to be thrown into a contest with our friend, Col. [James] Monroe." And although the ability to differentiate between "political and personal views" saved their friendship, Monroe's determined effort to make amending the Constitution a principal issue affected Madison. He was forced to concede in letters disseminated throughout the district that he now favored amendments to safeguard "essential rights." George Mason, who insisted that he continued to hold Madison in high esteem, claimed that Madison knew he would "not be elected without making some such Promises," and so he did. After his victory, "in order to appear as good as his word," Madison "made some motions in Congress."[20]

Jefferson's reservations about the absence of a bill of rights almost certainly caused Madison to rethink his earlier opposition. Shortly after the Constitutional Convention had adjourned and he was no longer "restrained from disclosing any part of their proceedings," Madison summarized for Jefferson, who was in Paris as the U.S. minister to France, the proceedings of the Philadelphia Convention. Jefferson replied that he found much to admire in the proposed Constitution but singled out the "omission of a bill of rights" as something "I do not like." The "people are entitled" to certain basic protections "against every government on earth, general or particular," Jefferson explained, and "no just government should refuse" them this guarantee. He understood the reserved powers argument that Madison endorsed in the Convention but found it unconvincing because it was applied inconsistently. The Constitution in fact contained specific provisions prohibiting the passing of ex post facto laws and bills of attainder, disallowing religious qualifications for office, proscribing titles of nobility, and limiting the suspension of the writ of habeas corpus to emergencies arising from rebellion or invasion. Clearly, the contention that "all is reserved . . . which is not given" is contradicted "by strong inferences from the body of the instrument." Although he generally approved of the proposed Constitution and wished to see it secured, Jefferson initially, as we have seen, also "sincerely wish[ed] that the 9 first conventions may receive, and the 4 last reject it." Thus the new federal government will at once become operational but be "oblige[d] . . . to offer a declaration of rights in order to complete the union." In this way, "we shall have all it's [*sic*] good, and cure it's [*sic*] principal defect."[21]

20. James Madison to Thomas Jefferson, March 29, 1789, *Republic of Letters*, 1:605; Harlow Giles Unger, *The Last Founding Father: James Monroe and a Nation's Call to Greatness* (Philadelphia, 2009), 83; Kenneth R. Bowling, "'A Tub to the Whale': The Founding Fathers and Adoption of the Federal Bill of Rights," *Journal of the Early Republic* 8 (Fall 1988):, 232–33 George Mason to John Mason, July 31, 1789, *PGM*, 3:1164.
21. Thomas Jefferson to James Madison, December 20, 1787, and February 6, 1788, *Republic of Letters*, 1:512–13, 529–30.

If Jefferson's reasoning affected Madison, however, it was not enough to convert him from a foe to a friend of a bill of rights. Jefferson himself admitted as much, writing to Madison that his likes and dislikes were conveyed "merely as a matter of curiosity for I know your own judgment has been formed on all these points." And indeed Jefferson seemed to have rightly assessed the situation, for in the Virginia ratifying convention, which met in June 1788, at least four months after Jefferson's letters, Madison opposed Patrick Henry's proposal for a bill of rights by arguing that it was both unnecessary and dangerous. Again, in October 1788, fully eight months after Jefferson's most deliberate letter on the subject, Madison continued to insist that the absence of a bill of rights did not amount to a "material defect" in the Constitution. What ultimately was the effect of Jefferson's objections? Although he did not accept Jefferson's assessment of the "principal defect" of the Constitution, by early 1789 Madison had come to share his friend's belief that a bill of rights was needed to "complete the union." Constantly monitoring the strength of the Antifederalist forces, he was convinced that the majority of the members gathering to meet in New York for the first Congress would be safely "on the side of the Constitution." But he was equally certain that at the state level the opponents of the new federal government were "formidable" and that they were "zealous for a second Convention." They were motivated by the "insidious hope of throwing all things into Confusion," thereby subverting the "fabric just established, if not the Union itself."[22]

The Role of Recommendatory Amendments

Underpinning Madison's fear of a second convention was his knowledge of the actions taken by five states during the ratification struggle. Following the example set by Massachusetts, four states had ratified the Constitution with recommendatory amendments. Ratification was an all or nothing proposition, to be sure, and all of the ratifying states had adopted the Constitution unconditionally. Nevertheless, recommendations do carry a certain amount of authority. Madison knew this. As a member of the Virginia convention, he was a party to the explanatory resolution that accompanied the state's ratification. That resolution recognized that many Virginians "dreaded" the operation of the new Constitution under its present form and tried to reassure them that its "imperfections" would be speedily addressed. Madison was also aware of the New York Antifederalist Society's letter to the states. Drafted by a committee of three headed by Melancton Smith, it noted that many of its members had

22. Pauline Maier, *Ratification: The People Debate the Constitution, 1787–1788* (New York, 2010), 297; *DHRC*, 10:1500–3, 1507; James Madison to Thomas Jefferson, October 17 and December 8, 1788, *Republic of Letters*, 1:564, 579–80.

voted to ratify the Constitution in spite of its "defects" because "they considered amendments as certain," regardless of whether these corrections came before or after ratification. For Madison, who was pleased by the outcome at Pough-keepsie and undoubtedly numbered Smith among the "intelligent Citizens" who were opposed to any proposition that kept "the state for the present out of the New Union," the letter's "suspicion" that implied "promises were made with a view to deceive" was personally distressing. The submitting and receiv-ing recommendatory amendments comprised a "tacit compact" between the parties that he felt bound to honor "as an honest man."[23]

What probably caused Madison some hesitation, however, was the nature of the recommendations themselves. As a member of the Wythe committee that drafted the forty recommendatory amendments adopted at Richmond, Madi-son was fully aware of the difficulties they posed. The first twenty, which fell under the heading of a "Declaration or Bill of Rights," were less problematic. These included broad statements of principle: that governments were insti-tuted for the common good; that the separation of powers doctrine must be observed; that the doctrine of nonresistance against arbitrary power was "slav-ish"; that magistrates and legislators have to return to their private stations at fixed periods so that they themselves may feel firsthand the consequences of their actions. Additionally, some conventional protections of individual liber-ties received particular mention: the right to a speedy trial and due process, the right peaceably to assemble, freedom of speech and press, freedom of con-science, protection against unreasonable searches and seizures, prohibition of cruel and unusual punishments, the right to bear arms, the right to confront one's accusers, and limits on the suspension of the writ of habeas corpus. All of these were unexceptional. Indeed, they were familiar to most Virginians because the Wythe committee relied heavily on George Mason's 1776 Declara-tion of Rights. The only point of contention in the original 1776 declaration centered on what is arguably its most famous passage, and that passage was noticeably absent from the 1788 proposals. Mason's 1776 draft declared that "all men are by nature equally free and independent, and have certain inherent rights." The 1788 recommendatory amendments stated more prosaically that there were "certain natural rights . . . which men" entering into a "social com-pact" cannot alienate. No doubt this change was inspired by the jarring incon-sistency of the largest slaveholding society in North America declaring all men to be born free and equal. Some Virginians also feared that any sort of lofty declaration that all men were entitled to the "enjoyment of life and liberty" as

23. James Madison to Richard Peters, August 18, 1789, *PJM*, 12:347; New York Antifederalist Society, proceedings, October 30–November 13, 1788, *DHRC*, 23:2475–77; James Madison to George Washington, July 21, 1788, *PJM*, 11:190.

well as the pursuit of "happiness and safety" amounted to an open invitation to slave insurrections.[24]

The second set of twenty recommendations Virginia submitted to Congress were far more troubling because they required changes to the "body of the Constitution." These were specific recommendations that would affect federal treaty-making powers, the enactment of laws of navigation and commerce, presidential terms, congressional authority within the planned federal city, federal control over state militias, the venue for impeachment trials, and the jurisdiction of the Supreme Court. These and other substantive revisions of the Constitution alarmed Madison and Federalists in general because they threatened to unhinge some of the compromises that had been struck in the Philadelphia Convention a year earlier. The enactment of laws regulating commerce, for example, had already been hotly debated in the Constitutional Convention. And, as we have seen, southern and northern delegates settled the dispute through a compromise linking federal legislation regarding commerce to the unfettered importation of slaves for twenty years. Virginia's proposed amendment requiring the consent of two-thirds of both houses of Congress to enact commercial laws would have reopened the debate not only on that issue but on the slave importation question as well.[25]

The recommendatory amendments brought forward by the other four states resembled Virginia's submission in being organized under two headings: those that protected individual liberties and those that altered the provisions of the Constitution itself. Massachusetts submitted nine amendments, three of which fell under the first heading and six under the second. New Hampshire's recommendations were identical to those of its larger neighbor with the addition of three bill of rights items that prohibited the quartering of soldiers in private houses, protected the freedom of religion, and secured the right to bear arms. South Carolina's submission was the briefest by far, including only a reserved powers declaration along with structural changes restricting the federal government's power to interfere with elections and restoring the requisition system for raising needed revenues. New York's list of explanatory and recommendatory amendments exceeded all others in length, but its fifty-seven items fell essentially into the same two categories. As with Virginia's first set of twenty amendments, the individual liberties singled out for protection by New York were the standard stuff of Revolutionary declarations. A conservative count of the substantive alterations proposed by all five states, however, yields a total of at least sixty separate recommendations. Some of these might properly

24. Veit, 17–18; *PGM*, 1:274, 275, 277, 283, 287–91.
25. Veit, 19–21.

be placed under both headings. New York's recommendation that the prohibition of ex post facto laws be limited "only to Laws concerning Crimes," for example, was both a protection of individual liberties and an alteration of the provision contained under Article 1, Section 9, of the Constitution. But even these hybrid recommendations threatened to revive issues that had been resolved in Philadelphia, and the most likely venue for such a reconsideration was a second federal convention.[26]

Congress or the States?

Under Article 5 of the Constitution, amendments may be initiated either by Congress or by the state legislatures. Congress may take the lead and with the approval of two-thirds of both houses propose amendments that would then be forwarded to the states for ratification. Alternatively, individual states may apply to Congress to call a convention for the exclusive purpose of amending the Constitution, and upon the application of two-thirds of the states Congress must do so. In either case, whether the proposals are generated by members of Congress or by convention delegates, they must be ratified by three-fourths of the states in order to become a part of the Constitution.

The Philadelphia Convention spent relatively little time and effort in crafting Article 5. The Virginia Plan, which Edmund Randolph introduced on May 29, 1787, recommended that some provision be made for amending the "Articles of Union whensoever it shall seem necessary," with the stipulation that the "assent of the National Legislature ought not to be required." George Mason explained the reason for this caveat. To require the assent of the national legislature would be inappropriate because its misdeeds may have led to the call for alterations in the first place. In that event, what were the chances that such a legislature would agree to modifications aimed at restricting its opportunities for abuse? The procedure for amending remained in this somewhat amorphous state—a decision by the convention to do something but precisely what left undetermined—until August 6, when the Committee of Detail delivered to each delegate a printed copy of the results of its deliberations. Among other things included in this report, which mainly summarized the convention's work over the preceding two weeks, was a provision for the national legislature to call a convention whenever two-thirds of the states requested it. In other words, the committee established the basis for the second of the two means of amending contained under Article 5. During the debate over this provision, Alexander Hamilton suggested that the national legislature also be empowered to call a convention, independent of the actions of the states, because it would be more "sensible to the necessity of amendments." Extend-

26. Veit, 14–28.

ing Hamilton's logic, Roger Sherman moved to enlarge the role of the legislature by allowing it to propose amendments directly to the states instead of limiting it to calling a convention at the discretion of two-thirds of both houses. Madison then offered a substitute motion that with minor revisions made its way into the final document as Article 5.[27]

By March of 1789, when the First Congress met, two states had already made considerable headway in their drive to amend the Constitution through the second of the two means specified under Article 5. In Virginia, Patrick Henry was determined not to allow Congress to take the lead in proposing amendments. He considered the state legislature better suited to look after the interests of the people than a distantly located and inadequately representative federal body. And with a compliant majority of the assembly behind him, Henry usually had his way. "*It is said,*" Washington told Madison, that the "edicts of Mr. H —— are enregistered with less opposition by the majority . . . than those of the Grand Monarch are in the Parliaments of France. He has only to say let this be Law—and it is Law." Not surprisingly, Henry succeeded in pushing through the assembly a resolution calling for a second general convention. Claiming that the delegates at the Richmond convention had voted to ratify the Constitution even though they "dreaded its operation under the present form," Virginia's application to Congress declared that only a "full expectation of its imperfections being speedily amended" could quiet "public apprehensions." The federal legislature could not meet that expectation because the "slow forms of congressional discussion and recommendation" foreboded delays at a time when the "anxiety with which our countrymen press for the accomplishment of this important end will ill admit of delay." The people needed some other means of advancing the necessary amendments. "Happily for their wishes, the Constitution hath presented an alternative." And that was the alternative on which Virginia hoped to capitalize by requesting a "convention be immediately called of deputies from the several states, with full power to take into their consideration the defects of this Constitution that have been suggested by the state conventions."[28]

A month later, in December 1788, Governor George Clinton, who had presided over the state convention in New York and voted against ratification in the committee of the whole, transmitted the Virginia resolution to the New York legislature. Declaring that the delegates at Poughkeepsie had acted in the belief that a second federal convention would soon meet to consider their list of amendments, the governor encouraged both houses to join Virginia in calling

---

27. Farrand, 1:22, 202–03, 2:177, 188, 558–59.
28. Richard R. Beeman, *Patrick Henry: A Biography* (New York, 1974), 166–67; George Washington to James Madison, November 17, 1788, *PJM*, 11:351; Virginia's application for a second convention, November 14, 1788, Veit, 235–37.

for a "speedy revisal" of the Constitution. The Antifederalist-controlled assembly readily endorsed Clinton's call for "a new Convention." The Federalist-controlled senate spent more time debating alternatives, but in the end it too "without hesitation, recommended a submission of the system to a general Convention." Both houses then adopted a resolution on February 5, urging that "an act to revise the said Constitution be among the first that shall be passed by the new Congress." New York's application to Congress for a "Convention of Deputies from the several states" differed from Virginia's in one important respect, however. It called for a convention "with full powers to take the said Constitution into their consideration." A casual observer might not have taken notice of the phrase following the words "full powers," but the legislators themselves knew what it signified. The New York Assembly adopted this rendering of its application after defeating a motion to limit the second convention to a consideration of those "amendments proposed by this or other states," meaning that the proposed convention's purview extended to the Constitution as a whole.[29]

Madison was alarmed by these proceedings. New York's circular letter "has a most pestilent tendency," he wrote Washington, because if the call for another "General Convention cannot be parried," the Constitution "may be at last successfully undermined by its enemies." The applications of the Virginia and New York legislatures were embodiments of this dangerous tendency. Designing men, self-professed opponents of the new system, wanted "to see a door opened for a re-consideration of the whole structure of the government." They knew it was unlikely that the door once opened would be shut "at that point which would be safe to the government itself." By contrast, friends of the Constitution may see a need for some "revisal," but not at the "risk of another Convention, whilst the purpose can be answered, by the other mode provided for introducing amendments." Because the "disaffected party" in both the House and Senate did "not exceed a very small minority," amendments drafted by Congress would effectively curtail any damage to the "particular structure" of the new federal government. But with five states having already proposed amendments and two states, including his own, explicitly requesting remedial action, momentum was on the side of those who favored a second convention. The time to act was now.[30]

29. New York Convention, circular letter to the executives of the states, July 26, 1788, *DHRC*, 23:2335–36; editors' note, New York recommends the calling of a second Constitutional Convention, *DHRC*, 23:2511–15; Veit, 237–38.

30. James Madison to George Washington, August 11, 1788, *PJM*, 11:230; Veit, 79; James Madison to Thomas Jefferson, December 8, 1788, and March 29, 1789, *Republic of Letters*, 1:579–80, 606.

Tub to the Whale

Madison's support of a federal bill of rights was thus a part of his strategic plan to outmaneuver the Antifederalists. His primary goal was to prevent any "possible injury" to the "main structure or principles" of the Constitution. A set of congressional proposals supplying additional safeguards for liberty "might be of use" by ensuring that any "revisal" was kept within proper boundaries. At the very least, "if properly executed" it would not hurt the existing constitutional arrangement and therefore "could not be of disservice." Additionally, his own tepid endorsement of a federal bill of rights notwithstanding, Madison was keenly aware that it "was anxiously desired by others." Many had opposed ratification for this reason alone, and if a simple enumeration of inviolable liberties would win them over, then he was for it. To Jefferson, Madison explained the basis of his reasoning: a congressional initiative would likely split the ranks of the opposition by distancing the "well meaning from the designing opponents" of the Constitution. Jefferson understood. He always numbered himself among the former but also always insisted that any "inconveniences" associated with a declaration of rights would be "shortlived, moderate, and reparable," whereas the "evil" that might result from the want of it was "permanent, afflicting and irreparable." Receiving his friend's thoughts with "great satisfaction," and convinced that "half a loaf is better than no bread," Jefferson sent his approval: "I am much pleased with the prospect."[31]

On June 8 Madison introduced his much anticipated proposal. Consisting of nine recommendations, it borrowed freely from Virginia's first twenty recommendatory amendments, that is, from its "Declaration or Bill of Rights." The heart of his proposal lay in its alteration of Article 1, Section 9, of the Constitution. This is the section that explicitly withholds from the federal government certain enumerated powers, such as suspending the writ of habeas corpus, enacting bills of attainder or ex post facto laws, granting titles of nobility, and most famously, interfering with the importation slaves prior to 1808. Madison, who favored incorporating all amendments into the existing text of the Constitution rather than attaching them as a separate supplement, proposed to insert into this section the equivalent of a federal bill of rights. In his fourth and longest recommendation—it was twice as long as any of the other eight—Madison included nearly all of the personal protections that would eventually constitute the Bill of Rights. Madison's insertion guaranteed freedom of

31. *Daily Advertiser*, June 9, 1789, Veit, 63; James Madison to Thomas Jefferson, October 17and December 8, 1788, *Republic of Letters*, 1:564, 579–80; Thomas Jefferson to James Madison, March 15, 1789; *Republic of Letters*, 1: 587–88.

conscience, press, speech, and assembly; the right to bear arms and to a fair and speedy trial; and protection against cruel and unusual punishment, excessive bail, unreasonable searches and seizures, the forcible quartering of soldiers, and double jeopardy. Indeed, in order to make clear that his listing of certain rights was not meant to imply that those not listed were vulnerable to governmental encroachment, Madison ended his lengthy recommendation with a disclaimer that was substantively identical to the assertion of reserved rights contained in what became the Ninth Amendment: an enumeration "in favor of particular rights shall not be so construed as to diminish the just importance of other rights retained by the people."[32]

Until the very moment that Madison rose from his seat in the House to present his proposed amendments, interested parties on both sides expressed a great deal of concern about the possible contents of his impending motion. Richard Henry Lee, the Virginia Antifederalist who had refused to serve in the Constitutional Convention and had subsequently, with the assistance of Patrick Henry, defeated Madison for a seat in the new Senate, wrote of Madison's anticipated motion that "his ideas and those of our convention . . . are not similar." George Clymer, the Philadelphia merchant and "lawyer of some abilities" who represented Pennsylvania at the Federal Convention, voiced the opposite concern. On the morning of June 8, Clymer informed Richard Peters, the Federalist speaker of the Pennsylvania Assembly, that Madison was preparing "to make an essay towards amendments," but whether he "will suffer himself to be so far frightened with the antifederalism of his own state as to attempt to lop off essentials I do not know." By that afternoon, however, having heard Madison's proposal, Clymer was no longer worried. "Madison's [proposal] has proved to be a tub," he informed Peters.[33]

To supporters and opponents of Madison's amendments, Clymer's assessment required no further explication. They understood it to be a literary reference to Jonathan Swift's allegorical *Tale of a Tub* (1704), in which the satirist explained that "seamen have a custom, when they meet a whale, to fling him out an empty tub . . . to divert him from laying violent hands upon the ship." For most of Madison's Federalist contemporaries, the June 8 proposal was nothing more than a tub to distract the Antifederalist whale in order to keep it from harming the constitutional ship. What about Madison's inclusion of a bill of rights in his proposed alteration of Article 1, Section 9? Was it an empty tub? Theodore Sedgwick thought so. During an extended debate over the freedom of speech and assembly provision in Madison's recommendation, Sedgwick, who represented western Massachusetts, could barely conceal his contempt. He suggested that the House might also consider declaring "that a

32. Veit, 11–14.   33. Veit, 241, 245; Farrand, 3:91.

man should have a right to wear his hat if he pleased, that he might get up when he pleased, and go to bed when he thought proper." Noah Webster, upset at Madison for having broached the subject of amending the Constitution in the first place, regretted that it now forced House members to waste "their time in throwing out an empty tub" while more pressing business was left unattended.[34]

Tranquilizing the Minds of Honest Opposers

In a spirited defense of his June 8 motion, Madison insisted that a bill of rights was both "proper in itself and highly politic," but even his admirers focused on the latter. Regardless of its propriety or necessity, a declaration of personal liberties would be politically advantageous. Edmund Randolph considered Madison's amendments as a kind of useful sedative, an "anodyne to the discontented." Abraham Baldwin, who had been the most influential member of the Georgia delegation at the Federal Convention and was now a representative from Augusta, explained to his brother-in-law Joel Barlow, the Connecticut Wit, that Madison's aim was to "tranquillize the minds of honest opposers" of the Constitution. Writing to Tench Coxe, a fellow Philadelphia merchant and Federalist, George Clymer said that Madison was a "like a sensible physician" administering a placebo, "bread pills" consisting of "powder of paste & neutral mixtures," to Antifederalist patients suffering "malades imaginaires" or imaginary illnesses.[35]

Federalists who were less well disposed toward Madison were far more unforgiving in their assessments. Fisher Ames, who in the Massachusetts ratifying convention had dismissed the notion of debating amendments as "too absurd" to warrant further discussion, ridiculed the "fruit" of Madison's "labour and research." Like Clymer, Ames thought Madison was acting as a political doctor but not a wise one. His "prodigious great dose" was too much "for a medicine." It was "rather food than physic," but it was hardly enough to sustain good health, as it consisted mainly of "an immense mass of sweet" designed to attract the undiscerning consumer. Senator Pierce Butler of South Carolina informed James Iredell, the champion of the ratification movement in North Carolina, that Madison, thirsting after popular approval, had gratuitously introduced "*milk-and-water* amendments" aimed at securing "liberty of conscience, a free press, and one or two general things already well secured." The problem with Madison, these critics agreed, was that he lacked the necessary "strength of nerves" to be an effective leader. To be sure, he possessed "first rate abilities," Federalist publisher John Fenno wrote, but he was handicapped

34. Veit, 175, 159, 276; Bowling, "'A Tub to the Whale,'" 237.
35. Veit, 84, 255, 256, 250.

by a "timidity of disposition" that prevented him from standing up to "artful, unprincipled, & disaffected" men whose sole desire was "to embroil & embarrass public affairs." Representative Sedgwick, who had successfully led a small army into battle against approximately a hundred of Shays's rebels in 1787 and consequently thought he knew something about courage in the face of demagogues and popular commotion, agreed that Madison's "talents [were] respectable" but attenuated by his "timidity." His "honorable intentions" were easily "lost to the public" because he could not set himself in "defiance [to] popular and factious clamors." Sadly, Sedgwick lamented, the House was forced to engage in "water gruel business" simply because Madison was "haunted by the ghost of Patrick Henry."[36]

Fisher Ames delighted his kinsman Thomas Dwight with a mocking description of Madison's proposal: "It contains a Bill of Rights—the right of enjoying property—of changing the govt. at pleasure—freedom of the press—of conscience—of juries. . . . There is too much of it—O. I had forgot, the right of the people to bear Arms." He closed with the Latin phrase "Risum teneatis amici," that is, "Could you forbear the laughter of a friend?" Ames and Dwight may have been amused, but Antifederalists were not. "Timid" was almost certainly not a word that they associated with Madison. Clever, scheming, deceitful, ambitious, and perhaps vain, they thought, but never timid. Madison's amendments were "calculated merely . . . to deceive," South Carolina representative Thomas Tudor Tucker observed. If successful, Madison's proposal would obstruct the progress of real efforts to secure meaningful changes in the federal frame. Ames and others dismissed his recommendations as insubstantial "hasty-pudding," but that was because they mistook their true significance and underestimated Madison. Boston lawyer James Sullivan, who as "Hampden" in 1788 had unsuccessfully argued for conditional ratification in Massachusetts, made no such mistakes. Sarcastically referring to the "great Man from Virginia," Sullivan urged his friend Elbridge Gerry to continue his "exertions" as long as Madison pursued his scheme to lay "aside the Amendments proposed by the several states in order to prevent any thing being done on the subject." George Mason, who claimed to have a "pretty thorough acquaintance" of Madison, accused him of carrying on a "Farce." Pretending to be the "Patron of Amendments," Madison put forward "some Milk and Water Propositions" that diverted attention away from more "important and substantial Amendments." Madison had thrown a "Tub to the Whale." South Carolina Antifederalist Aedanus Burke characterized Madison's amendments as "whipsyllabub, frothy and full of wind, formed only to please the palate." But unlike

---

36. Maier, *Ratification*, 202; Veit, 247, 248, 274, 258–59, 263–64; David P. Szatmary, *Shays' Rebellion: The Making of an Agrarian Insurrection* (Amherst, MA, 1980), 103.

his fellow Carolinian Pierce Butler, Burke did not view them as gratuitous. Madison was disingenuously offering his palate-pleasing froth in place of "those solid and substantial amendments which the people expect." Apparently, Burke grew so exercised during his speech that he finally launched into a personal attack on Madison. According to William Loughton Smith who witnessed firsthand his colleague's rant in the House of Representatives, Burke characterized the proposed amendments as "a mere *tub to the whale*" and then proceeded with some unkind "reflexions[,] . . . particularly on Madison," which were then "taken up warmly by Madison and others."[37]

Desultory Conversations

As Smith's account indicates, exchanges in the House of Representatives were becoming increasingly heated as Antifederalists, outvoted by large majorities on nearly every pivotal question, grew more agitated. Their goal initially was to have the House consider all of the amendments proposed by the states. Elbridge Gerry announced that it was not merely his personal "wish" that this occur; it was his duty in accordance with the instructions of the Massachusetts ratifying convention to "press the amendments" of his state until they had been "maturely considered by congress." These "same duties," he was certain, "were made incumbent on the members from some other states" that had also submitted recommendatory amendments. And mature consideration meant that the whole House had to be engaged as a committee of the whole, Thomas Tudor Tucker added. The subject was too important to be left to a small committee that, supposing itself to be "better capable than the house," might act unilaterally in rejecting "every proposition coming from the state conventions." Nevertheless, when Fisher Ames, contending that the House's time could be "illy spared" examining proposals that were "so various," moved that the business of amendments be referred to a committee of eleven consisting of one member from each state, his motion carried by a two-to-one majority.[38]

Antifederalist fears that a select committee would be hostile to their interests proved to be well founded. The Committee of Eleven consisted of ten Federalists and a lone Antifederalist, Aedanus Burke of South Carolina. Of the ten Federalists, five, led by Madison, had been "members of the convention that formed the constitution," Burke protested. "Such gentlemen having already given their opinion with respect to the perfection of the work, may be thought improper agents to bring forward amendments." Charged with the responsibility of deliberating on Madison's amendments as well as those submit-

37. Veit, 175, 247, 248, 256, 278; Maier, *Ratification*, 187, 193; James Mason to John Mason, July 31, 1789, *PGM*, 3:1164; James Mason to Thomas Jefferson, January 10, 1791, *PGM*, 3:1218.
38. Veit, 99–100, 101, 97; see 102 for vote of thirty-four to fifteen.

ted by the states, "without being bound" by either, the committee, predictably, chose to ignore all of the recommendations of the states. Perhaps equally unremarkable, the select committee's July 28 report was the nearly identical to Madison's June 8 proposal. Aside from reorganizing his nine recommendations into nineteen, which it managed to do mainly by assigning separate numbers to the individual liberties Madison lumped together in his bill of rights section, the select committee left Madison's work undisturbed.[39]

Having failed to gain what they thought was an obligatory hearing of the states' proposals, Antifederalists were determined to forestall any further action in Congress with regard to amendments. They adopted the tactic of confounding all discussion with "boundless" propositions and observations in hopes of postponing any resolution of the issue in the House and furthering the call for a second convention. At one point during the debates on August 15, John Fenno, the publisher of the Federalist *Gazette of the United States*, gave up trying to recount the specifics of a seemingly endless exchange over whether the freedom of speech and assembly also included the right of instructing one's congressional representative. He recorded simply that the deliberations "continued much longer" than was justified because a number of congressmen "appeared to take it for granted that they might touch upon collateral circumstances."[40]

For members of the press intent on keeping the public informed about the progress of business at the capital, these prolonged debates appeared pointless. Their favorite adjective was "desultory," as in the "desultory conversation" that ensued after a particular motion had been offered or the "desultory way" in which certain speakers made their case during the debates. What rendered these meandering, seemingly aimless, speeches puzzling to some spectators was that they were made amid incessant complaints about "being pressed for want of time." Even a few members of Congress were confused by the slow pace of proceedings in the House. Thomas Hartley of Pennsylvania thought it "very curious the Antis do not want any [amendments] at this time." Prior to the report of the Committee of Eleven, they had championed numerous amendments; now, "we are obliged . . . to force them upon them."[41]

Hartley's observation holds the key to the puzzle. Antifederalists were long winded because, as Massachusetts Federalist Benjamin Goodhue explained, "they say the propositions reported by the Committee of Eleven are only calculated to amuse without materially affecting those parts of the Constitution

39. Veit, 6, 97, 175. Madison's proposal and the Select Committee's Report are at 11–14, 29–33, respectively.

40. Benjamin Goodhue to Michael Hodge, August 20, 1789, Veit, 283; *Gazette of the United States*, August 19, 1789, Veit, 156.

41. Veit, 99, 156, 174, 279.

which were particularly objectionable." In other words, they did not want Congress to take the lead in amending the Constitution. The Federalists did, for essentially the same reasons. Thus while Antifederalists purposefully engaged in desultory objections, Federalists kept protesting that valuable time was being wasted. There was no contradiction here, as John Vining observed in the wake of his report from the Committee of Eleven. One side evidenced an "urgency to dispatch this business" while the other side engaged in "unnecessary delay and procrastination." John Brown, representing the Kentucky district of Virginia, went further and named names. The "Antis viz. Gerry, Tucker," and their cohorts seemed determined "to obstruct and & embarrass the business as much as possible." In a letter to Benjamin Rush, the Philadelphia doctor and outspoken advocate of the new federal government, Speaker of the House Frederick A. Muhlenberg described the Antifederalist strategy in full. "Mr Gerry & Mr. Tucker" professed to be the "greatest sticklers for Amendments," Muhlenberg explained, but they were throwing "every obstacle they could in their way . . . to mar their progress." That their "curious medley" of proposals could not possibly gain the assent of two-thirds of the House, and therefore would never be included in any congressional resolution pertaining to amendments, was inconsequential to them. The "Design" of these obstructionists was to so impede the conduct of business that eventually Congress would be forced to concede to "their darling Question for calling a convention."[42]

Political Thermometer High Each Day

For the majority of the members of the House, the obstructionism of the Antifederalists proved frustrating in the extreme. The press described the debates as "warm," "animated," and "copious." But the participants themselves preferred stronger adjectives: "disagreeable," "fatiguing," "wearisome," and "nauseous." The debate over amendments proved to be an ordeal, and it was so by design. Although Gerry's and Tucker's frivolous propositions met with the "rejection which they so justly merit," Goodhue reported, they consumed "precious moments" in the process. Delaware's Vining was clearly exasperated, scolding Gerry for coming into the House "day after day reiterating the same train of arguments, and demanding the attention of this body by rising six or seven times on a question." He longed to have "no more reiterations or tedious discussions." But Gerry was not so easily deterred. George Clymer, Pennsylvania's representative on the Committee of Eleven, was convinced that Gerry intended "to treat us with all the amendments of all the antifederalists in America."[43]

42. Veit, 170, 279, 280–81; Benjamin Goodhue to Michael Hodge, August 20, 1789, Veit, 283.
43. Veit, 191 ("warm"), 105 ("animated"), 107 ("copious"), 280 ("disagreeable"), 284 ("fatiguing" and "wearisome"), 281 ("nauseous"), 283, 170–71, 245.

By mid-August, Speaker Muhlenberg could not help but notice that tempers were flaring "so that a frequent call to Order became absolutely necessary." Massachusetts representative George Leonard confirmed: "Political Thermometer high each day." William Smith of Maryland noted that "intensely hot" summer temperatures contributed to the "bad temper" that prevailed in the House. Gerry questioned the integrity of the Committee of Eleven, whose members appeared too "ripe for a decision" on their report. He also insinuated that Madison, the "honorable gentleman from Virginia," was guilty of indulging his vanity. "It is natural, sir, for us to be fond of our own work," Gerry opined, but it would be unseemly if such fondness caused us "not to admit . . . an improvement." Madison, twice slighted, first as the draftsman of the June 8 proposal and then as a member of the select committee, refused to remain "silent" in the face of Gerry's insinuations. He placed his trust in those "who have heard the voice of their country," he said, to judge whether he was acting honorably. Others were not as forgiving. The climax to all of this "ill-humour & rudeness" came at the end of the first full week of debate. Maryland's Smith informed his son-in-law on August 22 that "very high words" were exchanged in the House that day, leading to an "*altercation*" that nearly ended in "direct challenges." The "weather was excessive & the blood warm," Smith summarized. Gerry, perhaps reflecting on the same episode, would later boast to his brother Samuel that he had faced down a challenge from a "gentleman . . . on Mr. Ames's side." This unnamed Federalist, claiming "to be offended by something" Gerry had said, threatened "to call him out" to a duel. In Gerry's telling, his own eagerness to "meet any proposition" that his challenger might think "proper to make out of the House" caused this would-be adversary to retreat, and "so the matter ended."[44]

There was method to the Antifederalists' madness. Taxing the patience of their colleagues was having an impact. Stalling seemed to be working. "We have sat so long," Speaker Muhlenberg lamented on August 18 that, given the "present temper of the House," the exchanges "from this day forward" must be "high." Soaring temperatures, escalating confrontations, and the threat of physical violence led Muhlenberg to conclude that "the sooner we close the Session the better." Muhlenberg's Pennsylvania cohort, Thomas Hartley, shared the speaker's dismay. "I am sorry that business [of amendments] was brought forward this session," he wrote on August 16. Encouraged by these expressions of exhaustion and regret emanating from the other side, Antifederalists bore down even harder. During the lengthy debate over the scope of free speech and assembly rights, as several members of the House repeatedly called

44. Veit, 281, 279, 278, 280, 169, 176, 285; for duel, see 279.

for the question, Gerry demanded to know why some "gentlemen seem in a great hurry." Tucker concluded that some congressmen were placing "private convenience" above public "duty"; otherwise, why the "haste"? Protesting the "undue precipitancy" of these "honorable gentlemen," South Carolina Anti-federalist Thomas Sumter suggested a solution. Perhaps "we had better drop the subject of amendments, and leave it until we have more leisure to consider the . . . business effectually." Aedanus Burke, still smarting over the treatment he had received in the Committee of Eleven, denounced the whole subject with the claim that "we have done nothing but lose our time." The best course of action for the House now would be "to drop the subject" and move on to other business.[45]

Madison Is Becoming Popular with the Antis

The suggestion to postpone or drop the subject of amendments might have resonated with some Federalists before July, prior to the appointment of the Committee of Eleven, but not in August. That battle had already been decided. Fatigue, frustration, and flaring tempers notwithstanding, few supporters of the Constitution were willing to lay aside the report of the select committee. To do so would almost surely have invited the state legislatures to take over the process of amending the Constitution, and for Federalists that was unacceptable. This was made evident earlier in June. As Federalists disagreed over whether it was better to discuss Madison's proposal openly in the committee of the whole or to relegate it to a select committee, several influential members argued that the entire subject of amendments was best left to a later date. Led by "father Sherman," the plain-spoken representative from Connecticut who had figured prominently in the Philadelphia Convention, they contended that the present was not the "proper time" for taking up any proposals for amending. Writing as "A Citizen of New Haven," Sherman staked out this position in an essay published in the *New-York Packet* at the outset of the first session of Congress: there was no immediate need to amend the Constitution. Experience alone would reveal the deficiencies of the new federal plan and thereby point out the nature and extent of the required alterations. By contrast, amendments made in anticipation of future "difficulties" were dangerous, suggesting a certain degree of "instability in government and laws" that might prove "detrimental, if not fatal to the union." Delaware's Vining agreed that the first order of business in the First Congress should be to make the new federal government fully operational. It behooved the House, therefore, to attend to the organization of the executive branch, the collection of taxes and imposts,

45. Veit, 281, 279, 169, 174, 175.

and composition of the national judiciary. Settling these issues would go a long way toward quieting the "perturbation of the public mind."[46]

Powerful arguments made by powerful friends of the Constitution were not easily dismissed. But John Page, a classmate of Jefferson's at the College of William and Mary who once gushed that Madison deserved the "immortal honor" of having laid the "foundation of this great fabric of government," trumped all of these objections by reminding the House of the "alternative" contained in Article 5. If Congress failed to act on Madison's motion, if it went from postponement to postponement in a manner that must eventually prove "very disagreeable," the people will turn their "attention to the alternative" promoted by Patrick Henry and the resolutions of the Virginia and New York legislatures. They will "clamor for a new convention," Page warned, and "you will not have power to deliberate" any longer or to control the extent of the changes to the Constitution. "How dangerous such an expedient would be, I need not mention." Granted there were other pressing matters before the House, and granted that ordinarily the test of experience should, as Georgia's James Jackson put it, precede any "talk of amending," but these were not ordinary times. Mindful of the probable consequences of congressional inaction, all "who dread the assembling of a convention, will do well to acquiesce in the present motion."[47]

That Federalists were united in their support of Madison's proposal while Antifederalists were divided in their opposition to it contributed to the failure of the stalling tactic and the suggestion to drop the subject of amendments. Madison claimed that the "great mass of the people" did not object to the Constitution because of its "structure"—that the president had no advisory council, for example, or that the senate exercised judicial powers in impeachment trials—but because "it did not contain effectual provision against encroachments on particular rights." Contrary to the wishes of "some respectable characters," a bill of rights would therefore satisfy the bulk of those opposed to the Constitution, making converts of a "great number of our fellow citizens." Madison may have exaggerated but, especially in the eyes of his Antifederalist opponents, not by much. William Grayson, who stood with Henry at the Richmond convention and who subsequently, with Henry's help, defeated Madison for a seat in the Senate, complained that too many "Antis are so extremely lukewarm as scarcely to deserve the appellation." These so-called Antifederalists seemed content to have nothing more than "amendments which

46. Veit, 73, 220–22. For Sherman, see 76. For "father Sherman" reference by Samuel Otis, see 224.

47. John Page to James Madison, August 6, 1788, *PJM*, 11:225; Veit, 75.

shall affect personal liberty alone." With this in mind, "some gentlemen" who support the Constitution have adopted a posture of "*divide & impera*" aimed at "break[ing] the spirit of the [Antifederalist] party by divisions." Grayson, purposefully resorting to the passive voice when he complained to Henry that "a string of amendments were presented to the lower House," must have known that Madison was the prime mover in the divide and conquer strategy. Edward Carrington certainly knew. As a member of the Virginia House of Delegates who worried that Henry and his companions favored the breakup of the United States into three confederations, Carrington rejoiced over the success of the Madisonian strategy. "Madison," he declared, "is becoming popular with the Antis."[48]

The seventeen amendments the House finally sent to the Senate on August 24, 1789, were "nearly the same as the special Committee of eleven had reported them," Speaker Muhlenberg remarked. There is no account of the debates in the Senate, but the alterations made by the upper house were relatively minor, consisting primarily of combining and reorganizing the House's seventeen articles into twelve. There was no extended consideration of substantive changes to the Constitution. Virginia's outspoken Antifederalist senator Richard Henry Lee informed Patrick Henry that the amendments proposed by the House fell "very far short of the wishes of our Convention" and that the modifications made by the Senate, if anything, "weakened" them even further. "The english language has been carefully culled to find words feeble in their Nature or doubtful in their meaning!" According to Lee, both he and Grayson spared no effort "to give success to all the Amendments proposed by our Country [Virginia]." But to no avail, indeed "we might as well have attempted to move Mount Atlas upon our shoulders." The very idea of securing meaningful amendments after ratification, what Lee referred to as the "doctrine of playing the after game," was "delusion altogether." A "careless reader" of the combined House and Senate resolutions might "suppose that the amendments desired by the States had been graciously granted," but a simple comparison would reveal that "nothing can be more unlike." To the Speaker of the Virginia House of Delegates and the governor, Lee and Grayson expressed their "grief that we now send forward propositions inadequate to the purpose of real and substantial Amendments." To Patrick Henry, Grayson spoke more bluntly, dismissing the suggested amendments as "good for nothing."[49]

48. Veit, 79; William Grayson to Patrick Henry, June 12, 1789, Veit, 249; Edward Carrington to Henry Knox, August 3, 1789, Veit, 271; Maier, *Ratification*, 231–32.

49. Frederick A. Muhlenberg to Benjamin Rush, August 18, 1789, Veit, 280; Richard Henry Lee to Patrick Henry, September 14 and 27, 1789, Veit, 295–96, 299; Lee and William Grayson to the speaker of the Virginia House of Delegates, September 28, 1789, Veit, 300; William Grayson to Patrick Henry, September 29, 1789, Veit, 300.

Five Days at Fayetteville

Madison kept Federalists in North Carolina apprized of the progress of his amendments in the First Congress, and they, unlike Grayson, greeted his efforts with "almost universal pleasure." Governor Johnston, to whom Madison had outlined his "twofold object of removing the fears of the discontented" without injuring the Constitution itself, heartily endorsed the "tub to the whale" strategy. He was opposed to any "material alterations," Johnston said, but not to "a little Flourish & Dressing." Madison's proposal, although nothing more that a "pompous Declaration of Rights" that added little of "intrinsic value" to the federal frame, might nevertheless be useful in converting "some well disposed men" who had "too hastily" opposed ratification at the Hillsborough convention. William R. Davie thought he witnessed this "happy effect" on many Antifederalists who were publicly expressing "great satisfaction" with Madison's motion. Similarly, after traveling from Wilmington to Warren, Benjamin Hawkins reported that residents of the five counties he traversed had undergone a remarkable transformation. Opposed to ratification a year earlier, "they have, most of them, changed their opinions, and are now friendly to it."[50]

The stage was set for another struggle over ratification in North Carolina, only this time the friends of the Constitution held the upper hand. Madison's proposal, coupled with the desire for federal assistance against Indians in the western counties and a general uneasiness over being classified with other "Foreign States," fueled Federalist victories in the post-Hillsborough elections. Friends of the Constitution were soon circulating petitions demanding another ratifying convention and getting positive responses even in previously hostile western and southeastern counties. When the legislature met in November 1788, the dominant issue was whether the state would hold such a convention. Staunch opponents of the Constitution, those not numbered among the "honest part of our Antifederalists" in Davie's estimation, dawdled over the question, but the most they could accomplish was to delay its opening until November 1789.[51]

Federalists found reasons to be encouraged in the months leading up to the new convention. First, the site of the meeting was more to their liking. Hillsborough, the county seat of Orange County, was situated in one of the hotspots of Antifederalism. Orange County voted against ratification twice, in 1788 and 1789. The new convention was to meet in Fayetteville in Cumberland County, one of only two southeastern Piedmont counties that had voted for

50. William R. Davie to James Madison, June 10, 1789, *PJM*, 12:210–11; Benjamin Hawkins to James Madison, June [July] 3, 1789, *PJM*, 12: 275.
51. Trenholme, *Ratification in North Carolina*, 230, 199, 212–13; *PJM*, 12:211.

ratification in 1788. Second, in response to a congratulatory note from Governor Johnston and the council, President Washington had written that he expected the Fayetteville convention to strengthen the Union and to make it more perfect with the addition of North Carolina. Acting on Madison's instructions, Federalists had the governor's address and Washington's reply published and circulated in the backcountry, where opposition to the Constitution had been most pronounced. One of James Iredell's correspondents subsequently informed him that the publication was having "the desired effect," meeting with the "approbation of all . . . except our friend (if he is within your number) Gen. Person." The reference to "our friend" was an insider's joke, hence the parenthetical qualification, for both men were probably familiar with Thomas Person's denunciation of Washington as a "damned rascal and traitor" for supporting the Constitution. Third, Madison had gotten Congress to act on his proposal before the Fayetteville convention met. North Carolina Federalists had been fearful that delays in Congress would redound to the benefit of their opponents, who were eager, as Benjamin Hawkins informed Madison, to "avail themselves of every thing to strengthen their party." Madison's motion and subsequent maneuvering, according to Davie, "confounded the Antis exceedingly." In this instance, Antifederalists actually hurt their cause by delaying the date of the state convention for as long as possible. The six months that elapsed between Madison's first mention of amendments in the House and the first day of business at Fayetteville allowed Congress more than enough time to, as Hawkins put it, "mend the constitution."[52]

The absence of Willie Jones from the Fayetteville convention was also a source of encouragement and no small delight among the supporters of the Constitution. No one had been more influential at Hillsborough than Jones, and the Federalists knew it. "I am persuaded we might have carried our point last year," the cantankerous Archibald Maclaine told Iredell two months before the Fayetteville meeting, "but for Wilie [*sic*] Jones." Unaware that Jones had decided not to stand for election as a delegate, Maclaine was "anxious to know whether he is [again] a member." Struggling to conceal his anxiety with a show of bravado, Maclaine boldly predicted that even if Jones did show up he would not have the run of the place this time. Jones had offended "a great number of well-meaning members," particularly among his former followers. Many of them, "ashamed of being led by the nose last year," had become "very restive" in the interval and would no longer do his bidding. Irrespective of

---

52. Samuel Johnston to James Madison, July 8, 1789, *PJM*, 12:284; Benjamin Hawkins to James Madison, June [July] 3, 1789, *PJM*, 12: 275; John Williams to James Iredell, September 11, 1789, and William R. Davie to James Madison, June 4, 1789, in Griffith J. McRee, *Life and Correspondence of James Iredell*, 2 vols. (New York, 1857–58), 2:266, 260; Trenholme, *Ratification in North Carolina*, 107, 219.

whether the gentleman from Halifax made an appearance at Fayetteville, therefore, "I think we shall succeed."[53]

Jones's absence was undoubtedly conspicuous, but the composition of the Hillsborough and Fayetteville conventions differed substantially in other ways that boded well for the Federalists. Nearly 60 percent of the 294 delegates who gathered at Fayetteville in 1789 were new, and of the 120 who served in both conventions, only 45 voted against ratification in the latter. Twenty Antifederalist delegates at Hillsborough in 1788 switched sides in 1789, but not a single Federalist delegate did. And while thirteen counties voted against adopting the Constitution at both conventions, twenty-four others reversed their earlier rejections and voted to ratify at Fayetteville.[54]

The outcome of the second convention, which met the week of November 16, was as predictable as the first. Much like its predecessor, the Fayetteville convention could have concluded its business quickly without altering the final decision. On the second day, Hugh Williamson, who had gained election as a delegate from Edenton and was known for his very public boast in 1788 that the proposed federal system was "more free and more perfect than any form or government that ever has been adopted by any nation," moved that the convention ratify the Constitution. It was the Antifederalists' turn to protest an early vote on so important an issue. The ensuing debates were not recorded, and although one Federalist delegate described Antifederalist arguments as "unreasonably tedious, trifling, and . . . absurd," they were neither long nor protracted. After a mere three days, the convention was set to vote for ratification. Antifederalists made a last-ditch effort to block unconditional ratification by proposing five amendments that they insisted had to be implemented before North Carolina's decision took effect. These were essentially the same as the ones Willie Jones had appended to the Virginia amendments in his 1788 resolution, but Federalists made quick work of the proposal, defeating it by a margin of 187 to 82. Proceeding to a final decision on November 21, the convention adopted the Constitution by a vote of 194 to 77.[55]

Pleasure, Joy, and Satisfaction on Every Countenance

Their victory complete, the Federalists adopted an Antifederalist-sponsored resolution instructing North Carolina's still-to-be-elected representatives to present to Congress a set of eight recommendations for altering the Constitu-

53. Benjamin Hawkins to James Madison, August 22, 1789, *PJM*, 12:358; Archibald Maclaine to James Iredell, September 15, 1789, McRee, *Correspondence of Iredell*, 2:266.

54. Trenholme, *Ratification in North Carolina*, 234–35.

55. Hugh Williamson, "Remarks on the New Plan of Government," *Daily Advertiser*, February 25–27, 1788, Bailyn, *Debate*, 2:227; John Dawson to James Iredell, November 22, 1789, in McRee, *Correspondence of Iredell*, 2:272; Trenholme, *Ratification in North Carolina*, 238.

tion "agreeable to the second mode proposed by the fifth article of the said constitution." They did this without hesitation because the resolution was essentially toothless. First, among its recommended amendments were a few that would have proven controversial had they been heard in Congress—requiring a two-thirds majority for laws regulating commerce, for example, or restricting congressional control over taxes and paper money, or removing impeachment trials from the Senate—but Madison's "tub to the whale" strategy had already seen to it that these, along with the other substantive constitutional changes proposed by the states, would not be debated. Second, the resolution sought amendments through the "second mode" provided for under Article 5, that is, by the applications of two-thirds of the states forcing Congress to call another federal convention. But Madison had eliminated that possibility by convincing Congress that it could not run the risk of a second convention unraveling the entire Constitution. Indeed, Madison would not allow the House even to consider North Carolina's recommendations or any state's application for a convention. When Theodorick Bland attempted to get the House to discuss Virginia's resolution for a "convention of deputies from the several states," Madison immediately interrupted. Congress, he objected, had no "deliberative power with respect to a convention." On this point, there could be no equivocation. Article 5 empowered the states individually to apply to Congress to call a convention, and upon the application of two-thirds of the states, Congress had to comply. There was no room for the exercise of discretion and therefore no point in allowing Congress to engage in deliberations. In short, the only thing the Antifederalists managed to salvage from their five days at Fayetteville was a meaningless concession.[56]

Federalists congratulated themselves on their achievement and were especially proud of the fact that the "great majority" at Fayetteville "in favor of the Constitution" exceeded "that at Hillsborough against it." Richard Dobbs Spaight, who had represented the state at the Philadelphia Convention and found the experience fraught with "severe and painful application and anxiety," rejoiced that North Carolinians had finally broken through the "cloud of ignorance, and villainy, which has so long obscured our political horizon." On November 23, the day the Fayetteville convention adjourned, its vice president, Charles Johnson, singled out Iredell for high praise. That Iredell had not been a member of the second convention was immaterial, for "nobody had it more at heart than you," Johnson declared, nor had anyone done more to bring about "this glorious event." A week later, Iredell's hometown of Edenton celebrated with flag displays, cannon blasts, bonfires, and toasts to the president of the United States and to the "Constitution as a blessing to the people." At day's

56. Trenholme, *Ratification in North Carolina*, 239–40 and n. 28; Veit, 57–61.

end, according to one account, "pleasure, joy and satisfaction sat on every countenance." In Congress, Elias Boudinot's face lit up with joy and relief in equal measure at the news, pronouncing North Carolina's ratification an event of "the very first magnitude." Madison's anticipated reunion of the "great American Family" was nearing completion.[57]

57. Charles Johnson to James Iredell, November 23, 1789, and Richard Dobbs Spaight to Iredell, November 26, 1789, in McRee, *Correspondence of Iredell*, 2:273; North Carolina delegates to Richard Caswell, September 18, 1787, Farrand, 3:83; Trenholme, *Ratification in North Carolina*, 241, 246; Veit, 66.

A New Generation Who Know Not Us

To the occasional observer, James Madison led a charmed life in retirement. Visitors to Montpelier—and there seemed to be an endless succession of them—described a "daily routine" of leisurely breakfasts and dinners, foot-races orchestrated by Dolley, playful "romping" with an assortment of nieces and nephews, and casual riding tours to different parts of the five-thousand-acre estate. "Freed from the cares of Public Life," Madison also entertained his admirers with lengthy one-sided drawing room "conversations" that were "various—sometimes didactic, sometimes scientific"—and always commingled with "lighter topics," during which "his small bright blue eyes would twinkle most wickedly." The elderly statesman was a "capital story teller," noted James K. Paulding, who had been a friend of Madison's since 1815, following his presidential appointment to the Board of Navy Commissioners. Regardless of the subject under consideration, whether literary, philosophical, or political, Madison seamlessly "relate[d] anecdotes highly amusing as well as interesting." The "*Sage* of his time," said Paulding, was a "man of wit."[1]

Margaret Bayard Smith, a Washington, DC, insider for nearly forty years and the accomplished wife of Samuel Harrison Smith, founder of the capital city's first newspaper, the *National Intelligencer*, was captivated by one of Madison's virtuoso performances. Even Dolley's invitation to "run a race" on the sixty-foot center portico against the Smiths' daughter Anna, during which "Mrs M.," who "looks young and says she feels so," proved she could "run very briskly" indeed, could not prod Smith away from the president's side. "His conversation was a stream of history," and "every sentence he spoke was worthy of being written down," she gushed at the end of a very long day that had begun for the Smiths with a difficult journey over a "rugged and broken" mountain road before arriving at Montpelier in a rainstorm. Madison's account of the "formation and adoption of the Constitution, the Convention and first congress, the characters of their members and the secret debates" was delivered with an authority "few men now living could have" commanded. "So rich in

1. Ralph L. Ketcham, ed., "An Unpublished Sketch of James Madison by James K. Paulding," *Virginia Magazine of History and Biography* 67.4 (1959): 435–37.

sentiments and facts" was his narrative, "so enlivened with anecdotes and epigrammatic remarks" that "my mind was full to over-flowing." All of that information in combination with the president's "very droll" sense of humor, which kept her laughing "very heartily" throughout the evening, made the hours pass so quickly that Smith "could scarcely credit [her] senses" upon discovering that it was 10:00 p.m. and time for them to be "separated for the night." Having monopolized the attention of her venerable host over such an extended period, she was a bit pensive at the end, but she had, she wrote, "feasted to satiety."[2]

Mr. Madison's Troubled Domain

Appearances of course can be deceiving. Reports of the good life at the "hospitable mansion" bordering on the Rapidan River, presided over by a master storyteller whose "blue eyes sparkled like stars" and his fleet-footed and forever youthful wife of thirty-five years who was "one of the happiest of human beings," were not constructed out of whole cloth by Paulding or Smith, but neither were they wholly descriptive of "Mr. Madison's domain." To begin with, Montpelier was a working plantation dependent on profits garnered from the production of agricultural commodities, and by the mid-1820s the collapse of the grain market in Europe, low tobacco prices, soil exhaustion, and successive years of poor harvests had resulted in losses that had begun to undermine Madison's once comfortable situation. Compounding the impact of these losses was the "disappointment," Madison wrote, "in collecting debts on which I counted," including a $5,000 loan to Dolley's brother-in-law Richard Cutts, a former Massachusetts congressman who had fallen on hard times, went bankrupt, and languished in debtor's prison for a while. In 1825, three years before the Smiths' memorable visit, which daughter Anna joyously announced marked "an epoch in her life," Madison himself attempted to borrow an amount "not exceeding six thousand dollars" from the Bank of the United States. Appealing personally to Nicholas Biddle, the bank's president, Madison explained that the "unfavorableness of the seasons" for the past several years had necessitated either a "moderate loan" or the sale of some of his property. Biddle's quick rejection of Madison's application, referencing the bank's policy, which forbade long-term loans that were secured by real estate only, even if such property was, as Madison had described his holdings, free of "flaw or incumbrance of any sort," left the ex-president with no other choice but to pursue the second of his two alternatives more vigorously.[3]

2. Margaret Bayard Smith, *Forty Years of Washington Society: Portrayed by the Family Letters of Mrs. Samuel Harrison Smith*, ed. Gaillard Hunt (New York, 1906), 235–37.

3. Smith, *Forty Years*, 233, 236, 234; Ralph Ketcham, *James Madison: A Biography* (Charlottesville, VA, 1990), 618, 623–24; James Madison to Nicholas Biddle, April 16, 1825, *Writings of Madison*, 9:221–22.

Madison told Thomas Jefferson about his increasingly gloomy economic prospects in 1826. The "unkind seasons" and the "ravages of insects" had limited his total yield for the decade since his return to private life to "one tolerable crop of tobacco and but one of wheat." Consequently, he was, Madison confessed to his best friend of fifty years, reduced to "living very much throughout on borrowed means." Of course, by this time Madison already knew that his failing to secure a loan from the Bank of the United States had severely curtailed any further reliance on borrowing and that "better crops and prices" alone could sustain a "more leisurely disposal of property." Continued bad times, however, made more leisurely sales unfeasible. Ultimately, in order to avoid economic ruin, Madison had to sell all of his land holdings in Kentucky, about a thousand acres, and to mortgage nearly half of Montpelier's five thousand acres.[4]

The urgency with which Madison liquidated his resources to "great disadvantage" in the face of falling land prices caused by the "quantity of land thrown into market by debtors and the defect of purchasers" was no doubt heightened by the burdens imposed on him by Payne Todd, Dolley's son from her first marriage, to the Quaker lawyer John Todd who died in the Philadelphia yellow fever epidemic of 1793. Uncontrolled and apparently uncontrollable, addicted to a dissipated life of drinking and gambling, Payne Todd was constantly in debt and in and out of debtor's prison. Madison made enormous economic sacrifices throughout the 1820s and early 1830s to clean up the mess left behind by his stepson, in one instance even paying a $1,300 tab twice because Payne, instead of paying off his outstanding obligations with the money sent to him, squandered it on a new round of gambling and drinking. By the mid-1820s the wastrel had reached, as Irving Brant, Madison's principal biographer, put it, "the full maturity of his extraordinary power to distress his family." Understandably mortified by her son's intemperance, Dolley pleaded with him to return home, saying "it will be best for your reputation," and repeatedly sent him the stage fare from Philadelphia or New York back to Orange County, Virginia. Madison also encouraged Payne to "come . . . to the bosom of your parents who are anxious to do everything to save [you] from tendencies and past errors and provide for [your] comfort and happiness." But such entreaties fell on deaf ears, and Payne persisted in what Madison termed his "strange and distressing career." All told, between 1813 and Madison's death in 1836, that is, from the time Payne Todd was twenty-one until he was forty-four years old, Madison spent approximately $40,000 covering his stepson's debts. It was a staggering amount—the equivalent of about a million dollars today—making "concealment" impossible. In spite of his best efforts to keep from Dolley the

4. James Madison to Thomas Jefferson, February 24, 1826, *Republic of Letters*, 3:1967.

full extent of her son's recklessness, Madison said she knew "enough to make her wretched the whole time."[5]

A Triple Alliance of Malady, Debility, and Age

Margaret Bayard Smith was certainly wrong then about her hostess having no "lodgement for care or trouble," but she may not have been mistaken in her observation that "time seems to favor her." When the Smiths visited Montpelier in 1828, Dolley was sixty years old, but Margaret, who was ten years her junior, doubted she would "ever look or feel like an old woman." James Madison, on the other hand, was not so fortunate in Smith's estimation. His blue eyes had not lost their "look of mischief," but they were set "amidst the deep wrinkles of his poor thin face" and partially concealed "under his bushy grey eye-brows." Anne Royall, who interviewed Dolley Madison in Richmond in 1829, confirmed Smith's observations. Contrary to expectations, Dolley was not some "little old dried-up woman," Royall said, but rather "tall, young, active, and elegant." Indeed, side by side with Madison, she appeared "young enough" to be his "daughter." Whereas Dolley favored fine gowns and stylish silk turbans, Madison stuck to his "customary black, old-fashioned clothes," and "excessively powdered" his thinning hair in the manner more common to the previous generation. Whereas Dolley was "as active on her feet as a girl," the former president's gait, although "firm," was "somewhat slow," and his "sight and hearing both somewhat impaired."[6]

What was left unspoken by Smith, Royall, and others was that Madison was considerably older than Dolley, seventeen years to be exact. And in 1828, at the age of seventy-seven, he had begun to suffer a decline in his health. Friends and correspondents routinely inquired after his physical well-being, and he just as routinely responded with reassurances that he was as healthy as "could be reasonably" expected "at the stage of life to which I am now advanced." What they in turn should reasonably anticipate were delays in his returns due to "frequent interruptions" dictated by recurring bouts of "bilious indisposition." When Joseph C. Cabell, who once acted as Jefferson's agent on educational matters in the Virginia senate and earned high praise for his efforts from his mentor at Monticello, wrote in 1829 asking for clarification of certain points pertaining to the Virginia doctrine of 1798, Madison did not send a timely response and had to apologize for the "tardiness of my attention," citing a "re-

5. James Madison to Nicholas Biddle, April 16, 1825, *Writings of Madison*, 9:222; Madison to N. P. Trist, June 26, 1828, *Letters of Madison*, 3:615; Irving Brant, *James Madison*, 6 vols. (Indianapolis, 1941–1961), 6:447–49; Ketcham, *Madison*, 615–16. The monetary conversion here is based on John J. McCusker, *How Much Is That in Real Money? A Historical Price Index for Use as a Deflator of Money Values in the Economy of the United States* (Worcester, MA, 1992), 326–27, 332.

6. Smith, *Forty Years*, 234–35; Ketcham, *Madison*, 620, 636–37.

turn of indisposition." This became an all too common excuse over the course of the next three years. Regretting the delays that were becoming too commonplace, Madison wished he could have answered "more promptly," and he would have, he reassured friends and acquaintances, but for "an indisposition . . . which has not entirely left me."[7]

In 1831–32 Madison's health took a turn for the worse, and he was "confined to [his] bed many days by a bilious attack." What he alternatively described as a "tedious illness," a "tedious indisposition," or an "obstinate attack," left him constantly "enfeebled." Even when he was not bedridden, however, Madison could not keep current with his correspondence. He informed James Monroe in the spring of 1831 that he was temporarily in "comfortable health" but that "stiffening fingers" had reduced his usual handwriting to "microscopic" size. "The older I grow," Madison told Monroe, whose own ailments would lead to his death within three months, the "smaller [my] letters" and "shorter [my] steps," while "progress" in either case was "more fatiguing as well as more slow." When Tench Ringgold later sent a note of commiseration accompanied by the "fullest account . . . of the death of our excellent friend" Monroe, Madison sent a hasty acknowledgment, remarking that very act of writing was painful with "rheumatic fingers." Rheumatism, Madison lamented on another occasion, "still cripples me in my limbs, and especially in my hands & fingers." To Nicholas P. Trist, a young disciple who three decades later would vote for Abraham Lincoln and publish extracts of the sage of Montpelier's letters in support of the Union, Madison summarized his ongoing health issues and added that "any convalescence . . . must be tedious, not to add imperfect" because "my malady, my debility, and my age" conspire together "in triple alliance against me."[8]

Majority Rule and Minority Rights

Having lived "a decade beyond the canonical three score & ten" and having been in poor health for "several years," Madison complained in 1831, he was constantly exhausted and wanted nothing more than "to be as little as possible before the public." And yet, the years during which he complained most frequently about maladies and indispositions coincided with the period of his

7. James Madison to Thomas Lehre, August 2, 1828, *Writings of Madison*, 9:315; James Madison to Joseph C. Cabell, August 16, 1828, *Writings of Madison*, 9:341–42; James Madison to Charles J. Ingersoll, February 2, 1831, *Writings of Madison*, 9: 439; Dumas Malone, *Jefferson and His Time*, 6 vols. (Boston, 1949–1981), 6:247.

8. James Madison to N. P. Trist, May [?], 1832, *Writings of Madison*, 9:479; James Madison to James Monroe, April 21, 1831, *Writings of Madison*, 9: 458–59; James Madison to Tench Ringgold, July 12, 1831, *Writings of Madison*, 9:462; James Madison to N. P. Trist, May 29, 1832, *Writings of Madison*, 9: 481; James Madison to General Lafayette, August 3, 1831, *Letters of Madison*, 4:193; Madison to ———, June 29, 1832, *Letters of Madison*, 4:223; and Madison to Benjamin Romaine, November 8, 1832, *Letters of Madison*, 4:226.

most sustained reentry into the world of national politics. In part, this inconsistency between protestation and performance may be explained by the solicitations of admirers like Richard Rush, his attorney general during the War of 1812, who hoped Madison's "useful, solemn testimony" might "still jarring elements" then threatening the general welfare. In part, it may be traced to his desire to correct the distortions made of the ideas he had presented in the Virginia Resolutions of 1798. But in the main, Madison roused himself from his "sick bed," as he put it, because of the "dangers hovering over our Constitution and even the Union itself."[9]

More than faltering finances or failing health, this last, a fear that the foolhardy actions of a few feckless firebrands were jeopardizing the legacy of the Revolution, effectively ended all dreams of an idyllic retirement for Madison. He was convinced that a new generation of Americans, "those who were not contemporaries with those interesting scenes in our Revolutionary drama, and are liable to be misled by false or defective views of them," needed to be instructed on the "state of things during the interval between the peace of 1783 and the adoption of the Constitution." The source of his apprehensions, what had him "reflecting in my sick bed," were the escalating challenges being mounted against the power of the federal government to impose duties on imports.[10]

In 1828 Congress raised import taxes from a third to nearly one-half of the value of the goods imported. As a rule, the southern states were opposed to protective tariffs, believing, not without reason, that they helped northern manufacturers at the expense of southern planters, largely because import taxes elevated the prices of manufactured goods in America and invited other nations to retaliate with protections of their own that would make southern staples less attractive abroad. It was a long-held belief, expressed first in 1787 at the Constitutional Convention. Southern delegations at Philadelphia, it will be recalled, had initially proposed to treat navigation laws as a separate category of legislation. Rather than a simple majority, they favored a two-thirds vote for measures enacted to regulate imports and exports. Only the bargain struck in the Committee of Eleven, signifying, as Madison noted, "an understanding" between the sections "on the two subjects of *navigation* and *slavery*," reconciled most of the southern delegates to the requirement of a simple majority for the passage of all laws.[11]

9. James Madison to James Monroe, April 21, 1831, *Writings of Madison*, 9:458; James Madison to Matthew Carey, July 27, 1831, *Writings of Madison*, 9:463; James Madison to N. P. Trist, May 29, 1832, *Writings of Madison*, 9: 480; Richard Rush to James Madison, January 10, 1829, in Drew R. McCoy, *The Last of the Fathers: James Madison and the Republican Legacy* (Cambridge, 1989), 121.

10. Madison to N. P. Trist, December 4, 1832, *Letters of James Madison*, 4:227.

11. Farrand, 2:449.

In the wake of the 1828 law, opponents were no longer quite so sure about the wisdom of the bargain reached forty years earlier at the federal convention. The so-called tariff of abominations would not have cleared Congress had the assent of two-thirds of both houses been required for all matters related to trade. South Carolina radicals, led by U.S. representatives James Hamilton Jr. and George McDuffie and South Carolina College president Thomas Cooper, were incensed that their state was "at the mercy" of a selfishly motivated and increasingly hostile majority faction. Voicing the sentiments of the low-country rice planters, Hamilton, who within two years would be elected governor, lambasted the northern majority for purposely sacrificing the "agriculture and trade of South-Carolina" in order to "foster the manufactures of New England." If present policies were allowed to continue unabated, Hamilton predicted, "ruin, unmitigated ruin, must be our portion." McDuffie, from the cotton-producing upcountry, had earlier, albeit anonymously, rejected the claim that "state rulers" retained the "right to resist the general government," denouncing it as "licentious" and "incompatible with the very notion of government." By 1828, he had done a complete turnabout because, he said, it had become clear to him that a program of "stupendous oppression" of the South was afoot and needed to be checked. The English-born Cooper, who traveled to France in 1792 and identified with the more zealous Jacobins of the French Revolution before he was forced to flee to the United States, outdid Hamilton and McDuffie in the vehemence of his opposition. Decrying the "series of successful attacks" launched by a "managed majority in Congress," Cooper warned his listeners not to "become the dupes" of northern manufacturers, not to allow the South to be converted into "colonies and tributaries" of the North, not to accommodate the servile doctrine of unlimited submission to arbitrary power, and not to put up with the unfair taxes and unwarranted "impositions" that steadily increased the power of the North while reducing the South to a "state of humiliation." In short, Cooper declared, it was "high time we should be 'up and doing.'"[12]

The problem with the general government, according to these critics, was that it had degenerated over time and could no longer be properly characterized as "federal." Yes, explained James Hamilton, "our delegates" at the Philadelphia Convention "thought they had assented to a scheme of government" composed of "separate and confederate sovereignties," each of which was privileged to manifest the dissimilarity of interests "created by the laws of God." But

---

12. James Hamilton Jr., speech at Walterborough, October 21, 1828, William W. Freehling, ed., *The Nullification Era: A Documentary Record* (New York, 1967), 50, 52; George McDuffie, *National and States Rights Considered* (1821) and speech at Charleston, May 19, 1831, Freehling, *Nullifcation Era*, 6, 105; Thomas Cooper, "Value of Union" speech, July 2, 1827, Freehling, *Nullifcation Era*, 20–22.

whatever their intentions were in 1787, the system as it had functioned for at least the past dozen years was "in *point of fact*, a consolidated government." And in a system founded on the principle of majority rule, this consolidated regime was unfortunately dominated by a northern majority that was apparently permanent. Concerns about the "general welfare" and "domestic tranquillity" fell by the wayside as Congress deferred to the whims of this majority, now emboldened to conduct itself "with the insolent officiousness of a Turkish Pacha."[13]

A State Veto

The problem of protecting minority rights from the encroachments of a self-interested majority was, of course, not a new one. In *Federalist* no. 10, Madison had confronted precisely this conundrum and famously prescribed a "republican remedy for the diseases most incident to republican government." Contrary to the accepted wisdom of the time, summarized best by Montesquieu in the *Spirit of the Laws*, Madison argued that a large republic was preferable to a small one; it would be infinitely more stable, more durable, and less invasive because its array of disparate, clashing "parties and interests" made it proportionately more difficult for a selfishly-motivated faction to form a majority of the whole. Presumably, these countervailing factions, rival groups of competitors promoting their own provincial causes, would at some point see the futility of pursuing only their narrow agendas and make the concessions necessary to appease the others. The sum of these concessions, once they had gained the assent of the majority, should be an approximation of the common good.[14]

Madison's remedy presupposed the existence of a multitude of kinetic factions, a fluid universe in which the composition of the majority might shift from issue to issue. In the view of the South Carolina radicals, however, if this supposition was grounded in reality in 1787 it was not by 1828. "Successive doses of federal legislation," epitomized by the tariffs of 1816, 1824, and 1828, too clearly demonstrated, McDuffie declared, that the components of the majority and minority parties were fixed and "predetermined." The best evidence of this was revealed in the adoption of "a permanently unequal and unjust system of taxation" expressly intended to enrich "one portion of the Union" as it "impoverish[ed] and enslave[d] the other." By heedlessly advancing discriminatory navigation laws "in violation of a solemn bargain between the parties" at Philadelphia, added Hamilton, the "selfish majority" situated in the North revealed itself to be indifferent to the spirit of the Constitution. Like McDuffie, who argued that the Union "cannot possibly be held together" without quick

13. James Hamilton Jr., speech at Walterborough, Freehling, *Nullification Era*, 49, 51.
14. *Federalist* no. 10, 129–36.

corrective action, Hamilton thought it unreasonable to expect southerners to endure for long the abuses of "the many-headed Potentate who sits on our throne."[15]

The surest way to save the Union, the Carolinians advised, was to check the designs of the despotic majority, repulse the forces of consolidation, and restore the original federal structure prescribed by the Constitution. And all of these ends might be achieved with a single remedy: a state veto. Hamilton described how this would work. A state would possess the right to veto any law enacted by Congress that it deemed to be unconstitutional, that is, to be beyond the scope of the powers delegated under Article 1. The implementation of the disputed measure would then be suspended and the law "nullified" unless the veto of the dissenting state was overridden by "an affirmative decision of three-fourths of the states in convention." In the confrontation over the 1828 tariff, this meant that the states would be the arbiters of constitutionality and that the decision of three-fourths of them would put the matter finally to rest. The procedure he outlined, Hamilton concluded, resting as it did on the solid foundation of the "sovereignty" of the states and remaining true to the "original principles which entered into the formation of this confederacy," must be dear to all who "venerate the Constitution" and the "sacred bond" of Union.[16]

Nullification by Any Other Name

John C. Calhoun—soon to emerge as the most feared and revered proponent of states' rights and nullification—maintained an uneasy silence on the matter of a state veto for the time being. As a sympathetic South Carolinian and an ambitious vice president of the United States, he was caught in a dilemma. He shared many of his countrymen's misgivings about the exercise of federal authority since the 1816 tariff, but he knew that if he "intermingled" on behalf of South Carolina, he would forfeit any hope of "future advancement" on the national stage, that is, he would reduce to zero his chances of succeeding Andrew Jackson as president. Besides, Calhoun rationalized, his power to direct public affairs was so limited that it would be an "act of madness" for him even to try. No, it was best for him, his home state, and the nation that he keep a low profile in the "great contest." To outsiders pleading with him to become more involved, he insisted that as a vice president in good standing operating behind the scenes, he might influence the "one man in this Union who can quiet the state, I mean the President of the United States." If he could persuade Jackson to recognize the "justice of the complaints of the South" and to commit

15. George McDuffie, speech at Charleston *Nullification Era*, 105, 113; James Hamilton Jr., speech at Walterborough, Freehling, *Nullification Era*, 52.

16. James Hamilton Jr., speech at Walterborough, Freehling, *Nullification Era*, 58–59, 61.

the full weight of his office to "equalizing the burdens and benefits of the Union," that would be his greatest work.[17]

Calhoun's protestations notwithstanding, South Carolinians who defended their state's right to veto the 1828 tariff knew that the vice president was much more actively engaged in their cause than he was willing to admit in public. Most significantly, acting on a request from the Carolina legislature, he anonymously drafted the "Exposition and Protest" of 1828, which denounced the "whole system of legislation imposing duties on imports" as "oppressive" and "calculated" to benefit one section of the country "exclusively" while it burdened the other. South Carolina thus behaved appropriately when it refused to abide by the terms of a protective tariff it judged to be an unconstitutional encroachment on the powers reserved to the states under the Tenth Amendment. Also, South Carolina was perfectly justified in assuming this elevated position because the "nature of our system" dictated that "sovereignty resides in the people of the several states," Calhoun said, and the "right of judging . . . is an essential attribute of sovereignty." Since the assertion of a right would be meaningless without a corresponding power to act on "contested points of authority," it was logical to conclude that South Carolina's right to judge necessarily "implies a veto . . . on the action of the General Government." Here was the "remedy" authorized by the Constitution "to prevent the encroachments of the General Government on the reserved rights of the states." This was the indispensable constitutional protection "afforded to the minority against the oppression of the majority" in a political universe no longer composed of shifting factions forging temporary alliances.[18]

By the middle of 1831, after President Jackson had made it abundantly clear that he was unequivocally opposed to the idea of a state veto and openly suspicious of his vice president's loyalties, Calhoun declared himself ready "to lay my opinions before the public." He expected to be "warmly assaulted," but he was prepared nevertheless to defend the "high ground of state sovereignty." One major outcome of this newfound determination was the "Fort Hill Address," which forcefully reasserted the claims Calhoun first articulated in the "Exposition and Protest." Protective tariffs had "divided the country into two great geographical divisions" and dangerously "arrayed them against each other." Indeed, because such legislation unfairly distributed their resulting burdens and benefits, "no two distinct nations ever entertained more opposite views of policy than these two sections do on all the important points." Fortunately, there was a constitutional "remedy" for this affliction. The several states that created the Constitution reserved to themselves the "right to judge of its

17. John Calhoun to Virgil Maxcy, September 11, 1830, Freehling, *Nullification Era*, 97.
18. John Calhoun, "Exposition and Protest," December 19, 1828, Ross M. Lence, ed., *Union and Liberty: The Political Philosophy of John C. Calhoun* (Indianapolis, 1992), 345, 348.

infractions." Thus whenever they detected a "deliberate, palpable, and dangerous exercise of power" on the part of the general government, they were empowered by that "compact" to check the "progress of the evil." This authority, "be
it called what it may—state-right, veto, nullification, or by any other name—I
conceive to be the fundamental principle of our system."[19]

Some were fearful that "a power of so high a nature may be abused by a
state" to the detriment of the Union, Calhoun continued, but such fears were
"unnatural and unreasonable." So far from posing a threat, the veto was the
safest guardian of the bonds that held the nation together. In other polities,
when "co-estates" were at loggerheads the only way to resolve the conflict was
through "compromise, submission, or force," all of which proved to be degrad-
ing to the "weaker" of the parties and to have a deleterious effect on the entire
system. "Not so in ours." Should a controversy arise between the general government and a state, "we have a higher remedy," namely, an appeal to the states
themselves. As stipulated under Article 5 of the Constitution, amendments become a part of the original compact as soon as three-fourths of the states agree
to the alteration or addition. In other words, three-fourths of the states "form a
power whose decrees are the Constitution itself." It stood to reason, then, that
the "voice" of three-fourths of the states "can silence all discontent."[20]

Nullification in South Carolina, 1832

To Calhoun, the advantages of the "safe and effectual" method he advocated
for resolving disputes between a state and the federal government were "incon-
trovertible." Anyone "who has maturely reflected on the nature of our institu-
tions" and the "principles of free governments" should see, he insisted, that the
"simple contrivance" of a state veto promoted domestic tranquility by removing the "necessity, and even the pretext," for a resort to "force." For the most
part, however, despite his disclaimer, the 1831 "Fort Hill Address" did not ven-
ture very far beyond a "general statement on an abstract question." Within a
year, Calhoun's abstractions were put to the test.[21]

In July 1832, Congress enacted yet another protective tariff. It did so, ironically as it turned out, in the hope that the new measure would quiet the protests stirred up by the 1828 tariff. President Jackson himself, whose 1831 annual
message called for a reduction of the "duties on imports with a view to equal
justice in relation to all our national interests," predicted that a downward revision of the tariff would leave the South Carolina radicals "without any pretext

19. John Calhoun to Francis Pickens, August 1, 1831, Freehling, *Nullification Era*, 138–39;
John Calhoun, "Fort Hill Address," July 26, 1831, Lence, *Union and Liberty*, 386–87, 371.
20. John Calhoun, "Fort Hill Address," July 26, 1831, Lence, *Union and Liberty*, 385, 377–78,
383.
21. John Calhoun, "Fort Hill Address," July 26, 1831, Lence, *Union and Liberty*, 376, 375, 383,
385.

of complaint." After the passage of the 1832 tariff, he announced that further claims of federal "oppression" were unfounded and must be seen as issuing solely from the "distempered brains of disappointed ambitious men."[22]

Distempered and disappointed they may have been, but discouraged they were not. Fueled in part by George McDuffie's simplistic projections on the devastating impact that the new rates would have on their staple economy, the radicals demanded that a state convention be held to draft a formal response to the 1832 measure. And by an overwhelming majority—79 percent in the house and 70 percent in the senate—the South Carolina legislature complied, calling for a convention of specially elected delegates to meet on November 19 in Columbia. Five days later, the convention adopted an Ordinance of Nullification, negating the 1828 and 1832 tariffs. Declaring both acts to be "unauthorized by the Constitution," the ordinance dismissed them as "null, void, and no law, nor binding upon the State, its officers or citizens." It also forbade federal officials from collecting the "duties imposed by the said acts within the limits" of South Carolina. Lastly, and most ominously for the Union, the ordinance warned the federal government not to resort to the use of force in attempting "to reduce this State to obedience." Should Congress enact coercive legislation of any sort, the people of South Carolina would "hold themselves absolved from all further obligation to maintain or preserve their political connection with the people of the other states, and will forthwith proceed to organize a separate government."[23]

Andrew Jackson reacted swiftly and firmly to the Nullification Ordinance. The "strange" doctrine championed by South Carolina—"that any one state may not only declare an act of Congress void, but prohibit its execution"—was "*incompatible with the existence of the Union*," the president proclaimed, and "*destructive of the great object for which*" the Constitution "*was formed.*" Admittedly, the tariffs were unevenly burdensome, as the nullifiers contended, but the same "objection may be made with truth to every law that has been or can be passed." The "wisdom of man" has "never yet contrived a system" of governing that operated with "perfect equality" on all of its constituent parts. If, therefore, South Carolina had the right to nullify the tariffs and to prevent their execution within its borders, then other states, many with competing concerns, possessed a similar right to void other federal laws they deemed to be "operating injuriously upon any local interest." In short, "if the unequal opera-

22. James R. Richardson, ed., *A Compilation of the Messages and Papers of the Presidents, 1789–1897,* 10 vols. (Washington, DC, 1896–99), 2:556; Andrew Jackson to Martin Van Buren, December 17, 1831, and Andrew Jackson to John Coffee, July 17, 1832, cited in William W. Freehling, *Prelude to Civil War: The Nullification Controversy in South Carolina, 1816–1836* (New York, 1965), 247, 248.

23. Freehling, *Prelude to Civil War,* 248, 260; Ordinance of Nullification, November 24, 1832, Freehling, *Nullification Era,* 151–52.

tion of a law makes it unconstitutional, and if all laws of that description may be abrogated by any state for that cause," then the Union was no longer sustainable and the Constitution degraded to such an extent as to be undeserving of the "slightest effort for its preservation."[24]

Civil War Must Soon Come

Jackson backed up his condemnation of South Carolina's "disorganizing ordinance" by announcing that he stood ready to use all of the resources available to him as the "First Magistrate of our common country" to ensure the collection of the duties set forth in the 1832 tariff. He would brook no defiance of the law. Indeed, "I have no discretionary power on the subject," Jackson explained in his Nullification Proclamation. The presidential oath of office obligates the chief executive to "preserve, protect and defend the Constitution," and Article 2 of that Constitution stipulates that it was his duty to "take care that the laws be faithfully executed." Accordingly, Jackson, taking the nullifiers at their word that they intended to obstruct the operation of the 1832 law, reinforced the troops stationed at the fortresses in Charleston harbor and ordered General Winfield Scott, who had won fame during the War of 1812 for professionalizing the American army and now commanded the federal forces in South Carolina, to be prepared for armed confrontations.[25]

Meanwhile the pace of change in South Carolina was accelerating. In what the historian William W. Freehling describes as the "Carolina version of musical chairs," Calhoun resigned as vice president in late December 1832 and took a seat in the U.S. Senate. To make room for Calhoun, Robert Y. Hayne resigned from the Senate and began his term as South Carolina's newly elected governor. Of the two, Jackson hated Calhoun more and threatened to hang him should hostilities commence, but Hayne was actually the more radical of the pair. Having forged his national reputation as a nullifier by defending the "South Carolina doctrine" during his widely publicized senate debate with Daniel Webster in 1830, Hayne was "violent & *inflammatory* in the extreme" by 1832. His inaugural address as governor, according to one firsthand account, "was full of 'usurpations of congress,' 'sovereignty of S. Carolina,' 'repelling invasion,' 'fighting and dying for their common mother.'" It was a powerful call to arms that generated great "excitement" among his "fellow citizens" and left "several of the legislators shedding *tears*."[26]

24. Andrew Jackson, Nullification Proclamation, December 10, 1832, Freehling, *Nullification Era*, 155–56.

25. Andrew Jackson, Nullification Proclamation, Freehling, *Nullification Era*, 161, 163; Andrew Jackson to the Senate and House of Representatives, January 16, 1833, Richardson, ed., *Messages and Papers of the Presidents*, 2:625.

26. Freehling, *Prelude to Civil War*, 264; Hayne-Webster debate (1830), Freehling, *Nullification Era*, 79; Samuel C. Jackson to William Truc, December 14, 1832, Freehling, *Nullification Era*, 165.

Hayne's speech, coupled with the emotions it stirred, portended the worst and convinced at least one observer that "civil war must *soon* come." When the governor proposed to assemble a force of some twenty-five thousand volunteers "as promptly as possible" in order to meet any "emergency" that might arise from federal efforts to impose the tariff or to interfere with the implementation of the Nullification Ordinance, that dire prediction seemed on the brink of being realized. The situation had become so dangerous and the chances of maintaining peace within the Union so problematic that some believed an unfortunate and unforeseen episode might trigger the "awful scourge." In fact, said General Scott, he was not particularly worried that "state authorities" would attack the forts under his command but was instead anxious lest "some unauthorized multitude, under sudden excitement, might attempt to seize them." Then calls for "wisdom & moderation," whether in the "Capitol at Washington" or in the "Statehouse at Columbia," would likely go unheeded. "What an awful position" for the nation. "Good God!"[27]

More Painful Than Words Can Express

To Madison, who characteristically advised "wise moderation" as the most effectual means of confronting the promoters of "rashness" and undercutting their appeal, the impending descent into violence was deeply troubling. Confined to his sickbed for long stretches of time as the crisis in South Carolina unfolded between 1830 and 1833, he urged others who shared the "same love of their country" to refute the "strange doctrines" and "unhappy aberrations" being advanced by the nullifiers. Their "mistaken causes" and "exaggerated sufferings" must not go unchallenged. The "absurdity of nullification" must be exposed; the "poisonous root" of secession removed. Even fingers so "stiffened with rheumatism" that they "abhor the pen" could not keep Madison from writing to thank his sometime correspondent Benjamin Romaine for his recent pamphlets on the subject of nullification, with regard to which "our judgments and feelings are without a difference." Upon learning that Nicholas Trist intended to publish a collection of documents dating back to the Confederation period, Madison wrote a note of encouragement, telling his young disciple that such a volume would be sorely appreciated as an antidote to the "rashness of the passions" of the "nullifying party." And during a brief period of improvement in his health, principally "an *occasional* relaxation of the terminal joints of my rheumatic fingers, which gives a degree of easy play to the pen," Madison dashed off a letter to Andrew Stevenson, the Virginian then

27. Samuel Jackson to William Truc, December 14, 1832; Freehling, *Nullification Era*, 165; Winfield Scott to William Campbell Preston, December 14, 1832, Freehling, *Nullification Era*, 175, 177.

serving as Speaker of the U.S. House of Representatives, thanking him for presenting the "doctrines of nullification and secession in lights that must confound, if failing to convince, their patrons."[28]

Madison was especially pleased whenever he heard that a repudiation of the Nullification Ordinance originated among the Carolinians themselves. After receiving a printed copy of Thomas S. Grimké's "letter to the people of S. Carolina," in which the state senator from Charleston addressed the "understandings" of his "erring fellow-citizens," Madison congratulated him for his "powerful and persuasive appeal." He only regretted, Madison wrote, that his "ill health, for a long time," had occasioned too many "omissions" in his correspondence. This, and not a lack of appreciation for the several "favors from your pen," Madison reassured the sometimes prickly South Carolinian whose principled eccentricities often discomfited others—he dressed like a pauper, he explained, because "every dollar saved in this way is an additional sum for the poor"—accounted for his belated expression of gratitude. Above all, he was grateful because Grimké's salutary contributions were sure to strengthen the "protest against the novel doctrines and rash counsels of the ascendent party" in South Carolina.[29]

In the end, however, Madison could not rely solely or even primarily on the contributions of friends and acquaintances, regardless of their talents, abilities, merits, or commitments. He might complain that bilious fevers, "crippled" fingers, and the unavoidable maladies associated with his "great age" left him so enfeebled, indeed "a prisoner in my own house," that others were "more able to be useful" to the cause, but he found it impossible to remain a cheerleader on the sidelines. Temperamentally and ideologically he could not stand by idly while the nullifiers propelled the nation headlong into a catastrophic confrontation. That a "Constitution which has been so fruitful of blessings, and a Union admitted to be the only guardian of the peace, liberty and happiness of the people of the States comprising it should be broken up and scattered to the winds" on the strength of nothing more than "misconceptions" and phantom oppressions was, Madison informed Nicholas Trist, "more painful than words can express."[30]

28. James Madison to N. P. Trist, December 4, 1832, *Letters of Madison*, 4:227; James Madison to Benjamin Romaine, November 8, 1832, *Letters of Madison*, 4:226; James Madison to Andrew Stevenson, February 4, 1833, *Letters of Madison*, 4:269; James Madison to Matthew Carey, July 27, 1831, *Writings of Madison*, 9:462, 463.

29. James Madison to Thomas S. Grimké, January 10, 1833, *Letters of Madison*, 4:267; Freehling, *Prelude to Civil War*, 180–81.

30. James Madison to Philip Doddridge, June 6, 1832, *Letters of Madison*, 4:221; James Madison to Matthew Carey, July 27, 1831, *Writings of Madison*, 9:463; James Madison to N. P. Trist, May [?], 1832, *Writings of Madison*, 9: 480.

Where Is the Fairness?

What made Madison's pain so excruciating, and what necessitated his direct involvement in the controversy, was the nullifiers' insistence that their case rested "upon the authority of Jefferson and of Madison." By invoking the principles "canonized" in the Virginia and Kentucky Resolutions of 1798, James Hamilton declared, "we put our citadel where no man can harm it." Three decades before, the advocates of the Alien and Sedition Acts had employed a tortured reading of the "necessary and proper" clause of the Constitution to justify a dangerous extension of federal powers, Hamilton said, just as the promoters of protective tariffs were doing currently. It made sense, therefore, for the Carolinians to reprise Jefferson's and Madison's "unanswerable commentary on the reserved and ultimate rights of the States." It was precisely those reserved rights that legitimized South Carolina's efforts to "interpose" to arrest the "progress of the evil" represented by the tariffs. Having judged the tariffs to be unconstitutional, the state was then duty bound to declare them "void." These were the lessons they had learned from Jefferson and Madison, and the Carolinians said they were proud to be following in the footsteps of the sages of Monticello and Montpelier.[31]

Hamilton's assertion that Jefferson and Madison were the fathers of nullification was hardly original. In fact, it was the commonest of claims made by the nullifiers. As Hayne argued in his debate with Webster, the "South Carolina doctrine" was identical to that "promulgated by the Fathers of the Faith," Jefferson and Madison. The "good old Republican doctrine of '98, the doctrine of the celebrated 'Virginia Resolutions,'" was all the authority South Carolina needed to negate federal legislation it deemed to be unconstitutional. "Mr. Madison," affirmed Calhoun, first in the Virginia Resolutions and subsequently in his explanatory remarks on the same, provided the "highest authority" for nullification by establishing the "constitutional right of the States to interpose, in order to protect their reserved powers" against federal encroachment.[32]

Madison found "much to be deplored" in the Carolina doctrine. It was, he said, "blotted with many strange errors." That this doctrine was "patronized" by men of supposedly "shining talents and patriotic reputations," whose appeals understandably generated a popular following, made it alarming. That these "statesmen" traced this error-filled doctrine back to him, identified him as their inspiration for nullification, made it personally offensive. They misinterpreted the Virginia Resolutions and "inferred" from that initial mistake

31. James Hamilton Jr., speech at Walterborough, Freehling, *Nullification Era*, 57, 59.
32. Robert Y. Hayne, *Several Speeches Made During the Debate in the Senate* (1830), Freehling, ed., *Nullification Era*, 79, 80; John Calhoun, "Exposition and Protest," Lence, *Union and Liberty*, 350–51.

"that I must then have been a nullifier." He was not and never had been. What had happened to common decency in this "hot-bed" state? "Where, indeed, is the fairness of attempting to palm on Virginia an intention which is contradicted by . . . a variety of contemporary proofs"? Who will undertake "that thorough consideration of the subject" and bring "justice" to it?[33]

The Distinction Was Intentional

Ultimately, there was only one person who could gainsay the claims of the nullifiers, and Madison knew it. If they were taking his name in vain, he needed to speak up. If they were misappropriating the Virginia Resolutions, he needed to take them to task. If they were wrong about the essential nature of the constitutional Union, he needed to set them straight. His involvement would leave him vulnerable to reprimands for engaging in the "warfare of politics unbecoming my age," or worse, expose him to "some not very candid attempts" to undermine his good name with accusations of "discrediting inconsistencies," but what was the alternative? Were he to remain silent, he might be suspected "of giving, by my silence, a sanction to erroneous criticisms" of the nullifiers. Thus although he typically closed his letters with a plea that the recipients of his missives keep their contents private and on at least one occasion asked his correspondent "to return the letter after perusal," his opinions became public soon enough.[34]

Madison opened his rebuttal with the "obvious" distinction between the 1798 Resolutions and the Nullification Ordinance. The former uses the "*plural number, States,*" instead of the singular, "a state," whenever "reference is made to the authority which presided over the [federal] government." And this was no accident. "As I am now known to have drawn those documents, I may say as I do with a distinct recollection, that the distinction was intentional." Only the states acting together in concert to oppose the Alien and Sedition Acts legitimated the "interposition" alluded to in the Virginia Resolutions by situating it "within the provisions and forms of the Constitution." The Nullification Ordinance, by contrast, "begins with a single State and ends with the ascendency of a minority of States over a majority," asserting the right of a single state to veto federal laws and put a stop their execution until its decision was reversed by a vote of three-fourths of the other states. Under the present circumstances, this meant that seven states in favor of a state's veto would "give it a prevalence over the vast majority of seventeen states." The "nullifying prerogative" thus

33. James Madison to Matthew Carey, July 27, 1831, *Letters of Madison*, 4:191; James Madison to N. P. Trist, December, 1831, *Letters of Madison*, 4:204; James Madison to Philip Doddridge, June 6, 1832, *Letters of Madison*, 4: 221.

34. James Madison to —— Townsend, October 18, 1831, *Letters of Madison*, 4:199; James Madison to N. P. Trist, December [?], 1831, *Letters of Madison*, 4:205; James Madison to W. C. Rives, March 12, 1833, *Letters of Madison*, 4: 291.

violated a fundamental principle of "all free governments": majority rule. It was hubris of the highest order, a "preposterous and anarchical pretension" for which "there is not a shadow of countenance in the Constitution."[35]

Madison's second point was directly related to his first. Although he dismissed as absurd the argument that tariffs were unconstitutional—Article 1, Section 8, delegated to the federal government the power to collect import taxes and to regulate trade, and Congress had exercised these powers for forty years, ever since the enactment of the first tariff in 1789, without incident—Madison went on to say that even if a state judged them to be so, secession was not justifiable under the Constitution. The American nation was founded in a "compact, the parties to which are mutually and equally bound." As with any contract, one or the other of the parties involved could not unilaterally abrogate the terms of the agreement. A single state, for example, could no more "at will withdraw from the others," than the others could "at will withdraw from her." No state, least of all South Carolina "until of late," would have supported the assertion that the Constitution empowered the states to expel one of their numbers "nolentem, volentem," unwillingly or willingly, "out of the Union." True to this contractual understanding of the Constitution, the Virginia Resolutions pledged to carry on the "protest" against the Alien and Sedition Acts while maintaining the "most scrupulous fidelity to that Constitution," and the Kentucky Resolutions vowed never to "cease to oppose in a constitutional manner" every attempt to violate the terms of the founding compact. The Ordinance of Nullification, on the other hand, outlined a course of action that was clearly extraconstitutional. As such, were it to succeed, South Carolina would deliver an "immediately mortal" blow to the Union and a "mortal wound" to itself.[36]

The "heresy of secession" also betrayed a profound misunderstanding of the nature of the political association created by the Constitution, Madison said. Its proponents mistakenly believed that the states entering the Union "never parted with an atom of their sovereignty, and consequently that the constitutional band which holds them together is a mere league or partnership." Nothing could be further from the truth. The "league of friendship," a creation of the now defunct Articles of Confederation, had been supplanted by a new Union possessing all of the "characteristics of sovereignty" that traditionally adhere to a single "nation." It was a "compound" nation, to be sure, a "new

35. James Madison to N. P. Trist, December 23, 1832, *Writings of Madison*, 9:490; James Madison to N. P. Trist, December [?], 1831, *Letters of Madison*, 4:206; James Madison to Andrew Stevenson, February 4, 1833, *Letters of Madison*, 4: 270.

36. James Madison to N. P. Trist, December 23, 1832, *Writings of Madison*, 9:489–90; Virginia Resolutions, December 24, 1798, Kermit L. Hall, ed., *Major Problems in American Constitutional History*, 2 vols. (Lexington, MA, 1992), 1:239; Kentucky Resolutions, February 22, 1799, Hall, ed., *Major Problems*, 1:241; James Madison to Andrew Stevenson, February 10, 1833, *Letters of Madison*, 4:272.

creation" in which, as he had tried to explain in *Federalist* no. 39, "national" and "federal" features were carefully combined so that the final product was "neither wholly *national* nor wholly *federal.*" But it was a nation nevertheless, "and acknowledged to be such by all other nations and sovereigns." By joining the new Union, therefore, the states acknowledged that they were component parts of a larger whole and that they were committing themselves to promoting the "general welfare of the United States." No longer were they at liberty to pursue their own ends, as some had too blithely done during the Confederation period. Secession "without the consent of the co-states" was simply the most extreme manifestation of this pursuit of individual ends at the expense of the general welfare. "A seceding state mutilates the domain and disturbs the whole system from which it separates itself." It weakened the Union, thereby necessarily damaging the nation's ability to manage foreign and domestic affairs advantageously, and for this reason secession was impermissible.[37]

Finally, Madison was deeply troubled by the nullifiers' casual disregard for the Union. He accused them of being either ignorant of the advantages of union or callously unconcerned about the consequences of disunion. Why else would they be exciting "unnatural feelings . . . against their brethren of other states"? Reflecting on Thomas Cooper's inflammatory 1827 speech, in which the transplanted English-born radical asked his audience to "calculate the value of our union" and suggested strongly that it was not "worth our while to continue this union of states," Madison lamented that southerners in general, but South Carolinians in particular, were "more and more disposed to calculate the value of the Union." Did they not realize that the "rupture of the Union" would be followed by "mutual enmity," "dreadful animosities," "rival alliances," "border wars," "standing armies," and "monarchical" governments trending toward despotism? He and Jefferson were certainly mindful of these repercussions; thus the Virginia and Kentucky Resolutions did not even hint at the prospect of breaking the Union apart. Rather, the former emphasized Virginia's "warm attachment to the Union" and reassured everyone that the "good people of this commonwealth" continued to feel the "most sincere affection for their brethren of the other states." And even the more radical Kentucky Resolutions of 1799, which sanctioned "nullification" as a "rightful remedy" reserved to the states, declared "unequivocally" an abiding "attachment to the Union."[38]

37. James Madison to Andrew Stevenson, February 4, 1833, *Letters of Madison*, 4:270; James Madison to W.C. Rives, March 12, 1833, *Letters of Madison*, 4: 289–90, 291; *Federalist* no. 39, 283–86.

38. James Madison to W. C. Rives, March 12, 1833, *Letters of Madison*, 4:291; James Madison to General Lafayette, August 3, 1831, *Letters of Madison*, 4:193; James Madison to Andrew Stevenson, February 10, 1833, *Letters of Madison*, 4: 273; Thomas Cooper, speech, July 2, 1827, Freehling, *Nullification Era*, 25; Kentucky Resolutions, 1798, Hall, *Major Problems*, 1:238; Virginia Resolutions, 1798, Hall, *Major Problems*, 1:239; Kentucky Resolutions, 1799, Hall, *Major Problems*, 1: 240.

Madison and Jackson Attune Their Defenses

Madison's evisceration of the Ordinance of Nullification helped to shape Jackson's response to the rapidly escalating controversy. Nicholas Trist, Madison's disciple on all matters political, became Jackson's private secretary in 1830. As one of Madison's most frequent correspondents throughout the nullification crisis, Trist was a readily available conduit for his mentor's arguments. Also, Jackson made a point of consulting with Madison in person, calling on the aged statesman at Montpelier a few months before he issued his proclamation in 1832 in order to "attune their defenses of the Union." The result of this collaboration may be seen in the phrases Jackson used to describe the Carolina doctrine: "strange," an "impractical absurdity," "fallacious," a "gross error," "confounding," "deluded," "perilous," "hideous," "fatal." It is better evidenced in Jackson's syllogistic justification for the actions he was prepared to take to neutralize the threat posed by South Carolina: the Constitution formed "a single nation" for the "benefit of all," instead of "a league" of sovereign states; the withdrawal of any member without the consent of the others was an "offense against the whole" because it "destroys the unity of a nation"; therefore, unilateral secession was not permitted under the Constitution.[39]

But Jackson was at his Madisonian best when he celebrated the blessings of union and the dreaded consequences of disunion. Under the Articles of Confederation, "we could scarcely be called a nation," he said. Divided at home and disrespected abroad, the prevailing "state of things could not be endured." A new frame of government, founded on the "authority of the people of the United States," was needed to secure all of the "important objects that are announced in the preamble" to the Constitution: justice, domestic tranquility, common defense, the general welfare, and liberty. But the "most important among these objects—that which is placed first in rank, on which all the others rest—is '*to form a more perfect union*.'" This the framers achieved through "mutual sacrifices," and the resulting "happy Union" after 1787 was soon the pride of an "increasing and happy population." Life was "agreeable." America became a beacon for the "wretched and the oppressed" of the world. The "lights of religion, morality, and general information" reached into "every cottage," however remote. "Look on this picture of happiness and honor and say, *We too are citizens of America*." Then contemplate, "if you can, without horror and remorse," the dissolution of the Union. The "picture of peace and prosperity we will deface," the "protection of that glorious flag we renounce," the "very name of Americans we discard," and once "fertile fields we will del-

---

39. Ketcham, *Madison*, 643–44; Brant, *Madison*, 6:485–86; Andrew Jackson, Nullification Proclamation, Freehling, *Era of Nullification*, 158–60.

uge with blood." "And for what, mistaken men? For what do you throw away these inestimable blessings?"[40]

The "emotional nationalism" apparent in Jackson's Nullification Proclamation resonated with others, including many whom Madison had earlier suspected of calculating the value of the Union. In fact, South Carolina stood alone. No other southern state supported the ultimatum contained in the Ordinance of Nullification, and some variously denounced it as "rash," "reckless," "unwarrantable," "dangerous," "dreadful," and "alarming." Mississippi went so far as to condemn South Carolina's "disorganizing doctrines" on the grounds that their continued pursuit would prove "fatal to the existence of the Union." Rather than persisting in its "delusion," South Carolina would be well advised "to hearken attentively to the paternal, yet ominous, warning of the Executive," for Mississippians were prepared to back the president in "preserving the integrity of the Union . . . holding it, as our fathers held it, precious above all price."[41]

Isolated, South Carolina was in an untenable position and open to compromise, which came in the form of the 1833 tariff. Introduced by Henry Clay, the new tariff proposed to lower existing duties in stages until 1842, by which time no import tax would exceed 20 percent. Calhoun, with whom Clay had already conferred and who had pledged his support for the compromise, immediately endorsed the proposal and all but guaranteed its passage. Soon after the enactment of the tariff, South Carolina rescinded its Ordinance of Nullification, and the crisis ended in a whimper rather than a bang.[42]

Fine Elements for Future Disunion

Madison was thankful for the compromise tariff, telling Clay that he was hopeful it would prevent "a renewal of the contest between the South and the North." The "lapse of nine or ten years," the duration of the "experimental period" set by the 1833 tariff, he reasoned, should result in improvements in domestic manufacturing that would make import duties unnecessary after 1842. It held out the promise, then, of removing forever one nagging source of potential conflict between the sections. Despite this expectation, however, Madison was hardly sanguine, primarily because of the "unceasing efforts" of the fire-eaters "to alarm the South by imputations against the North of unconstitutional designs on the subject of the slaves." That "no such intermeddling disposition exists" did not matter to these extremists who advocated "jumping into the fire for fear of the frying-pan." But "what *madness*" could possibly

40. Andrew Jackson, Nullification Proclamation, Freehling, *Nullification Era*, 155, 160, 162.
41. Freehling, *Prelude to Civil War*, 294; resolves adopted by the Mississippi Legislature, Freehling, *Nullification Era*, 172–73.
42. Freehling, *Prelude to Civil War*, 292–93.

sway otherwise rational people into thinking there was "greater safety in disunion"?[43]

The madness was slavery. When aggravated by the apprehension that a hostile northern majority intended to make intermeddling a federal policy, it was contagious enough to be more than "an over-match for the dictates of prudence" to which Madison appealed. South Carolina may have encountered the contagion sooner because it was the only state with a slave majority in the 1820s and 1830s, which made it supremely sensitive to perceived attacks on slavery and militantly defensive of slaveholding. By 1830 South Carolina was less willing than the other southern states to tolerate the slightest federal interference with the slave economy and more disposed to alienate itself from a union in which, according to Thomas Cooper, the "South has always been the loser, and the North always the gainer." Robert Barnwell Rhett, a low-country planter who espoused the "ultra opinions" that were gaining momentum in South Carolina, reversed the logic of Madison's question when he argued that "a people owning slaves are mad, or worse than mad, who do not hold their destinies in their own hands."[44]

As Madison feared, the secessionists were not satisfied with the compromise that ended the nullification crisis. Most accepted Cooper's assertion that the nullifiers were, as G. W. Featherstonhaugh, an Englishman who visited South Carolina after the nullification crisis, put it, "wrong to make peace with the Union men." According to Featherstonhaugh, Cooper thought the Carolinians should have "taken the field against General Jackson," and Rhett agreed that they should have settled the dispute on the "tented field." If South Carolina had taken up the "sword" and, in the worst-case scenario, been defeated, at least she would have fallen, Rhett suggested, "with her brow unsullied with the damp of timidity." By falling so nobly, the state would usefully have reminded the people that "preparation—armed preparation—energy unremitted—and vigilance, sleepless and untiring, were absolutely necessary to maintain their liberties." Clearly, defending the liberty to own slaves was not a job for sissies.[45]

As Madison also feared, the secessionists shared a common identity first and foremost as South Carolinians. That identification was confirmed by Featherstonhaugh. During his meeting in Columbia with Cooper and some of his colleagues, Featherstonhaugh could scarcely believe he was "amongst

43. James Madison to Henry Clay, June [?], 1833, *Letters of Madison*, 4:300–1.

44. James Madison to Clay, June [?], 1833, *Letters of Madison*, 4:301; Ira Berlin, *Slaves Without Masters: The Free Negro in the Antebellum South* (New York, 1974), 396–99; Freehling, *Prelude to Civil War*, 255–59; Thomas Cooper, speech, July 2, 1827, Freehling, *Nullification Era*, 25; G. W. Featherstonhaugh, *Excursions through the Slave States* (New York, 1844), Freehling, *Nullification Era*, 193; Robert Barnwell Rhett, speech, 1833, Freehling, *Nullification Era*, 189.

45. G. W. Featherstonhaugh, *Excursions through the Slave States,* Freehling, *Nullification Era*, 192; Robert Barnwell Rhett, speech, 1833, Freehling, *Nullification Era*, 190.

Americans." His hosts, for example, avoided the "self-laudatory" language Americans ordinarily used "when speaking of their country." Instead they spoke "openly against" a government based on majority rule. At one point, after "something very extravagant" was said, Featherstonhaugh asked "in a good-natured way" whether these men "called themselves Americans yet." The response, "No, sir, I am a South Carolinian," startled the Englishman, leading him to conclude that "here are fine elements for future disunion."[46]

A Beautiful China Vase

During his surprisingly testy Columbia visit, Featherstonhaugh, who said he "was in the habit of making autumnal visits" to Montpelier, ventured to offer the name of "Mr. Madison" as one deserving of respect. But he was "immediately stopped," cut short by a declaration that the Virginian was a liar. The secessionists disliked Jackson; they despised Madison. Jackson was a misguided commander in chief whom Cooper, a "little crooked octogenarian," dismissed with a "desperate cut with the hearth-brush." Madison, on the other hand, could not be dispatched with the symbolic swipe of a make-believe sword. He had been the darling of the nullifiers until he repudiated their appeal to his authority. And when he did, they turned on him. They accused him of inconsistency, of renouncing the very doctrines he had articulated in his Virginia Resolutions. He was a "false hypocritical dissembler." Indeed, in the estimation of Cooper's assembly, Madison was "one of the worst men the country had produced." Astounded by this assessment, Featherstonhaugh attributed it to the overheated political climate of the times. Madison's "inflexible opposition" to nullification had so discombobulated these "gentlemen" that they retaliated with churlish, defamatory comments of the sort they would never have condoned let alone uttered in "a period of less excitement."[47]

The rough treatment his friend received at the hands of the radicals unsettled the English traveler, but had he been informed, Madison would have been troubled more by the Carolinians' disparagement of the Union than by the barbs they directed against him. Whether these firebrands were driven by "an impenetrable stupidity" or an "incurable prejudice" mattered little, for their zealotry nourished the seeds of disunion. To be sure, their impassioned cries had failed to subdue "common sense, common good" in 1833, but there was no time to relax. When Edward Coles, a relative of Dolley's and another of Madison's disciples, remarked in 1834 that the nullification crisis being settled, the greatest danger to the republic now emanated from President Jackson's

---

46. G. W. Featherstonhaugh, *Excursions through the Slave States*, Freehling, *Nullification Era*, 193–94.

47. G. W. Featherstonhaugh, *Excursions through the Slave States*, Freehling, *Nullification Era*, 193.

usurpation of executive power, Madison lectured him sternly. The dangers posed by the nullifiers had not passed. Their doctrine continued to make advances "either in its original shape or in the disguises it assumes." Their numbers had increased "in most of the Southern states without a decrease in any one of them." Unopposed they might therefore succeed in conveying an "impression of a permanent incompatibility of interests between the South and the North." In other words, "nullification has the effect of putting powder under the Constitution and Union, and a match in the hand of every party to blow them up at pleasure." What could be "more dangerous" than that?[48]

Jackson, answered Edward Coles. It probably occurred to Madison, as the historian Drew R. McCoy has observed, "that fewer and fewer people were willing to listen to him or, even if willing, able to understand what he said." Coles belonged to the generation that was born or came to maturity after the framing and ratification of the Constitution. Richard Rush, the son of Benjamin Rush, the Philadelphia physician who was a signer of the Declaration of Independence, was a member of that generation. "Most of us now on the [national] stage," Rush wrote Madison, "were too young to retain a recollection of the day when we had no general government." It was a telling reminder. For Coles, Rush, and most of their cohorts, a strong union was a given, something they had always known. They had grown up understanding "our country" to mean the United States rather than their home state. They had no memory of a time when the states claimed sovereignty for themselves, ignored the requisitions of Congress, viewed one another as rivals, enacted discriminatory trade laws, entered into separate treaties, and defined their union as a league of friendship. Some undoubtedly had "read of the train of political and commercial evils" that plagued the nation under the Articles of Confederation, Rush added, but they "seem to have forgotten them."[49]

Rush's observation must have disappointed Madison because it confirmed his suspicion that too many members of the current generation failed to comprehend fully the repercussions of a demise of the constitutional Union, that it "would throw the states back into a chaos, out of which, not order a second time, but lasting disorder of the worst kind, could not fail to grow." Too many also assumed a lackadaisical posture on nullification, refusing to see that the "first and most obvious step is nullification; the next, secession; and the last, a farewell separation." And most distressingly, too many, including Coles, on whom he had showered "an affection truly fatherly," appeared uninformed

48. James Madison to N. P. Trist, September 23, 1831, quoted in McCoy, *Last of the Fathers*, 152; James Madison to N. P. Trist, January 18, 1833, *Letters of Madison*, 4:267; James Madison to Edward Coles, August 29, 1834, *Letters of Madison*, 4:357–58.

49. McCoy, *Last of the Fathers*, 157 (see also his illuminating discussion, 119–62); Rush to Madison, January 10, 1829, cited by McCoy at 121.

about the designs of "ambitious leaders," whose mission was to continue the pursuit of the "nullifying experiment" and to shatter the Union, a "beautiful China vase," into shards "which a miracle only could reunite."[50]

I May Be Thought to Have Outlived Myself

In January 1825, just three months shy of his eighty-second birthday, Jefferson wrote wistfully to an old acquaintance that the "solitude in which we are left by the death of our friends is one of the great evils of protracted life." Speaking for the isolated souls who remained, he lamented, "All, all dead! and ourselves left alone midst a new generation whom we know not, and who know not us." Madison was in a similarly contemplative mood six years later. By his own reckoning, Madison told Jared Sparks, who was then working on a biography of Gouverneur Morris and was soon to begin a multivolume edition of the writings of George Washington, he was the "only living signer of the Constitution," the "sole survivor" among those who had served in the Continental Congress before 1783, and the last living relic of the convention that created Virginia's 1776 constitution. It was an enviable record of longevity, but, Madison observed, "having outlived so many of my contemporaries, I ought not to forget that I may be thought to have outlived myself."[51]

The operative phrase here is "I may be thought." Madison knew that his critics, especially the supporters of nullification, had ungraciously suggested during the late crisis that he had descended into senility. Such mean-spirited insinuations notwithstanding, Madison's mind remained sharp to the end. Charles Jared Ingersoll, a Pennsylvania congressman during the War of 1812 and subsequently a friend of Madison's, was at Montpelier a month before Madison died in June 1836. Ingersoll found his host's "understanding to be as bright as ever; his intelligence, recollections, discriminations, and philosophy, all delightfully instructive." Dolley's younger brother J. C. Payne, employed by Madison to take dictation, reported on June 20, a week prior to Madison's death, that he was still expressing "his views on important subjects" with the "same soundness, clearness, vigor and felicity of expression" that had always "distinguished his compositions."[52]

That Ingersoll and Payne were not merely peddling the sort of puffery expected of sympathetic admirers is made evident by Madison's parting composition. In late 1834, in a clear hand indicative of one of those rare moments

50. James Madison to Richard Rush, January 17, 1829, McCoy, *Last of the Fathers*, 134; Adrienne Koch, *Madison's "Advice to My Country"* (Princeton, 1966), 150; James Madison to Edward Coles, August 29, 1834, *Letters of Madison*, 4:358.

51. Thomas Jefferson to Francis Van Der Kemp, January 11, 1825, *The Writings of Thomas Jefferson*, ed. Paul Leicester Ford, 10 vols. (New York, 1892–99), 10:337; James Madison to Jared Sparks, June 1, 1831, *Writings of Madison*, 9:460.

52. Charles Jared Ingersoll and J. C. Payne, cited in Brant, *Madison*, 6:518, 519.

when he experienced some measure of relief from a "crippled condition . . . which almost forbids the use of the pen," Madison completed his "Advice to My Country." His final message was simple and concise: "The advice nearest to my heart and deepest in my convictions is that the Union of the States be cherished and perpetuated. Let the open enemy to it be regarded as a Pandora with her box opened; and the disguised one, as the Serpent creeping with his deadly wiles into Paradise." Because his instructions were that these words not "see the light" until after "I am no more," Madison hoped they might "be considered as issuing from the tomb, where truth alone can be respected, and the happiness of man alone consulted." In effect, Madison's "Advice" was his epitaph, and given his unparalleled dedication to the cause for over half a century it would be hard to imagine a more fitting tribute.[53]

53. James Madison to William H. Winder, September 15, 1834, *Writings of Madison*, 9:542; James Madison, "Advice to My Country," Brant, *Madison*, 6:530–31.

The Perils of Originalism

In 1819 James Madison received an urgent appeal from Robert Walsh Jr., a thirty-five-year-old Philadelphia editor and abolitionist. Missouri, with a population of slaves rapidly approaching ten thousand, had applied for admission to the Union, and Walsh was seeking clarification on a constitutional question raised by an accompanying amendment introduced by Congressman James Tallmadge of New York. Tallmadge had proposed to amend the enabling bill so that no more slaves could be transported into Missouri and all slaves born after the effective date of statehood would be emancipated at age twenty-five. In other words, Missouri would enter the Union as a slave state in 1819 but gradually be converted into a free state. Tallmadge's proposal gained the assent of the House of Representatives but not the Senate. At issue was whether Congress had the power to restrict the movement of slaves within the United States, and the dispute centered on the proper interpretation of Article 1, Section 9, of the Constitution, which stipulates that the "migration or importation of such persons as any of the States now existing shall think proper to admit shall not be prohibited by the Congress prior to the year 1808."[1]

According to Walsh and the supporters of the Tallmadge amendment, "migration" and "importation" described two separate movements. Migration referred to forced relocations within the nation, and importation to the transportation of slaves from abroad. Congress had outlawed the importation of slaves into the United States after January 1, 1808; it should now assert its constitutional authority over the internal slave trade. To bolster his case, Walsh hoped to secure Madison's imprimatur on this rendering of Article 1, Section 9. Madison was a distinguished elderly statesman, a former president, but more importantly to Walsh, he was the authority on matters related to the Philadelphia Convention. "You are the one to whose judgment in this case, I would, of course, attach most weight," Walsh declared, because "no one can know as

---

1. William W. Freehling, *The Road to Disunion: Secessionists at Bay, 1776–1854* (New York, 1990), 144, 146; Ira Berlin, *Slaves without Masters: The Free Negro in the Antebellum South* (New York, 1974), 397, 401; Ira Berlin, *Many Thousands Gone: The First Two Centuries of Slavery in North America* (Cambridge, MA, 1998), 265.

well as you do, what were the views & intentions of the framers of the Constitution in regard to the extension or rather the restriction of negro-slavery."[2]

Unfortunately for Walsh, the "father of the Constitution" repudiated his reading of the disputed clause. "Whatever may have been intended by the term 'migration' or the term 'persons,'" (and Madison suggested that the ambiguity was a concession to "scrupulous" northern delegates who were loath to mention the ongoing trafficking in slaves) "it is most certain, that they referred exclusively to a migration or importation from other countries into the United States, and not to a removal, voluntary or involuntary, of slaves or freemen, from one to another part of the United States. Nothing appears or is recollected that warrants this latter intention." For Madison, the intent of the "framers" at Philadelphia was less consequential than the meaning imparted to the clause by the state ratifying conventions, and therefore he added that "nothing in the proceedings of the state conventions" would support Walsh's reasoning. Otherwise, among the numerous recommendatory amendments drafted by the states, and almost certainly among the forty submitted by Virginia, a principal exporter of slaves to Kentucky and Tennessee, would have been one that addressed slave "migration," but none "refers to the clause in question." Furthermore, Congress for three decades never assumed that it derived "from this clause a power over the migration or removal of individuals, whether freemen or slaves, from one state to another." For Madison, then, neither the intentions of the framers and ratifiers nor the proceedings of Congress since ratification supported the distinction Walsh was articulating between migration and importation.[3]

Walsh was disappointed by Madison's response but not dissuaded. He found Madison's letter "very interesting and instructive" and read his explanation with "an almost unbounded deference," and yet, he admitted, he "did not, in fact, wish to be convinced, as to the constitutional point." He had already made up his mind. Consequently, notwithstanding his deep respect for Madison, Walsh went on publicly to argue that the "*general intention* of the authors" of the Constitution—presumably Madison was a particular exception—was never "merely to guard against the importation of slaves . . . *from abroad*." If they had "intended to vest in Congress no other or further power than that of prohibiting *importation*," would they have included the word "migration" in the disputed clause? "Migration" and "importation" are not synonymous, and the framers were not careless wordsmiths. They expected "due force . . . to be given to every term" they used; therefore, "migration cannot be treated as null and without meaning." And it must not be extended

2. Drew R. McCoy, *The Last of the Fathers: James Madison and the Republican Legacy* (Cambridge, 1989), 105–13; Walsh's letter is quoted on 107.

3. James Madison to Robert Walsh, November 27, 1819, *Writings of Madison*, 9:3–5, 9.

beyond its "plain, acknowledged sense" to cover redundantly the same "act of emigrating across an ocean" that the word "*importation* alone" conveys "clearly" and "fully." In the end, Walsh concluded, "we are then left to understand by the word *migration* in the clause, the transportation or removal of slaves from one state to another, or from a state to a territory."[4]

Jurisprudence of Original Meaning

Walsh was among the first disputants to appeal to the authority of the "framers" in defense of a constitutional argument, but he was, fortunately or unfortunately, not the last. Indeed, since the 1980s appeals to the original "intent" of the framers of the Constitution or to the original "meaning" attached to its various clauses by the state ratifying conventions has become commonplace. "Constitutional originalism is all the rage these days," observed legal scholar Jeffrey Rosen in 2011, and shows no signs of losing any momentum in the immediate future. The combination of a patriotic devotion to the iconic leaders of the Revolution and an abiding reverence for the Constitution itself makes "originalism" enormously attractive to many Americans and to more than a few judges. How could it be otherwise, especially if the alternative is, as one of the most adamant defenders of the doctrine puts it, "freewheeling policy-making by Supreme Court Justices." It is worth our while, however, to examine some of the principal assertions of this influential and increasingly popular doctrine.[5]

A good starting point might be a speech delivered by Edwin Meese III before a gathering of the American Bar Association in 1985. Meese, then the attorney general of the United States, described the essentials of "a jurisprudence of original intention," which he characterized as "a jurisprudence that seeks to be faithful to our Constitution." This mode of proceeding begins with the simple premise that the framers "chose their words carefully" and therefore that the document they drafted "conveys meaning." Next, it assumes that this "meaning . . . can be known" because, as Meese argued, the "Founding Fathers" left behind a plethora of records pertaining to the creation and ratification of the Constitution. "The minutes of the Convention are a matter of public record. Several of the most important participants—including James Madison, the 'father' of the Constitution—wrote comprehensive accounts of the Convention. Others, Federalists and Anti-Federalists alike, committed their arguments for and against ratification, as well as their understandings of

---

4. McCoy, *Last of the Fathers*, 111–12; [Robert Walsh Jr.], *Free Remarks on the Spirit of the Federal Constitution* (Philadelphia, 1819), 19–20.

5. Jeffrey Rosen, "If Scalia Had His Way," *New York Times*, January 9, 2011; Lino A. Graglia, "How the Constitution Disappeared," in *Interpreting the Constitution: The Debate over Original Intent*, ed. Jack N. Rakove (Boston, 1990), 47.

the Constitution, to paper." By consulting these abundant records, "we know who did what, when, and many times why" and are thus privileged to advance a method of constitutional adjudication that "is rooted in the text of the Constitution as illuminated by those who drafted, proposed, and ratified it." Finally, although it is true that "unanimity among the framers and ratifiers" was not achieved "on all points," we must not lose sight of the fact that "meaning can be found, understood, and applied." Meese's last observation is crucial. Once meaning or intention is known, "it must be obeyed." Jurists are not free to base their decisions on "moral philosophies or personal notions of human dignity"; they must not allow vague "social theories" or the agendas of "various constituencies" to displace "fidelity to the Constitution." Those who ignore this rule may properly be charged with promoting an unreliable "chameleon jurisprudence" that, by "changing color and form in each era," puts at risk the very foundations of a "government of laws."[6]

Carefully Chosen Words

Meese was correct to assume that the Philadelphia delegates chose their words with care. But, as Madison explained to Robert Walsh in 1819, their choices were not always guided by a quest for precision and clarity. In fact, Gouverneur Morris, who with some justification once boasted to a correspondent that the final draft of the Constitution "was written by the fingers which write this letter," said he settled for a studied ambiguity in composing portions of the document. "Conflicting opinions had been maintained with so much professional astuteness" with regard to Article 3 on the federal judiciary, for example, Morris explained, that he resorted to phrases that while satisfying one party "would not alarm others." Article 4, Section 3, covering congressional powers over American territories, presented a similar difficulty. Anticipating the acquisition of new territories by the United States, including Canada and Louisiana, Morris said he and others preferred to "allow them no voice in our councils." However, he chose his words carefully, going only "as far as circumstances would permit" because had the exclusion of these provinces "been more pointedly expressed, a strong opposition would have been made." Compounding the difficulty of interpreting these instances of salutary ambiguity is the fact that, as Morris confessed candidly, "it is not possible for me to recollect with precision all that passed in the Convention, while we were framing the Constitution; and if I could, it is most probable, that a meaning may have been conceived from incidental expressions, different from that which they were intended to convey, and very different from the fixed opinions of the speaker."[7]

6. Edwin Meese III, "Interpreting the Constitution," in *Interpreting the Constitution*, 13–21.
7. Gouverneur Morris to Timothy Pickering, December 22, 1814, Elliot, 1:507; James Madison to Jared Sparks, April 8, 1831, Elliot, 1:508; Gouverneur Morris to Henry W. Livingston,

Casually Kept Records

Madison considered Morris "an able, an eloquent, and an active member" of the Philadelphia Convention and explained to an inquiring Jared Sparks that despite the "draft in detail" reported by the committee of the whole, "there was sufficient room for the talents and taste stamped by the author [Morris] on the face" of the Constitution. But why should the proponents of originalism be reduced to relying on someone so frustratingly irresolute? After all, as Meese said, the "period surrounding the creation of the Constitution is not a dark and mythical realm." The proceedings at Philadelphia "were carefully recorded" in the official journal of the convention and in the "comprehensive accounts" left by Madison and others. The former attorney general, however, is either unacquainted with the work of Max Farrand, whose *Records of the Federal Convention of 1787* remains the definitive edition of the available sources, or unaccountably indifferent to it. Farrand included in his volumes all of the minutes of the convention kept by its secretary, William Jackson, as well the notes of Robert Yates, James McHenry, Rufus King, William Paterson, and James Madison. Unfortunately, the minutes were "carelessly kept" by Secretary Jackson and therefore, "uncertainty and confusion" characterize his brief entries. Yates's notes are far from comprehensive. And because he and his New York colleague John Lansing left Philadelphia early, his narrative ends on July 5, well before the convention reached its two most contested compromises— the three-fifths clause and equal representation in the Senate. McHenry of Maryland intended to keep extensive notes, but his brother's illness kept him away from the convention from June 1 to August 6, and by September he had lost his enthusiasm for note taking. King from Massachusetts scribbled on loose sheets or scraps of paper, which he collated and put into better form in preparation for publication many years after the Constitution had been ratified. A revised copy of these notes, published by his grandson in 1894, was largely ignored. In any case, like McHenry, King seemed to have lost his early enthusiasm and kept few notes after the first week of August. New Jersey's Paterson kept notes "solely for his own use," Farrand observes, and therefore his entries provide "little help in studying the general proceedings of the Convention."[8]

Madison Sui Generis

Thus we are left with Madison. Seated next to Secretary Jackson at the front of the chamber, Madison heard "all that passed" in the convention and carefully

---

December 4, 1803, Farrand, 3:404; Gouverneur Morris to Henry W. Livingston, November 25, 1803, Farrand, 3:401.

8. James Madison to Jared Sparks, April 8, 1831, Elliot, 1:507, 508; Meese, "Interpreting the Constitution," 14; Farrand, introduction, 1:xi-xxi.

noted "what was read from the Chair [by George Washington] or spoken by the members." And he was so regular in his attendance that there is no reason to doubt his claim that he "could not have lost a single speech, unless a very short one." Also, Madison strove to ensure the "correctness" of the record he was creating by routinely fleshing out his daily notes of the debates, laboring long into the night because he wished to be "aided by the freshness of my recollections." Lastly, other delegates presented Madison with copies of their speeches and motions, apparently regarding him, not Jackson, as the reporter of record. Not surprisingly, as Farrand concludes, with the publication of Madison's notes, "all other records paled into insignificance."[9]

Diligent beyond compare, Madison nevertheless was able to record, the historian James H. Hutson estimates, "only ten percent of each hour's proceedings." To be sure, one might justifiably object to his "unscientific" method of comparing Madison's hourly production of notes against a verbatim transcript of an hour's discussion at a modern scholarly conference, Hutson concedes, but his experiment demonstrates that "there is a significant quantitative difference between what Madison recorded and what was said at the Convention." Of course, what is missing cannot be known and therefore need not discourage the advocates of the doctrine of originalism, but we are obliged to ask why, if the framers intended their decisions to guide future interpretations, they failed to keep more comprehensive records of their deliberations. In part, as Hutson points out, their crude form of shorthand did not allow a complete and accurate rendering of public discourse. But this would not explain why the official minutes of the convention comprise little more than a list of motions, frequently without dates, and decisions accompanied by inaccurately tabulated votes. Perhaps Jackson was ill suited to the role of secretary, but if the business they were conducting was intended for future application, surely the delegates would have found another, more competent scribe.[10]

A similar observation may be made with respect to Madison's conduct. Madison knew he had the most complete record of the convention debates, and yet, despite repeated requests from interested correspondents, he refused to have his notes published during his lifetime. He also refrained from referring to his notes as an authoritative source on the framers' intent during the acrimonious exchanges of the 1790s. In opposing the creation of the Bank of the United States in 1791, for example, Madison argued that such an institution was not authorized by the Constitution. Alexander Hamilton's appeal to the "necessary and proper" clause as justification was inappropriate, he contended, because

9. James Madison, "Preface to Debates in the Convention of 1787," Farrand, 3:550; Farrand, introduction, 1:xv.

10. James H. Hutson, "The Creation of the Constitution: The Integrity of the Documentary Record," in *Interpreting the Constitution*, 159, 166–67.

that phrase applied only to measures deemed absolutely essential for carrying into execution the powers enumerated under Article 1, Section 8, of the Constitution. When Hamilton countered that the common understanding of "necessary" was not as restrictive as Madison would have it, that the "popular sense of the term" covered things that were "useful or conducive" to the performance of an assigned task, and that this common sense usage "is the true one in which it is to be understood as used in the Constitution," Madison did not claim the advantage of his notes in making his case for the "true" definition of the word.[11]

In 1796 Madison was even more pointed in his rejection of the doctrine of originalism, this time in an exchange with Washington over the Jay Treaty. Although the treaty had gained the consent of the Senate in June of 1795, House Republicans, dismayed by the terms of the agreement with Great Britain, were determined to nullify it by refusing to appropriate the funds needed for its implementation. A disappointed Washington used the occasion to lecture them on the "principles on which the Constitution was formed." He had been "a member of the General Convention," Washington reminded them gratuitously, and thus knew firsthand that the "power of making treaties is exclusively vested in the President by and with the advice and consent of the Senate." The convention intentionally left the House out of the treaty-making process described under Article 2, Section 2, and since the adoption of the Constitution, no representative had ever expressed "a doubt or suspicion" that this construction of the relevant clause was not "the true one." No Congress, "until now," had assumed a power to approve or disapprove of treaties by enacting or refusing to enact the "requisite provisions for carrying them into effect."[12]

Madison, as the leader of the House Republicans, answered the president, first by questioning the precision of "any evidence drawn from the debates in the Convention, or resting on the memory of individuals," and then by dismissing altogether the very notion of relying on the intent of the framers. "Whatever veneration might be entertained for the body of men who formed the Constitution," Madison declared, "the sense of that body could never be regarded as the oracular guide in expounding the Constitution." The document created at Philadelphia "was nothing more than the draft of a plan, nothing but a dead letter, until life and validity were breathed into it by the voice of the people." In short, the intent of the fifty-five delegates who met in Philadelphia was inconsequential. "As a guide in expounding and applying the provisions of the Constitution, the debates and incidental decisions of the Convention can

11. Farrand, introduction, 1:xv; Alexander Hamilton, "Opinion on the Constitutionality of the Bank," February 23, 1791, in *The Reports of Alexander Hamilton*, ed. Jacob E. Cooke (New York, 1964), 88–89; Stanley Elkins and Eric McKitrick, *The Age of Federalism: The Early American Republic, 1788–1800* (New York, 1993), 229–33.
12. *Annals of Congress*, 42 vols. (Washington, D.C., 1834–56), 5:761.

have no authoritative character." Where, then, should we turn to look for the "meaning of the instrument"? To the state ratifying conventions, Madison said. The Federal Convention "planned & proposed" a new system of government, but the state conventions affixed the meaning and authority of the Constitution. "If we were to look, therefore, for the meaning of the instrument beyond the face of the instrument, we must look for it, not in the General Convention . . . but in the state conventions."[13]

The State Conventions

Madison was not suggesting that the meaning of the Constitution could be found in the proceedings of the state conventions. On the contrary, he said "if we were to look," then the state ratifying conventions, because of what they signified, would be more appropriate settings for such investigations than the Federal Convention. Ultimately, however, he thought the search for meaning in the former would prove as unrevealing as the search for intent in the latter was irrelevant. In the 1796 exchange, Washington ended his argument by invoking the authority of the ratifiers, claiming his construction of the Constitution agreed "with the opinions entertained by the state conventions." Madison responded that the president's confidence was unfounded. In the first place, the available records of the various ratifying conventions were not wholly reliable. "Referring to the debates of the state conventions as published," Madison refused to vouch for the "accuracy of them." Even the minutes of the Virginia convention, which were "taken down by the most skillful hand, (whose merit he wished by no means to disparage)," contained an "abundance of chasms and misconceptions of what was said." His examination of the published proceedings of the Richmond convention led Madison to conclude that some passages were "defective, others obscure, if not unintelligible, others again which must be more or less erroneous." The recommendatory amendments submitted by five states were more reliable, "but even here it would not be reasonable to expect a perfect precision and system in all their votes and proceedings." These amendments were the products of "compromise" and were drafted by delegates who, amid the "agitations of the public mind," were pressured into completing their work in a "hurry." This would explain the "inconsistencies which might be discovered" in their several proposals and should alert us to the difficulties of determining how provisions of the Constitution must be "understood."[14]

13. *Annals of Congress*, 5:761, 776; James Madison to Thomas Ritchie, September 15, 1821, and James Madison to Henry Lee, June 25, 1824, cited in Charles A. Lofgren, "The Original Understanding of Original Intent?," in *Interpreting the Constitution*, 136.

14. James Madison to Jonathan Elliot, November 1827, cited in Hutson, "Creation of the Constitution," 161; *Annals of Congress*, 5:761, 777–78.

Madison's words of caution about unwarranted assumptions of precision point to a second difficulty confronting those in search of meaning at the state conventions. Despite their best intentions, the delegates at the various ratifying conventions did not examine the Constitution systematically. Although they adopted procedural motions to discuss its provisions clause by clause and paragraph by paragraph, they violated those motions almost at will. Madison, as we have seen, protested such violations at the Virginia convention, but he too ignored the rule when the occasion suited him. In New York, the supporters of ratification used the procedure strategically to bog down the proceedings at Poughkeepsie as they waited on Virginia. And after they learned of the decision taken at Richmond, they kept comfortably silent as Antifederalists proposed a string of recommendatory amendments. The delegates at the Boston convention did the best job of sticking to the directive for most of their sessions and called violators to order more effectively than delegates elsewhere, but their deliberations took the form of a "free conversation" that glossed over whole sections of the Constitution.

Discounting all instances of desultory debates and muddled progression, there remains an even larger obstacle to assigning precise meanings to the clauses of the Constitution. Most of the ratifying conventions suspended all votes until the examination of the entire Constitution was completed. In other words, the delegates did not vote on a particular clause or section after it had been discussed. This was in keeping with the instruction forwarded by the Philadelphia Convention: the Constitution had to be accepted or rejected in toto. There were no allowances for partial or conditional ratification; thus it was reasonable for the state conventions to call the question at the end of their debates. Ultimately, objections mattered only if they in their totality were enough to justify a rejection of the Constitution. If they were not, then the Constitution ought to be ratified. It was that simple. What this manner of proceeding meant, however, was that there would be no expression of the sense of the convention on individual issues. In closely divided conventions, such as those of Massachusetts and Virginia, uncovering the meaning assigned by the majority to a given clause or paragraph is nearly impossible. In New York, where Antifederalists held a better than two to one majority, it is impossible. And in North Carolina, with supporters of ratification forced to ask and answer their own questions because the Antifederalist majority refused to engage them in debate, a search for meaning would be ludicrous.

Clio and the Originalists

Originalists are quick to profess their allegiance to Clio, the muse of history. To those who question the feasibility of deciphering original intent or meaning, Meese answers, "look at history." By ignoring "historical context," argues Lino A.

Graglia, another defender of the theory, judicial activists and their enablers find themselves free to insist that the Constitution "cannot be taken to mean what it rather clearly is known to mean." Justice Antonin Scalia, the Supreme Court's leading originalist, claims to be driven to historical sources in preparing his judicial opinions because "when I find it—the original meaning of the Constitution—I am handcuffed." In view of such declarations, it is fitting to ask whether these doctrinal champions are in fact capable historians, for the meaning they uncover can only be as good as their mastery of the craft of history.[15]

By now, it should be apparent that many if not most of the proponents of originalism are either unacquainted with the primary sources or engage them quite selectively. Meese appears to fall into the former category, Justice Scalia into the latter. According to legal scholar and biographer Bruce Allen Murphy, Scalia is a "kind of magpie historian, plucking these bits from the 18th century, those from the 19th, whatever it takes to reach his preordained result." To be fair, such handpicking of the evidence would not make Scalia unique. Fifty years ago, the constitutional historian Alfred H. Kelly traced the dubious use of history back to the Marshall Court. Except, in Kelly's analysis, originalism often supplied the "rationale for politically inspired activism." It provided "an almost perfect excuse for breaking precedent," for "if the Fathers proclaimed the truth and the Court merely 'rediscovers' it, who can gainsay the new revelation?" Contrary to Justice Scalia's assertion, then, the appeal to original meaning, rather than handcuffing justices, can and historically has set them free authoritatively to promote their predetermined opinions.[16]

Historians characterize the sort of history practiced by original-meaning justices as "law-office history." As the Pulitzer Prize–winning constitutional historian Leonard W. Levy explains, these justices "tend to reason backward from their decisions. They reach results first and then find reasons, precedents, and historical support." The problem as well as the temptation for practitioners to this genre of history is that neither the fifty-five participants at the Philadelphia Convention nor the more than sixteen hundred delegates at the thirteen state conventions thought "in one groove." The assurances of Meese notwithstanding, there is no "demonstrable consensus among the framers and ratifiers" waiting to be uncovered. Instead, as the historian Jack N. Rakove has pointed out, there was a "range of understandings" on the manifold provisions of the Constitution. Thus Rakove, the leading authority on the subject, casts his

15. Meese, "Interpreting the Constitution," 18; Graglia, "How the Constitution Disappeared," 39; Jeff Shesol, "Rightward Bound," *New York Times Book Review*, July 6, 2014.

16. Bruce Allen Murphy, *Scalia: A Court of One* (New York, 2014), cited in Shesol, "Rightward Bound"; Alfred H. Kelly, "Clio and the Court: An Illicit Love Affair," *Supreme Court Review*, vol. 1965 (1965), 119–58, quotations at 131–32.

analysis in the plural—"original meanings"—to reflect the "spectrum of complex views and different shadings of opinion" that lay behind "any clause." It is this reality that conveniently allows law-office historians to find the support they need for whatever decision they have reached beforehand.[17]

Walsh Redux

Madison's admirer Robert Walsh Jr., no lawyer himself, practiced law-office history. When Madison refused to validate his distinction between "immigration" and "migration," Walsh sought and found the backing of others. The young editor cited "the celebrated James Wilson" for proof of intent. The Constitution empowered the federal government to end the "reproachful slave trade" after twenty years, Wilson declared in the Pennsylvania convention, and "in the mean time" to keep slaves out of any "new states which are to be formed." Indeed, Wilson said he was surprised that the clause regarding the "migration and importation of slaves would be excepted to." Walsh also enlisted John Jay for support. Jay, he reminded his readers, had been a "venerable" delegate to the New York convention, was "one of the authors of the Federalist," and was the former chief justice of the Supreme Court. " To me," Walsh quotes Jay as declaring, "the constitutional authority of the Congress to prohibit the migration *and* importation of slaves into any of the states does not appear questionable." And in fact, Jay, a onetime slave owner who became a founding member and president of the New York manumission society in the 1780s, did begin publicly to endorse the Walsh's claim that the two terms, "migration" and "importation," were not synonymous. Here was all the "proof" Walsh needed of the "intention of the Convention to invest Congress with a power over internal transportation, and to exclude slavery altogether from the new states." In short, Walsh found the endorsements he needed to advance his preconceived ideas. That Madison balked at the distinction he insisted on making did not derail Walsh's decision to fortify his argument with an appeal to original meaning. Did a Wilson plus a Jay trump "the one" whose opinion Walsh said carried the "most weight" with him? He avoided the question. It did not matter to Walsh. And his followers are legion.[18]

17. Leonard W. Levy, *Original Intent and the Framers' Constitution* (New York, 1988), 299, 294; Jack N. Rakove, *Original Meanings: Politics and Ideas in the Making of the Constitution* (New York, 1996), 8, 9–10.

18. McCoy, *Last of the Fathers*, 107; Arthur Zilversmit, *The First Emancipation: The Abolition of Slavery in the North* (Chicago, 1967), 165–66; [Walsh], *Free Remarks on the Constitution*, 20, 23–24.

Constitutional Convention:
Attendance by States

	May	June	July	August	September
Connecticut	x	x	x	x	x
Delaware	x	x	x	x	x
Georgia	o	x	x	x	x
Maryland	o	o	x *from July 9*	x	x
Massachusetts	x	x	x	x	x
New Hampshire	o	o	o *until July 23*	x	x
New Jersey	x	x	x	x	x
New York	x	x	o *from July 10*	o	o
North Carolina	x	x	x	x	x
Pennsylvania	x	x	x	x	x
Rhode Island	o	o	o	o	o
South Carolina	x	x	x	x	x
Virginia	x	x	x	x	x
States Represented	9	10	10	11	11

Source: Farrand, 3:587–90.
Note: X=in attendance; O=absent.

Chronology of Ratification

Order of Ratification	State	Date of Ratification	Convention Votes: For/Against Ratification	Recommendatory Amendments?
1	Delaware	December 7, 1787	30 to 0	No
2	Pennsylvania	December 12, 1787	46 to 23	No
3	New Jersey	December 18, 1787	39 to 0	No
4	Georgia	January 2, 1788	26 to 0	No
5	Connecticut	January 9, 1788	128 to 40	No
6	Massachusetts	February 6, 1788	187 to 168	Yes
7	Maryland	April 28, 1788	63 to 11	No
8	South Carolina	May 23, 1788	149 to 73	Yes
9	New Hampshire	June 21, 1788	57 to 47	Yes
10	Virginia	June 25, 1788	89 to 79	Yes
11	New York	July 26, 1788	30 to 27	Yes
12	North Carolina	November 21, 1789	194 to 77	No*
13	Rhode Island	May 29, 1790	34 to 32	No*

*First Federal Congress already in session in New York.

Featherstonhaugh, G. W.: as friend of James
Madison, 265; observations on South
Carolinians by, 264–65

The Federalist: circulation of, 182; contemporary reaction to, 180–81; no. 10 of,
182; no. 40 of, 42; no. 54 of, 180; no. 55 of,
180; no. 84 of, 183, 219

Federalists: and Bill of Rights, 228–31; in
First Congress, 236; in Massachusetts
convention, 113–15, 124–25, 129, 131; and
minority strategy in New York convention,
177, 184, 193, 195–99, 203–4; in North
Carolina, 209–11, 213–15; in Virginia
convention, 150, 153–54, 157–58, 163–64,
172. *See also individual state conventions*

Fiske, John, *Critical Period of American
History*, 1–2

Floridablanca, Conde de, 6; on U.S.
alliance, 8

Franklin, Benjamin: on "coolness" in
debates, 38–39; formula for representation
by, 39; and two-headed snake, 74

Freehling, William W., 255

Gardoqui, Don Diego de, 8. *See also*
Jay-Gardoqui negotiations

Garrison William: on the Constitution, 58;
and the idea of compromise on slavery, 95,
97; on the union, 96

Georgia: and slave trade, 80, 82; ratification
in, 109

Gerry, Elbridge: and acceptance of Constitution by, 142–43; and altercation with
Francis Dana, 116–18; on amendments
in First Congress, 230, 231, 233–35; at
Massachusetts convention, 115–18; refusal
to sign Constitution by, 107–8, 115; on
Virginia Plan, 27

Gore, Christopher: on consequences of
rejecting Constitution, 126; on federal
taxing powers, 125

Gorham, Nathaniel: as chairman of
committee of whole, 52; on divisions
among Antifederalists, 130; as member of
Federalist caucus, 130–31; on recommendations of Grand Committee, 52–53; on role
of recommendatory amendments, 130,
133; suggestion of southern hypocrisy by,

67–69; on taxation and representation,
122; on taxing slave imports, 90

Graglia, Lino A., 277–78

Grand Committee: and large-state caucus,
56–57; recommendations of, 51; responses
to, 52–53; report accepted by convention,
55

Grayson, William: on amendments in First
Congress, 237; arrogance of, 160; on Jay's
proposal, 9; on lukewarm Antifederalists
in First Congress, 236–37

Hamilton, Alexander: arrival at Federal
Convention of, 19; on Bill of Rights, 219;
on centrifugal and centripetal forces, xi;
criticism of, 181; on disunion and despotism, xi–xii, 47–48; and *The Federalist*,
180–81; as member of informal committee
of four, 195; and miniature frigate *Hamilton*,
208; on moderate Antifederalists, 184–85;
on "necessary and proper" clause, 274–75;
participation in New York convention of,
179–80; post-convention reception of, 207;
and recommendatory amendments, 192; on
reservation to recede, 200–201

Hamilton, James, Jr.: on consolidated
government, 250; as leader of South
Carolina radicals, 249; on state veto, 251

Hancock, John: address in Massachusetts
convention by, 138–39; and Bowdoin's
friends, 132; and committee of twenty-five,
136–37; convention attendance of, 130–31,
133; Federalist appeal to, 131–32; infirmities
of, 130–31; as president of Massachusetts
convention, 130; recommendatory
amendments of, 133–35

Hayne, Robert Y.: as defender of "South
Carolina doctrine," 255; militancy of,
255–56

Henry, Patrick: on Articles of Confederation,
149; as "Demosthenes," 152; on disunion,
156–57, 159–60; and Thomas Jefferson,
155; on Jefferson's strategy concerning
ratification, 145; and James Madison, 173;
oratorical prowess of, 154–55; "painful
sensations" of, 173; and Edmund
Randolph, 149–52; and resolution for
second convention, 225; and rumors

Muhlenberg, Frederick A.: on Antifederalist strategy in First Congress, 233, 234; on threats of violence, 234

Nasson, Samuel, 123
navigation laws: sectional interests in, 84–85; and slave trade, 83–88, 90–93; two-thirds requirement for enacting, 83, 87–88; 90–92
New Hampshire: attendance at Federal Convention of, 30; ratification in, 109–10
New Jersey: ratification in, 110
New Jersey Plan: and introduction by Paterson of, 40; provisions of, 40–41; rejection by convention of, 44–45. *See also* Virginia Plan
New York Convention: Antifederalist majority in, 176–79; circular letter of, 226; Madison's assessment of ratification in, 110–11; recommendatory amendments of, 202–4, 223–24; rejection of coordination with Virginia by, 175–76; and right to recede, 199–201; and threatened separation of New York City, 187, 205–6. *See also* Hamilton, Alexander; Smith, Melancton
North Carolina Convention, Fayetteville: xiv; Antifederalist-sponsored amendments in, 241; comparison with Hillsborough of, 238–40; outcome of, 240
North Carolina Convention, Hillsborough, xiv; Antifederalist domination of, 210–11, 213; decision of, 216; on North Carolina as foreign power, 213–14. *See also* Iredell, James; Jones, Willie
Nullification Ordinance: Andrew Jackson's response to, 254–55; provisions of, 254; and Tariff of 1832, 253

Oothoudt, Henry, 177
Original Meaning: assumptions made by proponents of, 271–72; problems associated with doctrine of, 272–79

Parsons, Theophilus: on federal control of elections, 120–21; as mentor, 128, 138
Paterson, William: on illegitimacy of convention, 35, 99; impressions of, 35, 36; introduction of New Jersey Plan by, 40; notes of convention taken by, 273; as

proponent of equal representation, 31, 36; on three-fifths ratio, 75;
Paulding, James K., on Madison, 243–44
Pendleton, Edmund: as character of "most note," 153; on weaknesses of the Confederation, 162
Pennsylvania: minority report of, 141; ratification in, 109–10. *See also* Franklin, Benjamin; Massachusetts Convention; Morris, Gouverneur; Wilson, James
Pierce, William: on Rufus King, 78; on James Madison, 22, 33; on Luther Martin, 45; on Roger Sherman, 27, 38; on James Wilson, 36
Pinckney, Charles: arrival at Federal Convention of, 19; on counting slaves as "equal" to whites, 71; defends slave trade, 79; motion to keep two-thirds requirement for navigation laws, 90–91
Pinckney, Charles Cotesworth: on apportionment of seats in First Congress, 63–64; on the authority of convention, 25; as defender of slave trade, 81–82; on the legitimacy of the Federal Convention, 99; on "liberal conduct" of New England states, 94; proposal for Committee of Eleven (Grand Committee), 50
Platt, Zephaniah: "in confidence" votes of, 197–98; on voting for ratification, 205

Rakove, Jack, 278–79
Ramsay, David, 2; *History of the American Revolution*, 2–3
Randall, Benjamin, 139
Randolph, Edmund: and confrontation with Patrick Henry, 149–52, 165; as defender of the legitimacy of convention, 42; election to Constitutional Convention of, 18; and idea of a second convention, 104; and introduction of Virginia Plan, 23; and motion linking taxation and representation, 70–71; and proposal for a federal census, 65–66; propositions of, 24–27; on refusal to sign Constitution, 107–8, 149; and unconditional ratification, 150–51; on Virginia and the Union, 160–61; as "young Arnold," 150–51

ratification: all or nothing requirement of, xiii, 103–5; by the American people, 106; Federalist strategy for, 99–108; Madison's assessment of chances of, 109–10; nine-state requirement of, xiii, 100–101; by state conventions, 100; without prior congressional approval of, 101–3. *See also* Massachusetts Convention; New York Convention; North Carolina Convention; Virginia Convention

Read, George: arrival at Federal Convention by, 19; as defender of equal representation, 29–30; on Randolph's propositions, 28

representation: equal, xiii, 76; "equitable ratio" of, 67; in First Congress, 28, 62–65; proportional, xiii; and slavery, xii–xiii, 67–69; and taxation, 70- 73

Rhett, Robert Barnwell: militancy of, 264; "ultra opinions" of, 264

Rhode Island: absence from Federal Convention of, 30, 105; absence from First Congress of, 217; contemporary assessment of, 217–18

Ronald, William, 155,

Rossiter, Clinton, 69

Rush, Richard: appeals to James Madison by, 248; as member of new generation, 266

Rutledge, John: arrival at Federal Convention by, 19; as chair of Committee of Detail, 77; as defender of slave imports, 79; slaves of, 81; and threats of disunion, 79

Scalia, Antonin, as leading originalist on Supreme Court, 278

Schoonmaker, Cornelius C.: on Federalist victory in New York, 203–4; on ratification by Virginia, 184

sectionalism: and apportionment of seats in First Congress, 62–65; and definitions of "the South," 64–65; and equitable ratio of representation, 60–61; and slavery, 59; and slave trade, 87

Sedgwick, Theodore: on Annapolis Convention, 13; on James Madison's amendments, 228–29; preference for a northern confederation of, 13; on "timidity" of James Madison, 230

Shays's Rebellion, 14–16; Congress's response to, 15; and representation, 122. *See also* Massachusetts Convention

Sherman, Roger: on amendments in First Congress, 235; on Bill of Rights, 219; compromise proposal of, 38–39; as opponent of tax on slave imports, 89–90; respect for, 27–28

slavery: and fugitive slave clause, 92; in *Federalist* no. 54, 180–81; and sectionalism, 59; and three-fifths ratio, 60–62, 67–70

slave trade: and bargain involving navigation laws, 83–95; condemnation by William Lloyd Garrison of, 58; debates over, 77–83; federal taxes on, 88–90; linked to three-fifths ratio, 75; temporary protection of, 88–89; and threats of disunion, 79, 81–82

Smith, Jonathan: on anarchy of Shays's Rebellion, 126–27; "a time to sow and a time to reap," 127

Smith, Margaret Bayard, visit to Montpelier of, 243–44

Smith, Melancton: as Antifederalist leader, 181; circular letter of, 204; conditional stipulations of, 188, 198; and congressional actions, 189–90; detested "as much as Hamilton," 193–94; on *The Federalist*, 181; and meetings with Federalists, 204; as member of informal committee of four, 195; moderate disposition of, 187–88; and motion to recede, 193, 201–2; and motion to remove conditional stipulation, 197–98; post-convention reception of, 208; on preservation of the union, 204; on ratification in Massachusetts, 110; on representation in Congress, 179; second motion of, 191–93

Society of Cincinnati, 17

South Carolina: and slave imports, 78, 79, 89; threats of disunion, 79, 81–82

sovereignty, definitions of, 26

Strong, Caleb: as delegate to Federal Convention, 113, 115; on federal control of elections, 120–21; "free conversation" motion of, 113–14

Sullivan, James, on James Madison's amendments, 230